# The Professional Teacher's Handbook

*abridged second edition*

# The Professional Teacher's Handbook

A Guide for Improving Instruction in Today's Middle and Secondary Schools

## abridged second edition

## Kenneth H. Hoover
Arizona State University

**Allyn and Bacon, Inc.**     **Boston • London • Sydney**

**Library of Congress Cataloging in Publication Data**

Hoover, Kenneth H
   The professional teacher's handbook.

   Bibliography: p.
   Includes index.
   1.  High school teaching—Handbooks, manuals, etc.
I.  Title.
LB1607.H666 1976          373.1′1′02          76–43071
ISBN 0–205–05582–6
*Second printing . . . July, 1977*

*To the memory of*
*the late Mrs. Clio Clark,*
*a teacher whose influence*
*will be felt*
*for generations to come*

# Contents

## Unit III   Methods with a Focus on the Group

# Preface

In the four years since the publication of the third edition of *Learning and Teaching in the Secondary School,* the lines separating pre-service and in-service education have become blurred and indistinct. More and more the secondary schools of our nation have become the proving grounds for pre-service teachers. Indeed on-site teacher educational programs have sprung up in the colleges and universities throughout the country.

More importantly perhaps is the belated realization that new teachers need continued guidance and direction, especially during their early years of teaching. In response to this need many colleges and universities are cooperating with the public schools in setting up internship programs, teacher centers, and the like. Thus the demand for practical, performance-based textbook materials has accelerated. In response to this demand the author prepared *The Professional Teacher's Handbook,* patterned after the methods text. The book became popular with in-service teachers almost immediately. Surprisingly enough, the book was adopted by a substantial number of colleges and universities for pre-service teacher use, even though it was not advertised for this purpose.

In revising *The Professional Teacher's Handbook* the author has, at the same time, prepared an abridged edition of the book for college use. The basic approach used previously has been retained. The practical applications section, featured in the *Handbook,* has been added. In this way the prospective teacher is brought very close to the reality of actual classroom experience.

Chapters new to the second edition are "Discipline Problems," "Developmental Reading Techniques," "Drill and Practice Procedures," "Value-Focusing Activities," and "Individualizing Instruction." As with previous editions of *Learning and Teaching in the Secondary School,* this book is based on the premise that thinking is the key to educational method. While the processes of thought are still imperfectly understood, a great deal of knowledge has accumulated to indicate that analytical and intuitive thought processes account for much of man's interaction with his environment. Thus the teacher's function is seen as that of working with students in an appropriate selection, organization, and evaluation of those classroom experiences which will facilitate sound thinking. The function of the instructor is to help the learner grow and develop from trial-and-error learning, from superstition and prejudice, to more scientific ways of coping with problems.

For many decades there has been a controversy over subject matter preparation versus methods of teaching. Some teachers maintain that one who knows his subject matter can teach it. Others feel that almost any educational feat can be accomplished if one is well-grounded in teaching techniques. The argument becomes purely academic when learning is viewed as a process of cognitive thinking, as opposed to the older notion of learning as a process of knowledge acquisition. If one is to teach, one must teach *something*. Adequate subject matter preparation, then, is basic. A solid academic background in itself, however, offers no guarantee of effective teaching. Just as a student needs guidance in the processes of reflection, so does the teacher need guidance in the establishment of a proper environment for learning. In this book instructional method is conceived within the framework of analytical thought processes. Essential structural dimensions of each method are clearly identified. Each teacher is encouraged to bring his/her own creative ideas into focus *within such a framework*.

For convenience, this book is divided into three major units: Pre-Instructional Activities; Methods with a Focus on the Individual; Methods with a Focus on the Group. Each chapter features basic, fundamental properties, a basic instructional procedure, values and limitations, and method illustrations in different subject fields.

The writer wishes to express his gratitude to the many teachers and college students who have offered suggestions and provided illustrations for the various methods and techniques described. Their continued feedback is requested as the writer attempts to keep this book abreast of contemporary developments in a rapidly changing profession.

*Kenneth H. Hoover*

# The Professional Teacher's Handbook

*abridged second edition*

# Preinstructional Activities

Gaining the Concept
Establishing Instructional Objectives
Planning for Teaching

*Effective teaching represents the culmination of a series of preparatory activities. Long hours of careful preparation often go into one class period. In setting the stage for effective instruction the teacher must be a skillful predictor of events. Knowledge of students and a thorough knowledge of the subject field are necessary prerequisites to instructional excellence. Yet, of themselves, they are inadequate. The professional competence of a teacher ultimately rests on his ability to anticipate student needs and behaviors in advance of the actual experience. Instructional preparation, then, involves applied imagination in plannng for the experience. Such is the subject of this unit.*

*Instructional methods and techniques are designed to facilitate the teaching of content. One teaches algebra, American history, biology, foreign language. What aspects of such courses should be emphasized? If, as indicated, most facts are quickly forgotten, should they be taught at all? Chapter 1 indicates how specific facts may be so organized as to promote the attainment of the concept. Since concepts transfer readily from one situation to another, they become the foundations of all instruction.*

*Once basic concepts have been identified, instructional aims or purposes can be developed. The teacher, in establishing educational direction, focuses upon unit and lesson aims or goals. Once purpose has been determined, the rest of the instructional process begins to take shape. The key to effective planning and to effective teaching is the formulation of goals in behavioral terms. Attention also must be given to a variety of goal types and levels. Three basic taxonomies of objectives have been recognized: cognitive, affective, and psychomotor. These techniques have been treated in Chapter 2.*

*Long- and short-range planning, described in Chapter 3, remains a controversial instructional issue. The issue is not whether or not one should plan; rather, it is the nature and extent of planning necessary. There are effective teachers who prefer an unstructured classroom experience just as there are those who insist on a highly structured classroom experience. Both extremes can be beneficial in certain situations, depending upon the particular objectives involved. When lesson planning is viewed as a problem-solving experience the dilemma becomes much less ambiguous. Each person must resolve his problems in his own way. Planning needs will vary with each instructor and with each learning experience. Aside from the lesson objective, some teachers will need the psychological security of thoroughly developed lesson plans; other teachers will feel limited or boxed in with detailed lesson plans.*

*In an effort to provide a basis for the extreme needs associated with lesson planning, detailed long- and short-range planning techniques are offered. Every teacher needs some experience in detailed unit and lesson planning. Just as a beginning lawyer relies heavily upon his debate brief, so does a beginning teacher need the benefit of elaborate planning. As the lawyer gains experience he tends to carry an increasing amount of his debate brief in his head. The same holds for experienced teachers. The precise amount of written planning necessary must be decided by each teacher in each teaching situation. In the final analysis, the essential function of planning is to set the stage for learning. In a sense it is a dress rehearsal for the real thing. Even the best laid plans go awry. Nevertheless, the mere act of planning can prepare one for the unexpected!*

# CHAPTER 1

# Gaining the Concept

## OVERVIEW

### Key Concepts

1. Unit concepts, as defined in this chapter, are analogous to broad generalizations, principles, laws, or axioms.
2. Concepts exist at different levels.
3. Factual materials provide necessary background information essential to derivation of concepts.
4. Concepts are retained indefinitely; facts that are not used repeatedly are not retained.
5. Concepts are appropriately derived by students themselves from the school experience.
6. Instructional goals and class activities are derived from unit concepts.
7. Unit and lesson concepts are most useful when phrased as simple declarative statements.

### New Terms

1. **Unit Titles**—Derived from broad course concepts, unit titles are actually titles of the various instructional units. The term *theme, focus,* or *thrust* is used to suggest a planned focus or emphasis for the unit.
2. **Unit Concepts**—Basic structural properties (ideas) upon which a unit rests. Each unit concept embodies a real-life application.
3. **Lesson Generalizations**—The culminating product (ideas) of a specific lesson. Collectively they embody the unit concept upon which a lesson rests.
4. **Classificational Concepts**—A concept type useful in clarifying essential properties, processes, or events. Such concepts, usually derived from

facts, provide the learner with a much needed organizational pattern for isolated bits of information.

5. **Correlational Concepts**—A concept type useful in relating specific events, observations, or variables. Such concepts embody an "if . . . then" dimension.

6. **Theoretical Concepts**—A concept type useful in advancing from the known to the unknown. Such concepts go beyond existing facts but must be consistent with them.

7. **Concept Attainment**—This involves the total process of reflective thinking. Each instructional method is based upon this basic process of cognition.

8. **Intuitive Thought**—That type of thought that, although apparently based upon processes of reflection, does not seem to follow any order of logic. Frequently it is characterized by a sudden flash of insight.

## Questions to Guide Your Study

1. "Unit concepts, identified by the teacher in preinstructional activities, should be presented to students prior to the instructional experience." Defend or refute.

2. What is the relationship between concepts and instructional activities?

3. Why must a teacher avoid strict adherence to the steps of the cognitive or reflective process?

4. "Using concepts as an instructional foundation is more appropriate in some subject fields than in others." Defend or refute.

The mental images that we carry around in our heads are known as concepts. *A concept is a mental picture of an object, event, or relationship derived from experience.* Concepts help us classify or analyze; they help us associate or combine as well. These "mental images" gain meaning from subsequent experiences. As meaning becomes firmly established, we develop *feeling* about an idea or concept.

In the educative process, concepts are thought to form the basic *structure* of content areas. An understanding of the structural dimensions of a field of knowledge provides the learner with a frame of reference for thinking and for evaluating future experiences.

The structural properties of each teaching unit normally consist of from six to eight major concepts. These are the basic ideas that provide the focal point of instructional activities. Unit goals are derived from such concepts.

Concepts are derived from content. They are usually formulated as brief, concise statements. In essence, they are the basic ideas that hold a unit together. Thus the first step in unit planning is identification of the basic unit concepts (ideas) to be sought. To illustrate from a unit in a class in general business (Sales Promotion and Advertising):

1. Customer satisfaction is the most important product.
2. Customer needs are the prompters for purchasing decisions.

3. Advertising can be an effective means of preselling products.
4. Advertisements use customer motives that can be restated in the personal selling approach.
5. The customer market is in a state of constant change, and therefore continuous study is required to stay abreast of current developments.
6. Differences in the structure and style of a product can be stated as sales appeals.

## FUNDAMENTAL PROPERTIES

Concepts exist at many different levels ranging from highly abstract symbols to complex generalizations. They are also of different types. The specific level and type to be sought is dependent upon the nature of the content area to be studied.

### How Do Concepts Differ with Respect to Level?

The recent expansion of knowledge has focused attention on the importance of analysis, generalization, and application of knowledge. Rather than emphasizing specific content materials as ends in themselves, teachers have attempted to guide students in the processes of reduction of content learnings to basic ideas that, in turn, can be expanded or generalized to a wide variety of problems and situations. Three distinct concept levels are necessary for such an instructional approach.

*Unit Titles.* Unit titles represent the most abstract conceptual level of instructional planning. The first step in planning for teaching is identification of the broad content areas to be emphasized. Perhaps this task is best accomplished by examining several current textbooks in the subject field. The teacher is likely to find that most textbook writers emphasize many of the same broad content areas. (Final selection, however, usually is left to the individual teacher; it is *not* dictated by textbook writers.)

Once the broad areas are identified, they will be developed into appropriate unit titles. A unit (treated fully in Chapter 3) consists of a group of related concepts. Each unit title calls attention to the content area *and also to the major thrust or focus for the unit.* This thrust or focus serves as a constant reminder of the major reason for teaching a given unit. Thus it will suggest a real-life application. In deciding upon a major thrust or focus the teacher must ask himself the question, "Why should this unit be taught?" It is only after the teacher can provide some practical, real-life application, *immediate to the lives of students,* that he is ready to proceed further with planning activities. Popham and Baker[1] refer to this activity as the principle of "perceived purpose."

[1] W. James Popham and and Eva L. Baker, *Systematic Instruction* (Englewood Cliffs, N.J.: Prentice-Hall, Inc., 1970), pp. 80–82.

Each subject area has its own specific requirements. In Literature, for example, the content area involving the study of *Julius Caesar* might be focused on the unit theme of *ambition.* Thus the unit title might be, *Julius Caesar: Unbridled Ambition.* Such a unit appropriately would begin with a study of contemporary issues of vital concern to young people. Stress would be placed upon development of concepts of ambition and the characteristics that compose it. *Julius Caesar* would provide a basic content reference; indeed, the unit would appropriately culminate with an intensive study of *Julius Caesar.* Thus content emphasis is shifted from subject matter as an end in itself to its appropriate place as a means to attainment of more basic learnings. Other *thematic* units might be Frustration, Loneliness, Death. Some unit titles in the field of English, however, might be *topical* in nature, such as *Sentence Structure: Exploring Language.* In the latter illustration the title serves as a reminder that the unit focus will be on the easy, practical conveying of one's thoughts in writing. Unit titles in several different subject areas will suggest a variety of unit functions:

*History:* The Roosevelt Era: A Socialistic Trend.
*Home Economics:* Clothing: Improve Your Personal Appearance.
*Art:* Sketching: A Gateway to Good Design.
*Physical Education:* Team Sports: Cooperative Relationships.
*Chemistry:* Carbon: The Chemistry of Life.
*Mathematics:* Set Theory: Understanding Relationships.
*Business:* Economic Losses: Protection through Insurance.
*Humanities:* The Arts in Ancient Greece: Idealism as a Guide to Behavior.
*Biology:* Body Systems: Interdependency Functions.
*Foreign Language*: The Spanish Alphabet: English Parallels.

**Unit concepts.** Each unit, in turn, is broken into six or eight unit concepts. Based upon content, they provide the basic threads of a unit. Stating them specifically, *in advance of the instructional experience,* provides direction to the unit and ensures that none of the important threads will be omitted. It is usually best to state each concept in a simple, declarative statement form. Again, a *current* life application is essential. In many subject areas it is relatively easy to meet the criterion of current life application. In a few subject areas, however, this is a rather complicated, but nevertheless essential, task. In history, for example, a two-step process seems necessary. First, one must identify the major ideas of the unit; then he must expand into generalizations that are viable today. Without the second step, history teaching is likely to remain the dry and generally useless process of memorizing names, dates, and places. (See illustrations section of the chapter on Planning (pp. 44–46).)

In other subject fields the task of concept identification is often complicated by textbook organization. In literature, for example, textbook content may be organized around literary genres, historical themes, and the like. An historical theme on Colonial America, for example, offers the reader numerous selections, each with its own story theme. The teacher's task, again, is twofold in nature. First, it is necessary to identify major unit themes (e.g., major threads of thought that occur repeatedly); then one must identify the particular selections that can be used in teaching each given concept. This process also is fully illustrated on pp. 45–46 of chapter 3.

Here are some unit concept illustrations in other subject fields:

*Industrial arts:* Accuracy in measuring influences the work of those who must interpret meaning from a drawing.

*Home Economics:* Fabric content determines what can be made from a selected fabric.

*Physical Education:* One must be physically active to achieve a high level of physical fitness.

*Chemistry:* Sugars and starches are products of natural organic chemical processes.

*Humanities:* Idealism can result if a society believes that there is a rational order to the universe.

*Health:* Many aspects of health are personal; others are community problems.

*Business:* A personal budget helps one see exactly how his or her money is spent.

*Mathematics:* Sets can unite, intersect, or have differences.

*Art:* Inspiration for design can be found in almost everything in our environment.

As can be implied from the foregoing, unit concepts will vary from teacher to teacher, depending upon the individual teacher's frame of reference. This, in part, accounts for observed instructional differences between teachers of the same subject. Ultimately, however, many similar unit concepts receive attention. By jointly developing unit concepts teachers of the same subject field can maximize the parallel nature of different classes. Even so, differences must be expected since concept attainment rests with students.

*Lesson generalizations.* Each lesson is based upon a unit concept previously identified by the teacher. A lesson culminates in the derivation of a number of important generalizations (concepts). Lesson generalizations should be derived *by students* as an outgrowth of a given experience. Collectively they will embody the unit concept of the lesson. Thus a lesson generalization is more specific than a unit concept. To illustrate from a lesson on health:

*Concept:* Use of drugs may permanently damage an individual's health and well-being.

*Lesson generalizations:*
1. LSD users may incur permanent brain damage.
2. While under the influence of LSD, a person loses his or her ability to distinguish between reality and fantasy.
3. Use of LSD may render an individual emotionally dependent upon the drug.

Although generalizations can be derived by students in a number of ways, some authorities insist that they be written out. In this manner the teacher is able to provide assistance for those who are experiencing difficulty. In many practical situations teachers find it convenient to let students evolve generalizations through a culminating class discussion. Usually the more able students will quickly formulate key lesson generalizations. When they are placed on the chalk-board the less able students may write them out in their notes and then later memorize them for a test. Understanding may be partially or totally lacking. As a safeguard considerable probing is necessary. Such experiences cannot be rushed.

## What Are Some Basic Concept Types?

Concepts vary from axioms and propositions in mathematics to hypotheses and conclusions in science. Although the specific nature of concepts is dependent upon the nature of the unit under investigation, Pella has identified three basic types.[2]

*Classificational.* This is the most common type germane to classroom instruc-tion. Its function is basically that of defining, describing, or clarifying essential properties of phenomena, processes, or events. It is often based upon the classi-fication of facts into organized schemes or patterns. To illustrate in the field of science: An insect is an animal with six legs and three body cavities. It should be noted that the student is most appropriately provided a series of learning experiences that will inductively lead him to such a principle. For example, he might be asked to inspect a number of specimens, noting characteristics. He may conclude that there is a group of organisms that share this characteristic. We *classify* this group as insects.

*Correlational.* This type of concept is derived from *relating* specific events or observations; it consists of prediction. According to Pella, it consists of the formu-lation of general principles.[3] To illustrate in the field of science: When voltage is constant, the electrical current varies with the resistance. It will be noted that the concept consists of an "*if . . . then*" dimension. Involved is a *relationship* be-tween two variables.

*Theoretical.* A theoretical concept facilitates the explanation of data or events into organized systems. It involves the process of advancing from the known to the unknown. Examples: Unemployment leads to social unrest; indiscriminant bombing tends to stiffen enemy resistance; an atom is composed of electrons, protons, and other particles. A theoretical concept goes beyond the facts, but must be consistent with the known facts.

The list of concepts that follows has been derived from many different in-structional units in various content fields. The reader is urged to classify each according to concept type. It should be noted that some concept types are more typically found within a given field than are other types. In the social science area, for example, theoretical concepts usually predominate.

1. Ill-advised public expression may adversely affect statesmanship. T
2. As population increases pollution problems are increased. c-R

---

[2] Milton O. Pella, "Concept Learning in Science," *The Science Teacher* 33 (December 1966): 31–4.

[3] *Ibid.*

3. The world's population is increasing at a geometric rate. C
4. The conditions of the times influence the nature of literary contributions. C
5. Definitions, assumptions, and previously established principles become the basis for developing proof. C
6. Equations resemble a scale; both sides must be equally balanced. C-K
7. Absence of law leads to anarchy. C -K
8. State and local boundaries unnaturally divide regions that share common governmental problems. C
9. One's wardrobe reflects his life style. T
10. The frequency with which household equipment is used is related to convenience of storage and its arrangement in the work center. C

## What Function Is Served by Advance Organizers?

Basic to concept teaching is an overview of the major purpose of the forthcoming learning experience. In an inductive, problem solving type of experience students usually are guided into the development of their own questions that need exploration. This, in effect, serves as an anchor for subsequent activities. In an expository type of learning experience (which probably predominates) Ausubel[4] believes *advance organizers* are necessary. An advance organizer, according to Ausubel, is an abstract idea or concept that is introduced in advance of the material to be learned. Its purpose is to provide an initial conceptual base for facilitating the new learnings.

It should be noted that the advance organizer is *not* seen as the major concept upon which the lesson rests. Rather, it is a more abstract concept that "leads students in the right direction." Novak[5] offers an example in science when he cites that students might be instructed that the primary center of plant growth is at the ends of the stems. Subsequent instruction may lead students to observe the size of the leaves, the length of internodes, and the general contrast between the stems near the ends with lower regions. Although Novak fails to clarify the major lesson concept, it might well have been: Photosynthesis takes place in the leaves (and sometimes in the stems) of plants.

Advance organizers will vary somewhat with each given instructional method employed. They are not to be viewed as the basic means of developing interest in the lesson. Usually the advance organizer would be the very first part of a lesson. The "idea" might well be placed upon the chalkboard. If the idea can be worded in an interesting or challenging manner it may provide immediate interest. Its primary purpose, however, is to structure thinking around a basic idea. Although many teachers have responded that advance organizers are merely representative of common sense in teaching, Ausubel points out that they are not common in most conventional classes.

---

[4] D. P. Ausubel, *The Psychology of Meaningful Verbal Learnings* (New York: Grune and Stratton, 1963).

[5] J. D. Novak and others, "Interpretation of research findings in terms of Ausubel's theory and implications for science teaching," *Science Education* 55 (October 1971): 483–526.

# CONCEPT ATTAINMENT

Development of methods and techniques of guiding students in the formation of concepts is one purpose of this book. It seems necessary at this point to lay a foundation for the various teaching methods to be introduced in subsequent chapters. As indicated earlier, certain cognitive processes seem to be normally employed when an individual thinks. In this section each step of the analytical thought process is described. Although the steps will not always be followed in the order presented, nor all steps necessarily employed on each occasion, the classroom teacher should be aware of the sequence as a basis for preparation of classroom experiences.

## How Is the Problem Stated and Clarified?

A problem arises when an individual encounters difficulty in his regular activities. He recognizes that the concepts at hand somehow do not fit the observed events. This may produce a vague feeling of dissatisfaction with things as they are—from unhappiness with a definite snarl in the progress of events, or from mere curiosity. In any event, this is when the problem should be stated in as precise a manner as possible.

Frequently the teacher formulates a realistic problem from the unit concept that he has previously identified. As cited earlier, a concept in the area of general business was: Customer satisfaction is the most important product (of sales promotion and advertising). From this basic idea the teacher may formulate the problem: How might a customer feel when he is pressured into buying a product? He then decides upon an instructional method or technique that seems most appropriate for guiding students in solving the problem.

It should be noted that the teacher is involved in at least two separate creative acts: (1) the identification of important ideas (concepts) that are to be the "residue" of teaching, and (2) the designing of appropriate learning situations in which the concepts may be derived. One logically follows the other. If the concept is poorly formulated, it will become evident when one attempts to plan specific learning experiences. To illustrate with the concept illustrated on page 17 in the area of home economics, "Each family functions differently." In order to provide an appropriate learning experience, one must focus upon a particular area of family relationships. An appropriate problem might be: What policy should govern the financial aspect of family living? Again, various methods and techniques provide possible avenues for grappling with such an issue. The concept might have been more appropriately stated as follows: The management of family finances is dependent upon the personalities of the family members. Thus the teacher works constantly back and forth from concept to method as he engages in preinstructional activities.

In many instances students will be encouraged to develop their own problems for study and analysis. Problems may arise from ongoing class activities, or they may be planned with the help of the teacher. (See Chapter 18, "Processes of Inquiry.") Any preplanned experience is subject to modification as the need arises.

## How Are Facts Sorted and Analyzed?

The terms of a problem must be clarified, cause and effect relationships must be examined, and the importance of the issue must be established. This involves identifying and evaluating all the important facts and relationships that bear upon the problem. Students are prone to confuse personal opinion with facts and to confuse their opinion about facts with the facts. They also tend to jump to conclusions on the basis of limited evidence. Students, as well as most adults, tend to seek facts that will support a given point of view. Data on all sides of a question must be perused in the interest of intellectual honesty.

One of the most crucial aspects of the instructional process is the task of guiding students in their selection and analysis of facts. A common misuse of textbooks has contributed to an attitude of the text as the final answer. This also contributes to reliance upon the teacher as a final source of authority. It must be remembered that concept seeking is a searching, an inquiring process. Therefore the teacher must encourage students to seek widely for facts or data; he must guide students deliberately to uncover facts that will contribute to widely differing points of view. In discussion of the facts, students need to listen, need to actively pursue contrasting hypotheses and trace their ideas to their conclusions ("if . . . then"). As indicated in later chapters, buzz groups contribute to such an analysis. Students must be assisted in keeping to the problem and supporting their contentions with evidence. Whenever possible the student should compare conclusions based on personal experience with those drawn from the evidence.

## How Are Hypotheses Developed?

Once the problem has been stated and clarified, the individual has already moved into the "next step" in the analytical thought process. At this point he develops some hypotheses—bold guesses or hunches with respect to his problem. For the untrained individual there may be a tendency to accept the first guess (hypothesis) as correct. Thus further thinking is blocked. The trained individual delays reaction and deliberately "casts about" for several possible solutions. *It is important to remember that hypotheses are necessary as a guide in the acquisition of facts.* Hypotheses, of course, are based upon the facts in the original situation from which the problem grew.

Hypotheses cannot be guaranteed or controlled; they just appear. There are techniques, however, for minimizing ordinary inhibitions built up from past experience. One of these, brainstorming, for example, is discussed in another chapter.

### What Is the Role of Interference in Analytical Thought?

From an analysis of facts the individual formulates tentative conclusions. His ideas may be in the form of possible explanations to account for a chain of events, or they may represent several possible courses of action. An *inference* is a leap from the known to the unknown. This *movement* from present facts to possible (but not present) facts represents the heart of the thinking process. Each individual is continually making inferences as he grapples with large and small difficulties of his daily existence. Since the process is so commonplace there is a tendency to jump to unwarranted conclusions. It is the function of the instructional process to guide students in making *tested* inferences.

Both deductive and inductive reasoning processes normally are used in problem-solving experiences. Involved in the process of making inferences are *assumptions*. An assumption is anything taken for granted—anything assumed to be self-evident. A teacher may offer considerable assistance by requesting students to state their implicit assumptions, thus making them aware of them.

### How Are Conclusions Tested?

Although the processes of reflection ultimately result in a decision, the complexity of many instructional problems may render an immediate decision impossible. (See Chapter 16, "Discussion Methods.") In any event, however, the learner is encouraged to evolve pertinent generalizations (concepts) from the experience. These will not be identical to the major concept that gave rise to the problem. Rather, they will be supporting concepts that collectively encompass the major concept.

Lesson generalizations are derived by students. They are made most meaningful when written out and illustrated. Provision also must be made for their application to new situations, with emphasis on exploration of relationships, comparisons, and prediction of consequences.

### What Is the Role of Intuitive Thinking in Concept Formation?

Any treatment of the processes of concept formation would not be complete without some attention to those thought processes that do not seem to follow the scheme outlined on the preceding pages. It has long been recognized that many of the really great contributions to human knowledge have come in sudden flashes of insight. Frequently after an individual has labored over a problem for hours, days, or even weeks, the idea suddenly meshes. This very often occurs after the problem has been put aside. It was Archimedes who supposedly jumped from the bathtub shouting "Eureka" at his sudden discovery. Jerome Bruner describes the process as *intuitive thinking.*

Whether intuitive thinking follows a definite pattern or not is not known. Most writers, however, suggest that too much emphasis on the formal structure of analytical thinking processes is detrimental to intuitive thought. Routinized activities of any sort seem to be detrimental to the process. Bruner, however, stresses the complementary nature of the two when he says:

> Through intuitive thinking the individual may often arrive at solutions to problems which he would not achieve at all, or at best more slowly, through analytic thinking. Once achieved by intuitive methods, they should if possible be checked by analytic methods, while at the same time being respected as worthy hypotheses for such checking. Indeed, the intuitive thinker may even invent or discover problems that the analyst would not. But it may be the analyst who gives these problems the proper formalism.[6]

Accounts of thought-in-progress by individuals who have made singular intuitive leaps are beginning to accumulate. From this evidence a few characteristics of the process are beginning to emerge.

1. The idea comes as a sudden flash—a "Eureka."
2. It usually comes after a problem has been put aside, often when least expected. Thus an incubation period is necessary.
3. The Eureka does not seem to follow any logical sequence of steps.
4. It seems to be built upon a broad understanding of the field of knowledge involved.
5. Individuals using this process seem to be characterized by bold guessing. They seem to have the ability to cut through the conventional, the mundane, the expected.
6. They seem to be willing to abandon false hypotheses no matter how well they are liked.

## How Do Teaching Methods Relate to Analytical and Intuitive Thought Processes?

The preceding analysis of how we think has not been presented to suggest a formal outline to follow during the instructional process. A general, flexible scheme is not only possible but necessary. It means that teachers should conduct their classes so that students learn to take the steps as the normal way of going about learning, without self-consciousness. In an atmosphere that is reflective in quality, thinking may be expected to break out at any moment. As Burton, Kimball, and Wing so ably express the point, "The mind, contrary to widespread belief, has natural tendencies to generalize, to draw inferences, to be critical, to accept and reject conclusions on evidence."[7] The student learns to think through thinking. He needs guidance in perfecting this ability to select and clarify problems, to hypothesize, to secure and analyze facts, to make inferences from data, and to reach valid conclusions. The task of the school is to provide ample oppor-

---

[6] Jerome S. Bruner, *The Process of Education* (Cambridge, Mass.: Harvard University Press, 1961), p. 58.

[7] William H. Burton, Ronald B. Kimball, and Richard L. Wing, *Education for Reflective Thinking* (New York: Appleton-Century-Crofts, Inc., 1960), p. 292.

tunity to exercise the process of thinking, to the end that the natural tendencies to reflect and to draw inferences will be transformed into attitudes and habits of systematic inquiry.

A final word of caution is in order, however. To ask teachers to emphasize thinking is not to suggest that they keep students so occupied at all times. As indicated throughout this book, there is a valid place for drill, for lecture, and even recitation at times. The point is made, however, that whatever is done in the classroom should occur in a pervasive atmosphere of reflective behavior.

In the development of the various instructional approaches in this book, the reflective or problem-solving process has been used as a guiding theory for teaching. To suggest that such a theory is complete, however, would amount to gross oversimplification. Always they are viewed as avenues that follow the normal processes of inquiry. The patterns are flexible and offer ample leeway for each instructor to bring his own personal creativity and Eurekas into the picture. Still, their validity rests upon this unifying structure of how we think. Classroom instruction for too long has been a haphazard venture into techniques that seem to work. Some systematized, unifying structure is needed. This is seen as the natural cognitive process of thought. It accommodates intuitive thought processes as well.

## VALUES

Emphasis upon concept learning enhances transfer to related areas. Often referred to as *nonspecific transfer,* general ideas (concepts) transfer widely. The "higher" level concepts transfer more readily than do "lower" level concepts.

Concepts provide a basic structure for course, unit, and lesson planning. Essentially, it is the conceptual framework of a course that gives order to related experiences.

Evaluation, in terms of basic concepts, encourages retention of learning.

Concepts tell the learner what *facts* to look for and the meaning to assign to these facts. They are easily stored and rearranged for the derivation of new concepts.

## LIMITATIONS AND PROBLEMS

Inadequate concept formation provides a basis for distortions, biases, and prejudices. Since firmly established meanings are accompanied with *feelings,* improper concepts are often difficult to dislodge.

A teacher cannot "give" a student a concept. Since meaning is based upon concrete experiences, direct pupil involvement is desirable. Sometimes a mental image (concept) is so clear to the teacher that he is tempted to short-cut the essential learning processes. This temptation is especially great when one is running "short of time."

The different levels of concept formation necessitate selection of the appropriate
level(s) of learning experiences. Secondary students differ widely. Accordingly, group instruction may be ineffective for some of the lesser prepared
students.

Teachers who emphasize lesson "topics" tend to attempt too much in a given
lesson. Concept formation cannot be crowded or pushed.

It is extremely difficult to determine degree of concept attainment. Since concepts
gain meaning through experience, the teacher can never be certain of the
optimum number of experiences essential to adequate transfer of learning.


## CONCEPT ILLUSTRATIONS

It will be recalled that instructional concepts exist at three different levels: course
(unit themes), unit, and lesson. Lesson concepts (generalizations) are derived
*by students* as a culminating lesson experience. They essentially embody one basic
unit concept (formulated by the teacher in preplanning activities). Unit concepts,
in turn, embody one course concept (frequently called a unit or unit theme).
Course and unit concepts are illustrated below. Lesson generalizations are illustrated in the various chapters dealing with different instructional methods.

*Course Concepts (unit titles or themes)*

I. Useful in earth science classes

   A. Our dynamic earth and its materials
   B. Master cycle rules the earth's events
   C. The evolution of the earth's mountains
   D. Mother earth and her autobiography
   E. Planet earth and its environment in space
   F. The potential and kinetic climates of our planet earth

II. Useful in home economics classes

   A. Understanding ourselves and others
   B. The family
   C. Boy-girl interests
   D. Marriage
   E. Marital problems
   F. Parenthood
   G. Family finance

III. Useful in algebra classes

   A. Symbols: A new way to represent numbers
   B. Set theory: Understanding relationships
   C. Solving problems by equations
   D. Formulae: How mathematics saves time
   E. Polynomials: Expressions with more than one term
   F. Graphs: Visual representations

   IV. Useful in American literature classes

    A. The beginnings of the American tradition
    B. Democracy
    C. Internationalism
    D. Conflict
    E. Comic spirit
    F. Dissent
    G. Power structures

   V. Useful in American history classes

    A. Birth of democracy
    B. Reconstruction period in the South
    C. Influence of industrialization on the economy
    D. Problems and the growth of the worker
    E. City growth brings problems
    F. Immigrants and their contributions to the United States
    G. Isolationism and its effects on the United States

   VI. Useful in physical education classes

    A. Instilling self-confidence
    B. Developing a will to win
    C. Teamwork in sports and society
    D. Discovering recreational values
    E. Extending the body's capabilities
    F. Making the learner socially at ease

   VII. Useful in chemistry classes
    A. Matter and energy: Building blocks of the world around us
    B. Oxygen and hydrogen: Common chemical reactions
    C. Solutions and equilibrium: The states of matter that affect us
    D. Carbon: The chemistry of life
    E. Nuclear chemistry: A new source of energy

   VIII. Useful in art classes

    A. Developing sensitivity and awareness
    B. Relating the five elements of design
    C. Exploring new art media
    D. Perspective, structure, and composition
    E. Art appreciation and vocabulary: An introduction
    F. The three-dimensional experience

*Unit Concepts*

   I. Useful in earth science classes

   *Unit:* Our Dynamic Earth and Its Materials

   *Concepts:*
    1. Observations and measurements of the earth's surface con-
       tribute to knowledge about the earth's hidden interior.

2. The face of the earth is constantly changing.
3. The sequential order of events enables us to reconstruct the earth's history.
4. Minerals are the earth's building blocks.
5. Rocks on and in the earth's crust are continually changing in response to fluctuating environmental conditions.
6. A basic frame of reference is necessary to express motion.

II. Useful in home economics classes

*Unit:* The Family

*Concepts:*
1. Some form of family life is universal.
2. Each family functions differently.
3. Understanding of the family is essential to modern-day living.
4. Traditions, customs, and rituals play a major part in family development.
5. Families can be loving, noble, dictatorial, and possibly vindictive.
6. Families of today differ substantially from those of earlier times.
7. Each person, to some degree, is a product of his family.
8. The family stages offer new and varied experiences.

III. Useful in algebra classes

*Unit:* Formulae: How Mathematics Saves Time

*Concepts:*
1. The world is full of unknowns that can be represented by use of formulae.
2. Formulae allow one to express rules in a concise form.
3. The principles and facts that make a formula possible are more important than memorizing the formula itself.

IV. Useful in American literature classes

*Unit:* The Beginning of the American Tradition

*Concepts:*
1. Political writers influence the development of American ideals.
2. Conflict of interests (as in the American colonies) inspires political writers to reflect the revolutionary spirit.
3. Talented political leaders (scientists) are responsible for some of our most valuable documents (e.g., the Constitution of the United States).
4. American tradition is rooted in the colonial period.
5. The men who created the literature of colonial America (just as modern writers) were, by and large, not professional writers.

V. Useful in United States history classes

*Unit:* Birth of Democracy

*Concepts:*
1. Communication between people is essential.
2. Responsibility is the partner to freedom.
3. The United States Constitution is a series of compromises.
4. The United States President's office is one of the most powerful offices in the world.
5. The check and balance system is an integral part of all forms of democratic life.

VI. Useful in physical education classes

*Unit:* Teamwork in Sports and Society

*Concepts:*
1. We are on teams all our lives.
2. Each player has a responsibility to the team.
3. It is as important to bring others into team participation as it is to make a large individual team contribution.
4. Principles of teamwork are readily transferred to teamwork in the larger society.
5. All people must be able team workers to function effectively in society.

VII. Useful in chemistry classes

*Unit:* Carbon: The Chemistry of Life

*Concepts:*
1. Methane, a common fuel gas, is a building block for all other organic compounds.
2. Alcohol, a hydrocarbon in which one hydrogen has been replaced by an $-OH$ group, serves many uses.
3. Sugars and starches are products of natural organic chemical processes.
4. Photosynthesis, the "food"-producing process of plants, is a complex organic reaction.
5. Many important drugs and vitamins, such as penicillin, are organic compounds.
6. Rubber, plastic, and synthetic fibers are the result of research in organic chemistry.
7. Proteins and the genetic code (DNA) are complex organic compounds that control all living things.

VIII. Useful in art classes

*Unit:* Developing Sensitivity and Awareness

*Concepts:*
1. Art originality and uniqueness stem from awareness and sensitivity.
2. An artist must continually search for new stimuli of various backgrounds and details.

3. Eagerness and an open mind are necessary ingredients for allowing the growth of awareness and sensitivity in art.
4. The "odd ball" approach encourages the artist's search for new ideas and ways of using art media.
5. The fully developed awareness of such men as Van Gogh, Michelangelo, Arnason, and Frank Lloyd Wright have set these artists apart from their peers.
6. The importance of individual awareness can become evident when we observe its absence in the extreme.

# CHAPTER 2

# Establishing
# Instructional Objectives

## OVERVIEW

### Key Concepts

1. Instructional objectives are categorized into three somewhat overlapping domains: cognitive, affective, and psychomotor; each essentially embodies the problem-solving process.
2. Attainment of outcomes in one domain does not necessarily entail attainment of outcomes in the other domains.
3. Objectives are derived from basic concepts of the unit.
4. Instructional objectives range from simple to complex. "Higher"-order outcomes incorporate "lower"-order outcomes.
5. Instructional objectives are culminated in terms of projected pupil behavioral outcomes.
6. Degree of outcome specificity will vary, depending upon whether it is a minimum-essentials or a developmental outcome.
7. Instructional objectives with their behavioral outcomes provide a sound basis for subsequent instructional and evaluational experiences.

### New Terms

1. **Cognitive Objectives**—A domain of objectives, ranging from simple to complex, which involves basic reasoning (problem-solving) processes.
2. **Affective Objectives**—A domain of objectives, ranging from mere attention to characterization of a value complex. Attitudes and emotions are involved.
3. **Psychomotor Objectives**—A domain of objectives which incorporates the necessary steps in the acquisition of mental and motor skills.
4. **Behavioral Outcomes**—Actual pupil behaviors which may be anticipated at the culmination of a given learning experience or sequence.

5. **Minimum Essentials Outcomes**—Most appropriate in the mental and motor skills area, such outcomes must indicate the specific *conditions* and the *minimum level* of performance anticipated.
6. **Developmental Outcomes**—Most appropriate in the "academic" areas, this group of outcomes suggests a "class" or group of anticipated behaviors. Since *maximum* achievement is sought, anticipated conditions and minimum level of performance criteria are not needed.
7. **Entry Behaviors**—Behaviors indicating competencies which are assumed as a prerequisite for a given learning experience. Some type of pre-assessment such as a pretest is essential.
8. **En Route Behaviors**—These intermediate behavioral outcomes deemed prerequisite for attainment of final (terminal) outcomes.
9. **Terminal Behaviors**—Those behaviors that are indicative of ultimate goal achievement.


## Questions to Guide Your Study

1. How do behavioral stated outcomes (as a preinstructional activity) set the stage for learning and evaluational experiences?
2. Since the three-goal taxonomies overlap, why bother to treat them separately?
3. It has been stated that the higher, more complex levels of educational objectives also include the lower, less complex objectives. The reverse, however, does not necessarily apply. Explain and indicate the implications for teaching.
4. "Developmental outcomes which specify the conditions and minimum level of performance expected are of the recall variety." Defend or refute.


The most fundamental aspect of teaching is the formulation of worthwhile aims or goals.[1] Just as a list of educational purposes is useful in determining the nature of the curriculum, so do course and unit goals guide the teacher and student in selection, in organization, and finally in evaluation of learning experiences. Actually, goals or purposes constitute the hub around which all other instructional activities revolve.

Unless goals are stated in meaningful terms, they do not serve a worthwhile purpose. Although most teachers acknowledge the importance of instructional goals, relatively few actually use them effectively as a guide for selecting appropriate learning activities. The almost inevitable consequence is an unimaginative, memoriter-type of experience, commonly known as textbook teaching. When this situation exists, there is a tendency to emphasize textbook facts as ends in themselves. Accordingly, relatively little transfer or application to related life problems can be expected.

Once the teacher has identified major unit concepts to be emphasized, he is in a position to develop unit objectives. Each major concept must be analyzed for the purpose of determining the precise nature of the objective (purpose or

[1] In this chapter the words *aims, goals, objectives,* and *purposes* are used interchangeably.

goal) to be sought. It may be that an understanding or comprehension is desired; sometimes an attitude or value must be developed and/or altered; frequently a mental or motor skill will be emphasized. This basic decision will determine the nature of the unit experiences.

## FUNDAMENTAL PROPERTIES

The ends of instruction (goal attainment) become basic ideas (concepts) in one's repertoire of experience. Ideas are internalized, however, in different ways. One idea, for example, may represent a mere basic understanding, while another idea will be accompanied with strong emotion. Still another idea may be associated with some mental or motor dexterity. All three components are usually associated, in some measure, with each idea or concept. Nevertheless, the instructional experience will vary considerably with the nature of the outcome sought. Attainment of one does not guarantee the attainment of another.

### What Are the Properties of Cognitive Goals?

Such goals are usually expressed as *understandings.* They vary from simple recall of facts to highly original and creative ways of combining and synthesizing new ideas and materials. A useful taxonomy of cognitive goals has been developed by Bloom and his associates.[2] They describe six cognitive levels.

1. *Knowledge.* This involves the lowest level of learning including recall and memory. At this level the learner is expected to recall specifics with concrete referents. They include terminology and specific facts such as dates, events, persons, places. Also included is *recall* of basic principles and generalizations.

2. *Comprehension.* This represents the lowest level of understanding. The individual is able to make use of the materials or idea without relating them to other materials. For example, he is able to paraphrase or even interpret something he has gained from reading or listening. At the highest level of this category the learner may be able to *extend* his thinking beyond the data by making simple inferences. Thus in science class he is able to draw conclusions from a simple demonstration or experiment.

3. *Application.* This intellectual skill entails the use of information in specific situations. The information may be in the form of general ideas, or concepts, principles, or theories which must be remembered and applied. The science student, for example, who draws conclusions from a particular experiment at the comprehension level is now able to *apply* the basic principle(s) to *related* experiments or scientific phenomena.

[2] Benjamin S. Bloom, ed., *Taxonomy of Educational Objectives, Handbook I: Cognitive Domain* (New York: David McKay Co., Inc., 1956). Copyright © 1956 by David McKay Co., Inc.; David R. Krathwohl, "Stating Objectives Appropriately for Program, for Curriculum, and for Instructional Materials Development," *Journal of Teacher Education* 16, no. 1 (March 1965): 83–92. Used by permission of the publisher.

4. *Analysis.* This involves taking apart the information and making relationships. The purpose is to clarify by discovering hidden meaning and basic structure. The student is able to read between the lines, to distinguish between fact and opinion, to assess degree of consistency or inconsistency. Thus the science student is able to distinguish between relevant and extraneous materials or events. Likewise, the social science student is able to detect unstated assumptions.

5. *Synthesis.* At this level the learner is able to reassemble the component parts for new meaning. This recombining process permits the emergence of a new pattern or structure not previously apparent. Thus the learner may develop new or creative ideas from the process. While a certain amount of combining is involved at the lower levels, at this level the process is more complete. He draws upon elements from many sources *in addition to* the particular problem under consideration. The science student, for instance, may propose a unique plan (to him at least) for testing a hypothesis. The mathematics student may make a discovery or generalization which is not evident from the given communication.

6. *Evaluation.* This highest level of cognition involves making judgments on the materials, information, or method for specific purposes. This represents the end process of cognition, involving distinct criteria as a basis for such decisions. When conceived in relation to the problem-solving or cognitive process, it involves selecting one of the proposed alternatives over all the rest.

It is seen from Bloom's taxonomy that intellectual or cognitive learnings vary from simple to the complex, from concrete to the abstract. Attainment of the higher cognitive levels is dependent on satisfactory progress at the lower levels of cognition. Attainment of the lower levels, however, does not assure attainment of the higher levels. Implicit in the taxonomy are the processes of critical or reflective thinking, sometimes merely described as the problem-solving or cognitive process.

## What Are the Properties of Affective Goals?

Along with the attainment of intellectual or cognitive objectives, teachers have emphasized emotional or affective purposes. Such goals are often expressed as interests, attitudes, or appreciations. As Krathwohl, Bloom, and Masia point out, "we need to provide a range of emotion from neutrality through mild to strong emotion, probably of a positive, but possibly also of a negative kind."[3] They have developed such a taxonomy. As with the cognitive domain, the affective taxonomy ranges from the simple to the complex. This is described in terms of relative degrees of *internalization.*[4] By internalization they mean a process through which there is first an incomplete and tentative adoption of the desired

---

[3] David R. Krathwohl, Benjamin S. Bloom, and Bertram S. Masia, *Taxonomy of Educational Objectives, Handbook II: Affective Domain* (New York: David McKay Co., Inc., 1964), p. 26.
[4] David R. Krathwohl, "Stating Objectives Appropriately for Program, for Curriculum, and for Instructional Materials Development," *Journal of Teacher Education* 16 (March 1965): 83–92. Used by permission of the publisher.

emotion to a more complete adoption of the feeling in the latter stages of learning. The five levels of the affective domain follow:

1. *Receiving (Attending).* At this first level the learner merely becomes aware of an idea, process, or thing. Thus he is willing to listen or to attend to a given communication. From a purely passive role of captive receiver he may advance to one of directing his attention to the communication, despite competing or distracting stimuli. For example, he listens for rhythm in poetry or prose read aloud.

2. *Responding.* This level involves doing something with or about the phenomenon other than merely perceiving it. At this low level of commitment the student does not yet hold the value. To use a common expression of teachers, "He displays an *interest* in the phenomenon." From obedient participation, the student may advance to voluntary response, and finally to a *pleasurable feeling* or *satisfaction* which accompanies his behavior. This feeling may be expressed by the goal, "reads poetry for personal pleasure."

3. *Valuing.* As the term implies, at this level a thing, phenomenon, or behavior has worth. Behavior at this level reflects a belief or an attitude. Thus it might be said that he "holds the value." This level is characterized by motivated behavior in which the individual's commitment guides his behavior. At the lower end of the continuum the learner might be said to hold the belief somewhat tentatively; at the other end, his value becomes one of conviction—certainty "beyond the shadow of a doubt." Indeed at the upper end of the continuum he is likely to try to persuade others to his way of thinking.

4. *Organization.* Here the individual has established a conscious basis for choice-making. He has organized his values into a system—a set of criteria—for guiding his behavior. Accordingly, he will be able to defend his choices and will be aware of the basis of his attitudes.

5. *Characterization.* At this level the internalization process is complete. Values are *integrated* into some kind of internally consistent system. Thus the person is described as having certain controlling tendencies. He has a recognized philosophy of life.

Prior to development of the affective taxonomy, teachers experienced considerable difficulty in providing adequate evaluational experiences in this area. Consequently, instructional emphasis tended to neglect the emotional aspects of learning. The affective taxonomy is an extremely useful technique of clarifying the problem.

Complex affective goals are not as easily achieved as complex cognitive goals. Indeed the levels of "organization" and "characterization" are not reached in any one course. They represent a culmination of many years of educational experience.

## What Are the Properties of Psychomotor Goals?

A third major instructional domain is in the area of mental and motor skills. Teachers recognize that as a result of certain instructional activities, students should acquire such motor skills as playing tennis or basketball; that they should also develop certain mental skills, such as those required in writing and talking. Although all skills require some understanding and are usually accompanied with varying degrees of emotion, it is recognized that *emphasis* in this area must be placed upon development of the skill. The psychomotor taxonomy clarifies the essentials of this process.

1. *Observing.* At this level the learner observes a more experienced person in his performance of the activity. He is usually asked to observe sequences and relationships and to pay particular attention to the finished product. Sometimes the reading of directions substitutes for this experience. Frequently, however, reading is *supplemented* by direct observation. Thus the beginning tennis student may read his manual and then watch his instructor demonstrate certain techniques.

2. *Imitating.* By the time the learner has advanced to this level he has begun to acquire the basic rudiments of the desired behavior. He follows directions and sequences under close supervision. The total act is not important, nor is timing or coordination emphasized. He is conscious of deliberate effort to imitate the model. The tennis player, for example, may practice a prescribed stance or stroke.

3. *Practicing.* The entire sequence is performed repeatedly at this level. All aspects of the act are performed in sequence. Conscious effort is no longer necessary as the performance becomes more or less habitual in nature. At this level we might reasonably say that the person has acquired the skill.

4. *Adapting.* The terminal level is often referred to as "perfection of the skill." Although a few individuals develop much greater skill in certain areas than do most individuals, there is nearly always room for "greater perfection." The process involves adapting "minor" details which, in turn, influence the total performance. Such modifications may be initiated by the learner or by his teacher. This is the process a basketball player goes through, for example, when a "good" player becomes a better player.

It is obvious that the psychomotor domain also involves a graded sequence from simple to complex. By deciding upon the degree of skill development needed, the instructor is able to plan his instructional activities most efficiently. Likewise, evaluational techniques will vary considerably with the different levels.

### What Are the Essential Differences in Formulating Minimum Essentials and Developmental Outcomes?

Culminating instructional goals with specific behavioral outcomes is a relatively simple task. There is considerable controversy and confusion, however, relative to how specifically such outcomes should be stated. Many leaders in the field suggest that along with specific behaviors the teacher should also specify the *conditions* under which the behavior is exhibited and the *minimum level of performance* expected. To illustrate with an example by Esbensen.[5]

---

[5] Thorwald Esbensen, "Writing Instructional Objectives," *Phi Delta Kappan* 48 (January 1967): 246–7.

"Given 20 sentences containing a variety of mistakes in capitalization, the student is able, with at least 90 percent accuracy, to identify and rewrite correctly each word that has a mistake in capitalization." Such an outcome, according to Gronlund,[6] might be considered one of several *minimum essentials* expected of all students. They are relatively easily achieved and serve as prerequisites to further learning in the area. Although minimum level standards are easily established, an acceptable basis for such standards is much more difficult to defend. In the preceding example one might just as logically establish a minimum standard of accuracy of 89 or 92 percent. Defensible minimum levels may be adjusted on the basis of instructional experience. Certain standards, as in typing accuracy, have evolved over a period of time. Thus a maximum of two mistakes may be tolerated in a typing exercise.

*Developmental* outcomes, according to Gronlund,[7] should normally account for a major portion of preplanned instructional outcomes, especially in "academic courses." The teacher emphasis is on encouraging each student to progress as far as possible toward predetermined goals. Thus such outcomes are more general than those at the mastery level. At the developmental level *maximum achievement* is sought, rendering levels of performance practically impossible to define. The developmental outcome, ". . . ability to identify fallacies in arguments," for example, appropriately does not call for a minimum standard of performance. This will depend upon each student's interpretation. Furthermore, the terminal activity being merely representative of previous instructional experiences would not necessarily elicit any minimum number of "fallacies."

Both minimum essential and developmental outcomes are useful in most classes. In skill areas (e.g., typing, shorthand, physical education and shop courses) more emphasis is usually placed upon the minimum essential type of outcome. In the academic areas (e.g., English, biology, history, and general business courses) the developmental type of outcome should be more in evidence. Generally, outcomes should be stated as simply and concisely as possible. They are characterized by "action" words, such as identify, name, construct, describe, order, and so on. These verbs are less ambiguous than other (more commonly used) verbs. Such verbs as *know, appreciate, understand, master, apply,* and *evaluate* tend to carry many meanings.

## What Are the Differences Between Entry, En Route, and Terminal Behaviors?[8]

Basic to all instruction is this question: "What learnings must the student possess if he is to reach the intended goal?" In answering this question a systematic program of *preassessment* is recommended. According to Popham and

---

[6] Norman E. Gronlund, *Stating Objectives for Classroom Instruction* (New York: The Macmillan Co., 1970), pp. 33–6.

[7] Gronlund, *Stating Objectives,* pp. 33–6.

[8] The reader is urged to refer to learning outcomes illustrated in sample lesson plans. Attempt to classify relative to domain, level, and type.

Baker[9] such a pretest will include terminal behaviors as well as a sampling of essential entry and en route behaviors. The number of hours on instruction which are wasted each year on developing skills that learners already possess would be staggering to the imagination. Literally thousands of students suffer through lessons designed to teach facts that they already know simply because teachers do not pretest. Likewise, those students who do not possess the skills necessary for success in a course are doomed to failure unless appropriate corrective action is taken.

A *terminal* behavior might be illustrated as follows: ". . . writes a paragraph which includes a topic sentence" (from Popham and Baker). Entry behaviors include such learnings as what constitutes a paragraph and a topic sentence. They also include ability to write sentences, appropriate spelling, punctuation, and the like. These are assumptions that teachers normally make with respect to readiness of students to cope with the problem under consideration. Today's emphasis upon "social promotion," regardless of previous achievement, renders such assumptions increasingly tenuous.

*En route* or intermediate behaviors are those deemed necessary to lead the learner to the terminal behavior. A logical question to ask is "What must the learner do before he can successfully perform the terminal behavior?" This provides clues to planning of instructional activities.

Instructional outcomes (at the unit level) will generally focus upon those terminal behaviors anticipated from the learning experiences. It should be observed, however, that they may sometimes feature en route behaviors also. Frequently they will suggest a terminal behavior that will be identical to one or more en route behaviors. The case method, for example, may be used during the instructional sequence (en route) and also as a terminal activity. Likewise, students may do a written exercise along the way and do a similar one as a terminal activity. *Lesson* outcomes will always emphasize en route behaviors within the total unit context.

## What Is the Role of the Student in Goal Formation?

Throughout this section emphasis has been placed upon preplanning activities of the teacher. The teacher identifies the unit concepts, goals, and behavioral outcomes to be sought through the instructional experience. He then communicates purposes to students in language that they can understand. This is usually a basic function of a unit overview. (See course and unit introductions, treated in chapter following.) It should be repeated frequently during the learning experiences.

As a result of revealing instructional purposes to students, certain changes are usually in order. Some purposes may be altered on the basis of pupil feedback. Planned activities (en route behaviors) frequently will be altered. In some instances the process of revealing purposes to students will provide a springboard for joint teacher-student planning of instructional sequences.

[9] W. James Popham and Eva L. Baker, *Systematic Instruction* (Englewood Cliffs, N.J.: Prentice-Hall, Inc., 1970), pp. 72–4.

# GOAL FORMULATION

For many years teachers have been stating worthwhile goals. Unfortunately, however, goals have been stated so vaguely as to hold little meaning. The result has been overemphasis on textbook teaching and relatively little application to related life problems. The procedure recommended below represents one way of correcting the difficulty.

### How Are Goals Constructed?

A great deal of confusion exists today over the relationship between the concept, goal, and behavioral outcomes. Some authorities advocate the omission of the general goal or objective entirely. They would have the instructor proceed directly from the concept to specific behaviors students are to display at the culmination of instruction.[10] To illustrate: "Defines selected technical terms in his own words." This technique is most useful in programmed instruction and at the training level of performance. For conventional class instruction, however, it tends to suggest that the identified behaviors are ends in themselves. Thus, *instruction* in the specific identified behavior would be emphasized, e.g., defining technical terms. To assess degree of achievement the student logically would be expected to merely recall previous learnings.

Another approach and the one recommended by the author has been clarified by Gronlund.[11] This involves stating the general instructional objectives (derived from a given unit concept) and then listing samples of specific behaviors which are acceptable evidence of goal attainment. To illustrate: "Understands the meaning of selected technical terms by defining the terms in his own words." Thus the *goal* is now one of understanding. Specific outcomes of defining, using, identifying, relating, or whatever are merely *samples* of behaviors which would suggest goal attainment. This opens the door to many types of learning experiences. Assessing degree of goal achievement now calls for responses not directly taught. The student must indicate his ability to *generalize.*

When achieved, an instructional goal is internalized as an idea or concept. The nature of ideas, however, will vary according to the three broad domains previously described. Either stated or implied in a worthy goal is a real-life application. As a means of focusing attention upon the student, it is recommended that each instructional goal begin with the introductory clause, "After this unit (or lesson) the student should. . . ." In this way the emphasis tends to be shifted from teacher wants to student needs.

The next step is identification of the domain to be emphasized. The words *understanding, attitudes and appreciations,* and *skills and habits* are commonly employed to denote the cognitive, affective, and psychomotor domains, respec-

---

[10] R. F. Mager, *Preparing Instructional Objectives* (Palo Alto, Calif.: Fearon Publishers, 1962).

[11] Gronlund, *Stating Objectives,* pp. 4–6.

tively. For example, "After this lesson the student should have furthered his *understanding* of. . . ." Each goal should be restricted to a given domain and to a single idea.

## How Are Pupil Behaviors Incorporated into Instructional Goals?

Although learnings are internalized as ideas or concepts, there are many outward manifestations of that which is learned. A student's behavior offers the best clues to that which is learned. These are referred to as behavioral outcomes. For each instructional goal a number of pupil outcomes will suggest goal achievement or means to achievement. Accordingly, for each goal the teacher should select those specific behavioral outcomes which seem most likely to reflect progress toward goal achievement. It is usually desirable to identify as many outcomes as possible and then to select those which seem most practical for use as a guide to instructional activities.

Behavioral outcomes are usually incorporated within the goal framework. For example, "After this unit in American literature the student should further appreciate the social inequalities resulting from a social class structure, as evidenced by (1) his realistic *responses* in a class discussion on the problem "What should be the United States's policy with respect to migrant workers?" (2) his willingness to examine feeling reactions resulting from a sociodrama designed to portray feelings in a specified social situation, and (3) his greater cooperation with underprivileged students in class and society." It should be noted that outcome (1) relates to level two of the affective domain (responding), while outcomes (2) and (3) suggest different levels of number three (valuing) of this domain. By becoming thoroughly familiar with the various levels of each instructional domain, the teacher can select those outcomes which seem most appropriate for any given set of circumstances.

Unit outcomes provide definite clues to desirable class activities. The foregoing illustration, for example, pinpoints at least two *intermediate* behaviors which might be elicited as avenues to goal achievement. This applies to outcomes (1) and (2). Outcome (3) is a *terminal* behavior but one which can hardly be measured under normal school conditions. Its usefulness seems to be primarily that of reminding the teacher of the ultimate behavior being sought.

In *evaluating goal achievement,* the teacher must direct attention to *terminal* behaviors. The behaviors identified in the foregoing illustration, however, provide a useful *basis* for this task. Outcome (1), for example, can be rendered sufficient for evaluational purposes by identifying various processes essential in a problem-solving class discussion. These might include one's ability (1) to identify the central issue, (2) to recognize assumptions, (3) to evaluate evidence, and (4) to draw warranted conclusions.

In considering techniques which may be used to judge goal achievement one can focus upon actual overt *behavior* or the *products* of learning obtained from tests and the like. All too often emphasis has been placed upon the latter to the exclusion of the former. Performance on tests and various other written assignments are indeed valid indicators of achievement. More *overt* behavior, however, is an equally valid and sometimes superior indicator of goal achievement. If, for example, a speech student can render an effective impromptu speech at the culmination of a unit, this may be the best indication of goal attainment possible. This assumes, of course, that records of preliminary experiences have been kept so that progress can be effectively measured.

## VALUES

Appropriate formulation of goals provides the basis for development of consistent learning and evaluation experiences.

The process of formulating goals, in terms of behavioral outcomes, emphasizes the transfer of learnings to related areas.

Preliminary formulation of lesson goals, with their appropriate behavioral outcomes, tends to expand one's perception of the many avenues available for reaching these ends. Thus a variety of instructional techniques may be employed.

Appropriate goal formulation tends to relegate the selected textbook to its proper place, as only one of many instructional resources.

## LIMITATIONS AND PROBLEMS

Goals or aims, when inappropriately formulated, are a waste of time. Thus many teachers consider them the *least* important rather than the *most* important aspect of the instructional process.

Many worthy instructional outcomes cannot be observed or evaluated within the context of a given course. As a consequence, certain important learning experiences may be minimized, simply because they cannot be evaluated effectively. One solution to the problem involves the formulation of longitudinal goals, evaluated by several teachers over an extended period of time.

Since each student is expected to progress toward common goal achievement, there is a tendency for some teachers to follow with a common set of learning and evaluational activities. Such a practice ignores all we know about individual differences. Different students achieve instructional outcomes in different ways.

Many worthwhile goals can be derived for each instructional unit. There is a tendency to emphasize the cognitive over the affective domain. Again, this practice is apparently related to the ease of evaluating cognitive, as opposed to affective, learning. With the recent appearance of a taxonomy of educational objectives in the affective domain, it is hoped that this imbalance will be adjusted.

Considerable confusion exists between those behaviors sought *during* the learning experience and those sought as *terminal* behaviors. The teacher's first concern must be with those behaviors which are likely to contribute to growth toward goals. Eventually, however, he must direct attention toward final goal achievement. The latter must be more specific than the former.

## ILLUSTRATIONS

Additional unit goal illustrations are provided in Appendix A. Lesson goals are illustrated in the sample lesson plans provided in each methods chapter.

CHAPTER **3**

# Planning for Teaching

## OVERVIEW

### Key Concepts

1. The unit concept is fundamental to instructional planning.
2. A functional unit concept is broader than specific content material; it embodies a current-life application.
3. Unit concepts are not passed along to students; rather, students are expected to derive their own generalizations as a culminating experience of each lesson.
4. Although preinstructional planning is essential, adjustments based upon specific student wants and needs are to be expected.
5. Lesson plans are generally based upon a single unit concept.
6. Behavioral unit outcomes foreshadow instructional methods and techniques.
7. A lesson plan, essentially, consists of a proposed analytical development of a selected problem.
8. Since the resolution of a given problem may extend well beyond a single class period, the *daily* lesson plan is a misnomer.

### New Terms

1. **The Yearly Plan**—The overall course plan, consisting essentially of unit titles (evolved from general course concepts).
2. **The Teaching Unit**—A group of related concepts from which a given set of instructional and evaluational experiences is derived. Units normally range from three to six weeks long.
3. **The Lesson Plan**—Those specific learning activities which evolve from a given unit concept. Each lesson plan is structured around a problem specifically designed to guide the processes of reflective thinking.

### Questions to Guide Your Study

1. Why do textbook units often make rather poor teaching units?
2. "Unit planning is more appropriate for academic courses than for skills classes." Defend or refute.
3. In what ways has the unit approach to instruction affected the nature of lesson planning.
4. What are the basic differences between the content outline and a list of major unit concepts?
5. It has been observed that experienced teachers are more likely to omit lesson goals than any other segment from their planning activities. Yet, experts consider a statement of goals among the most basic aspects of planning. Evaluate this apparent discrepancy between theory and practice.

Planning, like map making, enables one to predict the future course of events. In essence, a plan is a blueprint—a plan of action. As any traveler knows, the best-laid plans sometimes go awry. Sometimes unforeseen circumstances even prevent one from beginning a well-planned journey; other times, conditions while on the trip may cause one to alter his plans drastically. More often, however, a well-planned journey is altered in *minor* ways for those unpredictable "side trips" which may seem desirable from close range.

Likewise, teachers must plan classroom experiences. They must plan the scope and sequence of courses, the content within courses, the units to be taught, the activities to be employed, and the tests to be given. While few teachers would deny the necessity of planning, there is some controversy with respect to the scope and nature of planning. Indeed, methods specialists themselves differ relative to the essential scope of planning. Some seem to feel that unit planning renders lesson planning almost unnecessary. Others stress the importance of lesson plans while minimizing the value of unit plans. While the planning needs of teachers will vary markedly, there is considerable justification for *both* unit and lesson planning.

# THE YEARLY PLAN

The process of planning begins when a teacher sets out to determine what major ideas or dimensions will be emphasized during the year. All available textbooks in the area, curriculum guides, and course-of-study aids should be surveyed for this purpose. Although each teacher often prepares his own yearly plan, increased emphasis is being given to joint participation by all members of a department. This promotes appropriate integration of related courses and enables teachers of the same course to develop desirable commonalities. At the same time it leaves each instructor free to develop various aspects of the course in his own way.

Oddly enough, some teachers have limited their preparation for yearly planning to a single selected textbook. Such a practice, in effect, makes both teacher and students slaves to a single frame of reference. Textbook units, chapters and topics, accordingly, are studied in a chapter-by-chapter and page-by-page manner. It must be emphasized that a textbook, at its best, merely provides all learners with one comprehensive source of information. Since textbooks are designed to fulfill the needs of as many people as possible, they usually contain some materials which will be of marginal value to individual instructors. As each textbook writer tends to emphasize certain aspects over others, it behooves the teacher to survey as many such sources as possible for the purpose of ascertaining what aspects *he* will emphasize.

## How Are Major Course Concepts Identified?

As indicated in the chapter on "Gaining the Concept," concepts exist at different levels. The most abstract level, for instructional purposes, is identification of several broad ideas (concepts) which should be developed during the course. At this point they will be broad and suggestive only. There may be as many as a dozen of these. It is usually desirable to state them as complete thoughts. To illustrate from a course in general business:

1. Production standards in the United States make this nation the distribution center of the world.
2. Retail markets in the United States are consumer-oriented.
3. Selling is a joint process of communication between buyer and seller.

After several tentative course concepts have been stated, they are revised and reworked until six or eight basic ideas remain. (Some teachers prefer to incorporate course concepts into course objectives. This step is not essential however.)

Frequently a need for two or more units may be developed from a single major concept. This suggests the need for more specific concepts. Eventually there usually will be a unit for each major concept. Appropriate unit titles, based upon the illustrated concepts in a general business course, follow:

1. The United States: Distribution Center of the World
2. The Consumer Determines the Market
3. Sales Promotion and Advertising

After major unit titles have been tentatively established, an approximate time schedule for each unit is established. This will reflect relative degrees of emphasis to be given to each unit. It may be that time limitations will necessitate basic changes. Sometimes certain proposed units must be deleted. Units are seldom less than three or more than six weeks long.

## How Are Major Course Purposes Developed with Students?

After major units have been selected, the teacher is in a position to develop for students an overview of the major aspects of the course. Purpose of this experience is to give students an opportunity to develop a series of expectations relative to the course. Basic purposes, at their level of understanding, are offered. Students, in turn, are provided an opportunity to ask questions and to offer suggestions. The effect of such an experience is that of creating initial interest in the experiences which are to follow.

Such an introductory statement may be handled as a lecture-discussion experience. With a little added imagination, however, an atmosphere of eager anticipation may be established. Almost any instructional method or technique may be a useful means of attracting students to the particular course of study. There is an abundance of instructional media available for such purposes.

At least one class period should be devoted to this activity. A course introduction can be found in the unit plan illustrated in Appendix A.

# THE TEACHING UNIT

The teaching unit is designed to center the work of the class around meaningful wholes or patterns and to make the work of different days focus on a central theme until some degree of unified learning is attained. *The basic elements of a teaching unit consist of a group of related concepts, unified for instructional purposes.*

The process is essentially one of combining related ideas into some intellectual pattern. It provides opportunities for critical thinking, generalization and application of ideas to many situations.

Unit titles, as illustrated in the yearly plan, do not usually correspond to textbook units. In order to make instruction attractive to boys and girls, a teaching unit most appropriately focuses upon a central, practical idea or theme. Although some English teachers would attempt to structure a unit around Julius Caesar, for example, youngsters would likely be more attracted to a unit dealing with "ambition." Such a unit, of course, would focus upon Julius Caesar as an avenue to realizing the major objectives.[1] Instead of studying evolution, a science teacher might construct a unit around the concept of "change." The idea of evolution would become one dimension of a much more comprehensive theme. Such a unit concept approaches what Jerome Bruner has termed the basic structure of knowledge.[2]

Implicit in unit planning are three different phases: initiating activities, developing activities, culminating activities. The first phase of unit planning is similar to the steps in yearly planning. Unit planning is necessarily more

---

[1] John B. Chase, Jr., and James L. Howard, "Changing Concepts of Unit Teaching," *The High School Journal* 47, no. 4 (February 1964): 180–7.
[2] Jerome Bruner, *The Process of Education* (Cambridge, Mass.: Harvard University Press, 1961), pp. 17–18.

restricted and specific than the latter. In all cases, however, the process must be consistent with, and fit into, the overall framework established in the yearly plan.

### What Purpose Does the Content Outline Serve?

As an aid in developing a series of cohesive experiences, a content outline of each unit should be developed. Various aspects of the unit can be readily developed if basic content is clearly delineated in either detailed or topical fashion. Basic textbooks serve a most useful purpose in this phase of unit planning.

The content outline must be detailed enough to indicate points of emphasis, yet brief enough to be useful in the derivation of major unit concepts. The content outline which appears in the illustrated unit is rather brief. In a subject such as history or political science a more elaborate outline would be appropriate.

### How Are Major Unit Concepts Identified?

Using the unit outline as a broad frame of reference, the teacher develops from six to ten unit concepts. They are most appropriately expressed as complete thoughts. In essence, they are to become the structural foundations of the unit. As indicated in Chapter 1, "Gaining the Concept," if properly developed, concepts have high retention and transfer value. Although based upon content, they must possess generalizability. *Thus they are most appropriately phrased as generalizations suggesting current life applications.*

The illustration which follows is based upon a unit in general business, Sales Promotion and Advertising.

1. Customer satisfaction is the most important product.
2. Customer needs are the prompters for purchasing decisions.
3. Advertising can be an effective means of preselling products.[3]

In many subject areas it is relatively easy to meet the criterion of current life application. In a few subject areas, however, this is a rather complicated, but nevertheless essential, task. In history, for example, a two-step process seems necessary. First, one must identify the major ideas of the unit; then he must expand them into generalizations that are viable today. Without the second step, history teaching is likely to remain the dry and generally useless process of memorizing names, dates, and places.

To illustrate from a unit in United States history on World War I (*To Make the World Safe for Democracy*):

1. *Major unit idea*—Wilson's mistakes due to the peace treaty caused his unpopularity at home.

---

[3] A complete list of concepts for this unit is provided in the illustrated teaching unit in Appendix A.

2. *Major unit concept*—Ill-advised public expression (e.g., riots, etc., against Wilson) can adversely affect statesmanship.[4]

It is seen from the foregoing that each major unit concept is derived from an idea which is specific to a given era of history. Many of the concepts will occur again and again as the student studies other history units. In this way the learner can become aware of the repetition of diplomatic errors. New concepts, of course, also will be emphasized in each subsequent unit.

In other subject fields the task of concept identification is often complicated by textbook organization. In American literature, for example, textbook content may be organized around the broad themes of literary forms, historical themes, and the like. A historical theme on colonial America, for example, offers the reader numerous selections, each with its own story theme. The teacher's task, again, is two-fold in nature. First, he must identify major unit concepts (e.g., major threads of thought which occur repeatedly); then he must identify the particular selections which can be used in teaching each given concept.[5]

### How Are Instructional Goals and Behavioral Outcomes Derived from Unit Concepts?

Based upon unit concepts, appropriate unit goals with their accompanying outcomes are developed. Unit goals provide a necessary transition from what the teacher views as the ends of instruction to statements of pupil behaviors necessary for and indicative of the desired learnings. Frequently each unit goal will embody a different unit concept, but sometimes two or more *may* be embodied within a single goal. Indeed there are usually more concepts than goals.

By referring to the previous chapter the reader will note that instructional outcomes may apply to *minimum essentials objectives,* or they may be applied to *developmental objectives.* If they are of the minimum essentials variety, the specific conditions and expected level of performance must be specified. If, however, outcomes are developmental in nature, this degree of specificity is not appropriate. In academic courses the latter is emphasized. Accordingly, the illustration which follows is *developmental* in nature.

*Concept:* Customer needs are the prompters for purchasing decisions.

*Instructional Goal and Accompanying Behavioral Outcomes:*
After this unit the student should have furthered his understanding of the role of basic human motives and wants in selling, as evidenced by:
A. His ability to apply appropriate psychological principles in simulation games.
B. His interpretation of sales resistance evident in a sociodrama.

It should be noted that the named behavioral outcomes are complex, calling for a whole *class* of responses. They do suggest, however, specific

[4] This process is further illustrated in the last section of this chapter.
[5] This process is illustrated in the last section of this chapter.

methods and techniques which would represent appropriate *means* of goal achievement. Lesson outcomes are much more specific than unit outcomes.

## How Are Learning Experiences Evolved from Anticipated Behavioral Outcomes?

As indicated in the foregoing, each behavioral outcome suggests one or more methods or techniques which will contribute to goal achievement. Both a simulation game and a sociodrama were suggested in the illustration. At this point the teacher identifies the specific methods problems to be developed. To illustrate:

1. *Simulation Game:* "People, U.S.A."

2. *Sociodrama*

   *Problem:* How does a customer feel when he is pressured into buying a product?

   *Broad Situation:* Mary wants to buy a gift for her husband's birthday. Jim is a salesman in a department store.

The act of preplanning some of the activities does not mean that the teacher must assume the role of taskmaster. Students may actively participate in the planning of class activities, but this does not replace the need for a certain number of preplanned activities *suggested* by the teacher. As in the sample unit, different pupils often will be involved in different activities; thus provision for individual differences may become a reality. For beginning teachers it may be necessary to make a special point of this in the unit plan.

## How Is Goal Achievement Assessed?

Although unit evaluation is not a preinstructional activity, it is foreshadowed during preinstructional planning. Indeed, a unit plan may be rendered ineffective if students anticipate being asked to recall specific facts while the teacher focuses his planning around specific unit concepts. Measurement and evaluation must be consistent with unit goals and anticipated behavioral outcomes. As indicated in the previous chapter, behaviors which are appropriate as learning activities are usually not adequate for evaluating learning. They do provide sound bases, however, for development of the needed evaluational experiences. For example, the case analysis activity (cited as one of the learning activities) should help students identify pertinent facts, feelings, and relationships associated with selling. Thus test items based on another case might well be utilized for these purposes.

Essentially, activities of the unit are designed to provide *practice* essential to achievement of identified behavioral outcomes. This practice will tend to be *identical* to terminal assessment experiences when minimum essentials objectives are involved (e.g., a minimum level of typing). When developmental objectives are involved, the unit experiences usually will not be identical; rather they will be analogous or similar. A case analysis, for example, will not necessarily be followed with another case analysis as terminal assessment activity. Since the case method is designed to emphasize human emotion in a conflict situation, any test item which emphasizes such a situation would be appropriate.

### How Are Major Unit Purposes Developed with Students?

As with yearly planning, it seems desirable to assist students in gaining an overall perspective of the unit. Major objectives and some of the anticipated unit activities should be discussed with students. This not only creates a state of learning readiness, but it can provide valuable feedback from students. A teaching unit is *not* preplanned for the purpose of prescribing all aspects of the learning experience; rather it is designed as a basis for further planning with students. Modifications must be expected.

The unit introduction essentially entails setting realistic expectations with students. While it is *most inappropriate* to identify specific unit concepts for students, it is appropriate to impress upon them the nature of the concept approach to teaching and learning. (After a unit or two has been completed, this activity may need no further reinforcement.) By following this with suggestions for activities which should promote goal achievement, the student at least begins to see the need for various unit activities and assignments.

## LESSON PLANNING

A lesson plan is an expanded portion of a unit plan. It represents a more or less detailed analysis of a particular *activity* described in the unit plan. For example, one of the unit activities is called *class discussion*. While the problem title was stated in the unit plan, no indication was given as to *how* the problem would be developed. In discussing a *problem of policy*, as described in Chapter 16, careful planning is essential. The lesson plan serves such a purpose.

The essentials of a lesson plan are somewhat similar to the important elements of a unit plan. Although forms and styles differ markedly from one teacher to another, a lesson plan usually contains a goal, lesson introduction (approach), lesson development, and lesson generalizations. Depending on the nature of the lesson, it also may include a list of materials needed, provision for individual differences, and an assignment.

The common elements of lesson planning erroneously suggest a more or less standard routine. While it is true that most plans will be structured around the common elements described, significant differences will be observed within this framework. Different teaching methods often are designed for different instructional purposes; they involve different sequences. Thus lesson plans must be modified accordingly. Sample lesson plans, prepared for the purposes of illustrating each of the major teaching methods, appear in the respective methods chapters. A comparison of some of these plans is recommended. The particular style of lesson planning illustrated in this book is suggestive only.

## What Role Does the Unit Concept Play in Lesson Planning?

Each lesson plan is based upon a *unit* outcome, deemed essential for achievement of a *unit* concept. Thus back of every lesson plan is a concept. Two or more lessons may be essential to ensure the attainment of a single concept. It is desirable to restate the concept prior to development of a lesson plan. Although some feel that in certain contexts the concept may be stated for student guidance, most authorities apparently feel that students should be guided inductively toward concept achievement.

By restating the unit concept with each lesson plan, subsequent aspects of planning are simplified. Furthermore, one tends to focus upon one and only one major idea during the lesson.

## How Are Lesson Goals and Outcomes Evolved from the Unit Concept?

From each unit concept the teacher must decide what major goal domain must be emphasized, for example, cognitive, affective, or psychomotor. It may be that two or even all three of these should receive emphasis. Usually there will be a different lesson for each major goal domain to be emphasized. Sometimes, however, more than one domain may be stressed in a single lesson. This applies especially to certain inquiry methods which, in effect, involve several unified lessons.

By way of illustration, unit concept 3 from the illustrated unit is reproduced along with unit goal II.

*Unit concept:* Advertising can be an effective means of preselling products.

*Unit goal:*    After this unit the student should have furthered his understanding of the relationship between impulse buying and advertising, as evidenced by:
1. His ability to test hypotheses of impulse buying in a class discussion.
2. His ability to apply appropriate advertising principles in role-played situations.

Unit outcome 1 suggests class discussion and the cognitive domain (although the affective domain can be stressed in certain types of discussion). Using the unit concept as a guide, then a lesson goal with appropriate lesson outcomes can be derived. To illustrate: After this lesson the student should have furthered his understanding of the importance of impulse buying, as evidenced by (1) the questions he asks during the discussion, (2) his ability to offer and/or evaluate hypotheses posed during the discussion, (3) his ability to derive generalizations from the discussion.

It will be noted that the specific learning outcomes represent behaviors which can be expected during a problem-solving discussion experience.

## How Is the Lesson Problem Developed?

Every major instructional method is based upon a problem. With the exception of the lecture method, instructional methods problems usually involve some form of policy problem. The above illustration, for example, calls for a discussion problem. One example might be, "What can we as marketers do to stimulate buying?"

Since the processes of reflection demand a constant referral back to the basic problem, it is usually placed on the chalkboard. In this way, it functions as an effective guide for the learning experience. An inappropriately worded problem usually results in an ineffective lesson.

## What Is the Function of the Lesson Approach?

Every lesson must be so designed as to capture student interest at the outset. This may range from two or three introductory questions in a class discussion to a five- or ten-minute demonstration in a science discovery-type lesson. Whatever technique is employed the purpose is essentially that of preparing the learner for subsequent class activities.

The lesson approach is comparable to the course and unit introductions except that it applies to a specific lesson. Caution must be exercised or the activity may be overextended. It, in effect, merely sets the stage for learning.

## What Are the Essentials of the Lesson Development?

Major activities of the lesson are incorporated in this phase of a lesson plan. Subdivisions of the lesson development will vary with the particular method to be used. The teacher must first identify the different aspects of the reflective process germane to the particular method involved. He then writes out points, questions, and/or comments deemed essential in the instructional process. In class discussion, for example, this may consist of only two or three key questions in each area to be explored. At this point the reader will want to study the illustrated lesson plans provided in the methods chapters.

The sequence of key questions (or events) is extremely important in achieving lesson objectives. Essentially, questions serve a dual role. They focus on the content being discussed and on the cognitive processes as well. Instructional processes that foster critical thinking must be sequenced. As illustrated in discussion lesson plan (page 265), the first sequence of

questions pertains to analysis of the problem. These, in turn, are followed
with key questions which pertain to the higher levels of cognition, analysis,
and synthesis of hypotheses or proposed solutions. Finally, some attention is
given to the highest level of cognition (evaluation).

### How Is the Lesson Culminated?

The culminating portion of a lesson is often neglected or rushed. This is
particularly unfortunate, since it is at this point that students are expected
to derive concepts or generalizations. The culmination of almost every lesson
should involve students in the derivation of generalizations, based on the
current lesson experiences. The lesson generalizations are collectively equal
to the basic unit concept upon which the lesson rests. Thus any one lesson
generalization cannot be identical to the basic unit concept upon which the
lesson rests.

Lesson generalizations should be derived by students. Some authorities
insist that they be written out by students. In many instances students will
verbally derive lesson generalizations which are written for all to see. Students
are expected to record them in their notes, however.

Basic unit concepts, contrary to lesson concepts or generalizations, are
derived by teachers as they plan for instruction. Concepts, at the unit level,
are sometimes inductively derived by students as a *culminating* unit activity.
(See Chapter 22 on review method.) As an aid in teaching, the instructor
usually writes out one or two anticipated lesson generalizations in his lesson
plan. They are to be used as an instructional guide only. To illustrate from the
cited lesson problem:

1. Buying is associated with personal status.
2. Quality products sell themselves through satisfied customers.

## VALUES

Unit planning provides a basic course structure around which specific class
   activities can be organized.
Through careful unit planning, the teacher is able to integrate the basic course
   concepts and those of related areas into various teaching experiences.
Unit planning enables the teacher to provide adequate balance between various
   dimensions of a course. By taking a long-range look he is able to develop
   essential priorities in advance of actual classroom experiences.
The unit plan seems to be the best technique yet developed to enable a teacher
   to break away from traditional textbook teaching.
Emphasis upon behavioral outcomes in both unit and lesson planning tends to
   result in a more meaningful series of learning experiences.

## LIMITATIONS AND PROBLEMS

A teacher may become a "slave" to his plans. This is a special hazard for those who prefer detailed lesson plans.

Excessive planning may promote an authoritarian class situation. This factor may become apparent when the changing needs of students are largely disregarded.

Unless adequate caution is exercised, lesson plans may become a mere outline of textbook materials. If practical lesson goals, along with specific behavioral outcomes, are developed *as a basis for* class activities, this need not be a hazard.

Thorough planning takes time—more time, in fact, than is available to some first-year teachers. Furthermore, it is usually impractical to construct lesson plans more than three or four days in advance of the experience. (By making substantial use of marginal notes a teacher may use effective plans as a basis for subsequent planning.)

## ILLUSTRATIONS

I. A unit plan is illustrated in Appendix A. Lesson plans are provided in each of the chapters dealing with instructional methods.

II. Useful in history classes

The following illustration depicts the two-step process (described on pp. 37–38) of changing unit concepts of historical events into concepts with viable and current life applications. Instructional goals are derived from the latter.

This illustration is based upon a unit in United States history called, *World War I: To Make the World Safe for Democracy.*

| *Content Ideas* (specific to a given unit) | *Major Unit Concepts* (generalized understandings) |
|---|---|
| 1. The assassination of Franz Ferdinand of Austria was the "kick off point" that led to war. | 1. Insignificant events often lead to unforgettable disaster. |
| 2. Wilson's personal belief that democracy could save all mankind greatly affected the United States and its involvement in World War I. | 2. The misleading notion that "Democracy can save all mankind" originated with Woodrow Wilson. |
| 3. America's entrance into World War I was related to her isolationist policy. | 3. Isolation and lack of communication whether it be between nations or individuals, lead to inevitable conflicts. |
| 4. Wilson's idea of peace without victory was impractical. | 4. Peace without victory may set the stage for later conflict. |

*Content Ideas* (cont.)

5. Germany's submarine warfare influenced our decision to enter the war on the side of the Allies.

6. The United States was solidly united due to the war effort.

7. Bitter feelings of the Allies toward the Central Powers made peace terms very demanding.

8. The Big Four's acceptance of the League of Nations necessitated compromise which led to its ultimate demise.

9. Wilson's stance on the peace treaty led to his unpopularity at home.

10. High reparations and other demands assessed against the defeated countries contributed to the depression of 1929.

*Major Unit Concepts* (cont.)

5. Aggression (e.g., submarine warfare during World War I) tends to widen gaps between peoples.

6. A common cause (e.g., the U.S. during World War I) tends to unite peoples.

7. Bitter feelings between individuals and nations (e.g., the Allies toward the Central Powers following World War I) make peaceful relationships difficult to establish and maintain.

8. Unwanted compromise (e.g., the League of Nations) tends to lessen the effectiveness of peacekeeping organizations and treaties.

9. Ill-advised public expression (e.g., riots, etc., against Wilson) can adversely affect statesmanship.

10. Misuse of power by the victor (e.g., reparation demands of the Central Powers following World War I) may adversely affect intergroup relations for many generations.

It is seen from the foregoing that each of the major United States history concepts is derived from an idea which is specific to a given era of history. Many of the named concepts will occur again and again as the student studies other history units. In this way the learner can become aware of the repetition of diplomatic errors. New concepts, of course, also will be emphasized in each subsequent unit.

III. Useful in literature classes

Illustrated below is the two-step process of identifying major unit ideas (concepts) and then organizing content selections which tend to develop each idea. The illustrated unit in American literature is entitled "Colonial America: Birth of a New Culture."

*Concept:* The conditions of the time influence the nature of literary contributions.

*Illustrated by:* *Of Plymouth Plantation*
*The Prologue*
*The Author to Her Book*
*The Preface*
*Upon a Spider Catching a Fly*
*Sinners in the Hands of an Angry God*
*Diary of Samuel Sewall*
*The History of the Dividing Line*
*From the Journal of John Woolman*
*Letters from an American Farmer*

*Concept:* Puritan ideals have had and still have an influence on our social system.

*Illustrated by:* *The Prologue*
*The Author to Her Book*
*The Preface*
*Upon a Spider Catching a Fly*
*Sinners in the Hands of an Angry God*
*Diary of Samuel Sewall*

*Concept:* Reaching worthwhile goals involves hardships and struggles.

*Illustrated by:* *Of Plymouth Plantation*
*The History of the Dividing Line*
*From the Journal of John Woolman*
*Letters from an American Farmer*

*Concept:* Freedom embodies responsibility and interdependence of man.

*Illustrated by:* *Of Plymouth Plantation*
*Sinners in the Hands of an Angry God*
*The History of the Dividing Line*
*From the Journal of John Woolman*
*Letters from an American Farmer*

*Concept:* Realities of life are not always consistent with ideals.

*Illustrated by:* *Sinners in the Hands of an Angry God*
*Diary of Samuel Sewall*
*The History of the Dividing Line*
*From the Journal of John Woolman*
*Letters from an American Farmer*

*Concept:* If ultimate ideals are to be achieved, one's perception of reality must change.

*Illustrated by:* *Of Plymouth Plantation*
*Sinners in the Hands of an Angry God*
*Diary of Samuel Sewall*
*The History of the Dividing Line*
*From the Journal of John Woolman*
*Letters from an American Farmer*

## SELECTED BIBLIOGRAPHY

Bruner, Jerome S. *The Process of Education* (Cambridge, Mass.: Harvard University Press, 1960).

Carin, Arthur A., and Sund, Robert B. *Developing Questioning Strategies,* chs. 4 and 5 (Columbus: Charles E. Merrill Publishing Co., 1971).

Coop, Richard H., and White, Kinnard. *Psychological Concepts in the Classroom* (New York: Harper and Row, Publishers, 1974).

Hager, Herbert K. *First Steps in Secondary Teaching* (Columbus: Charles E. Merrill Publishing Co., 1973).

Hanson, Kenneth T. *Secondary Teaching: A Personal Approach,* ch. 3 (Itasca, N.Y.: F. E. Peacock Co., 1974).

Harrow, Anita J. *A Taxonomy of the Psychomotor Domain* (New York: David McKay Co., Inc., 1972).

Kim, Eugene C., and Kellough, Richard D. *A Resource Guide for Secondary School Teaching,* Parts II and III (New York: The Macmillan Co., Inc., 1974).

McAshen, H. H. *Writing Behavioral Objectives* (New York: Harper and Row, Publishers, 1972).

Mager, Robert. *Goal Analysis* (Belmont, Calif.: Fearon Publishers, 1972).

Martorella, Peter H. et al. *Concept Learning: Designs for Instruction* (Scranton, Pa.: Intext Educational Publishers, 1972).

Strom, Robert D., and Torrence, E. Paul. *Education for Affective Achievement* (New York: Rand McNally & Co., 1973).

Tanner, Daniel. *Using Behavioral Objectives in the Classroom* (New York: The Macmillan Co., Inc., 1972).

## ANNOTATED FILM LIST

*Concept Formation*—Intermediate Level
    16 mm film; 20 minutes
    Demonstrates a concept development discussion with sixth grade students, using South America as a basis for the discussion.
    Addison-Wesley Publishing Co., Inc.
    Off South Street
    Reading, Mass. 01867

*The Concept of Function*
    16 mm film; 16 minutes
    Illustrates how to use "SET" in considering function.
    From the *Teacher Education in Modern Math* Series
    McGraw-Hill Textfilms
    1221 Ave. of the Americas
    New York, N.Y. 10020

*Motivation Through Unit Teaching*
    16 mm film
    Shows steps in teaching by the unit method and how psychological

principles are realized through its use. Although a bit older than the
other listed films, this one is still very useful.
State College of Iowa
Audio-Visual Center
Ames, Iowa

*Unit Construction I, II, III: Techniques for the First Garment Fitting*
16mm film; 5, 8, and 4 minutes
"Techniques for Applying the Collar"; "Techniques for the Second Fitting";
"First Garment Fitting."
Shows how the unit method saves time and energy in constructing a
garment.
Doubleday Multimedia
1370 Reynolds Ave.
Santa Ana, Calif. 92705

## SELECTED FILMSTRIPS

*Concept Learning*
Filmstrip with script
Based upon three teaching strategies for the social studies series.
Science Research Associates
259 E. Erie St.
Chicago, Ill. 60611

*Concepts in Ecology—A Series*
Filmstrip
Focuses on the environment with a view to developing an appreciation
for the interrelationships of living things, including man; appropriate for
junior high school level.
Contron Educational Films
1255 Post St., Suite 652
San Francisco, Calif. 94109

*Concepts of Modern Math,* Parts 1, 2, and 3
Filmstrips
Focuses on most of the basic, practical math computations needed in
everyday life; appropriate for intermediate to high school levels.
University Education and Visual Arts
221 Park Ave. S.
New York, N.Y. 10003

*Concepts in Science,* Sets I, IV, and VI
Filmstrip
Treats a variety of concepts in the realm of physical science; appropriate
for intermediate and high school levels.
Eye Gate House, Inc.
146–01 Archer Ave.
Jamaica, N.Y. 11435

*Developing and Writing Performance Objectives—A Series*
Sound filmstrip
Describes a system for developing and evaluating performance objectives.
Multi-Media Associates
4901 E. 5th St.
Tucson, Ariz. 85732

*Identifying Affective Objectives*
   Sound filmstrip
   Provides a strategy for developing and using affective objectives.
   Vimcit Associates
   P.O. Box 24714
   Los Angeles, Calif. 90024

*Preparing a Unit*
   Filmstrip
   Shows how to develop all aspects of a unit plan.
   Bel Mort Films
   619 Cascade Bldg.
   Portland, Ore. 97204

## SELECTED OVERHEAD TRANSPARENCIES

*Concept Learning and Programmed Instruction*
   8 x 10 prepared transparency, master available.
   University of Iowa
   AV Center
   Iowa City, Iowa 52240

*Writing Behavioral Objectives*—A Series
   8 x 10 prepared transparencies
   Langford Publishing Company
   P.O. Box 8711
   1088 Lincoln Ave.
   San Jose, Calif. 95155

## FREE AND INEXPENSIVE LEARNING MATERIALS

*Curriculum Bulletins.* No. 166–05.
   Free, with 20 cents postage
   Each bulletin is addressed to the teaching of secondary school English.
   Joseph Mersand
   Highland Ave.
   Jamaica, N.Y. 11432

# Methods with a Focus on the Individual

Motivational Activities
Discipline Problems
Providing for Individual
Differences
Independent and
Semi-Independent Study
Individualizing Instruction
Value-Focusing Activities

Encouraging Creativity
Questioning Strategies
Sociometric Techniques
The Sociodramatic
Method
The Case Method
Developmental Reading
Techniques

*Instruction at its best is beamed at the individual. Many instructional methods and techniques focus on the individual directly despite the fact that the student may be in a crowded classroom. Others use the group as a vehicle to reach the individual. The chapters in this unit feature essentially teacher-focused instructional activities.*

*Even the most careful planning cannot produce beneficial results unless the student himself feels a need for learning. Students are continually solving problems of immediate concern. Activating a desire to learn in a particular area, however, is another matter. As indicated in Chapter 4, motivation cannot be taught—rather, it has to be caught. As Frymier points out, motivation is an aspect of personality. Capitalizing on the basic needs and curiosities of students is an art that is basic to all instruction. Like all other dimensions of instruction, students differ in the desire to learn. Accordingly, motivational techniques must vary with the needs of those involved. Chapter 4 suggests how to provide such a basis for learning.*

*A symptom of inadequate or misdirected motivation will be reflected in student misbehavior, treated in Chapter 5. Discipline has been a major concern of teachers for many years. The problem is even more acute today than it was two or three decades ago. A number of factors have contributed to this state of affairs, among them: (1) greater emphasis on compulsory education, (2) social promotion practices, (3) emphasis on secondary education for everyone, (4) school integration policies, and (5) larger classes.*

*Beginning teachers especially are prone to seek quick solutions to discipline problems. They reason that if this one problem—discipline—can be worked out their chances of survival are assured. While the reasoning process is valid, the problem is considerably more complex. Discipline problems are usually symptoms of more serious difficulties. They may indicate a lack of student interest, the need for recognition, or problems of group acceptance. Effective corrective action, then, must be directed to the underlying cause(s).*

*Closely associated with motivational activities and discipline is the problem of providing adequately for individual differences (Chapter 6). It is the rare student indeed who will not create disturbances when class expectations are too high or too low for his capacities. Yet some teachers typically expect all students to read the same books, to do the same problems, and to keep up with all other members of the class. As might be expected, these teachers often find they are devoting most of their energies to problems of class control.*

*Students, in whatever manner they may be grouped, will vary widely in any number of ways. With the typical class size of thirty to forty students, individualization of instruction can be most difficult unless some systematized approach is employed. Accordingly, a useful technique for subgrouping within the classroom is presented in Chapter 6. Subgrouping on the basis of achievement and/or ability, employed widely in the elementary schools, also can be effective at the secondary level. The function of such an approach, of course, is to facilitate individualization of instruction.*

*Most departures from conventional instruction are aimed at providing increased learner independence. Modular scheduling techniques, for example, would provide ample opportunities for independent and semi-independent study, treated in Chapter 7. The ultimate goal of teaching, of course, is purely individualized instruction and learning. When each student is permitted to progress at his/her own individual rate some modification of conventional class and grade lines is needed. Fortunately modern technology has made such an arrangement feasible. In Chapter 8 some exciting innovations are treated. Some assistance is provided for the classroom teacher in a conventional setting who desires to move in the direction of independent study and individualized instruction.*

*Closely associated with learner independence are values and creativity. A fully functioning individual must be free to examine and explore his/her own values and to apply imagination in solving problems. Most values are caught in the process of growth and development; all too often they are confusing and contradictory. Young people can and should be assisted in value clarification. Some useful techniques are offered in Chapter 9. Techniques of encouraging creativity are provided in Chapter 10.*

*Questioning techniques, presented in the next chapter in this unit, are foundational to all instructional methods and procedures. Just as the entire reflective process rests upon an appropriately phrased problem question, so do various aspects of the process depend upon adequate questioning techniques. It has been established that about 90 percent of all classroom questions are at the memory level. Yet, if concepts are to be inductively derived, emphasis should be focused upon the higher levels of cognition. The Bloom taxonomy of educational objectives provides a basis for the questioning techniques developed in this chapter.*

*Education at its best must help the individual cope with the affairs of everyday life. Achievement in the various content fields is of secondary importance to the social and emotional development of the high school student. Whatever one does, wherever one goes, the complexities of modern day living must be met. It is not enough to expect that all individuals will somehow make the necessary adjustments as they interact in the school society. The accelerated pace of school integration, the mobility of the population, and the sheer weight of increased enrollments are but a few of the factors that have accentuated the problem during the last decade. Systematic instructional strategies are essential to the growth and development of healthy emotions and values. They are the focus of Chapters 12, 13, and 14.*

*Finally, teachers are discovering that the basic skills are not necessarily mastered in the elementary school. Many secondary students need remedial instruction in reading, for example. All students need special instruction in coping with the language of different subject areas. This is the logical task of each classroom teacher. Accordingly, developmental reading techniques are treated in Chapter 15. Emphasis is placed upon comprehension and variable reading techniques needed in specialized areas.*

CHAPTER **4**

# Motivational Activities

## OVERVIEW

### Key Concepts

1. Motivation is a basic aspect of personality that changes slowly over a period of time.
2. Basic needs, special interests, and incentives are prompters of motivation.
3. Motivational techniques are essential aspects of all instructional activities.
4. Group efforts to activate the desire to learn must be supplemented with attention to the special interests of a few students whose desire to learn is especially low.
5. Motivation and discipline are aspects of the same problem.

### New Terms

1. **Basic Psychological Needs**—Inner forces which drive and direct an individual's behavior. Needs (e.g., recognition, acceptance, approval) must be continually fulfilled if adequate self-adjustment is to be realized.
2. **Intrinsic Motivation**—That motivation which originates from within the individual.
3. **Extrinsic Motivation**—Incentives which are advanced by others to encourage learning.
4. **Self-Concept**—One's assessment of his own capacities and worth.
5. **Leadership Patterns**—The amount of teacher domination in general class discussion activities.

### Questions to Guide Your Study

1. It has been contended that some students have no desire to learn. Defend or refute.
2. In suggesting an integration of motives for effective teaching the author would use incentives as a last resort. This is strangely at odds with common practice. What justification do you see for such a recommendation?
3. Contrast effective motivational techniques for students with a relatively low desire to learn with those who might be classified as self-motivated.
4. Using the four dimensions of personality which influence motivation (internal-external, intake-output, approach-avoidance, reflection-impulsivity), suggest their instructional implications in the areas of assignments, instructional activities, and evaluational procedures.
5. Are some students highly motivated in some areas while possessing low motivation in other areas? Relate your answer to Frymier's contention that motivation is an aspect of personality which changes gradually.

Motivation is that part of the self which impels a person to learn—to work toward a goal. It is thought to represent a basic aspect of personality structure. Accordingly, motivation is a fairly stable characteristic. Yet one's motivational structure may be altered over a period of a few months or years. The teacher has the responsibility for encouraging and cultivating desirable motivational patterns. Alteration of existing patterns, however, is an involved process related to basic personality changes. It is usually approached indirectly through the avenue of interests.

Perhaps a more satisfactory definition of motivation may be offered in terms of teacher behavior. By viewing motivation as a process of creating a climate whereby a person will want to do his best, one gets the notion that a teacher can indeed do something to motivate students, even though actual motivation must come from within. Perhaps an appropriate subtitle might be "activating the desire to learn."

## FUNDAMENTAL PROPERTIES

Since teachers often must work with students in groups, an examination of the universal mainsprings of human behavior is important. As emphasized throughout this book, however, a more individualized learning experience is needed. Among the more important—and neglected—aspects of individual differences are motivational differences. Teachers are just beginning to realize that students differ as much in their motivational structure as they do in general ability. The properties which follow emphasize *both* aspects of the problem.

### What Psychological Needs Must Be Considered?

The basic physiological and psychological needs of man have long been emphasized. They are common to all people in all societies. The avenues through which needs may be fulfilled, however, vary from one society to the next. As will be seen, the "adolescent society" in our culture represents an especially difficult problem of need fulfillment. Maslow[1] offers a thorough analysis of basic psychological needs which he classifies into four basic types.

He believes that there is a hierarchy of need satisfaction. This he calls a *prepotency* of need fulfillment. Thus each physiological need (water, food, protection, sex, etc.) is satisfied systematically and in an order of prepotency. One must, for example, satisfy his thirst before he can enjoy eating; likewise, protection is relatively unimportant to an extremely hungry person. In a similar manner Maslow sees a prepotency of the psychological needs which emerges when the physiological needs are satisfied.

*Safety needs* are almost as prepotent as are the physiological needs and, for most individuals at least, are first satisfied at an early age. One strives for protection and security from life's major hazards. An indication of a child's need for safety is his preference for some kind of undisturbed routine. Maslow points out that young children seem to thrive better under a system of "permissiveness within limits" rather than the extremes of control.

*The belongingness and love needs,* which emerge after the safety needs have been fairly well gratified, include the desire for affection, love, and a feeling of belonging. The family is ideally suited to the fulfillment of these needs. According to Maslow, the thwarting of these needs is the most common source of maladjustment in our society.

*The esteem needs* in our society are represented by man's desire for a "stable, firmly based, usually high evaluation" of himself. He needs self-respect. He needs to achieve, to feel adequate or competent, to have confidence enough to "face the world." At the same time the individual desires a favorable status or reputation to be bestowed upon him by others. Satisfaction of the self-esteem needs leads to feelings of personal worth, of adequacy, of being useful or necessary in the world.

*The need for self-actualization,* according to Maslow, is the highest of all need groups. Even when all other needs are reasonably well fulfilled a person is discontented and restless unless he is doing that for which he is best fitted. This desire for self-fulfillment, in essence, is the need to become what one is capable of becoming. This need may take many forms. In one person, for example, it may be the desire to become an ideal mother; in another individual it may be the desire to play ball, and so on.

Maslow cautions the reader against assuming that each set of needs must be 100 percent gratified before the next emerges. As a matter of fact, most people are partially satisfied and partially unsatisfied in all their basic needs at the same time. However, a certain degree of fulfillment of the "lower" needs is essential before the individual can effectively concentrate upon the "higher" needs. Furthermore, a need cannot be fulfilled once and for all. A suitable environment for constant "recharging" is essential. It also is apparent that a number of needs can often be gratified in a single act.

[1] Based on Abraham H. Maslow, *Motivation and Personality* (New York: Harper & Row, Publishers, 1954), pp. 80–106.

The theory of need prepotency appears to be a very useful concept in understanding motivation. The adolescent years are of a transitory nature. The youngster who suddenly finds himself with a new body must assume a new life role. Thus he is disrupted from established routines of living. His *safety needs* are disrupted. In accepting this new role the family can no longer fully satisfy his *belonging and love needs.* His physiological development brings sex to the fore, forcing him to take a new look at the opposite sex. As an adolescent he is no longer a child, nor is he accepted by society as an adult. Consequently, he must seek security and affection from his peer group. If he does not "belong" to the peer group he does not belong! Thus conformity becomes the order of the day. Rejection by the adolescent crowd causes him to lose confidence in himself—his self-respect or *self-esteem.* Furthermore, on top of all the other difficulties the teen-ager is expected to think of the future. He knows that within a relatively short period of time he will be expected to pursue a career or vocation for which he is "best fitted." Frequently his preoccupation with the more basic needs will thwart his positive efforts toward *self-actualization.*

## What Are the Comparable Roles of Intrinsic vs. Extrinsic Motivation?

Intrinsic motivation is that which originates from within the individual. Certain basic needs compel each individual to perform in various ways as he strives for need fulfillment from his own frame of reference. Closely associated with basic needs is the element of curiosity. All individuals are curious. From the small child who asks "Why?" a thousand times a day to the elderly person who rushes to the scene of a fire or accident, individuals display a compelling urge to "know." Miss Webster, the chemistry teacher, capitalized on this natural urge when she set off a hydrogen explosion which literally shook the windows. "What happened? Why? How? What caused it?"—such questions came from all corners of the room. The problem was no longer one of interest, but one of directing the enthusiasm displayed.

For many years teachers have attempted to capitalize on the *individual interests* of youngsters as an avenue for developing interest in course instruction. One must help the student relate the needs and values associated with his special interest to the needs and values associated with the course values. Almost any special interest *can* be related to course values *provided* the teacher allows himself to think creatively about the issue. The illustration which follows is designed to suggest ways a special interest can be related to different subject fields.

Mary indicated an interest in collecting stamps. She frequently showed her rather large collection to friends and neighbors.

The *history* teacher can capitalize on this interest by encouraging Mary to make a study of the historical events related to certain stamps.

The *mathematics* teacher can help Mary develop a graph depicting the relative value of the dollar indicated by the price of stamps at given times.

The *biology* teacher might use Mary's stamp collection to illustrate the value of a hobby by having Mary present an oral report of activities involved in stamp collecting as a hobby.

The *English* teacher can develop Mary's interest in writing a theme pertaining to a particular event portrayed on a highly treasured stamp.

*Incentives or extrinsic instructional devices* have been included among classroom activities for many years. Some of the better known of these are threat of failure, emphasis upon marks, demanding certain marks as a basis for competitive sports eligibility, honor roll lists, and scholarship eligibility.

Although extrinsic pressure *may* spur some students to greater effort, it is not without serious hazards. Motivation for high grades usually has a favorable impact on only those individuals who have a chance to win! In most class situations this will be a very small percentage of the group. Certainly by the age of adolescence the child is well aware of his chances of this type of success. Moreover, those who are most likely to be motivated by competition usually need it least. They are the individuals who are self-motivated to do high quality work, with or without special motivational activities.

The impact of keen competition for marks on the less able student is likely to be quite unhealthful. Having failed before, he tends to be overly anxious at the outset of the learning experience. Added pressure tends to result in *less* effort in academic areas and a turning to other, less desirable, avenues of fulfilling his needs for success.

Extrinsic devices *can* be effective if the learner has a fair chance of winning *as he sees it.* Some teachers, for example, have devised ways of permitting a student to compete with *his own past record.* For instance, in typing class a student can attempt to improve his speed and accuracy as measured by past performances; in English class one may keep a list of his own grammatical errors; the tennis player may keep a list of his performance in serving the ball.

## What Basic Personality Determinants Influence the Effectiveness of Instructional Activities?

Traditionally, teachers have concerned themselves with motivating students to do good work. They have sought to help students see the fundamental values and purposes of education, of a particular course, or of a particular unit within a course. All too often, however, those students who seem highly motivated at the outset continue to exhibit such behaviors, while those who appear to lack this quality seldom change their behaviors very dramatically. Every teacher is aware of those students who have self-sustaining motivational qualities. They need relatively little encouragement. They already have an abundance of it! Too many other students tend to have little drive to achieve in any subject.

Such observations have led investigators to examine the personality determinants of motivation. Mounting evidence suggests that motivation is an aspect of personality; *that motivation is something a student already possesses.*

It is *not* something which a teacher does to students directly. The teacher *can activate and direct* the student's natural drive and desire for learning, however.

Four basic learning styles have been identified by various researchers: Internal-external, intake-output, approach-avoidance, and reflection-impulsivity.[2] They have been treated in Chapter 19. The reader should examine these (pp. 301–2) for the purpose of understanding basic personality differences that have a direct bearing on learning.

The effect of various personality traits upon learning is the production of varying degrees of motivation. A brief look at the two extremes should provide valuable clues to needed motivational techniques.

Highly motivated students tend to have a positive picture of *themselves.* They feel competent to handle the problems of their everyday existence. They feel accepted and respected. Being free of their own problems they tend to have a positive concept of others, as evidenced by a willingness to trust and rely upon the integrity of others.

On the other hand, students with low motivation tend to have a low self-esteem. They feel that they are not liked and respected; that they are not worthy, not important. Accordingly, they feel that other people cannot be trusted, that others will take advantage of them if possible.

The *values* associated with motivation seem to be related specifically to the time dimension. As Frymier points out, "Highly motivated students tend to have an awareness of the future, a consciousness of the present, and a realistic appraisal of the past." The low-motivated student, in contrast, tends to be fearful or to ignore the future; he is obsessed with the past or is completely preoccupied with the present. He seems to become fixated on one segment of time.

The highly motivated student tends to accept education as a challenge, feeling that he can cope with school and class situations and problems. He seems to view specific problems within a broad perspective. Conversely, the low-motivated student tends to feel threatened by specific school or class experiences. He tends to build the task up to a point that is out of proportion with the other aspects of his environment.

### What Role Does the Self-Concept Play in Motivational Activities?

A student's performance is based upon his actual capacities *as well as* what he perceives them to be. If one's perceptions of his capacities are below his actual capacities he will not achieve to his capacity. Psychologically each person needs to maintain an intact self-structure. This serves as a sort of gyroscope by helping him guide his own behavior. Such behavior tends to be compulsive and unconsciously motivated.

One's perception of himself grows within a social context. To a marked

---

[2] The first three of these are based upon the Frymier studies. They have been synthesized in Jack R. Frymier, *The Nature of Educational Method* (Columbus, Ohio: Charles E. Merrill Books, 1965). The dimension of reflection-impulsivity is based upon research by J. Kagan and his associates. See p. 302.

degree it is determined by how one incorporates his impact on others and what they expect from him. Inferiority feelings result from many negative experiences with others over an extended period of time.

The symptoms of low self-esteem, as outlined by Hamachek,[3] are:

1. *Sensitivity to criticism.* Any kind of criticism is viewed as further proof of one's inferiority.
2. *Overresponsiveness to praise.* Praise and flattery are seen as testimony against the inferiority one feels.
3. *Hypercritical attitude.* This is usually a divisionary strategy to direct attention from one's own limitations.
4. *A "nobody likes me" feeling.* One does not like himself very well. Thus he does not see how others could like him either.
5. *Negative feelings about competition.* One wants to win as much as anybody else but is far less optimistic than most people of the probability of his success.
6. *A general tendency toward seclusiveness, shyness, and timidity.* Although one's fear may be accompanied by feigned self-assurance, it is more commonly expressed as timidity and shyness.

As one grows older his self-concept becomes increasingly difficult to change, but it can be done, either through one's own effort or through the guidance of a skilled therapist or sensitive teacher.

### How Does Knowledge of Results Influence Learning?

Of all the psychological principles of learning, knowledge of results seems to be most basic in keeping students motivated. Immediate, specific knowledge of results, in addition to providing needed feedback for improved performance, has the advantage of providing an incentive toward increased effort. Furthermore, such feedback enables one to use his time more productively by minimizing needless rehearsal of that which is already known.

The evidence clearly indicates the importance of immediate feedback. Work which is returned two or three weeks after it is turned in has little appreciable impact on motivation. An even less acceptable practice is that of merely showing a letter grade. Mistakes, if they are to be avoided in the future, must be pointed out, along with some indication of why they were made. Ideally, such feedback should be managed within a single class period. Such knowledge of results tends to make one compete with his own past performance. This is the most healthy form of competition known.

## MOTIVATIONAL TECHNIQUES

Motivation, like other aspects of learning, basically is an individualized task. It is a practical impossibility, however, to give individualized attention to each student in large classes. In fact, basic motives of all human beings render group

---

[3] Don E. Hamachek, "Self-Concept: Implications for Teaching and Learning," *School and Community* 55 (May 1969): 18–19. Used by permission of the author and the publisher.

motivation not only possible but desirable. This, however, should be supplemented with individualized techniques for those who do not readily respond to such treatment.

### How Are Motives Integrated for Effective Learning?

Since *all* people have certain *basic needs and a basic curiosity,* the teacher might focus his attention *first* upon these areas. Thus if the unit or lesson approach were effectively executed *most* of the students might respond. One might reasonably expect a *few* students to show relatively little response, simply because their most urgent current needs are little affected by the motivational device(s).

The teacher's second line of attack might be in the area of *special interests.* While this might be just as desirable as the first, it is not likely to be as economical of time and effort. If, however, the desire to learn can be effectively activated in *most* students through basic needs or through the element of curiosity, the teacher can afford the time needed to work through the area of special interests.

Finally, a teacher can hold out incentives to students who have not yet responded to previous efforts at motivation. A good incentive makes a connection between the learner and the task. As interest is developed the incentive fades out. Honors, awards, commendations, publicity, and group approval are good incentives *if recognition of improvement* as well as final accomplishment is made.

On occasion a teacher *may* find it necessary to employ a negative incentive. For example, it sometimes may be necessary to warn one or two students that failure to do the work will most certainly mean failure to receive credit for the course. A great deal of discretion is needed, however, in terms of the individual involved. Sometimes such a threat will provide the stimulus needed for development of interest. In the overwhelming majority of cases, however, threats can do more harm than good to those students who are in greatest need of motivation. Far too many teachers rely almost exclusively on the use of incentives as an approach to motivation.

Studies indicate that for middle-class students knowledge of results is adequate reinforcement. Praise or blame may be used as a supplementary technique. However, it must be recognized that it has different effects on different students. Those with a high regard for themselves and their abilities tend to be challenged by a critical approach to their work. Students with a low self-concept tend to work harder when praised frequently. Students from culturally diverse homes seem to respond to reinforcers of a material nature (e.g., candy or similar tokens), while such rewards are usually unnecessary with middle-class children.

### What Techniques Seem to Work Best for Low-Motivated Students?

In reporting the findings of the Forest Hills High School experiments, Brandwein, Watson, and Blackwood develop the categories of "Science Shy" and "Science Prone" students.[4] They suggest, however, that the techniques might just as readily be applied to other areas of instruction outside the field of science.

Prior to an analysis of teaching techniques which seem appropriate for students who find school a frustrating experience, it is important to know something about the common characteristics of such individuals. First and foremost, most of the group fall into the category of *slow* learners. This slowness may be directly related to a lack of ability, low motivation, or both. They have lost interest in school, in the teachers, and especially in themselves. In the Forest Hills High School studies this seemed to be because:

1. Stress in the ordinary course was on memorization of materials unrelated to life.
2. Slow learners generally had inadequate academic tools, as indicated by low reading and arithmetic scores.
3. Low reading and arithmetic scores usually (but not always) went with low IQ scores.
4. The majority, though far from all, of the slow learners came from low socioeconomic groups where the expectancy of entering college was rarely a motivating factor.

In the first place, it was found that joint teacher-pupil planning of class activities was an exceedingly useful technique. Such planning, when intelligently done, tended to develop self-confidence in planning one's own work, in the present and in after-school years.

The class period of 40 minutes was divided into three subperiods of approximately 10, 15, and 15 minutes. *The first subperiod* (10 minutes) was an *activity* in which *all participated.* Some examples follow:·

*Biology:* Take the calipers on your desk and press both ends to your finger, the palm of your hand, your arm, your leg. Did you feel pain from both points in all locations? Explain.

*Art:* Look at the painting. Jot down your impressions. Working in pairs, find out your neighbor's impressions.

*History:* From papers on your desk find three articles dealing with some current problem of historical importance. Discuss these with the two other students in your subgroup.

Whenever possible the initial motivating activity included *reading* for a clear purpose. Also, whenever possible the activity included *working with others.*

Following the initial activity students were asked to *write* a summary of what they had done and observed. At this point consulting with neighbors was discouraged, but students were encouraged to consult their texts, the dictionary, and other references. During this time the teacher *visited with students;*

---

[4] Paul F. Brandwein, Fletcher G. Watson, and Paul E. Blackwood, *Teaching High School Science: A Book of Methods* (New York: Harcourt, Brace & World, Inc., 1958), chapters 8 and 9.

he simply sat down with each individual and talked briefly with him as he examined what was being written.

*The second subperiod* (15 minutes) involved a *discussion* of the topic of the lesson proper. Students followed a rule that only one person was to talk at a time. A student simply raised his hand to the student speaking. Each speaker faced the class. The teacher did *not* lead the discussion; indeed, he sat among the students and raised his hand when he wanted to speak. Most of the teacher's questions were designed to move the discussion toward the solution of the problem, or to question an incorrect statement.

During the discussion the students were expected to write a *summary*. When the discussion was completed they were expected to read this summary to the class. (Slow learners seem to have difficulty writing summaries of what they hear.)

*The third subperiod* (15 minutes) consisted of an extension of the lesson and preparation for the next day's work. Students *read* material in class and took *notes* on it. The last three to five minutes were given to an examination of the next day's work in the text, on the bulletin board, or in some other visual aid.

In short it was found that in all of the activities the students who *did* the activity, *discussed* it, then *read* about it, in a continuous time sequence, reinforced their understanding of what had been happening. Furthermore, each time they culminated the experience by *writing* a summary of their understanding. The sequence of events seemed to help these students gain *status* and *self-esteem*.

In addition to the daily pattern described in the foregoing, one class period *each week* was spent in supervised study of written instructional material. Students were asked to read a paragraph and then write out the major thought as briefly- as possible, preferably in one sentence. This activity was designed to help these individuals read for meaning.

Every *two weeks* students were given a short test which they themselves corrected. For the first two months they did not turn in the test unless satisfied with their marks. For the first two tests they could use texts and notebooks; for the next two tests, only their notebooks. Thereafter they were permitted to use neither of these.

Each month the students had a full-period test for which preparation was made in class. Two class periods were spent in review of materials learned. Some attention was given to how to take a test. Another period was given to discussing the test. The first month's test was a sample and was not turned in unless a student wished to do so. Thereafter tests were turned in.

Not only did the foregoing teaching techniques stimulate this group of students greatly, but it was found to be effective for *all* students. Even the highly motivated students benefited from the special helps for learning involved.

## What Factors Are Associated with Self-Motivated Students?

One becomes a writer by writing, a painter by painting, a scientist by "sciencing," a mathematician by "mathematizing." And the sooner he writes, or paints or does science and mathematics, the sooner he creates, the sooner he actually becomes a writer or painter or scientist or mathematician. A course in which a youngster has an opportunity to create fits our gifted . . . who are expected to become, among other things, our "doers," our "creative minds," our innovators and inventors, our originators in all areas.[5]

The individual who possesses a high potential for originality and creativity must have an opportunity to be "original" and to "create" on his own level. This demands both time and motivation within an encouraging school atmosphere.

Before any systematic attempt can be made in the realm of cultivating high creative potential it is important to recognize factors which seem to be associated with such potential. Although it is quite difficult to identify *all* factors which are needed for high motivation, Brandwein, Watson, and Blackwood have provided a framework for identification of the "science prone," which in many respects parallels Frymier's description of the highly motivated, well-adjusted individual.

1. *Genetic factors.* High scholastic ability, especially in the verbal (oral and written) and mathematical areas, seems important. The upper 15–20 percent of a normal school population which falls within the academically "bright" category contains many individuals who may have a zest for school and for learning. This group usually scores 115 or over on a Stanford-Binet intelligence test. In this group resides the highest creative potential.

2. *Predisposing factors.*
   a. Persistence, which according to Brandwein, Watson, and Blackwood consisted of at least three attitudes:
      1) A marked willingness to give unusually long hours to a given task, including a willingness to schedule one's own time. This frequently carried one beyond a 9–5 day.
      2) A willingness to withstand discomfort, such as shortened or no lunch hours, working holidays, withstanding fatigue, strain, and at times even minor illness.
      3) A willingness to face failure—in essence, having "undying" faith in oneself and the task(s) involved.
   b. Questing. This predisposing factor is indicated by a continuous discontent with present explanations of various aspects of reality.

3. *Activating factors.* This, it seems, is closely related to *opportunity* and *encouragement.* Here the classroom teacher seems to play an especially vital role.

Such an individual, then, is a high achiever who produces in depth and scope, who displays an unusual degree of originality, invention, and innovation; one who holds a high degree of tolerance for uncertainty, resisting early and simple solutions to complex situations. He may be almost ruthless with himself and others when involved in the pursuit of an intellectual commitment. A good part of his reward is in the activity itself, rather than the recognition which it may bring.

---

[5] Brandwein et al., *Teaching High School Science,* p. 167.

## What Is the Relationship Between Leadership and Motivational Patterns?

Described in the foregoing were students who are characteristically low and high in their predispositions toward school work. Specific instructional strategies were offered. Discussion was seen as a basic activity for those low in motivation. It is equally important with all students. Indeed some form of "discussion" is probably employed more than any other technique. This has been treated in another chapter. The degree of teacher-dominance as a discussion leader will influence the learning situation in different ways, depending upon one's personality structure. Six different instructional approaches have been described by Frymier.[6]

*Manipulative.* This strategy is characterized by an *apparent* equalitarian relationship between teacher and student. In the final analysis, however, the teacher always gets his way. Through skillful maneuvering, the teacher's predetermined ends are followed, regardless of the desires of the group. Students are moved in a predetermined direction, despite the fact that they are led to believe that they themselves are involved in the decision-making process. Not only is the strategy undemocratic, but it is dishonest as well.

*Directive.* In this situation the leader openly directs the learner. He prescribes class activities and expects students to follow. His methods are primarily teacher-centered, e.g., lecture and recitation. His purpose is to bring the group to a predetermined end. In contrast to the manipulative strategy, the directive approach is openly a superior-inferior relationship. Students know where they stand. Under appropriate conditions it is fully legitimate in a democracy.

*Persuasive.* This type of leadership emphasizes the equalitarian role of the teacher. Along with the ideas of others he offers his own ideas for consideration. He urges the adoption of his views on the basis of merit. As Frymier says, he is ". . . effective in a pulling sort of way." The position, in many ways, resembles that of manipulation, except that the teacher does not insist upon his own way when group consensus is against him.

*Discussive.* This position embodies the true discussion spirit, described in the chapter on class and panel discussion. Here the leader pools his ideas along with the rest of the group. Each idea, regardless of its source, is considered for its own merit. The usual result is the evolution of new ideas, new avenues of thought.

*Supportive.* This instructional strategy features the student "in the driver's seat." Students set direction—map out areas of concern—and then proceed with the support of the teacher. The teacher's role is relegated to that of guidance and assistance as needed.

*Nondirective.* A final strategy is called nondirective since it permits students to do just as they please. The teacher does not provide any sort of direction,

[6] Frymier, *Educational Method,* pp. 175–84.

except as an individual may ask for it. It is completely open-ended. This strategy, according to Frymier, is not appropriate for secondary use. He suggests it is a form of educational anarchy, since students have no walls to press against.

## What Is the Relationship of Learning Patterns and Personality?

When some form of subgrouping is feasible on the basis of motivational structure, at least four different patterns emerge. When combined with the appropriate leadership strategy each produces an ideal learning situation.

*High motivation–adequate personality.* This sort of individual would probably respond best to a *supportive* instructional strategy. Here the student creates his own structure.

*High motivation–inadequate personality.* The insecurity and apprehensiveness of such a student calls for an abundance of teacher structuring, characteristic of the *directive* approach.

*Low motivation–adequate personality.* Such an individual does not want to learn. Thus he probably responds best to some kind of *discussive* strategy. According to Frymier, such a student is encouraged by the extensive involvement and participation made necessary.

*Low motivation–inadequate personality.* This most difficult student to work with needs a strong leader. He needs someone to tell him what to do and to attract him to the learning task. Thus the *persuasive* strategy is favored.

Although Frymier's analysis seems to presuppose an ideal situation in which students with like motivation are grouped together, the implications for accommodating individual differences within the classroom are many. In Chapter 6, for example, an instructional model for classroom grouping is offered. Although this model is based upon academic achievement, it is entirely possible that such an arrangement could be based upon differing motivational patterns. The legitimate leadership strategies introduced here are more fully developed as instructional methods in various chapters of this book.

# VALUES

Motivational experiences give direction and focus to class learning activities.

If developed appropriately, motivational techniques may lead to continued interest in the subject areas.

Motivation which is generally acceptable to the group tends to spread. Thus those who have minimal interest in specific class activities may develop interest through their need for acceptance and approval.

Effective motivational experiences tend to release the creative potential possessed by each student. Self-directed and even self-actualizing activities may result.

## LIMITATIONS AND PROBLEMS

Incentives which are effective for one individual may be ineffective for another. This especially applies to class marks, honors, and awards. For example, students who work for "A's" will be only those who see a reasonable chance of attaining them. This problem can be minimized if recognition for *improvement* is also given.

Motivational activities can easily become ends in themselves. Today it is recognized that class marks all too often become the ends of education in the minds of students.

*Daily* motivational activities may become more extensive than necessary. If held to a maximum of five or ten minutes this hazard may be minimized. It must be recognized that not all class experiences require *formal* motivational techniques.

While immediate reward or reinforcement (such as an approving smile or word) is usually immediately encouraging, more *basic* rewards must be forthcoming if *continuing* interest is to be maintained.

This merely suggests that the learner must clearly perceive the connection between task and outcome.

Interests are both transitory and basic. Transitory interests may result in a basic interest and continued motivation after basic knowledge in the field has been achieved. Mere expression of interest, however, is no guarantee of learning.

## ILLUSTRATED MOTIVATIONAL TECHNIQUES

I.  Useful in science classes.[7]

   *As Set Induction* (when introducing a lesson, a unit, or any segment of instruction).

   A.  Begin by passing out toothpicks.
   B.  Ask students to use a toothpick to poke themselves in the palm, the abdomen, the calf, and the top of the foot.
   C.  Students compare sensations.
   D.  Then they move into a lesson on the nervous system.

II. Useful in journalism classes.[8]

   *As Set Induction*

   A.  The experience begins by asking a boy and a girl to come forward and stand facing the class.

[7] William L. Hinckley, "Set Induction: What a Teacher Does to Introduce a Lesson," *School and Community* 57 (May 1971): 11. Used by permission of the author and the publisher.
[8] Hinckley, "Set Induction."

    B. Blindfolds are put in place and each student is asked in turn to describe the other—color of clothes, eyes, hair, and the like.

    C. Blindfolds are removed and lesson topic is introduced: observation and reporting of physical details.

III. Useful in any class.[9]

*For students with low motivation* (Burlington, Vt., High School)

    A. Involves twenty-four tenth-grade students who are just on the fringe of educational success (from a student body of 1,700 students).

    B. Selection is voluntary. Once selected, however, students work on a contractual basis.

    C. Course essentially entails a week of group discussion, followed by the students' own special projects. They may select a Mass Science course or an American Studies course. The program is self-contained. The group spends all its time apart from the rest of the school.

    D. The only formal "curriculum" is that planned and directed by students. For example, one boy rebuilt a car that he bought for a dollar. A girl elected to work voluntarily with orphans (at a nearby children's home).

    E. Since its basic purpose is a more positive self-concept, students usually need to perceive something that they can make.

    F. Credit is based upon completion of certain contracted activities and is on a point basis.

    G. Teachers (called by their first names) assume a counseling role. Physical education requirements have been dropped and replaced with such excursions as bowling, skiing, horseback riding, hiking, and fishing by the entire class.

*Note to the reader:* It should be noted that many of the illustrations provided in the various chapters of this book can be adapted to the motivational needs of a group.

[9] Diane Divoky, "What to Do About the Ones Who Don't Care," *National Schools* 85 (February 1970): 60–62.

# CHAPTER 5

# Discipline Problems

## OVERVIEW

### Key concepts

1.  Misbehavior is a symptom of other problems.
2.  Punishment must not be associated with school work.
3.  Physical force must be avoided whenever possible.
4.  Students want and have a right to active participation in policy development.
5.  Student misbehavior must not jeopardize the learning environment of other students.
6.  Discipline procedures must be adjusted to individual differences among students.
7.  The teacher's legal right to chastisement of students rests in the common law concept of *in loco parentis*.

### New Terms

1.  **Discipline**—A classroom organization conducive to orderly social conduct, leading to a self-disciplined individual.
2.  **Developmental Tasks**—Tasks an adolescent must learn if he is to be judged and to judge himself as a reasonably happy and successful person.

3. **Corporal Punishment**—The process of administering physical chastise-ment (inflicting physical pain or suffering) for the purpose of maintaining classroom (or school) discipline.
4. **Common Law**—A body of legal principles based upon the customs of the people or the judgments of the courts.
5. **In loco parentis**—A legal term that means standing in the place of a parent for the purposes of a student's education.
6. **Reinforcement**—The process of rewarding (reinforcing) desirable be-havior immediately following the act, thereby "stamping in" the behavior.
7. **Contingency Management**—Pairing a highly desirable response with a less desirable one for the purpose of reinforcing the latter.
8. **Extinction**—Allowing an undesirable behavior to diminish and die out by refusing to reinforce it.
9. **Punishment**—Negatively reinforcing (administering an unpleasant or aversive reward) undesirable behavior or simply withdrawing positive reinforcement (e.g., a privilege or an object). Although punishment can be effective it may be temporary if no new desirable behaviors are learned.

### Questions to Guide Your Study

1. "Motivation and discipline are part of the same problem." Defend or refute.
2. Why are different approaches suggested for stable and "disturbed" students?
3. "Discipline, essentially, should be conceived as another method of teach-ing." Defend or refute.
4. Many experienced teachers recommend "starting out tough" and gradu-ally relaxing behavior standards as the school year moves along. Discuss in terms of the principles of consistency and self-discipline.
5. Why is corporal punishment considered an undesirable form of discipline? Can you think of some instances when it might be justified?
6. What advantages do you see in developing some plan of action prior to the development of discipline problems? How would you alter the plan offered in this chapter to meet your own needs?

## FUNDAMENTAL PROPERTIES

The word *discipline* is apparently derived from the root word *disciple*—meaning to follow or study under an accepted leader. In early civilization discipline im-plied teaching or helping one to grow or achieve. Later it became associated with blind conformity. Today it means many things to many people. It is probably the most talked about but least understood of all problems of teaching. As a matter of fact, there is practically no substantive research on the subject. Perhaps this condition is due to the fact that it was originally a very comprehen-sive and amorphous concept that has become smaller and smaller as different parts are crystallized and separated into different categories. For example, such problems as delinquency, emotional disturbances, and problems resulting from mental and educational retardation now tend to be handled as separate problems as contrasted with the situation a few years ago. The aim of good discipline is to help the individual adjust to the *personal* and *social forces* of his experiences.

First, the adolescent must learn to adjust to himself as a growing and developing individual. He must achieve certain *developmental tasks* of the teen-age period if happiness and success in later tasks are to be achieved. These tasks include: (1) achieving new and more mature relations with his peer group, (2) achieving emotional independence of adults, especially his parents, (3) desiring and achieving socially responsible behavior, and (4) acquiring an adequate value system to guide behavior.

Second, the secondary school student must adjust to the existing culture and institutions within which he participates. A reasonable degree of cooperativeness, conformity, and consistency of behavior is expected. Above all, he will have to accept certain basic cultural contradictions. For example, the democratic concept of "equal treatment for all" must be adjusted (temporarily at least) to abuses of adolescents, racial and religious minorities, and nationality conflicts. Finally, he often will have to adjust standards of his home environment to those of the school.

Thus the problem of discipline today consists mainly of helping the student develop disciplined and *acceptable inner controls*. The concept has shifted from uniform demands on everyone to the acceptance of variations in behavior by individuals and even the toleration of variations for a single individual as he is faced with changing conditions.

This portion of the chapter deals with those aspects of the problem that set the stage for effective class control.

## What Variables Tend to Provoke Discipline Problems?

The room was hot and stuffy. It was the last period of the day. Everyone was excited about the district basketball tournament scheduled for the weekend. Could the home team conquer the neighboring school to the south which had barely defeated them in previous encounters?

Mrs. Burns was more than a little disturbed. It had all started when three of the team has been excused from class by the administration. She had planned her lesson well, but after a few minutes most pretenses of interest had disappeared. Finally one student blurted out, "Why do we have to study Shakespeare, especially the day before the big game?"

At this point Mrs. Burns could contain her emotions no longer. She assured the group that the study of Shakespeare was good for their cultural development—that there would be no need for such questions if they would study literature with the enthusiasm with which they studied basketball.

About this time somebody dropped a book. A few students giggled and began talking among themselves. Mrs. Burns, visibly shaken, rapped for attention and said, "All right, if you are not mature enough to discuss the lesson intelligently you can do an open book test on the material. Papers will be due by the end of the class period."

A few students grumbled cautiously, but most of them made at least some pretense of conforming to the request.

What caused Mrs. Burns's problem? Was it the coming basketball game? the students? the content of the course? Or was it caused by Mrs. Burns herself? An examination of the situation discloses a number of contributing factors. In the *first* place, there was the coming basketball game. Such circumstances are numerous in the public schools of today. A typical secondary school may have fifteen to twenty-five clubs—to say nothing of the sports events! A number of school situations tend to contribute to disorder in the classroom:

> The last period of the day, usually.
> The last five minutes of the class period before lunch.
> The last period of the day on Friday.
> The whole day just before some extra-class function like a sports event.
> The first part of the period following a school assembly, fire drill, or exciting rally.
> At a time of all-school crisis, such as a basketball tournament, conflict between students, students and teachers, or teachers and teachers.
> Before a holiday.
> The first few days of school.
> Fridays in general; sometimes the first half of Monday.
> Appearance of a substitute teacher.
> The first few minutes of the period.

*Another variable* contributing to Mrs. Burns's discipline problems was *teacher-caused.* She was unable to develop an important purpose for studying Shakespeare and tended to put the blame on students. Few people are able to make effective progress when they are uncertain as to why they are working at a task. Secondary school students need constant reminders of purpose, interpreted in language they can readily understand. This means that it must be near their operational level of behavior. Would it have been possible to relate the study of Shakespeare to the immediate interest in basketball? The resourceful teacher would likely say "yes."

Furthermore, Mrs. Burns permitted her emotions to interfere with sound teaching techniques. In the first place, it is not psychologically sound to assign school work as punishment. Neither is it appropriate to discipline a group for the transgressions of a few. Many discipline problems are, in fact, teacher-caused. Some of these have been listed below:

> Sarcasm
> Inconsistency
> Being impolite and inconsiderate
> Having favorites
> Gossiping about students in public places
> Failure to make class and lesson purposes clear to students
> Using the same method day after day
> Failure to provide for individual differences
> Talking "over" noise
> A classroom that is either too hot or too cold
> Taking time out for calling roll every day
> Confusion resulting from class routines
> Vague assignments
> Emphasizing factual-type tests

A *third variable* contributing to disorder within Mrs. Burns's classroom was *student-caused.* Students are usually quick to exploit an unfortunate situation. Some of them dislike school and most teachers associated with it. Others, just like all human beings, react in terms of health, emotions, and passing interests. More will be said of pupil-caused problems later.

While there is no "quick" solution to Mrs. Burns's problem, the resourceful teacher might have openly acknowledged the student's preoccupation with basketball by comparing the sport with recreational activities during Shakespeare's time. Furthermore, the influence of healthful (and unhealthful) competition is evident in most of Shakespeare's writings, providing an easy approach to problems associated with interscholastic competition.

## How Do Students with Problems Differ from Problem Students?

You are working with . . . American children. This is not the same as training animals; a dog, a horse, a rat, or a cow or a team of oxen. Animals are never supposed to rebel . . . burn the lessons . . . into their brains, and into every pore of their bodies.

. . . Only the leaders think in dictator countries. The people obey.

Your job is different. Your children must think *and* obey. They must fit in *and* break out. They must follow accepted paths *and* break out on their own.

Jesus was a rebel.

Columbus was a rebel.

Washington was a rebel.

Every significant scientist who has made your life the good life it is was a rebel. . . .

Americans are rebels. And your approach to teaching discipline has to fit into this framework.[1]

The adolescent is tasting independence for the first time. This independence in a democratic society is most important. Yet without some conformity chaos follows. Two decades ago Hymes[2] suggested that teachers must make a distinction between *students with problems and problem students.* He pointed out that the vast majority are "well individuals" who need no more than "straight" teaching. Like all human beings, they have problems from time to time. With these students the teacher discusses, explains, interprets, and talks. This Hymes called the logical approach.

With a few students, however, one must do "remedial teaching." These are the individuals whose past experiences have "hurt" them. They tend to be

[1] James L. Hymes, Jr., *Behavior and Misbehavior* (Englewood Cliffs, N.J.: Prentice-Hall, Inc., 1955), pp. 8–9.
[2] *Ibid.*

suspicious, resentful, and overly egocentric. By every act they "cry out" for attention, for success, for love, for security. With these few individuals (the "problem children") the teacher frequently must say "no" and mean it. These are the students who will hurt others and create an undesirable learning situation. Although they need and demand attention, they must be "stopped"—compelled to conform to class rules—*and then treated with all manner of kindness possible.* In Chapter 4 specific instructional techniques were offered for dealing with low motivated students. These are frequently the persons who need the so-called remedial approach to discipline.

### What Activities May Reveal Clues to Personal-social Adjustment Problems?

Although symptoms of individuals with difficulty sometimes are revealed when least expected, certain activities are especially likely to provide clues. Reference is here made to fairly stable individuals who, like all human beings, need help from time to time. As indicated in the foregoing section, seriously disturbed students are readily detected. The teacher is in an ideal position to prevent normal but serious problems from seriously disrupting class activities. Certain activities tend to reveal valuable clues to personal-social adjustment.

1. *Any period when controversial issues are discussed.* Significant clues to adjustment are indicated by the individual who rigidly defends his own ideas just because they are his own. He sometimes rejects opposing views because he dislikes the individual proposing them. In all probability, such a student is experiencing some difficulty in satisfying his need for security.

2. *Self-directed activities.* Among the many advantages to the lengthened class period is the opportunity it provides for the teacher to observe the work habits of youngsters. Students who display overdependence on others, those who are easily distracted, and those who "give up" easily can undoubtedly profit from immediate attention. Some of these individuals may lack a sense of personal worth; others may be bothered with home or other out-of-class problems; while still others may merely need goals clarified or reemphasized.

3. *Group activities.* Even casual observation during group activities will disclose those who have difficulty in cooperative behavior, those who dominate, and those who tend to react negatively when their ideas are rejected. It is in such activities that a teacher can partially determine why certain individuals are always on the fringe of the group. While the behavior pattern may not be serious enough to result in total rejection, it can seriously impede one in reaching his maximum potential.

4. *Role-playing activities.* The type of role that one chooses to play may offer valuable clues to personality adjustment. Even more revealing are those roles assigned or suggested for certain individuals. During the unrehearsed play acting, clues are derived from those who show unusual hostility, tenseness, and so on.

5. *Student-led committee activities.* In these situations it is easy to spot those who have difficulty in accepting responsibilities from members of the peer

group. Sometimes a student who usually displays high initiative in teacher-directed activities will show very little progress in student-led activities. This type of behavior indicates difficulty—perhaps too much parental domination.

6. *Extra-class activities.* Here the instructor notes the spontaneous groupings that prevail. Sometimes students who seem at ease in the formal classroom situation will show quite different reactions in informal social situations. They may withdraw, display shyness, or even become aggressive when classroom inhibitions are released.

All adolescents have problems or difficulties. Many such problems are of a transitory nature. The reasonable well-adjusted student can cope with most problems. Sometimes, however, problems persist or one's adjustment to them is inadequate for healthful living. Clues are available to guide the close observer in isolating the difficulty. The remedial action necessary will, of course, depend on the unique circumstances associated with each case.

### How Does One Recognize and Cope with the Mental Health Needs of Teen-agers?

In describing his experiences with troubled students, a school psychologist once cited the following incident:

I recently taught in a well-to-do suburban school where 80 per cent of the children go on to college and the other 20 per cent seem to become lost. I thought we should offer a program for this 20 per cent, the "lost" seniors. Most of them were uneducated and unable to read above a grade five level. They were trouble-makers, seventeen- and eighteen-year-old seniors who would graduate because the teacher got the signal, "Let this guy through." It was agreed that I might offer them an enrichment course, an "Introduction to Psychology," where we could talk about sex, hypnosis, the unconscious, etc. But I couldn't get them to listen to me. On the first day I was greeted with, "Hi Doc. I'm the class nut, analyze me." Another one said, "Hi Doc, I run this class. Nobody teaches anything without my permission." He was a six-foot-three leading basketball player. To my relief, he said, "I'm going to have a little snooze, so you just go ahead." Soon he was snoring. I finally said, "Jimmy, how would you like for me to analyze you?" He woke up. Yes, he was interested, and so were the other members of the class who cheered him on.

Improvising, I said, "Jimmy, you have difficulty with your masculinity. You're trying to prove yourself all the time." After a moment he said, "You come to the bathroom and I'll prove it." I said, "I'm not interested in your physical self but in your feelings."

Considering this statement, he replied, "Doc, in this class I'm leader and speak for the hidden feelings of everyone in it. We're the generation nobody cares about. But I will never let anybody forget us. I'll cause so much trouble that no one will be able to." The class was astonished, the whole atmosphere was changed, but they all knew what he meant.[3]

[3] Sol Gordon, "Education and the Impulse Life of the Child," *Phi Delta Kappan* 47, no. 6 (February, 1966): 310–14.

In working with these individuals the psychologist found that they were as bright as the group going on to college. They were unable to pay attention to teachers, it seems, because they equated learning with submission.

Another characteristic of emotional maladjustment is dependency, characterized by leaning heavily on others for ego satisfaction and for the solving of life's problems. Such an individual does not like his self-image. He tends to project blame on others for his shortcomings. Frequently he relies heavily on the common adjustment mechanisms of escape, such as denial, rationalization, and fantasy. He is rigid, compulsive, and burdened with guilt feelings.[4]

Mental health, like physical health, is a relative term. Progress toward a realistically oriented, well-balanced state is a never-ending process. Descriptive statements by mental health authorities suggest a number of characteristics. A mentally healthy individual:

1. is independent; relies on others but not until he has first utilized his own resources;
2. lives by the reality principle, facing problems head-on rather than circumventing or postponing attempts at solution;
3. stands behind his actions;
4. accepts himself, including those limitations that he is unable to overcome;
5. yet is ever emergent in those areas where growth and change are possible, moving toward the goal of optimum development;
6. is flexible, not becoming easily upset by changes in living routines;
7. is uncompartmentalized, applying values in a consistent way in all of life's areas;
8. relates effectively to others;
9. keeps basic needs satisfied, as best he can, so as to increase his effectiveness in solving life's problems;
10. remains free of debilitating guilt;
11. works in the present but makes reasonable plans for the future; and
12. has a high tolerance for frustration.[5]

In coping with the mental health needs of students the teacher must realize that teaching consists of delicate human interaction. His authority over pupils is maintained at the minimum level necessary for producing a climate of emotional security. This implies a guiding, rather than a demanding role. It means sharing, as opposed to meting out tasks. It means encouraging pupils to become progressively more independent of the teacher.

A second requirement for building mentally healthy learners is acceptance. The teacher must accept all students. This means the ability to respect, to listen, and to distinguish the individual from his disagreeable behaviors. The process of reaching the emotional life of an unmotivated youngster is not easy. This attribute, more than anything else, is probably best characterized by an emotional climate which conveys the basic notion that somebody really cares. It is the climate that reassures the learner that his resentments, thoughts, and wildest

---

[4] Gail M. Inlow, *The Emergent in Curriculum* (New York: John Wiley & Sons, Inc., 1966), p. 52.

[5] *Ibid.*, pp. 51–52.

dreams are likely little different from those of other, normal youngsters; that energy can be used in constructive ways.

A third essential for building mental health is a mentally healthy teacher. Although teachers, like all human beings, vary considerably in this respect, most psychologists agree that an individual can improve his own mental health through introspection and ordered activity. Such introspection can be gained through a variety of ways, some of which are listed below.

1. Look at yourself. Become aware of your own beliefs, attitudes, needs, and motivation and predict their consequences to the learning process. You may not like what you find, but this provides a basis for building a satisfactory self-image.

2. Recognize that change is not only possible but inevitable. The choice is merely between drift and ordered change. Sometimes it may involve reestablishing an appropriate balance between physical, mental, and social aspects of existence. Adequate social relationships, for example, can be established satisfactorily if one is willing to work at the task.

3. Recreation is useful for a change of pace. It not only relaxes but often enables one to gain a new perspective or outlook.

4. Human beings are continually in the process of becoming. Graduation from college should be viewed as merely the beginning of a lifetime of professional and personal growth. Boredom and discontentment are often reflections of one's inability to grow intellectually.

Respect for the individual is the essence of democratic living. It is through our activities and behavior that this respect is communicated. Mental health depends not on being free from problems but on facing them realistically.

### How Is a Working Relationship Established?

In any working relationship the parties involved must fully understand the rules of procedure. A set of expectations, including limits, must be established. Adolescents are especially sensitive to "fair play." Although this is characteristically a period of challenge of constituted authority and cultural norms, the adolescent respects the teacher who consistently enforces realistic class policies. He is usually intolerant of unnecessary regulations or any rule that makes him feel he is being "treated like a child."

Implied in the foregoing is the desirability of working *with* students in establishing class policies and rules of procedure. Teen-agers readily respond to perceived needs in such situations. In fact, they may be too hard on themselves unless the teacher can interject some measure of restraint.

Once school policies are thoroughly understood and class policies have been clearly defined, the teacher is expected to see that they are carried out. Prompt and consistent enforcement is necessary as rules are tested. Minor problems are not permitted to grow into crises. Complete consistency to every member of the group is neither necessary nor desirable, however. Complete inconsistency, on the other hand, would render the stiuation impossible. Indeed, total inconsistency would be as rigid and inflexible as complete uniformity. As implied, then, consistency means expecting all individuals to follow the rules with ample allowances for individual differences and the reality of actual situations.

Experienced teachers sometimes claim they "start out tough" and gradually relax the rules as the school term moves along. This is a form of inconsistency and is not recommended. What actually happens sometimes is that as the students and teacher become adjusted to class policies and procedures they tend to *feel* progressively less restricted in daily activities.

### What Is the Legal Status of Corporal Punishment?

Corporal punishment, causing physical pain or suffering as a means of modifying behavior, for many years was an unquestionable right of the teacher. Today, however, such practices are generally not recommended for secondary school age students. Nevertheless, many school authorities insist on maintaining the *legal right* to use corporal punishment in extreme cases. In many schools this "right" is seldom, if ever, exercised. (The psychological damage that can result is treated later in this chapter.)

The teacher's legal right to chastise a student rests in common law (derived from the customs of the people and from the judgments of the courts).[6] Teachers, administrators, and even school board members stand *in loco parentis* to their students. Essentially this means that an educator stands in the place of a parent for the purpose of educating a young person. The courts have ruled that the parent has delegated authority over the youngster to the teacher for educational purposes. This is so, despite the fact that the parent has lost the right to determine *if* he will send his child to school or not. A parent's wish cannot override this authority.

Neither a parent nor the teacher can legally abuse a student, however. Immoderate use of corporal punishment is illegal and may result in a charge of assault and battery (the intent to injure). This falls under the category of a criminal offense. The individual states, in many cases, have exercised their legal right to modify rules governing corporal punishment. Only two states (Massachusetts and New Jersey) and the District of Columbia presently ban corporal punishment. Many other states have regulated its use. Generally a teacher is not permitted to strike a student about the head or face. Usually the punishment must not be administered in anger and must be witnessed by another teacher or administrator.

In any event, the courts decide cases on the basis of common law principles that function within the state and also on the basis of *in loco parentis*. From this, two distinct lines of authority have evolved:

1. The accused is within the protected privilege of a parent to discipline his child unless permanent injury results from the punishment or unless the act was

---

[6] Many of the ideas expressed here are based upon Samuel N. Francis and Emma J. Hirsheberger, "Corporal Punishment in the School," *Educational Leadership* 30 (April 1973): 591–5.

done with legal malice. Under this line of authority the accused parent or teacher is the sole judge of both the necessity for and the amount of the punishment.

2. A jury is permitted to determine both the necessity for and the amount of the punishment. This line of authority is followed in many states.

The legal right to corporal punishment recently has been challenged in the courts. A landmark case from Texas (*Ware* v. *Estes*) recently was allowed to stand by the United States Supreme Court (November, 1972). In this case the plaintiffs contended that corporal punishment violated the 8th (cruel and unusual punishment) and the 14th (due process of law) Amendments to the Constitution. At the time of this writing several other cases were pending.

Even though at the time of this writing the legal right to corporal punishment has successfully withstood court tests, a number of recent federal court decisions have forced school authorities to recognize that pupils are citizens with the *legal* right to fair and impartial hearings. It has been established, for example, that students have the right to wear clothing and hair styles that promote individualism rather than conformity; they have the legal right to free speech in the school newspaper. In school after school, arbitrary regulations are being effectively challenged in the courts. The traditional precedent of doing things *for* students rather than *with* students apparently needs an immediate reappraisal.

# MANAGEMENT AND DISCIPLINE TECHNIQUES

For years various individuals and groups have formulated prescriptions for maintaining class control. Generally such "techniques" have been somewhat ineffective simply because each situation is different and each teacher must act within his own philosophical and personality framework. Techniques that may be quite effective for one individual, for example, often are rather ineffective for another. Yet, evidence indicates that prospective and new teachers worry more about discipline than any other aspect of teaching.

In an effort to strike a balance between the general and the specific, the writer has approached the problem from the standpoint of individual differences and those techniques that may provide a broad framework from which a teacher may operate. Included are psychological principles that have been employed effectively in typical class situations.

### How Can Discipline Be Taught to Stable Students?

Discipline is hard for students to learn because it is made up of innumerable specifics. Truths, honesty, dependability, respect for property, privacy, personality, helpfulness to others, and protection of smaller people are just a few of the rules of society that each new generation must learn to uphold. Some children learn such lessons at home and need only *apply* them at school. Others, especially those who are the products of lower social class homes, must *learn* the rules of the game. This is no small matter because, in a typical, unselected group of youngsters, more than half of the individuals come from the lower socioeconomic classes. The acquisition and alteration of attitudes and values take time. Patience is essential. One's teaching task in discipline is similar to his task in any other field. Students learn some things by listening, but they are more likely to remember and act on their *own words and ideas.* They need to solve their own problems: to make proposals, seek out and analyze the available data, test their own hypotheses, and examine their own results. The emphasis in this book has been just that!

Placing emphasis on group and individual problem-solving techniques demands that one have a lot of faith in the capacity of teen-agers to develop and uphold high standards of conduct. Students want, and have a right to expect, reasonable limits on their actions. Indeed, they often will impose unnecessarily high standards on themselves if given a free hand. In the final analysis, the boys and girls must do most of the thinking and most of the talking. They must do all the learning.

Students will learn more quickly if they are permitted to assist in setting up their own rules of conduct. The teacher, however, must retain the right to determine what action is necessary when rules are broken. This is made necessary because behavior results from many *different* causes. The action to be taken must be consistent with the cause(s) and the individual involved. For instance, a class may decide that late assignments should not count as much as those turned in on time. There are times, however, when such action would be most inappropriate (sickness, special emergencies, etc.). The instructor must weigh each case separately.

How does one respond to misbehavior of stable children? First he must determine the cause(s). If the teacher decides that the individual does not yet know or understand what is expected, he should *talk, discuss, and explain.* If, however, the act seems directly related to a teen-age developmental task, it may be appropriate to simply *ignore* the disturbing behavior. Boy-girl relationships frequently fall into this category. If a boy-girl situation is too bothersome to ignore, it may be necessary to *channel* the behavior into a more acceptable area. For example, the couple can be placed together on a project, committee, or report. Sometimes difficulties result from the immediate environment, in which case it will be important to move the individual or otherwise *alter the environment.*

Occasionally a behavior problem demands more extreme action than that suggested in the preceding paragraph. Should the teacher then punish? Psychologists often refer to punishment as that action which blocks a given behavior. For example, the warning, "Don't talk while Mary is giving her report," is a punishment. This is the negative approach. Reward also can be used to control misbehavior. The teacher can say, "Now if we pay very close attention to Mary we should determine just how the———process works." Both reward and punishment are effective—both are appropriate techniques to use. Whenever possible, however, reward (the positive approach) should be used. Punishment causes one to remember because of pain, discomfort, or fear, whereas reward gives pleasure or satisfaction.

According to Hymes,[7] punishment should be used with caution. He offers some helpful guidelines in the appropriate use of punishment:

1. *Use it with stable students only.*
2. *Use it when students are "ignorant of the law."* One must sometimes say, "Do not touch this machine"; "Do not move this microscope"; "Do not tamper with the chemicals in this cabinet."
3. *Use it only when they must learn the law quickly.* The pressure for quick results, however, does not often originate with what the student is doing. It is more often associated with the way the teacher is feeling!
4. *Use it only when the law is a specific one, applicable to a definite situation.*

The use of physical or corporal punishment is not mentioned in the preceding discussion, because it is usually considered an inappropriate technique to use with students.

### How Can Discipline Be Taught to Disturbed Students?

The thirsty man knows his trouble. He can tell you: "I want water." The hungry man can verbalize his emptiness: "Food. Give me food." The sleepy one can say to you: "I'm so tired I cannot keep my eyes open." These . . . youngsters do not know their trouble. They have no words to explain how they feel. They cannot say: "This is where it hurts." . . They hurt, but they cannot tell you where or why or how.

. . . These psychological hungers are not nicely located—in the belly, in the throat, in the eyelids. They are all through the body . . . everywhere . . . in every pore, muscle, and nerve.[8]

A few students—probably not more than three or four in an average classroom—have not had their basic psychological needs adequately fulfilled. The result is a "gnawing emptiness" that tends to dominate their behavior patterns. They are the problem children. They are the ones whose problems seem to obscure the individuals behind them! Identification is easy—just look for the individuals who are always getting into trouble; the ones with school reputations; those who have acquired nicknames: Jughead, Toughie, Weasel, Loudmouth.

Instead of proceeding with a straightforward approach to *teaching*, a reverse order of procedure is in order for these students. They first must be stopped. They will hit others, make wisecracks, talk back, or do anything to attract attention. As a professionally trained person, the teacher knows why. They are trying to satisfy nagging hungers. They seek—*they demand*—recognition, success, love and affection, a sense of personal worth. These behaviors represent their attempts

[7] Hymes, *op. cit.*, pp. 71–72.
[8] Hymes, *op. cit.*, pp. 83–84.

to adjust. Although they realize that such behaviors often get them into difficulty, they know of no other alternatives. Some recognition, transitory as it is, is better than no recognition. The teacher must be firm with these individuals; otherwise, they will take over. Without firmness, without limits, the learning environment of 35 other students will be seriously jeopardized. One must be firm—say *no* and mean it—but he must also be *gentle*. As Hymes states in his book *Behavior and Misbehavior*, the teacher must be firm but not severe. He will stop the child but not try to hurt him. *He* understands. The feeling is inside. It will not let him look with angry eyes—sympathy will show through. The misunderstood person "feels" the difference, simply because he has had. ample experience with the other kind of treatment—when the correction was cold and hard. As a professionally trained person, the teacher puts himself inside others' skins, thinks with their brains, sees with their eyes. Then, and only then, can he understand that in spite of all the deviltry "inside" these students they are not at fault.

Teachers know what these individuals want. They will say with assurance: "He wants attention, to have his own way, to be boss." The analysis is easy because the clues are obvious. The next step also would be simple, except for the fact that one sometimes allows emotions to blur his vision. The classroom is a miniature society. Some people will lead, get the headlines, receive the glory. In many situations the instructor has the power to determine who receives these rewards. Who needs them the most? At this point the "starved" individual for the first time may be able to satisfy his hungers in a socially acceptable manner. But what about the stable individuals? Do they not deserve such rewards too? Yes but they can wait, for their basic needs are not nearly as demanding as are those of problem students. Furthermore, they have developed acceptable techniques of achieving such rewards on their own initative. *Good behavior for stable students is an avenue to rewards. With problem students the rewards must come first so that they can develop good behavior.*

The problem is by no means solved, however, when such individuals are given opportunities to lead or otherwise gain recognition. They tend to overact or overrespond. The *new* experience for them is almost more than they can handle. Sometimes they may identify the reward as an excuse to disturb even more. This is a natural consequence, for such persons have been accustomed to gaining attention in such a manner. In other words, they may get worse before they get better. As indicated in Chapter 12, when students are grouped sociometrically those who need the added security of close proximity with their mutual choices tend to overreact. Even so, this is a sign of progress. The teacher "looks the other way" or, if necessary, channels the behavior into more constructive areas. A doctor does not expect a severely wounded patient to recover overnight. He has faith in himself, the patient, and the treatment being prescribed. These individuals are also sick—not just for a day, a week, or a year. Their "sickness" may extend over a period of ten or fifteen years. Time and patience are essential. Cooperation with other teachers, with administrators, and with parents is needed. Indeed a school-planned program of treatment is vitally needed.

There is one group of disturbed young people that is not easily recognized as needing help. These are the quiet ones—those who are not causing anyone else trouble but are nevertheless in trouble themselves. They are specialists at covering up. The trouble is there, but is bottled up inside. They are the ones who seek perfection, hide their emotions, or daydream. They are often fearful of social interaction, sometimes refusing to recite in class. "Pushing" is not the answer, nor is exacting high demands upon them a satisfactory approach. They lack confidence in themselves, but clues to the causes are not readily apparent from their behavior. Thus it often becomes necessary to turn to their pasts for answers to the problem. Parents, earlier teachers, and friends can often provide useful sources of data. In the meantime one can establish situations that provide a release for these "tightly sealed" feelings. Opportunities for composing stories, essays, or plays will help. Role playing may also provide the needed release. Although they may cause little or no trouble within the classroom, they are actually in greater trouble than those who overtly misbehave. It is a serious mistake to ignore them. They are the ones who can suddenly explode someday and literally destroy those with whom they associate.

## What Guidelines Are Useful in Dealing with Common Class Disturbances?

Although it is essential that the teacher distinguish between "normal" and "disturbed" students, there are a number of general guidelines that many teachers have found to be effective. The reader, however, is cautioned against assuming any fixed procedure in class disturbances.

*Disturbing conversation.* Sometimes such a disturbance can be ignored. If it threatens to spread, the teacher can move to the area of disturbance. He may offer to help the students get started on an assignment. If the teacher is talking to the entire group, a pause or a question to one of the disturbing students can effectively solve the problem. Although some teachers are quick to separate students who disturb, this is often an inadvisable procedure. The practice may create resentment and serve to spread the problem to other parts of the room.

*Passing notes.* Such activities are symptomatic of a boring experience or lack of appropriate challenge. Frequently a change of pace takes care of the situation. It is not appropriate to read notes aloud to the class.

*Overdependence of one student on another.* This problem will usually work itself out. The students sometimes need each other until wider social acceptance is possible. Wider social acceptance is encouraged through emphasis on group work in which students are grouped sociometrically.

*Hostility between individuals and/or groups.* Talk with each of the participants individually. Try to find the cause prior to any drastic attempts at reformation.

*Flirtations.* It is natural for individuals to become attracted to the opposite sex at adolescence. As one of the developmental tasks it is best to permit more, rather than less, socialization (within proper limits). The resourceful teacher usually is able to find many areas where this type of socialization will produce a minimum amount of class disturbance.

*Cheating.* As indicated earlier, cheating usually occurs as a result of over-emphasis on grades or the establishment of unrealistic standards. In the chapter treating individual differences, the importance of making assignments and tests commensurate with students' abilities was emphasized. If the task is too hard for the person he will be forced to cheat in order to meet the requirement.

Sometimes students cheat primarily because of the opportunities provided. This can be discouraged by separating students when they are assigned individual work. In the case of crowded classrooms alternate forms of a test can be constructed. A class discussion of the consequences of cheating may be very effective. Frequently the problem can be alleviated by permitting students to redo poor work for some credit.

*Refusal to comply with a teacher request.* Sometimes a teacher makes a simple request, only to discover that the student refuses to obey. What should be done under the circumstances? Should the refusal be ignored? Should the teacher meet the conflict with force? The action to be taken will, of course, depend on the nature of the request. Refusal to comply with simple requests usually is associated with high emotional tension. Some teachers simply handle the situation by saying: "I could possibly make you move, but will certainly not try it. I suppose we will need to talk this over at the end of the class period." The student usually decides to follow through with the suggested action. If the situation is too serious to ignore, a teacher can say: "I believe I had better find someone who *can* persuade you to comply." The student usually follows the teacher out the door or suddenly decides he had better move after all. It is very important, however, that teacher requests be followed. Failure to comply should be subject to certain consequences. Unreasonable requests should be avoided. A reasonable request for one student may be unreasonable for another.

### What Are Some Questionable Practices of Classroom Discipline?

"You forget about the things they taught you while in college. I have discovered some things that really work."

Miss Brown was perplexed. "Why," she asked herself, "was there such a discrepancy between college instruction and classroom practice in the area of discipline?"

The dilemma is a real one. Many teachers discover and adopt some "pet" technique that "works" in maintaining order in the classroom. By "works" they usually mean "keeps students quiet or orderly," and "here and now." Professional educators and, indeed, many classroom teachers tend to look beyond surface and temporary conformity. It has been established that forced conformity does not equip youngsters to become progressively more able to cope with their own affairs. The overwhelming majority of lawbreakers who serve time in penal institutions continue their criminal records when they are released. Forced conformity in the classroom is apt to "boil over" at any time. In such cases the teacher eventually finds himself devoting a major portion of his energies to maintaining order.

One of the most important functions of education in a democracy is to help boys and girls develop skills in working and playing together. Socialization with those who differ in so many different respects is not an easy goal to attain. Application of democratic principles as a way of life can hardly be cultivated by authoritarian disciplinary techniques. Learning to apply the rules of democracy is a slower and more difficult procedure than forced conformity, but as students develop these techniques they need progressively less assistance from the teacher. The disciplinary techniques that follow generally are considered inappropriate or at least of questionable value:

*Corporal punishment.* As indicated earlier, this is a dangerous technique for the teacher (the student may strike back!). It can be both physically and psychologically damaging to the student. Furthermore, there have been a number of court actions against teachers who have used corporal punishment. Students themselves tend to resent this sort of punishment, claiming that adults seldom if ever know all the facts in the situation.

*Isolation.* Separating a student from his peers tends to reinforce the craving that induced the behavior in the first place. It may be necessary to isolate a student *temporarily* as a stop-gap measure, but continued use of the technique can only lead to greater frustration, deeper feelings of guilt, and resentment.

*Imposition of school tasks for punitive purposes.* Such a technique, in essence, punishes a child by making him do school work. Thus he tends to *associate* misbehavior with school work.

*Forced apologies.* Forcing a student to verbalize an apology he does not feel is a way of forcing him to lie. It solves nothing!

*Sarcastic remarks.* This creates resentment and lowers the esteem of the teacher in the eyes of students.

*Removal from the situation.* While there will be times when an individual must be removed from the classroom, it should be used only as a last resort. In such instances the teacher is admitting his inability to handle the situation. When the practice becomes necessary the offender should be sent to a specific member of the teaching or administrative staff. In other words, he should not be sent from the room without adequate provisions for supervision.

*Demerits.* One's conduct witihn the classroom should not be associated with academic marks. The two are important yet distinct aspects of learning. The act of penalizing a student in one area for transgressions in another area tends to establish an undesirable association. To illustrate: a child penalized academically for misbehavior may develop an attitude of "What's the use?" toward his school work. Likewise, a child who is rewarded academically for "good" behavior may substitute "being nice" for academic achievement.

## What Techniques Tend to Prevent Discipline Problems?

Some teachers experience more than their share of difficulty in maintaining class control. Often it is noted that the same students who "give some teachers a hard time" are very well behaved in the classes of other teachers. Why is this?

Although there are undoubtedly many variables in classroom management, it is generally agreed that a well-organized class situation is an effective means of preventing class disturbances. The following directions are suggestive only:

1. Plan carefully. Attempt to see that every minute is covered with organized activities.
2. Keep the class moving. Change activities every 15 minutes or so. When students become restless it is time to introduce a new activity.
3. Minimize the time for putting points on the chalkboard. Do this before class; use overhead projector transparencies; enlist the help of a student; shorten points to a few key words.
4. Make certain that visual aids are ready for use before the class arrives.
5. Read constantly in your subject area. This enables one to keep his teaching vitality and to bring in timely anecdotes of human interest.
6. Whenever possible, enlist students in planning their own learning activities. In any event, discuss the purpose of their learning activities.
7. When class presentations are planned be sure to prepare each individual (or group) for his presentation. Students, as well as teachers, must fully understand the methods they will use.
8. Maintain high and definite standards for all normal students. Any normal student who does not attain a minimum standard of performance should be expected to repeat. Less able students, likewise, will attain a minimum level of achievement. This, however, will be commensurate with their own limited abilities.
9. Out-of-class assignments must be fully explained. Whenever possible, put directions in writing; follow up all assignments, especially those which involve reading only.
10. Even though an assignment may have been poorly done, create the impression that most of the students did quite well. This tends to build peer pressure.

Although important to the orderly functioning of a large school, many routine tasks interfere with the teaching process. Most teachers recognize a need for techniques of streamlining routine tasks. Many are so preoccupied with the major functions of teaching, however, that they permit undesirable situations to jeopardize seriously the classroom situation. Each teacher must become an efficiency expert in clerical and routine aspects of teaching so that his work week will be shortened. Thus he can be freed to devote his major energies to the creative elements of teaching. The following suggestions are indicative of efforts to streamline such tasks:

1. Eliminate all superfluous motions when doing such routine chores as correcting objective tests, stapling, correcting duplicated copies, and making trips to the office.
2. Keep expendable and often used items such as paper, blotters, pencils, passes, chalk, rubber bands, and manila folders in good supply and in convenient places.
3. For each class use a different colored manila folder with its two big pockets as a handy container for papers to be marked, papers to be returned, and lesson plans.
4. To evaluate other than test papers concentrate on a few revealing

points common to all papers and rapidly scan the remainder of each pupil's work.

5. Make heavy use of typewriting and shorthand skills. Duplicating services also will expedite work.

6. Leave two or three desks unassigned, to serve as places for distribution and collection of materials. These desks also can be used to take care of students who need to be moved for disciplinary reasons.

7. Be prepared to *use* additional moments when one ordinarily would be waiting. A pencil and note pad should be available for immediate use at all times.

8. Use students to check attendance, collect monies, change bulletin board displays, and operate media equipment.

9. When reteaching must be done, permit the best student in class to teach the two lowest pupils, the second highest student to teach the third and fourth lowest pupils, and so on until all students in the class are accounted for. This, according to Zafra, tends to increase motivation.

10. Use discriminating and valid test items from other classes and other years. Although desirable improvements should be made, many items can be used more than once.

11. Let pupils correct one another's objective quiz papers under your supervision and direction.

12. Use a daily date-book for keeping track of prearranged committee meetings and forthcoming chores.

13. When stencils are cut, run off enough copies to last for a considerable time. Save the masters for future use.

14. Whenever possible, make duplicated quiz papers nonexpendable. Adapt them to machine-scored answer sheets or hand-scored forms that can be corrected rapidly.

15. Manage to build up a class library, consisting especially of encyclopedias and other reference books in your subject area.

16. Use a rubber stamp with the teacher's name on it, to save time and writer's cramp for such things as report cards, class schedules, passes, and attendance reports.

17. Let pupils help make attractive posters, with a supply of poster paper readily available, together with a yardstick, shears, and a variety of felt pens.

Clerical and routine tasks can take the fun out of teaching. They can effectively prevent a teacher from making his job the creative endeavor that is so important. A little thought and advance preparation will greatly minimize these troublesome tasks.

### How Can the Principles of Reinforcement Be Applied to Classroom Management?

One of the most important conditions of learning is that of reward or reinforcement. As a matter of fact, according to many psychologists, *learning occurs only when an act is reinforced or rewarded.* Thorndike, in the early years of the present century, came close to the problem in his well-known *law of effect:* "Of several responses made to the same situation, those which are accompanied or closely followed by satisfaction . . . will . . . be more . . . likely to reoccur . . ."[9] Later psychologists showed that Thorndike's law of effect, in itself, was inadequate and must be supplemented by *purposeful* behavior. In essence, then, the law can be stated as follows: Learning occurs only when one is able to determine that he is making progress toward his goal.

In using reward as a technique for shaping human behavior a series of steps and conditions are necessary.

First, observe behavior during free time periods. It may be useful to ask students to specify in writing how they would prefer to utilize any free time in class.

Next, develop a system of pairing a lower problem behavior (e.g., studying) with a higher problem behavior (e.g., talking to one's friend). For example, the learner can be informed of the opportunity to talk, play a game, etc. *after* he has completed his reading assignment. In this manner the less desirable behavior gradually acquires the characteristics of the more desirable behavior. Psychologists refer to this as *contingency management.*

Provide opportunities for students to earn free time activities. Perhaps a point system can be developed that can result in up to five minutes of free time daily, cumulative by week. Undesirable behavior would not be reinforced. This technique of permitting undesirable behavior to die out from lack of reinforcement is known as *extinction.* An extinguished behavior may reappear later (spontaneous recovery). If not reinforced it will disappear and rarely reappear a second time. It should be noted that even though a teacher may refuse to reward an undesirable behavior such reward may be acquired through the peer group. In such cases the behavior will not be extinguished. Most behavioral changes accomplished through extinction are noted within a period of two weeks.

Whenever possible a student can be assisted in adapting behavior by pairing with another student who exhibits such desirable behavior. Known as *modeling,* this technique is effective only when the paired associate himself exhibits strong and consistent patterns of desirable behavior.

While the desirable behavior at first may be rewarded through a point system, later a timely word of praise or commendation may be all that is needed. Shaping behavior is at best a slow, tedious task. Thus reward must be based upon *successive approximations.* In other words, the teacher must not expect too much; he must allow ample time for both quality and quantity of the desirable behavior patterns to emerge.

In some cases *negative reinforcement* (punishment) may be necessary. A student may be reprimanded or points may be taken away for disturbances that demand class time for correction. The results of this technique, however, may be temporary and uncertain, since the learner may be at a loss as to what desirable behavior is needed to replace the old one. In short, desirable behavior may be stamped in but undesirable behavior cannot be stamped out.

Finally, as a practical matter, if a student's behavior should become extreme enough to disrupt the school he should be referred to school specialists. Eventu-

[9] E. L. Thorndike, *The Principles of Teaching* (New York: A. G. Seiler, 1906), p. 244.

ally such an individual may be referred to his or her parents or even to the police.

## What Action Can Be Useful in Coping with Defiant Students While under Extreme Stress?

It has long been established that individuals do not act rationally while under extreme emotional stress. Due to changes of the internal body chemistry, the person involved tends to act first and think later. This is normally a valuable protective mechanism essential to man's survival. In a highly industrialized society, however, one's emotional reactions can be quite detrimental to his survival at times. This is especially true of the classroom teacher. We expect adolescents to experience difficulty in controlling their emotions from time to time. Teachers, however, are expected to control their emotional reactions. Nevertheless, there are times when any adult may lose some control over his emotions. It is at such times that a teacher may impose some form of discipline that later seems quite inappropriate. In order to avoid more loss of face or obvious inconsistencies, he usually finds it desirable to let the punishment or impositions stand.

In times of extreme emotional stress many persons tend to revert to a form of infantile behavior. And, of course, discipline for a very young child tends to be more authoritarian than discipline for an older child because of his limited reasoning ability. What action can be useful in coping with the well-known tendency to revert to infantile behavior under extreme emotional stress? It is easy to admonish one not to lose control over his emotions, but the danger is ever present, even with the best of us.

> Miss Jones asked Johnny to stop talking with his neighbor in as kind a manner as possible, but the conversation continued. After three or four other reminders she decided that the boy should be moved from his friend. Johnny refused, saying, "You can't make me move."

What is to be done under the circumstances? The infantile tendency is to apply force. Yet our rational senses tell us that such action is inappropriate.

It is proposed that teachers (especially those who tend to become upset easily) determine *in advance* a general plan of action designed to cope with the defiant student. This plan of action might well be memorized—"burned" into the brain cells—so that it will be remembered at times when emotional responses tend to dominate rational thinking. While it is recognized that any such plan must have its limitations (the discipline should fit the individual), it *may* prevent one from applying even more inappropriate measures. The following plan of action is designed to serve as a guideline only. Each teacher should develop his own approach to the problem in terms of school policy.

> *Situation:* Bill is conversing with his neighbor while the teacher is explaining an important point.
> 1. Stop and look directly at the offender.
> 2. Call his name.

3. Politely ask for his attention.
4. Request that he move to another seat.
5. Isolate him from the rest of the class.
6. Remove him from the situation.

*Occasionally* a student will defy the teacher by refusing to change seats or leave the room. If this happens the teacher needs to plan in advance a course of action, in the event of high emotional tension. He may agree with Bill by saying, "You may be correct. I probably could not force you to move. Perhaps we had better discuss this after class." The offender then usually follows through with the requested action. If he does not and the disturbance continues, the teacher might be forced to resolve the situation by getting help from the administrator.

While the suggested plan of action may not be fully appropriate for any given student, it is at least preferable to the incidents described below:

When Bill refused to move Mr. Jones grabbed him and shoved—hard. Bill fell and broke his arm.

When Tom refused to move, Miss Mika assigned him an hour in the detention room. The boy said, "I don't care. Why don't you make it five hours?" Miss Mika made it five hours; whereupon Bill dared her to make it more.

One should not infer from the foregoing that such defiance is likely. Indeed, it never will be experienced by some teachers. Usually when it does occur the teacher is somehow at fault. What of it? When the situation arises it cannot be wished away. The problem must be dealt with immediately! Furthermore, a student should not be permitted to get by with such behavior without some corrective action. This can only encourage others to act in a similar manner. An appropriate learning environment must be provided for all students!

## VALUES

A well organized and managed class can contribute immeasurably toward an appropriate learning environment. Students who know what to expect tend to be less anxious and thus better prepared to cope with learning tasks.

By creating adequate and reasonable behavior standards the adolescent may develop a standard of values useful in interacting with others.

Students who themselves become involved in establishing appropriate standards of behavior may gain valuable insights into the elements of fair play.

Group-imposed limits represent a preliminary step toward self-imposed behavior standards.

Some attention to class rules and conduct promotes consistency of behavior. This is a necessary ingredient in classroom management.

# LIMITATIONS AND PROBLEMS

Misbehavior is merely a symptom of more basic difficulties. Although the teacher may be forced to deal with the symptom as an expediency measure, underlying causes must not be neglected.

Some misbehavior provides clues to extreme maladjustment, demanding referral to a school specialist. Unfortunately, some teachers and administrators traditionally have attempted to deal directly with all types of misbehavior. Withdrawal behavior, for example, demands professional attention although it seldom interferes directly with learning environment.

Youngsters enter their classes with a set of expectations based upon their respective home situations. Since home patterns vary widely, one must *teach* students how to behave. All too often it is assumed that students already know expected behavior standards.

Unfortunately, some teachers and administrators equate successful teaching with one's ability to control the behavior of students. Thus an overly restrictive environment may lead to pupil resentment and increased misbehavior. A "noisy" classroom may be indicative of a most desirable learning situation.

Class control techniques, like other methods of teaching, preferably are viewed from the framework of problem solving. Such a frame of reference contributes to much needed flexibility in the area.

# ILLUSTRATED TECHNIQUES

I. Enlisting student assistance in establishing class rules and procedures. Early in the course the teacher may want to identify some potential "problem areas" and enlist student suggestions for handling them. Some of these areas are the following:

A. Absences and tardiness
B. Late or incomplete assignments
C. Disturbances that interfere with the learning environment
D. Cheating, stealing, etc.
E. Defiance of reasonable requests

When students assist in setting up rules of conduct the teacher is then placed in a position of merely carrying them out. Due caution must be exercised, however, in making sure that rules are reasonable, flexible, and pedagogically sound.

II. Sociodrama (Simulation)

Perhaps after certain problems have arisen it is useful to enact selected situations for study and analysis. This technique enables students to perceive a problem from the frame of reference of another person. Illustrations follow:

*Broad Situation*

A. Johnny is caught cheating on an important examination. Both the teacher and a number of students become aware of the situation.

    B.  Timothy and Mike are talking while Mr. Jones is trying to explain an important point. Despite the usual warnings they continue until Mr. Jones asks Mike to move to the opposite side of the room. Thereupon Mike responded by saying, "No, I don't want to move."

    C.  Four girls are working on a committee. One of them is black. The three white girls deliberately "snub" the black; she suspects her skin color accounts for the girls' behavior. She desperately wants to develop a working relationship with the girls.

The foregoing problems could be role-played and analyzed as indicated in Chapter 13 on Sociodrama. (They should *not* be selected as a result of an almost identical class situation, as this would tend to embarrass those involved.)

In the analysis, emphasis might be replaced upon the importance of a "face-saving" technique for *both teacher and students.* For example, when Mike says, "No, I don't want to move," an alternative satisfactory for both teacher and Mike is needed. The teacher may say, for example, "All right, but do keep quiet so that all of us can follow the points in class."

III.  Case study

Rather than enact a situation, the teacher may want to write one out. This technique has the advantage of providing more structure and complexity than is possible in the sociodrama. It also can be tailored to fit a specific problem. (See Chapter 10 on The Case Method.)

### A Defiant Student

Mr. Martin accepted his first teaching assignment on February 10 at Central High School. Having recently completed an extended tour in the armed forces, he felt more than ready to embark on his chosen career. He felt that his considerable teaching experience while in the military service should be an asset. Moreover, he received considerable experience in judo tactics in hand-to-hand fighting. Although he aspired to be a biology teacher, he had agreed to take the eighth grade science position for the remainder of the year on the condition that he step into the biology position the following fall.

Students, under Mrs. Jenks's direction, had been given considerable freedom. After the first few weeks she became stricken with internal cancer, resulting in several intermittent absences during the fall semester. As her health continued to deteriorate and various substitute teachers were called in, students became progressively more unruly. By the end of the fall semester Mrs. Jenks realized that she would be no longer able to continue. Her resignation necessitated employment of one substitute teacher after another for a period of six weeks. Most of the substitute teachers reported that the class was unmanageable.

Realizing the situation, Mr. Martin decided to engage the students themselves in formulation of "ground rules" for class behavior. The group seemed enthusiastic and more than willing to cooperate. Minor class disturbances were corrected before they could spread. Such correction usually consisted of verbal reminders, with an occasional change of seats to break up disturbing combinations.

Lacking interest in school, Bill had established a reputation of "giving teachers a hard time." Although he was not accepted by the class group, students seemed to admire his ability to make things tough for the teacher. He liked Mr. Martin, however, and enthusiastically joined in formulation of basic class rules. In fact, he had been appointed to write major points on the chalkboard during the planning sessions on discipline procedures. For several days thereafter, Bill was a model student. (His classmates could hardly believe it!)

The first science test was a crushing disappointment for Bill. For once in his life he had actually tried to pass a test. Although his score was by no means the lowest in class, it was still below passing.

Later, in his own words to the principal, Bill explained his feelings and behavior: "I just had to let off steam, so I started talking to those seated next to me." Mr. Martin first attempted to silence Bill by moving him to another seat. Not only was the technique ineffective but Bill appeared to be enjoying his success in disrupting class activities. Finally, Mr. Martin asked Bill to report to the principal at once. Bill immediately responded by saying, "I won't go and you can't make me."

1. What is the major problem in this case?
2. What are the issues involved? (An issue is not a fact.)
3. What action would you take and why?

It may be desirable to let each student write out his own solution to the problem. This can be followed with a class discussion of the various solutions offered.

In deriving generalizations from the experience students are likely to observe that the situation need not have developed if more appropriate action had been taken early in the situation. This provides an opportunity to help students perceive how the offending party himself can avoid "backing the teacher into a corner."

# CHAPTER 6

# Providing for Individual Differences

## OVERVIEW

### Key Concepts

1. Students differ in numerous ways relative to the school experience.
2. Individual enrichment techniques are ideally suited for individual differences; since they often become unwieldy in large classes, however, some form of subgroup is often necessary to facilitate such practices.
3. Subgrouping techniques (within class) are characterized by flexibility in at least three ways:
   a. Students can move from one group to another as the occasion demands.
   b. Individual differences within each subgroup must be recognized.
   c. For many activities, students from different groups work with members of other groups.
4. Grouping between *classes* may create or enhance psychological adjustment problems; flexible grouping within a class need not be fraught with such a problem.
5. Retention and acceleration are often discouraged on the basis of social adjustment problems.

### New Terms

1. **Dull Students**—Those students who are well below average in academic aptitude.
2. **Bright Students**—Those students who are well above average in academic aptitude.

3. **Homogeneous Grouping**—The practice of placing students with similar academic aptitude (usually high, average, and low) in separate classes.
4. **Ability Grouping** (within given classes)—The practice of placing students with others of similar class *achievement* (usually high, average, and low) in separate subgroupings, based upon the wishes of the individual student involved.
5. **Enrichment Activities**—The provision of different (sometimes additional) materials for able learners.
6. **Culturally Diverse**—Students whose experiential backgrounds have been significantly different from the great majority of secondary school youth. Sometimes referred to as culturally deprived, disadvantaged, or different.
7. **Stigma**—A feeling of inadequacy, often arising from some sort of unfavorable comparison with the peer group.

## Questions to Guide Your Study

1. What is the extent and nature of individual differences among secondary school students?
2. In view of the recent trend toward mixing inner-city students with those of the suburbs, what problems are encountered when instructional activities are directed toward the "average" student?
3. "Students whose scholastic aptitudes differ substantially from the norm or average should be segregated for instructional purposes." Defend or refute.
4. What advantages does the suggested model for classroom grouping have over homogeneous grouping?
5. Subgrouping at the secondary level would seem to be more important than in elementary school since achievement levels tend to spread out as youngsters advance in school. Yet this is strangely at odds with common practice. How do you account for this?

Today's teacher is caught in the horns of a dilemma. On the one hand he is asked to work with groups of students. These groups or classes are gradually increasing in size as enrollment pressures mount. On the other hand he is expected to provide for the individual differences of students. Each year new important differences are discovered, all of which have an impact on learning. The situation is being further complicated by the accelerated mixing of all races, creeds, and different cultural groups.

One solution to the problem has been a trend toward individualization of instructional patterns in which class lines are eliminated. (See Chapter 8.) This requires a complete restructuring of the educational program, however, along with a considerable outlay of equipment and supplies. Meanwhile, the vast majority of teachers must continue to individualize instruction as much as possible *within* a group or class structure. This chapter provides some guidelines for accomplishing such a task.

# FUNDAMENTAL PROPERTIES

Each individual is unique. Many differences, however, are unimportant for the purposes of instruction. Other differences are important at different times and in different ways. Some of these are briefly described in this section.

## What Is the Impact of Ability Differences on Learning?

Since the turn of the century the importance of general or academic aptitude (IQ) has been stressed. For many years it was thought that one's IQ imposed rather rigid limits on learning potentialities; IQ changes were thought to be slight and inconsequential.

Although academic aptitude is still regarded as one of the more important individual differences among students, it is presently conceived as a highly flexible concept which merely provides a useful starting point for instructional diversity. An IQ score is an indirect measure of many attributes including memory, spatial relationships, quantitative and qualitative reasoning, and the like. Many aspects of ability are not tested by most IQ tests (creativity, for example). Other factors such as motivation, reasoning patterns, state of one's health, and cultural determinants influence IQ scores in unknown ways.

Within broad limits IQ scores do enable us to identify students who are likely to experience considerable (or little) difficulty in learning. It is grossly unfair, for example, to expect a slow student to do the same assignments as and to otherwise compete with bright students. To illustrate: Slow students tend to:

1. have a slow reaction time, needing a lot of practice
2. be inept at finding new solutions
3. have a short attention span
4. be weak in initiative, versatility, and originality
5. be poor in working with abstractions
6. be weak in making associations and relationships
7. be inept in making generalizations
8. be weak in self-criticism
9. be weak in detecting absurdities
10. have a narrow range of interests
11. be impressed with the physical, the concrete, or the mechanical[1]

On the other hand, the bright student is usually strong or the opposite in each of these areas. Thus it becomes apparent that instruction which is most appropriate for the slow is highly inappropriate for the bright and vice versa. Even though IQ scores do not necessarily identify such students, along with other tools and observational techniques, they serve as useful guides for busy teachers.

[1] Georgia S. Adams and Theodore Torgerson, *Measurement and Evaluation for the Secondary School* (New York: Holt, Rinehart, and Winston, Inc., 1956), p. 83.

Contrasting academic abilities suggest differing life styles which *can* become a positive instructional force in today's classroom. Slow students, for example, have a lifetime of personal experience behind them which if shared appropriately with bright students can become the basis for much needed empathy and understanding.

## How Do Reading Differences Influence Learning?

By the time a student reaches high school he is expected to have mastered the three Rs. Mastery, however, is one of degree. The fact remains that some students are woefully weak in these areas. Reading is used constantly in every aspect of learning. If a student is unable to comprehend his text and related materials, content learning becomes virtually impossible. It has been demonstrated that in a typical ninth-grade class, reading and mathematical abilities will vary from third-grade to junior college levels. Even with a multiple textbook selection *some* students must be provided individually prescribed reading matter. It should be pointed out that while slow students will tend to be deficient in the three Rs, *some* reasonably able students as well can be expected to be deficient in these areas.

## What Physiological and Psychological Differences Should Be Considered?

All too often neglected are those physiological differences which influence learning. Certain physical defects are readily apparent; others, equally important, are not so obvious. These include hearing and seeing difficulties along with such problems as epilepsy and various heart and nervous conditions.

Each individual has psychological needs which must be fulfilled continually throughout life. These include the need for acceptance, security, belonging, success, esteem, and the like. As an individual matures, a certain degree of need fulfillment is essential if he is to develop into a well-adjusted human being. A need which is frustrated has a decided influence on the behavior of the individual. An adolescent who is rejected by his peer group, for example, may lose confidence in himself—his self-respect or self-esteem. Such students, often identified as "problem students," need special attention and assistance in their quest for need fulfillment.

## How Do Cultural Differences Influence Learning?

The neighborhood school concept is rapidly giving way to a cosmopolitan school which must meet the needs of every facet of our society. The deliberate mixing of students from the inner cities with those of the suburbs has disclosed sharp contrasts of values among different segments of our population.

As the culturally diverse have come into the main stream of education, they have questioned the relevancy of many instructional activities. In short, many instructional techniques which may be appropriate for a white, middle-class youngster seem inappropriate for one from an inner-city slum. Riessman[2] has pointed out that the cognitive or mental style of the culturally diverse student often makes him appear to be dull, inasmuch as he may be slow in performing intellectual tasks. This "slowness," however, is not to be associated with dullness. Such a person may be slow because he is extremely careful, meticulous, or cautious. He may be slow because he cannot understand a concept unless he, in some manner, uses his hands in connection with the idea. Furthermore, such an individual may be viewed as inarticulate and nonverbal when he actually may be quite verbal in his out-of-school environment. There is merely a gap between formal language and public language, between the language of the textbook and the informal everyday language. Finally, the culturally diverse youngster is often erroneously judged as having a dislike for education. Most such individuals (and their parents) consider education a "good thing." They may dislike school, however, because it is not adapted to their cultural mores and because its emphasis is often upon knowledge for its own sake.

## INDIVIDUALIZATION TECHNIQUES

For the past thirty years various techniques and "plans" have been advanced for meeting the varying needs of students. Many of these have become eclipsed by the sheer force of increased class size; others have not stood the test of research and experience. Those that have been most fruitful are emphasized in this chapter.

### What Part Do Retention and Acceleration Play?

Retention on the basis of insufficient progress was at one time quite common. Today, however, the technique is not nearly so extensively used. While "high" standards of competence are desirable, it is also recognized that "high" for one individual may be "low" for another. Retention on the basis of limited capacity merely tends to aggravate the problem. Not only does it tend to contradict the social and emotional needs of the child, but it frequently does little in solving the problem of intellectual progress. Indeed, most studies have clearly shown that deficient students who have been "passed" tend to achieve more than those who are retained. Arbitrary class standards of achievement, of course, *assume* equal or near-equal potential. This assumption was disproved some fifty years ago.

There are instances when retention *is* recommended. These may be asso-

[2] Frank Riessman, *The Culturally Deprived Child* (New York: Harper and Row Publishers, 1962), pp. 3–10.

ciated with physical immaturity usually most evident in the lower elementary levels. In the secondary school, retention sometimes is recommended when lack of effort is evident. This, of course, presupposes the adaptation of instruction to individual needs.

Acceleration, for similar reasons, is usually discouraged. There *are* some recent renewed attempts to admit unusually capable children to institutions of higher learning one or two (or sometimes more) years earlier than normal. Preliminary evidence seems to indicate adequate intellectual adjustment. The social and emotional results can hardly be evaluated for some years, however.

### What Part Do Elective Courses Serve?

The assumption that students, with adequate guidance, will themselves select courses which are somewhat commensurate with their needs has led to an expanded secondary school curriculum. Today this is standard procedure, within certain limits. Many new problems and abuses have emerged, however. One of these is the question of how many and what courses should be required. Another problem is that some students elect courses on the basis of "easy credit" rather than on the basis of real need. This abuse seems to be related to a general overemphasis on school marks and the inadequacies of school guidance programs. Much current school controversy is concerned with this area.

### What Is the Role of Special Classes?

A rather recent development has been the practice of bringing unusually capable high achievers into a group for special study in designated areas. Students generally work in their own areas of specialized interest. The work frequently is college level, even with the services of a college professor as the instructor. Such classes may or may not carry college credit. In any event, the special talents, motivation, creativity, and originality of students are emphasized. This practice has gained a great deal of favor in recent years.

Likewise, special classes may be established for extreme underachievers who are unlikely to profit from ordinary class instruction. Sometimes such classes are made up almost entirely of racial or ethnic minorities who have recently been brought into the school. This practice has led to charges of discrimination within the school itself and is thus being discouraged in many areas.

### What Are Some Problems Associated with Homogeneous Grouping Between Classes?

For years now school after school has attempted some form of student selection for classes—often on the basis of scholastic aptitude. While the idea initially has had wide popular appeal, it frequently has been less satisfactory in practice. Results of several surveys have revealed that fewer schools were utilizing homogeneously grouped classes than twenty years ago. At least half of the schools polled in one nationwide survey, for example, reported some such plan. The subjects most frequently mentioned for homogeneous grouping were English, mathematics, social studies, and science. A number of schools had tried and abandoned the plan. Reasons most often given were parental objections, social stigma, results not apparent, inconsistency with the philosophy of the school and staff preferences to adapt instruction to the individual. The problem of scheduling classes, especially in the smaller schools, often has been difficult if not impossible to circumvent. More recent reviews of research in the area have revealed no clear-cut advantages with homogeneous grouping arrangements.

### How Is Class Enrichment Provided?

Ask any substantial number of secondary school teachers how they provide for individual differences and the majority is likely to mention "enrichment." The term, as commonly used in teaching, refers to the provision of either or both *additional* and *different* assignments for unusually capable students. Some teachers seem to associate *additional* work only with enrichment activities, however. Ask them how they meet the needs of slow students and they are frequently less definite. What actually happens, in too many instances, is that the label acts as a "smoke screen" for doing very little in the area. With the mounting pressure of numbers, combined with more heterogeneous groups, the pressure of time may seriously curtail one's efforts, despite the best of intentions. It is the writer's contention that some systematic plan of enrichment is necessary before the task may be adequately accomplished in large classes.

### How May Programmed Instruction Be Employed?

Although closely associated with purely individualized instructional techniques (treated elsewhere), instructional programming has found its place as an effective tool in conventional classes. When used in conjunction with a teaching machine or even as a programmed textbook, the learner may proceed entirely on his own through the provided program. For diagnostic purposes and for students who have been absent for extended periods of time the technique has no equal. As most current programs are commercially developed, one must make sure that local objectives are effectively met. Instructional programs are most effective in the area of mental skills.

### How May Flexible Class Grouping Be Utilized?

Student differences within a given classroom, despite efforts to make the group homogeneous, are exceedingly great. Attempts to provide adequate enrichment experiences for each individual becomes most difficult in large classes. One way of expediting this technique is a system of flexible grouping within classes. Such groupings, if adequately organized and flexible, are highly recommended. The model, provided in the next section of this chapter, involves such a plan.

# A MODEL FOR CLASS GROUPING

This section of the chapter deals with *an* approach to grouping within the classroom. Just as any one teaching method is inadequate, the model which follows cannot be employed per se in all classes in all subject fields. In one important respect, however, it is more than just another teaching method. Its purpose is to offer a useful framework for coping with the many individual differences to be encountered. Certain aspects of the basic framework are highly controversial and will probably need some alteration in adjusting to the individual needs of students.

Prior to any description of a systematic plan for classroom grouping, a list of criteria must be established. Any plan which can successfully satisfy these requirements is worthy of consideration.

1. Subgrouping within the classroom must be flexible. Students must be permitted to shift from one group to another when the need arises. Furthermore, students from each group must have ample opportunity to work with members from other groups.
2. Class groups must be handled in such a manner as to minimize any feelings of stigma or superiority from becoming associated with different groups.
3. Subgroups must *increase* the potential for *individualizing* instruction. As with homogeneously grouped classes, there is danger in the assumption that a subgroup is homogeneous and that instructional materials and procedures can be adjusted to the needs of the group as a whole. Grouping the elementary school student for instruction in reading, for example, has all too often resulted in a new type of "lock-step" teaching simply because the teacher has tended to treat the *groups* as homogeneous. Giving identical assignments to all students in a group is little better than no grouping at all.
4. Subgroups must provide adequately for the social and emotional needs of youngsters.
5. Group *and* individual cooperation and competition must be provided.
6. Each student must have an opportunity to meet the goals of instruction commensurate with his capacities.

### How May a Teacher Initiate Grouping Within the Classroom?

For the first unit of a course (usually 3–6 weeks) it is proposed that the teacher organize a class along traditional lines. Instruction generally will be adapted to the needs of the "average" student. During this initial period students will be adjusting to each other, the instructor, and the course. Then, *on the basis of achievement during this period,* three subgroups can be organized:

*Group I.* This group will be composed of those students who achieved considerably more than the average during the unit. In terms of marks those individuals will have earned high "B's" and "A's." Also included in this group will be those students who by their own desires elect to join it. The instructor recommends but leaves the final decision to each individual.

*Group II.* Members of this group will be those who made near average progress during the unit. They will have received grades of "C" or low "B." The group might, in addition, include certain individuals who decided, against the teacher's recommendations, to identify with the group. This usually will be the largest group.

*Group III.* This group will consist of individuals who achieved considerably less than the average, as evidenced by marks of "D" and "F." As with the other groups, it may also include other students who, for some reason, prefer to be associated with this group.

## How May Students Be Prepared for Grouping?

Imposition of any new classroom technique on a group of adolescents can be hazardous. Most people tend to reject that which they do not understand. Therefore, it is recommended that students actively participate in planning the system. Many teachers have found that students generally are acutely aware of the injustices of expecting every individual to reach similar standards. A discussion of the problem can do much to clarify the issues. The teacher can then explain, in some detail, the plan to be attempted. It is desirable at this point to clarify with students five important characteristics of the plan:

1. Final decision as to who works in what group is made by the student.
2. The *recommended* grouping is made wholly on the basis of achievement in the first (or previous) unit of the course, rather than on the basis of ability.
3. An individual may shift from one group to another with the approval of the teacher. Frequently the instructor will recommend that a student move from one group to another. The final decision rests with the student. In the final analysis, decision to shift from one group to another usually should be based on past achievement. Flexibility of the groups in this respect is especially important.
4. Even though the three groups will be the *basis* for instructional purposes, the class will work as a single unit much of the time. Also, there will be the usual variety of other groups and committees which will *cut across* achievement-group lines.
5. Some teachers have found it desirable to have each group together when subgroup instruction is needed.

## How Do Goals and Activities Vary from Group to Group?

Instructional objectives usually will be the same for each subgroup, but the expected behavioral outcomes may vary considerably. (See Chapter 2.) If the expected behavioral outcomes are different, it would then seem to follow that pupil *experiences* thought necessary to achieve the goals (outcomes) also must vary.

This would indicate that *all* students will be expected to make some progress toward class goals. For the dull or otherwise low achievers, progress will be limited. The teacher must judge what basic core of content is essential to ensure at least nominal progress toward the lesson goals. The other two groups would be expected to achieve more.

Activities will vary for and within each subgroup. The major objective is to provide explicit directions for each subgroup so that it can function for varying periods of time without direct assistance from the teacher. (Teacher aides or assistants greatly facilitate the attainment of such an objective.) One of the most critical, yet difficult, aspects of the technique is that of varying depth and scope of instruction between subgroups. Accordingly, a specific class (biology) is used for illustrative purposes.

An appropriate instructional goal might be: "After this lesson the student should have furthered his understanding of inheritance as applied to plant and animal improvement. One class or group of behavioral outcomes might be proper application of these principles to genetic problems which involve their use." The teacher first would instruct the class as a single group, helping, insofar as possible, each student develop an understanding of basic principles involved in the simple dominant-recessive crosses. Then all students would be afforded the opportunity of applying the principles to problems involving basic genetic crosses. The low-achiever group (Group III), however, would have a number of problems, all of which would involve the simple dominant-recessive crosses. In this manner the element of repetition would be introduced—so essential for this group.

Group II (the average achievers) would be assigned fewer of the "basic genetic cross" problems, but it would, instead, be expected to solve some problems involving more complicated crosses. For example, these students might be able to understand and apply the concepts of the dihybrid (two-factor) cross. This, of course, would require some class instruction. While the low achievers would be practicing the application of "simple genetic crosses" Groups II and I could be receiving instructions on the dihybrid cross concept.

The high achievers (Group I) would be assigned a minimum number of the simple dominant-recessive cross problems; they would have some problems involving the dihybrid cross; an additional number of problems might relate to still more complicated concepts. These students have demonstrated, repeatedly, their capacities for making appropriate applications which involve multiple alleles (black-white cross, for example), crossing-over and the attached-X (which may result from the use of X-rays). Not only are they generally capable of handling such complicated crosses, but often they seem to enjoy work of this type demanding some originality and creativity. Of course, the teacher must expect variations within the group just as he would expect variations in any instructional activity. Thus, while Group III and II members are occupied with assignments the teacher can work briefly with members of Group I in clarifying the new principles involved. Since this group has the quickest reaction time and needs a minimum of repetition, explanatory remarks usually need not be extensive.

Through such activities we usually find that the goal has been achieved, in some measure, by every student. As the teacher supervises class work he soon discovers that Group III needs more individual attention than the other groups. Members of Group I, who tend to become bored and disgusted after the third or fourth explanation of a point, are exposed to a minimum of repetition and have maximum opportunity for creative, original thinking. Those in Group II also are better provided for, as they fall between the extremes.

The same principles of teaching may apply in other areas of a biology class and in other courses. If a laboratory-type lesson is planned members of Group I can be given the responsibility of setting up the microscopes and doing research identifying an unknown organism. Members of Group II then may look at the organism (already focused under the microscope). They can be directed in completing other activities appropriate to their achievement levels. Those of the third group might merely look at the organism. Such activities would undoubtedly vary with each group and with the philosophy of the instructor. Depth and scope of activities necessarily would depend on the value system of the teacher involved. The foregoing illustrations are meant only to indicate the *type* of diversified activities recommended.

## How Can Students Be Evaluated in Different Ability Groups?

It follows that if the depth and scope of class activities vary from one group to another students should not be expected to take the same tests. Each member of a given group, however, can be evaluated on the basis of his accomplishment as compared to the other members of that group. This means, in effect, that any individual within the group may earn any mark from "A" to "F." There still is competition, but the competition now is among those with approximately equal achievement and ability. Such a scheme seems closely to approximate competition evidenced in the larger society. For example, teachers do not compete *directly* with engineers, but they do compete with other teachers in their particular fields. Likewise, carpenters compete more directly with other carpenters than with electricians.

If, as in the case of many schools, the teacher is required to base course and report card marks on the relative achievement of *all* students in a class he may be forced to limit those in Group III to a top mark of "C," those in Group II to a top mark of "B," and those in Group I to a top mark of "A." This is inconsistent with what is here recommended, but if explained thoroughly to students and to parents most of them readily accept the idea. One important compensating factor is the opportunity for any individual to shift to a more difficult level whenever his achievement warrants it.

In some schools the teacher is permitted to indicate group differences on grade reports as follows:

*Group I*—$A_1$, $B_1$, etc.
*Group II*—$A_2$, $B_2$, etc.
*Group III*—$A_3$, $B_3$, etc.

Directly on the school report or transcript can be entered an explanatory note to the effect that the subscripts are indicative of *class* level. For example, "$A_3$" would represent top performance in the lower third of the class.

### How Serious Is the Danger of Stigmas?

There is always the potential threat of stigmas, regardless of the teaching method utilized. Much depends on techniques of handling details. It must be remembered that each adolescent knows his own capacities and limitations better than anybody else. The peer group also is aware of each person's capacities and limitations. If, when the approach is first initiated, achievement is used as the basic criterion for establishing groups, the problem likely will be minimized.

The foregoing description of essential instructional differences between subgroups should not cause the reader to lose sight of the flexible nature of the program. As indicated in the essential criteria (listed on p. 104), students from each group must have ample opportunity to work with members from other groups. Indeed a majority of the activities would appropriately involve members from different subgroups working on a common problem. Division of labor, often quite naturally, would be developed on the basis of capacities of various individuals to complete self-assigned tasks. Rather than assigning some students "easier" references, for example, a multiple listing of references might be made available. Those who experience comprehension difficulties quite naturally will tend to select "easier" references. Individual evaluational procedures must be made in terms of individual growth.

### What Is the Role of the Teacher?

In addition to establishing a basic instructional and evaluational framework for each subgroup, the teacher must see that instructional resources and adequate space are available. While one group is using laboratory facilities, for example, a second group can be engaged in some sort of written work. A third group may be in the library or instructional resources center. This requires careful coordination with other school personnel, especially if the teacher himself cannot be present at all times. Time schedules and deadlines must be developed. Selected students may provide nominal direction to groups in lieu of the teacher. Although subgroup activities are emphasized, total group instruction at intervals must remain a vital aspect of the program.

## VALUES

Systematic subgrouping within large classes calls attention to important differences. Thus it facilitates the individualization process.

Providing for individual differences places learning on a realistic basis. The bright student is afforded opportunities to move ahead as he desires; at the same time, the slow student is not expected to achieve at an unrealistic rate.

Many instructional techniques that are appropriate for the bright are inappropriate for the dull and vice versa. Class subgroupings tend to minimize this paradox.

The instructional framework tends to emphasize a desirable type of competition. The student, for example, more often competes with himself and the members of his own subgroup, rather than with all members of his class.

The formation of subgroups tends to result in increased pupil interest. This can probably be attributed to the fact that instruction under this approach is more consistent with student abilities and interests.

## LIMITATIONS AND PROBLEMS

The system demands a great deal of the teacher's time. For some of the activities at least, he must prepare three basic instructional approaches, corresponding to the basic needs of accelerated, average, and slow students. Instead of constructing one unit test, for example, he may find himself constructing three of them! This additional work, however, is greatly diminished after the basic framework has been established.

Some teachers who have adopted the system have tended to treat all members of each subgroup alike. This, in effect, is merely another form of lock-step teaching and is little better than treating all students in a class or grade as if they were equal. (The problem has emerged at the elementary level where subgrouping is expected in reading and related areas.)

As in homogeneous grouping *between* classes, psychological damage may occur if a subgroup is labeled "bright" or "dumb." For this reason, it is probably preferable to establish groups on the basis of achievement in the given course, rather than on the basis of academic aptitude.

Subgroups that are ill-conceived will be ineffective. For example, the groups must differ substantially or the system may evolve into some sort of status order.

The system does not readily fit in with traditional marking practices of evaluating each student along with other students in the class. Adaptations can be readily developed, however.

Physical facilities within the classroom sometimes impede the success of such a system. Classrooms too small for the number of students or seats that cannot be moved, for example, may create obstacles. The resourceful teacher, nevertheless, is usually able to overcome such handicaps.

## ILLUSTRATED TECHNIQUES

I. Modified Class Grouping

Sometimes particularly adverse conditions may reduce the flexibility of a subgrouping plan. Such was the case with one algebra teacher who found himself in a room with unmovable seats. They were in rows and every seat was filled.

After observing that five or six students usually completed all assigned problems with no more than two errors he decided to establish a special "brain-teaser" group. These students switched places with other students so that they occupied the back row of seats for the day. While the rest of the class received further instruction in areas of difficulty, the "brain-teaser" group was occupied on special problems constructed for this purpose.

After a few weeks the group more than doubled in size. The "older" members of the group were even given responsibility for constructing some of the "brain-teaser" problems for their fellows. The system proved its effectiveness in initiating and sustaining interest as well as its contribution to learning effectiveness.

II. College Credit Classes

Today a number of colleges and universities have a policy of awarding college credit for special classes of high school students. Especially able students are permitted to advance at an accelerated pace in regular classes, enabling them to enroll for such classes early in their high school years. (Some students may earn as much as a full semester or year of college credits by the time of high school graduation.)

The plan has the advantage of keeping the student with his age mates, enabling him to participate in the regular social and physical education activities which may be essential for a full rounded individual. At the same time he is able to advance intellectually according to his full potentialities. Such a plan has many similarities with purely individualized instructional programs, treated in a separate chapter.

III. Work-Experience Programs

There is a trend to mix vocational course work with actual experience on the job. This plan varies considerably from school to school. Generally, however, formal education is reduced to half day sessions, with a planned program of work-experience for the remainder of the school day. Such is the principle of many distributive education programs. Such plans have been particularly effective for underprivileged students. It not only provides needed financial assistance but helps learners adjust to actual work conditions while under the close supervision of teachers. Work-experience programs can be applied to a few students in two or three classes, or they can become a regular feature of the entire school.

IV. Contract Plan

Such a technique often involves a signed contract between teacher and student for specified work, due date, and the grade for which he will work. In one such class a business education teacher allocated two class periods a week to contracts and the remaining three days to regular class activities. Students could continue contractual activities at home if desired. Failure to "live up" to the terms of the contract resulted in a penalty for the next contract. In essence, learners planned their own assignments and determined their own grades in cooperation with the teacher. It was observed that interest and initiative were usually high and that students generally offered a realistic appraisal of their work. If they felt they could have done better, they readily discussed this with the teacher.[3]

The contract approach in some schools has been extended by employing what they term "LAPs": Learning Activity Packages. LAPs usually consist of rather elaborate instructions, including alternatives to guide boys and girls in individualized learning activities. LAPs may be made for each unit of instruction. In those schools which have adapted wholly individualized instructional programs the LAP program has been extended to entire courses of work. This concept is explained in greater detail on pp. 130-31.

## V. Computer-Assisted Instruction

The computer can contribute to the individualization of instruction in many ways. Perhaps the most widely used, thus far, is a drill-and-practice type of lesson. Brief lessons are administered to the pupil at a computer terminal as follow-up exercises to the teacher's presentation.

A problem-solving program also has been developed in which the computer presents a verbal math problem along with all the relevant mathematical data involved. The student is free to use any sequence of steps toward the solution to the problem. The computer provides him with the necessary calculations and an evaluation of his progress at each step. The computer can store, summarize, and feed to the teacher the student's sequence of attack. Somewhat similar approaches are being employed in "inquiry labs" in the natural and social sciences.[4]

## VI. Tutoring Plans

In one school a remedial reading teacher uses students to tutor younger students. One gains the opportunity to tutor by fulfilling certain basic library reading assignments. Students, through the tutoring activity, in addition to gaining a feeling of importance, were able to fill in their own personal reading gaps. In preparation for their tutoring instruction it was necessary to prepare picture cards representing various vowel and blend sounds, diphthongs, and the like. This necessitated knowing these sounds themselves in order to make the cards. Thus there was a learning set established for the teacher. Inasmuch as the cards were being constructed for use on younger children they did not scorn material that might have been considered too babyish.[5]

[3] Nagle, K., "Contract for Individual Projects," *Business Education Forum* 24 (April 1970): 19–20.
[4] Arthur D. Roberts and Perry A. Zirkel, "Computer Applications to Instruction," *Journal of Secondary Education* 46 (March 1971): 99–105. Some nine different techniques are summarized in this article.
[5] M. M. Harris, "Learning by Tutoring Others," *Today's Education* 60 (February 1971): 48–9.

A number of high schools across the nation have adopted systems whereby selected students tutor elementary students. In some cases culturally diverse students may tutor culturally diverse elementary students. Usually the tutor receives a fee for his help. In one school, college bound students, during their "free" period, were provided the opportunity for assisting teachers, tutoring students, or participating directly in the instructional process. From a student body of two thousand, one student in four elected to work as a student assistant. Benefits were apparent to both the tutor and the tutee.[6]

[6] Herbert A. Thelan, "Tutoring by Students," *School Review* 77 (September 1969): 229–44. Several different tutoring patterns are summarized in this article.

CHAPTER **7**

# Independent and Semi-Independent Study

## OVERVIEW

### Key Concepts

1. The instructional resource center is the key to independent and semi-independent study activities.
2. Independent study evolves gradually during the secondary school years.
3. Some students may not be capable of purely independent study.
4. Independent and semi-independent study rest upon adequate study skills.
5. Textbook and library study skills must be systematically developed.
6. Textbook material is seldom read line by line and page by page.

### New Terms

1. **Criterion-referenced Measure**—An absolute scale for determining achievement relative to some established criterion (standard) without reference to other students.
2. **SQ4R Method**—A method of selective reading for increased meaning. Includes a sequence of *Skimming, Questioning, Reciting* answers in one's own words, *Riting* [sic] key words as cues, *Recalling* complete answers, *Reviewing* questions formulated earlier.
3. **Skimming**—Reading for general impression or main ideas.
4. **Scanning**—Looking for specific information by using such indicators as italics, capitalized words, and figures.
5. **Ready Reference Materials**—General sources of ready information such as dictionaries, encyclopedias, almanacs, atlases, indexes, and the like.
6. **Primary Sources**—First-hand reports, based on direct observation, diaries, and the like.

7. **Copyright Laws**—Laws designed to adjudicate between the rights of author and publisher, on the one hand, and the rights of the user of published materials, on the other.

### Questions to Guide Your Study

1. Distinguish between independent and semi-independent study.
2. How do the SQ4R method and the question-outline prepare one for independent study?
3. "Fully independent study is an unrealistic goal for the majority of secondary school students." Defend or refute.
4. What is meant by honesty in the handling of reference materials by scholars? To what extent can the same standards and principles be required of secondary school students?
5. How can evaluation problems raised through independent and semi-independent study programs be resolved?

The basic purpose of formal education is the production of self-directed learners. In accomplishing this objective, the student not only learns how to direct his own learning, but he develops initiative and major responsibilities for his own learning as well.

The importance of developing learner self-direction has long been recognized. Traditionally, the home assignment was designed to accomplish this purpose. This was followed later by the study hall approach, which finally gave way to class-directed study activities. The inadequacies of such approaches have long been recognized, however. Since individuals apparently have various styles of learning, an individualistic approach to the problem seems essential.

## FUNDAMENTAL PROPERTIES

Independent study embodies concepts that are contrary to certain conventional notions of teaching. First, the teacher must rid himself of the notion that he is not teaching unless he is standing in front of his students every day. Furthermore, he must reexamine the assumption that students are not learning if they are not in their appointed classrooms, study halls, or cubicles. Finally, the teacher must recognize that, as opposed to transmission of knowledge, teaching is basically a process of stimulating individual inquiry, which is facilitated when situations are created whereby the learner can discover for himself.

### What Is the Objective of the Self-Directed Experience?

Self-directed learning is a process that begins in the elementary school and is accelerated during the high school years. Maturity and experience are its two basic ingredients. Psychological (like physical) maturity is an extremely variable process during the adolescent years. Some freshmen, for example, are more capable of learning independence than are some seniors. The basic objective, however, is to make each individual a more independent learner as a result of appropriate school experience. This calls for an extremely variable program featuring different levels of independence.

## How Much Learner Independence Is Realistic?

The writer recently asked a school superintendent for his assessment of the current emphasis upon independent study. "Independent study," he said, "is a misnomer. Very few students are capable of such responsibilities." When asked if he thought most students were capable of more independence than the typical school presently provides, he responded with an emphatic "Yes." By way of explanation he added, "Although most youngsters should be provided increased independence from the teacher, relatively few are capable of working entirely on their own."

Essentially the notion of independent study represents an ultimate goal. It is accomplished gradually by a program featuring various levels of independence. Some students will continue to need constant supervision and attention. A few will be capable of purely independent study with a minimum of teacher guidance. Others (perhaps most) will fall between the two extremes.

## What Evaluation Problems Are Raised?

Oddly enough, some teachers object to independent study programs because of increased difficulty of evaluation. Since the turn of the century teachers have relied heavily upon norm-referenced measures. Such measures are used to ascertain an individual's performance in relation to that of other individuals in the same class. An individual's score acquires meaning by comparing it with other scores. Obviously, individuals at various levels of achievement and independence often cannot be appropriately measured with a norm-referenced test.

Attention is currently being directed to a new type of measure, called a *criterion-referenced measure* (or scale).[1] Such a measure is used to ascertain an individual's status with respect to some established criterion without reference to other students. Such measures specify minimum levels of performance expected at the culmination of the experience. This is usually set at a level of 85 or 90 percent. The criterion-referenced measure is seen as an alternative method of evaluation in conventional school organization. The technique would seem especially appropriate to independent study programs.

---

[1] W. James Popham, *Criterion-Referenced Measurement* (Englewood Cliffs, N.J.: Education Technology Publications, 1971).

# INDEPENDENT AND SEMI-INDEPENDENT STUDY TECHNIQUES

Independent and semi-independent study techniques vary widely from school to school. They are usually (but not always) associated with some type of flexible scheduling. Likewise, they are often associated with individualized study programs. It should be emphasized, however, that individualized study does not necessarily emphasize independent study. The techniques that follow are suggestive only.

## How Does Independent Study Apply in Actual School Situations?

Independent study consists of much more than merely providing free time for learning. If an individual is to make effective use of such time he must know what to study, how to proceed, where he can work and find needed materials, and when to confer with his instructor. At least three distinct phases of independence, based upon student responsibility, are recognized. Students may be assigned to a particular phase of the program on the basis of counselor, teacher, and parent recommendation.

*Phase I—Directed Study.* In every school there are students who have demonstrated their need for help in developing basic, responsible study habits. The basic purpose of this phase is to prepare such individuals for semi-independent or wholly independent study activities. After four years of experience with an independent study program (Claremont [California] High School), Wiley and Bishop reported that approximately 10 percent of the school's student body of two thousand were assigned to directed study.[2] The number was being reduced as skill was developed in preparing learners for greater independence.

The program features work with teacher aides in supervised study for a part of the time and with an assigned teacher the rest of the time. Students frequently meet in groups of seven or eight to discuss study problems, how to use the resource centers, the library, or laboratories. They may discuss related study problems such as how to do research, how to prepare a research paper, or how to make effective class reports.

The Claremont School Program of Independent Study assigns to this group two types of students. First, there are those individuals who are notably deficient in appropriate study skills. They often lack confidence in themselves, but with close supervision they can develop into at least average students. In the other category (often referred to as "problem students") are those who are bright and capable but for one reason or another have become alienated from school. Such individuals require highly interested teachers who are unusually skillful

---

[2] W. Deane Wiley and Lloyd K. Bishop, *The Flexible Scheduled High School* (West Nyack, N.Y.: Parker Publishing Co., Inc., 1968), p. 44. Much of the material in this model is based upon the Claremont experience.

in developing rapport with teen-agers. Such students seem to respond better in small groups than in other school situations.

*Phase II—Semi-Independent Study.* This category, usually consisting of a majority of the student body, involves a program of limited independent study. At the outset, students are given guidance in planning constructive use of their unscheduled time, which is usually limited to no more than three modules in any one day. For the remaining study time these individuals are scheduled for open laboratories or resource facilities where roll is taken and records are kept. Others are scheduled for supervised study in certain specific areas for a specified period of time each week. Students themselves, however, decide the particular time for study.

In providing for limited independent study, a syllabus is used effectively at the Nathan Hale High School (Seattle, Washington).[3] It contains assignments in reading, writing, and speaking as well as instructions, references, conference dates, and examination dates.

A large part of the syllabus consists of a study plan wherein each unit is divided into small parts. A poetry unit, for example, may be divided into analysis of the theme, content and structure, and the relationship of literary trends or historical implications. Each student activity is clearly defined, enabling the student to proceed on his own. Each of the small segments contains options or different means of achieving similar goals. Conferences are provided two or three times for each seven-day cycle. Instructors meet with small groups (seven or eight students) or with individuals as deemed appropriate.

*Phase III—Independent Study.* This is the highest level of independent study and is student-initiated. Sometimes called the "quest" program, it is de- signed for selected students who are responsible, self-disciplined, and motivated. The student is involved in a self-directed type of activity with limited assistance from the teacher. Such students may study in any of the resource centers, in the library, in open classrooms, and in laboratories as they choose.

Such study is initiated when a student decides that he wants to explore a problem *in depth* for a given period of time. He asks a teacher to be his advisor in the project, submitting a brief plan indicating what is to be explored, ideas for exploring it, his reasons for pursuing the problem, and the way he feels he might want to conclude his exploration. The advisor then assumes responsibility for guidance and evaluation of the result. Such students usually meet with their advisors about once a week.

Under a *quest* program at one school a student is permitted to drop out of a regularly scheduled subject to strike out on his own for a period of nine to eighteen weeks and receive a grade or credit in that subject.[4] Such a request is initiated when an individual finds one particular area of a course of sufficient interest to warrant exploration in depth. A student may, for example, conduct

[3] Dale F. Fleury, "Independent Study: Foreign Language Seminars," *Bulletin of the National Association of Secondary School Principals* 53 (September 1969): 90–99.

[4] D. Wright, "Try a Quest," *English Journal* 59 (January 1970): 131–33. It should be noted that this program was initiated in a conventional classroom setting.

science research utilizing the science laboratory and the assistance of the science staff; he may elect to do a research paper in history; or he may even decide to do a project such as the production of clothing in home economics. Findings are usually reported in writing, orally, or in some type of presentation to a class, a small group, or a teacher. The chapter on research methods offers an approach that seems particularly appropriate for programs involving total independent study.

### How Are Printed Materials Used Most Effectively?

Learner independence is impossible if basic book study skills are lacking. The all-too-familiar quote, "I've read and reread the chapter but can't remember anything it says," suggests deficiencies in this area.

Effective textbook usage demands a systematic methodology. This includes the preliminary textbook survey, meaningful reading and retention (SQ4R method), and effective skimming and scanning techniques. All of these techniques have been treated in the chapter on "Developmental Reading Techniques."[5]

Even after the learner has developed skills in the use of printed materials, continued guidance is essential for various class assignments. If, for example, one special reading technique is appropriate for a given assignment this should be called to the student's attention. A teacher might say, "For this assignment skimming is all that is necessary." Such practices may easily reduce study time by as much as one half. It is also desirable to check out students' actual textbook usage from time to time. Familiarity with appropriate techniques is no guarantee of continued application. There is a strong tendency to revert to earlier, often less efficient, habits.

### How Are Library Resources Utilized?[6]

Semi-independent study usually involves the scheduling of a series of pre-liminary meetings in the library or resource center for the purpose of developing appropriate "library research" skills. The library staff will want to know the nature of the work to be done and the number of students involved. Library instructors should understand that they are only to guide the search, not pre-assemble the material or spoon-feed students. Students should understand that while they are expected to do as much as possible on their own, requests should be in terms of "Where can I find . . ." rather than "Give me what you have on. . . ." Some specific suggestions for such a work period are:

[5] The reader should reexamine these techniques at this point.

[6] This topic and the one that follows were prepared by Evelyn Cornish, Director of Libraries, Bellevue Public Schools, Bellevue, Washington. Used by permission.

1. *Prepare carefully.*
   Make sure each student has his problem outline with him.
   Encourage experienced students to do preliminary searching before the work period. This relieves congestion.
   Stress the fact that card catalog, periodical indexes, and other special indexes are *keys to the collection,* designed to save the user time and fruitless effort.
   Group students who will need the most help, and put them close to the card catalog and reference section.
   If the class is large, decide in advance which students are to begin with the card catalog, which are to go to the periodical indexes, etc. Give the slower students names of specific reference books.
2. *Stay with the class and assume responsibility for their conduct.*
   Require quiet, orderly behavior with a minimum of talking. Conform to the rules set by the instructional center staff; discourage and break up disruptive behavior.
3. *Move about and assist students in locating materials.*
   Insist that students attempt to find materials on their own first. In giving help, start with the question, "Where have you looked?"
4. *Require that something definite be accomplished by the end of the period.*
   Encourage students to return to the center during study hours or after school to complete assignments. Schedule another work period the following day if needed.
5. *Stress responsibility in the library, particularly care of materials, proper check-out, and sharing limited materials.*
6. *End the period effectively.*
   Make sure materials are returned to place. Ask students to check off on their problem outlines the points they have satisfactorily covered. Caution against losing material and suggest they plan to continue work at earliest possible time. Answer questions. Summarize what is to be done at the next class meeting.
7. *At the next class meeting, discuss what was done and the difficulties encountered.*
   Make deadlines flexible if added work is required, so that all students will have a chance to complete the assignment.
8. *Do not allow too much time to elapse before another opportunity to practice reference techniques is given.*
   Any skill requires frequent practice, particularly in its initial stages.

## How Are Skills in Note-Taking and Use of Reference Materials Developed?

The first impulse of untrained students is to copy material from source books word by word and to hand it in as their own. Many never get past this style of "research." The teacher must make the student realize the basic principles of responsible scholarship—that credit should be given to the intellectual work of others and that the raw materials gathered in library reference must then be reworked so that the thought of the student is evident. While one gets the material from another writer, he should organize it and phrase it in his own way, for his own particular purpose. The support of reliable authorities for statements of fact or opinion is lost unless the student identifies the sources of his information.

The formally written "term paper" with carefully arranged footnotes and separate bibliography is *not the best first step* in making students realize these principles. It is too artificial, too complicated, and too demanding for the beginner; it frequently forces him to quote what he does not understand and to give more attention to form than to thought and content.

Have the student number items in his problem outline. Then have him put each piece of information he finds on a separate card or sheet of paper, numbered to correspond with the main point to which it relates. *The source of information should be noted on each of these slips of paper, which may be called source notes.* The student will have several source notes for some points; for others, he may have nothing, in which case he must do further searching. *Any material taken down verbatim should be enclosed in quotation marks on the source note.* With experience the student will learn to distinguish between what is worth copying word for word for transfer to his paper, and other material that may be summarized in his own words or phrases. (This, too, requires a specific reference.)

Using his problem outline and the source notes alone, the student will be able to write a brief paper. *The teacher must require that the outline and notes be handed in with the paper,* in lieu of a formal outline and bibliography. No time should be spent in reworking or polishing the notes and outline; they are simply the "working papers" similar to an artist's preliminary sketches or a scientist's experimental data. By comparing the student's "working papers" with the finished product, the teacher can guide the learner in developing his own creative imagination.

Students also should have considerable practice in taking notes from lectures, tapes, recorded speeches, films, and filmstrips, and the like. It will be necessary to allow additional time to locate, set up, use, and note these sources.

What is important is not so much the form in which sources are acknowledged as the basic attitude of respect for the work of others. Assigning a number of short papers that set these habits and attitudes firmly is more important than mastery of a specific form of footnoting or of typing a bibliography.

While most beginning papers will be factual in nature, the student very quickly finds materials that present more than facts—interpretations and the author's opinion. How is he to judge which materials should be credited and which should be questioned? With increasing maturity comes the realization that the printed word is not always reliable. Whatever the student has learned about logic, the different types of propaganda, and the existence of special interest groups can be applied here. We can only discuss a few general considerations the teacher can bring to the attention of his students.

*Primary Sources.* Preference in research is given to primary sources, such as official records, the results of carefully controlled experiments, firsthand reports based on direct observation, diaries, and letters. New reproduction processes are making facsimiles of important original documents and of rare books available at modest cost to instructional resource centers.

Photocopying devices and cooperation between libraries make it possible for scholars to consult books that may be housed hundreds of miles away. These should be made available to students whenever possible, and should be used in preference to reprints, selected passages of original works, summaries, or secondary sources of all kinds. Moreover, the encounter with an original document, particularly if it is an old one, is interesting and exciting to students. The teacher will want to emphasize the unique value of such documents as part of our cultural heritage, and stress the importance of their care and preservation.

Students and teachers alike should understand the implications of our copyright laws, which are designed to protect the author and publisher in the field of information storage and retrieval and reproduction of printed materials.

Copying such material is lawful only when it is acknowledged, when the excerpt does not represent a major portion of the work copied, and when its use does not affect the possible sale of additional copies of the original. Thus copying, whether by hand or machine, should be clearly limited to brief excerpts, well identified. Teachers should beware of duplicating materials such as printed workbooks or exercises that are ordinarily purchased in classroom quantities. We can look forward to closer scrutiny of such uses and further legislation to control the newer methods of reproduction of printed material.

*Expert Opinion.* Students must be taught to value expert opinion and to check the qualifications of the authorities they use. This usually can be done by reference to biographical sources such as *Who's Who in America* or the *Directory of American Scholars.* Furthermore, they should understand that an expert is only qualified in his own field; his opinions in other areas are not superior to those of other highly educated and intelligent individuals. It is also useful to point out that qualified experts sometimes disagree.

*Sponsorship.* Studies undertaken and published under the aegis of learned society or leading professional groups usually are regarded as reliable sources of information. Statistics and studies released by governmental agencies would be included in this category.

*Recency.* As indicated earlier, the importance of recency of information varies with the subject. It is best to teach students to check the date of each publication carefully and to assess its importance in each case. The latest book, however, is not always the most useful and reliable; care in scholarship and clarity of information are also important considerations. As the student becomes more sophisticated in reference work, he will recognize that scholarly work follows an historical pattern and that in each field there are basic reference works. Fortunately these are the very books most likely to be found in a carefully stocked resource center.

*Bias.* It is only by comparing a number of sources that the bias of a single author can be discovered and allowance made. The teacher will do well to call to the attention of the whole class, repeatedly, cases in which authorities differ in their interpretation of facts. This is particularly important in the field of social science, but also is evident in literary criticism and even in certain fields of scientific research. Excellent examples can be found in the area of current events.

*Nonprint Sources.* It is particularly difficult to apply the tests of scholarly worth to material that is viewed or heard rather than read from print. Once an item is in print, it can be studied, compared to other documents, analyzed, and later reviewed. The impression made on different students by the same film or recording will vary widely; it is also difficult to review such sources for further analysis. Emotional appeal is strong in many such presentations. Students should be trained to take notes when possible and to realize the limitations of such material as a reliable source of detailed information.

### What School Facilities (in Addition to the Library) Are Needed?

In addition to the library, which is used primarily for projects requiring use of library materials, a number of other facilities are necessary for an effective independent study program. The Claremont Independent Study Program has made wide use of *resource centers.* Former classrooms have been provided with individual study carrels and shelving for storage of books and related materials. The centers are used for doing assignments in subject areas. Teacher aides or regular teachers are in charge of the resource centers all modules of the school day.

*Open laboratories* are available for use during unscheduled time whenever a student desires. The Claremont Program also makes use of a *structured laboratory* where students are scheduled from the more restricted phases of the program. A foreign language student, for example, could use an open laboratory to practice articulation of the language, listen to tape recordings, or make tapes of his own speech. A teacher or laboratory technician is available for assistance at all times.

*Clinics,* as used in the Claremont Program, are fundamentally remedial in nature. They are open to all students. Sometimes known as "skill development clinics," they are specifically designed for remedial reading, writing, and work in mathematics skills. Although some students are assigned to these facilities, other students can use them as needed. They are closely supervised.

### What Is the Role of the Instructional Staff?

As has been implied, the teacher's role in an independent study program shifts from that of a taskmaster to one of counselor, guide, and friend of the student. Fundamentally, he is available to guide an active learner into productive activities as he makes use of varied school facilities.

No longer is he responsible for neatly organized classes where attempts are made to have each student cover the same materials. Instead, he often finds himself working with students on a one-to-one relationship. Usually this relationship is initiated by the student himself. A teacher who is himself continually questing and curious seems to be ideally suited for such a role.

In discussing an appropriate staffing arrangement, Brown sees the need for two new staff positions: a coordinator and a preceptor.[7] The *coordinator* (needed

---

[7] B. Frank Brown, *Education by Appointment: New Approaches to Independent Study* (West Nyack, N.Y.: Parker Publishing Co., 1968), pp. 80–82.

if the program comprises more than fifty students) should be released from all instructional responsibilities. He would be responsible for establishing checkpoints and safeguards along the way to ensure that students do not simply waste time. He also would be responsible for directing all projects and serve as a liaison between independent study projects and the conventional rules of the school.

The *preceptor* (at least one for each subject area) would be responsible for identification of area facilities, approval of specific activities, and coordination of seminars. In addition he would meet with students on a regular basis for small group and individual conferences. Brown suggests that as a general rule a teacher should be provided with one hour released time for each twenty-five students in a particular discipline.

### How Is Independent Study Evaluated?

Above all, teachers must resist the temptation to compare independent study results among students. The fundamental goal of such a program is a self-directed learner who works at his own pace according to his particular interests and talents. Thus he must be evaluated in terms of his own potential and development at a given stage.

As indicated earlier, a shift to criterion-referenced measures is desirable. Unfortunately, absolute scales of performance have not been adequately developed in many areas of the curriculum. In moving in this direction, some schools have asked for a "thesis paper" from each student wherein he demonstrates the scope of his major activities. The student may be marked on a scale from "A" to "E" or on a "Pass-Fail" plan.

Perhaps a more valid approach is the requirement of a seminar presentation in which the student reports on his investigation. He is questioned by a faculty committee as well as by his colleagues in the seminar. This plan, borrowed from the university doctoral program, contains a lot of merit. It has the disadvantage, however, of being time-consuming.

Still another alternative is the development of criterion-referenced examinations for measuring performance in terms of objectives. Theoretically, this is perhaps the most appropriate evaluational scheme of all. It is presently limited, however, by a dearth of systematically developed scales (criteria) and examinations in many areas of the curriculum. It should be emphasized that performance on such measures is based upon an absolute scale without regard to progress of any other student. A major baseline is established by using the results of pretests in the area.

## VALUES

As the term implies, independent study produces self-directed learners. The able student is permitted to forge ahead of others in his grade level.

Since a variety of instructional materials are essential for independent study, the

instructional resource center (formerly school library) is replacing traditional home assignments.

Independent study teaches the student to learn how to learn. It encourages
him to reach his own conclusions after he has explored a problem of personal
interest.

Provision for independent and semi-independent study during the school day
tends to develop "library" skills essential for self-directed learning.

Learning is dissociated from teaching and is adjusted to the style of the individual. Teachers are available to help the learner in his quest for knowledge. Independent study techniques contribute to the development of
reflective thinking.

## LIMITATIONS AND PROBLEMS

Independent study competence is a gradual process that demands careful guidance. Study independence, before the learner is ready for it, produces confusion and chaos.

Provision for independent study demands an alteration of conventional class
activities. Large-group instruction and small-group discussions, for example, must raise more questions than they resolve.

Students differ in degree of study independence needed. Thus differentiated
assignments must be developed. (Differentiated assignments have been
advocated for years, but in actual practice relatively little differentiation is
evident.)

Since independent study tends to replace conventional home assignments, parents
must be educated to accept the new conditions. (Students frequently study
at home—as an extension of independent project work started in school.
The nature of the activity differs from conventional homework, however.)

Some students need restraint. They may literally "burn themselves out" in independent study, if appropriate guidance is not provided.

## ILLUSTRATED INDEPENDENT STUDY PROJECTS

Since the ultimate aim of an independent study program is a fully self-directed
learner, this section will emphasize a "quest" type of experience. Such an
experience features an individual who is self-motivated to explore a problem
"in depth" with minimal faculty assistance.

    I.  Useful in science or social science classes

        A.  Flood control
           In a locality where flooding tends to occur a student may develop
           a flood control plan. Such a project would necessitate considerable in-

vestigation of local terrain and run-off patterns, local soil conditions, climatic factors, and the like. Such a project might well be limited to a localized area within the community. Sometimes local school property is so affected.

B. Pollution control

Since pollution is currently a matter of general concern to young people, a study of local conditions might be well received by the local citizenry. Sometimes an enterprising team of high school students can, with minimal funds and considerable imagination, develop adequate measuring devices for determining the concentration of air pollutants. Another team can then develop an overall plan for needed action. Such a project can be broadened to include soil and water pollution as well. Eventually the project can influence school policies relative to such matters.

C. Landscaping

Landscaping often fits in readily with independent study quest programs. Individual students may develop a landscape project for their own homes. Others may want to team up for the purpose of developing a landscape plan for a local municipal building or complex that has been allowed to deteriorate over the years. In any event, such a project should include cost-accounting estimates.

D. Insect damage

In various sections of the country insect damage occurs periodically. Although farmers are continually alert to such problems, sometimes whole communities are involved. Grasshoppers, for example, sometimes increase so rapidly that every plant in their path is stripped of its foliage. Interested students, by becoming fully knowledgeable with the life cycle and habitat of such insects, may be able to offer predictions when such damage is most likely and to offer suggestions for controlling the local environment in such a manner as to minimize the danger of such scourges.

Useful in English, literature, or journalism classes    *N. B.* !

A. How writings are produced

It is one thing to study the writings of others but quite another to become concerned with the actual production of such writings. An interesting project can focus upon the habits, skills, and motives of local writers in the community. Although relatively few produce poetry or prose that may find its way into a literature book, writings of all kinds have certain commonalities. To illustrate: news and editorial writings; journal articles; popular and professional books; free-lance writing of all kinds. After gaining some notion of how a writer produces, some students may themselves decide to emulate the disciplined behavior evidenced by successful writers. Such an experience can produce a "feel" for making important contributions at a later date.

B. Social issues

American literature characteristically draws attention to important social issues. In a quest program social issues may be pursued relative to the local community. The issue of exploitation of underprivileged groups, for example, may provide the groundwork for an investigation of such problems in the area. If such problems exist what action, if any, may be taken? Is such a problem also reflected in the school itself? If so, what specific programs may be introduced to correct the situation? Certain limitations, of course, may be imposed to protect an overly zealous individual from pressing his "fight" beyond the readiness of the controlling elements involved. Such action does have the advantage of adding an important dimension to most literature classes.

III.  Useful in home economics classes

Many young girls, unknowingly, do considerable damage to their bodies in their quest to maintain a heavy suntan during the summer months. An interesting project could entail a study of the effects of the sun's rays over extended periods of time. An appropriate schedule for "sunbathing" can be developed. Finally a study of the use of suntan lotions may be useful. A related project could deal with the possible damage associated with various cosmetics.

Although the foregoing suggestions for independent study projects have been grouped into content areas, it should be noted that projects of this kind tend to cut across subject matter boundaries. The projects treated under home economics, for example, could just as easily be launched in a science class. Likewise, a study of social issues can originate in social science classes. Such projects tend to illustrate the arbitrary nature of subject matter boundaries.

# CHAPTER 8

# Individualizing Instruction

## OVERVIEW

### Key Concepts

1. Individualized instruction programs enable the learner to progress at his own pace without regard to any other student.
2. A basic premise of individualized instruction is that the individual is capable of learning on his own with minimum direction from teachers.
3. With the increasing trend toward individualized instruction, a great variety of preplanned learning sequences (learning packages and minipacs) have become available.
4. Individualized instruction programs create the need for differentiated staffing, cluster classrooms, and the like.
5. The individual teacher in a conventional class setting can move toward individualized learning.

### New Terms

1. **Learning Packages**—Instructional materials and resources (including tests) needed for a given learning sequence.
2. **Individualized Study Units** (minipacs)—Instructional materials and resources needed for a particular unit of instruction.
3. **Learning Centers**—Usually individualized study booths featuring earphones, learning programs, recordings, etc. Such centers usually are adjacent to needed resource materials.
4. **Differentiated Staffing**—Trained personnel at more than one level of instruction. Often includes teacher aides, master teachers, and specialized staff members.
5. **Placement (Preassessment) Test**—A test especially designed to determine at what level the student's learning should be initiated.

6. **Self-assessment Test**—A test administered at different check points, enabling the learner to evaluate his own progress.

### Questions to Guide Your Study

1. "A conventional class setting blocks the emergence of an individualized instruction program." Defend or refute.
2. There is a trend toward an increased ratio of pupils per teacher. On the other hand, there is a trend toward more individualized instruction programs. How do you account for these seemingly contradictory trends?
3. What steps might a regular classroom teacher take toward greater individualization of instruction?
4. "Individualized instruction programs are needed more in some content fields than in others." Defend or refute.

Educators, for many years, have emphasized the importance of individual differences in learning. They have repeatedly recommended taking a student from where he is to as far as he can go. Traditional classroom patterns, however, have generally defeated such an ideal. Group instruction in some form has been viewed as the only alternative to mass education.

Recent technological developments are enabling educators to translate individualized instruction from dream to reality. An individual learning system provides the learner with substantial responsibility for planning and carrying out his own organized program of studies, with the assistance of teachers. It is a highly flexible system involving a multitude of materials and procedures. Achievement is based upon individual performance in terms of pupil goals.[1]

## FUNDAMENTAL CONCEPTS

In considering a move toward individualized learning, attention must be directed to several crucial concepts. While most of these are recommended for instruction generally, they emerge as especially crucial in the organization and development of an individualized learning system.

### What Individual Needs and Abilities Are Met?

Since the program is tailored to *each* student, particular attention in overall planning must be given to the needs and abilities of the individual. Entry level behaviors must be carefully delineated. Selection of objectives, the sequence of study, and the choice of materials and procedures will vary with each student.

---

[1] Gail L. Baker and Isadore Goldberg, "The Individualized Learning Program," *Educational Leadership* 27 (May 1970): 775–80.

Those with limited abilities, for example, are provided ample opportunity for overt activity and practice needed for conceptualization. Those with limited reading skills are provided printed material at their particular level. No longer is an individual expected to use books designed for a particular grade or level.

Conventional boundaries of grade levels and courses, along with arbitrary time units for content coverage, are eliminated. Each learner works at his own level and moves ahead as soon as he masters the prerequisites for the next level of work. Such programs, unlike conventional programs, are based upon the assumption that the student is capable of learning on his own. Although teachers are available for remedial assistance, their major function is to provide materials and learning sequences at the time they are needed. Usually a mastery level of 85 or 90 percent is expected.

## What Is the Place for Behavioral Objectives?

The anticipated outcomes of prepared learning sequences are carefully developed. These may be in the form of terminal behaviors or particular products of behaviors. The learner is fully aware of the objectives toward which he is working. They are usually written out so that he can refer to them from time to time as he progresses from one objective to the next one.

By providing appropriate feedback, the learner soon develops self-confidence in his ability to learn on his own. No longer must he "wait" for others to "catch up"; no longer must he listen to a teacher explain something for the fourth or fifth time simply because a few students lack the needed background for the experience. When one outcome is achieved, he proceeds immediately to the next one.

## What Type of Activities Is Needed?

Recognizing that there is no one essential set of learning techniques, the teacher encourages the learner to select (from recommended experiences) those materials and techniques which he wishes to follow. In a sense he enters into a "contract" with the teacher. He moves freely from place to place and talks freely with others, as necessary in achieving his objectives. Objectives may be pursued individually, in small groups, or with teachers, depending upon learning needs. This aspect of the program has led to the introduction of such terms as the "open classroom," or the "open school." The term merely connotes the relaxed and informal control, the ease of communication and the mutual supportiveness between teacher and student in an individualized learning setting.

## What Evaluation Techniques Are Needed?

The use of effective tests, in terms of behavioral objectives, is emphasized in individualized learning programs. Initially, a *placement test* is administered for the purpose of determining functional level of achievement in an area and for the purpose of a general grouping. After determining one's approximate level of achievement, *pretests* are administered in order to detect those specific skills needed for further development. This guides the teacher and the student in prescription of suitable learning experiences for strengthening weaknesses. Learning experiences may be individual, small group, or even large group as students temporarily pursue common problems. A variety of educational media are available. Choice of activity rests primarily with the student, with teacher approval.

Frequent *self-evaluation tests* are employed as a means of providing information and reinforcement relative to student progress. Trouble areas are carefully diagnosed and additional assignments made as needed. It is at this point in the program that diversity becomes most apparent. Individual needs demand the availability of many approaches to the resolution of a problem area.

Finally *posttests* are administered to determine level of achievement. As previously indicated, an 85 to 90 percent mastery level is usually expected. Failure to succeed on posttests indicates a need for further diagnosis and additional learning experiences. A student is not advanced to the next area until he has performed satisfactorily on the posttests.

## What Function Do Learning Packages Serve?

Every individual learning program is accompanied by a "learning package." As opposed to the older notion of a "textbook package," consisting of a basic text and its supplementary workbook, today's package contains a variety of *complementary* materials. A social science package, for example, may bring in programs, games, films, field trips, organized discussions, projects, and written work exercises all integrated into the basic continuity of the course. Many, if not most of the parts, are inseparable.

The larger, more complex, packages are conceived as *programs* instead of materials. The basic aim is creation of a new curriculum, based upon the notion of individualized instruction. This usually means that a package is based upon broad course concepts organized into coordinated units.

From this basic structure pretests and behavioral objectives are developed. This, of course, leads to the creation of a system of instructional media and materials. Since people learn in different ways, a variety of instructional activities must be included. These are usually organized into clearly defined alternatives or pathways for achieving the objectives. Through appropriate observation and diagnosis, the teacher guides the learner in selecting the alternative most appropriate for his needs.

Since each component of the package is integral to the system, the selected pathway of learning must be followed rather closely if the validity of the program is to be realized. This has led to the criticism of "teacher proof," for example, leaving few or no instructional decisions to the teacher. The current trend is toward increased flexibility. While retaining some basic structure, alternatives in media, in approach, and even in subject matter coverage are provided.

The package also contains self-evaluation tests, along with posttests. Thus every aspect of the instructional process is provided in the package. The text is relegated to one of many essential components of the package.

## What Is the Place for Learning Centers?

As individualized instruction gains momentum, the concept of the individualized classroom will give way to learning centers. Presently learning centers are often associated with the library or the instructional materials center. Sometimes they are decentralized facilities associated with teaching departments. Others represent an extension of specialized facilities such as science laboratories.

One of the most comprehensive individualized learning patterns has been developed in Pittsburgh, Pennsylvania.[2] Its learning center is located in a large room with inexpensive record players and their attached earphones along the walls. A student, working on a program, obtains a reading disc and places it in a recorder. Following directions, he completes his lesson, takes it to a teacher aide for scoring purposes. The teacher then evaluates it, listens to him read, asks some questions and then, if satisfactory, tells him to continue. When the prescription is completed he is tested. The test is corrected immediately. If he falls below 85 percent the teacher suggests a series of alternative activities to correct the weaknesses. This often includes special tutoring exercises.

## What Are the Staffing Needs?

The demands of an individualized learning program call for trained personnel at more than one level of teaching. Included are regular teachers, teacher aides, master teachers and specialized staff members. While each has his own specific domain of responsibility, the members must work as a professional team in carrying out the various tasks of the program. Although most learning packages are developed by separate teams of experts, a number of basic instructional decisions must be made by the teaching team. Furthermore, instructional programs call for a considerable number of diagnostic and testing activities which must be fed back to the learner as soon as possible following his initial responses. The team spends more time answering questions of individual pupils and working with small groups than lecturing to a class. Learning is couched in an informal, relaxed atmosphere. The teacher lends support and guidance to the individual's learning activities.

## What Computer Assistance Is Needed?

With the advent of modular scheduling, the computer found its place in the secondary schools (1963). Individualized learning requirements of record

[2] The Pittsburgh program for its first three years has been limited to K-6th grade. It is presently being expanded to the junior and senior high school.

keeping, testing, diagnosing learning deficiencies, records of student progress, individualized schedules, and student assignments demand computer assistance. The computer, more than anything else, has contributed to the move toward individualized instruction.

# INDIVIDUALIZED INSTRUCTIONAL PROCEDURES

Various techniques for providing for individual differences *within group settings* have been proposed. As indicated in Chapter 6, most of these have been somewhat ineffective. The more effective techniques certainly demand skillful and resourceful teachers. Individualized instructional procedures depart from the group or class concept of teaching. Thus a major restructuring process is necessary, even when restricted to a relatively few instructional areas. The procedure, outlined below, is recommended for those who wish to move gradually into an individualized learning program.

### What Preparation Is Needed?

Once a school decides to launch an individualized learning program, a project director should be appointed. Although an individualized learning program for an entire school is usually recommended by experts, most school systems begin with one or two instructional areas, moving into the program gradually. The project director guides the instructional team in developing appropriate learning centers and individual study units.

Although an ideal learning center involves a cluster classroom arrangement, individual classrooms may be adapted for this purpose, especially in the initial phases of the program. The cluster classroom arrangement usually involves six to ten classrooms in a cluster. Provision is made for individualized study, small-group instruction, seminars, and large-group instruction. Likewise, the individual classroom can be organized into cluster areas for such purposes. Sometimes appropriate adjustments may be made by taking out walls to adjacent classrooms.

Although development of individual study units can be contracted for by some outside agency (such as a private firm or university), local teachers usually choose to develop their own materials. This often can be facilitated through an in-service education and work program during the summer months. The skill areas of the curriculum are most amenable to the initial stages of an individualized instructional program. Many schools, for example, have begun with the area of mathematics.

### What Function Is Served with Individual
### Study Units (Minipacs)?

Whereas a learning package usually deals with the overall curriculum area, an individualized study unit (sometimes called a minipac) deals with a particular unit of a given subject. Individualized study units are derived from course concepts that have been arranged in a sequential order. Each study unit is based upon a single concept.

A study unit involves a rationale for the unit, unit objectives, learning activity options, and a variety of tests. The rationale is a statement clarifying *what* the student is going to learn, and *why* it is important for him to learn the unit. Many times a short, succinct statement is all that is necessary. To illustrate:

> The purpose of this unit is to familiarize you with the common usage of topic sentences and to enable you to use them effectively in communicating your own ideas.

Sometimes, when the purpose is more remote, an introductory paragraph or two may be necessary. This is followed with a statement of purpose. It should be noted that such statements establish learner purpose. Thus they must create a need or motivation for learning.

## How Are Unit Objectives and Behavioral Outcomes Developed?

Unit objectives have been fully described and illustrated elsewhere. It should be emphasized that the minimum-essentials type of objective is emphasized in the individualized learning unit. Accordingly, each objective must be developed in behavioral terms which describe the *conditions* under which the behavior is exhibited, the *specific act or performance* to be accepted as evidence of achievement, and the *minimum level of performance* expected. To illustrate:

> Given twenty sentences containing a variety of mistakes in capitalization, the student is able, with at least 90 percent accuracy, to identify and rewrite correctly each word that has a mistake in capitalization.

As in any instructional program, emphasis should be placed upon the higher level objectives (see Chapter 2). The use of certain "action" verbs in objectives offers clues to the cognition levels involved. At the highest level (evaluation), for example, action verbs might include: *judging, resolving, discriminating.* At the analyzing and synthesizing levels, action verbs may be: *comparing, distinguishing, identifying, classifying, restructuring, establishing.* The action verbs for the foregoing illustration are *identify* and *rewrite.* The first is at the remembering level while the latter would appear to involve the translating level of cognition.

## What Learning Activity Options Are Needed?

Goals, when stated in behavioral terms, suggest learning experiences which will contribute to goal fulfillment. It has long been recognized that a variety of learning experiences may be equally effective in the attainment of desired outcomes. The individualized learning program capitalizes upon this factor by providing several learning activity options.

Instructions must be explicit, however, in describing when and how the options are to be employed. According to Lewis,[3] no more than 40 percent of the total number of options should be required for initial completion of the unit. Thus if a student must be recycled through the unit at some future time, acceptable alternative options can be employed. The student checks off those options which he selects.

Options should be characterized by variability. The different methods and techniques treated in this book are suggestive of the many techniques available. They will include reading, writing, simulation, listening and observing activities. Above all, the options will exist at varying levels of difficulty and complexity. Several different reading levels must be provided.

## What Role Do Tests Play?

One of the most fundamental features of the individualized learning experience is the systematic use of tests. It should be emphasized, however, that their use is in many ways quite different from current testing procedures.

The placement test is usually of a general nature. Its purpose is to determine at what level the student's learning is to be initiated. A number of standardized achievement tests are available in the skills areas. Before being used, however, one must determine how well they match stated objectives.

A pretest, administered just prior to the learning experience, is designed to measure achievement of particular skills needed for attainment of unit objectives. According to Lewis,[4] the student should first be given an opportunity to give the pretest his cursory perusal to ascertain for himself whether he thinks it is possible for him to complete it successfully. If he feels it is too difficult, then he should not attempt it. An established level of accuracy (e.g., 90 percent) is expected if one is to be exempt from completing the unit.

The self-assessment test provides the learner with check points which enables him to evaluate progress as he proceeds through the unit. It is composed of such items as:

Explain the following:
  1. Topic sentence
  2. Coherence and transition
Give an example of the following:
  1. Topic outline
  2. Sentence outline

The student periodically refers to self-assessment items as he progresses through the unit.

Similar to the pretest, the posttest determines if a satisfactory level of performance has been attained. It is developed in terms of the behavioral objectives set for the unit. If the established minimum level of performance is

---

[3] James Lewis, Jr., *Administering the Individualized Program* (New York: Parker Publishing Co., Inc., 1971), p. 96.
[4] Lewis, *Administering the Individualized Program,* p. 82.

achieved the student proceeds to the next unit. If not, he is recycled through a portion or all of the learning activity options. He is then retested for an indication of further achievement. He does *not* progress to the next unit until the established minimum level of achievement has been attained.

## How Can an Individual Teacher Work Toward Individualized Instruction?

Emphasis in this chapter has been placed upon techniques employed by an entire school faculty or at least two or more teachers in moving into individualized instruction programs. Frequently, however, an individual teacher will want to move *in the direction of* individualized instruction within the confines of a conventional class setting. The recommendations which follow might be considered a series of steps. They are suggestive only.

1. Some type of subgrouping might well be established. Such a model was offered in Chapter 6.
2. By establishing subgroups, it becomes necessary to provide somewhat different materials for each group. At the top of the list will be books at different reading levels.
3. As one becomes conscious of individual differences within each subgroup, the need for more specialized materials will become apparent. Self-instructional devices and programmed materials are among the most useful tools available for this purpose. As a beginning, the use of programmed textbooks (perhaps beginning with one instructional unit) is recommended. Then, as demonstrable results are accumulated one may move toward more comprehensive programming.
4. Since learning programs characteristically rely heavily upon preassessment as well as self-assessment tests, the teacher will want to begin constructing such instruments for each subgroup. (Eventually these can be further differentiated to meet individual needs.)
5. The reader will recall that each subgroup is characteristically provided *different* instructional experiences for meeting common class objectives. It is recognized, however, that even the in-depth learning expected from the top group may be completed *prior* to minimal achievement of the objectives by another subgroup. At this point the teacher has an important decision to make. Should the one group be provided review materials until the other groups catch up? Or should it be permitted to move ahead into the next unit? If the latter choice is made, an individualized instruction program comes into existence.
6. If the choice is to move one subgroup ahead, the need for teacher aides, cluster study areas, and the like becomes apparent. Thus a "full blown" individualized instruction program begins to take shape.

It is emphasized that instruction designed to meet individual needs and abilities is the aim of all instruction. Subgrouping techniques may represent the first step in that direction. This, in turn, leads to greater individualization as individual differences are portrayed. While the ultimate goal may be a purely individualized instruction program, conventional class restrictions need not prevent the resourceful teacher from moving as far as he can in this direction.

## VALUES

Individualized learning programs combine the freedom of independent study with the necessary structure to insure attainment of objectives.
Competition is based upon one's own past achievement.
The program is tailored to the individual needs of each student.
The teacher's role is relegated to a diagnostician and a facilitator of learning.
Learning is measured on the basis of specific behavioral objectives.
Immediate feedback is available to the learner.

## LIMITATIONS AND PROBLEMS

Individualized learning programs demand a vast quantity of materials to fill the various learning needs of students.
The program tends to limit teacher flexibility, e.g., once a learning option has been selected the activities are prescribed and outlined for the learner without much teacher involvement.
Current individualized learning programs are primarily applicable to the skills areas.
Some slow students have experienced difficulty in adjusting to existing individualized learning programs.
Individualized learning programs provide a minimum of pupil-pupil interaction.
Frequent testing is essential. Adequate placement tests especially are nonexistent in some subject areas.
Individualized learning programs demand a restructuring of existing facilities and instructional personnel relationships.

## INDIVIDUALIZED INSTRUCTIONAL ILLUSTRATIONS

Individualized instructional programs are springing up in all parts of the country. Although they are characterized by diversity they have one common element: The traditional pattern of instruction, in which all students are taught the same content at the same time, is being abandoned. Instead, instructional teams are creating learning conditions which enable individuals to proceed at their own pace, often on self-selected subjects, toward self-evaluated and self-satisfying goals.[5] Some of the better publicized patterns have been described briefly below.

    I.  The nation's largest individualized learning project, Individually Prescribed Instruction (IPI) was developed at the University of Pittsburgh in cooperation with the USOE regional laboratory (1964). By 1967 more

[5] Jack V. Edling, "Individualized Instruction," *Audiovisual Instruction* 15 (February 1970): 13–16.

than a thousand school systems had asked for assistance in setting up IPI programs. By 1970 IPI was being used by 75,000 students in 264 schools.

Materials have been developed in elementary mathematics and language arts. Plans are being developed for its expansion through high school. Based upon carefully sequenced behavioral objectives, empirically developed materials permit students to plan and proceed independently. Provision for continued diagnosis and pupil progress and regular feedback are provided.

II.  Project PLAN (Program for Learning in Accordance with Needs), the nation's second largest effort to individualize instruction, has been in existence since 1967. Unlike IPI, PLAN is representative of a private venture. (It was created by Westinghouse Learning Corporation and American Institutes for Research, in Palo Alto, California.) It utilizes available commercial materials, adjusting them to the individualized program. Computer assistance provides vital individual feedback on a daily basis. The program involves all grade levels in language arts, reading, social studies, mathematics, and science. Cost is estimated to be an extra $100 per pupil per year.

III.  The NOVA plan (developed at Nova High School, Fort Lauderdale, Florida) was developed by a staff of eight educators through funds from the U.S. Office of Education. The group, located at the educational research and development center for the Broward County Board of Public Instruction, Broward County, Florida, has been working on the Interrelated Mathematics Science Project.

Specially designed booklets called Learning Activity Packages (LAPs) are being written in both mathematics and science areas. The primary function of the LAP system is to guide the student through a highly structured program of learning materials. LAPs, outlining a model program with blank spaces for individual schools to design and write their own program of instruction, are being used widely in the Florida area.

IV.  The Tutorial Community utilizes student tutors (presently advanced sixth graders) to assist younger students (first graders) who are experiencing difficulty in a specific learning skill. Financed by the System Development Corporation, Santa Monica, California, the program is a seven-year project being conducted by the Pacoima Elementary School, Los Angeles, California. Its basic purposes are to analyze the processes and skills involved in tutoring and to evaluate the long term effects of tutoring on both tutor and learner.

V.  The Quintile Plan (McComb, Mississippi), in effect, forces teachers to individualize instruction. The plan divides the school year into four nine-week sessions, in addition to a special summer session. A student may enroll in five basic subjects, but he studies only one subject at a time for nine weeks. (Physical education and special interest subjects such as art and music are taken with the core subject.)

Teachers have discovered that they cannot maintain interest and attention when they lecture for five periods a day. This has resulted in a decided change in instructional activities. Students now proceed individually toward course objectives; teachers provide guidance and assistance as needed.

The foregoing are merely suggestive of the varied approaches to individualized instruction being developed across the country. Edling summarizes eighteen such representative programs that were in existence in 1970.[6] In looking for generalizations he finds that support money usually is obtained to initiate programs; that programs are initiated by school administrators; that the movement is not located in any one section of the country; that the older programs employ an abundance and variety of instructional technology; and that there is a broadening of traditional educational objectives.

[6] Edling, *"Individualized Instruction,"* pp. 13–16.

# CHAPTER 9

# Value-Focusing Activities

## OVERVIEW

### Key Concepts

1. Values are acquired, subconsciously in many ways. While some are the products of reflection, many are acquired from various social groups such as the family, the church, or the peer group.
2. Values possess both affective and cognitive dimensions.
3. Values can be structured and restructured through processes of reflective thinking. Such instruction must be *personalized,* however.
4. Expressions of beliefs, interests, and feelings provide clues to one's values.

### New Terms

1. **Value**—A guide to human behavior.
2. **Attitude**—A predisposition to behave in a prescribed manner.
3. **Belief**—Essentially cognitive in nature; represents one of the early signs of an emerging value.
4. **Feeling**—The emotional dimension of a value. Not all feelings are associated with values, however.
5. **Value Indicators**—Expressions of aspirations, purposes, attitudes, interests, beliefs, and the like.
6. **The Clarifying Response**—A brief verbal exchange between teacher and student designed to help the learner think about and perhaps clarify his values.
7. **Values Sheet**—A stimulator (e.g., short story, poetry, cartoon, etc.) followed with a few key questions about the values problem raised. Usually designed as a group experience.

8. **Value-clarifying Discussion**—A short, informal discussion designed to raise issues. Often directed informally to a small group of students as opposed to the entire class.

### Questions to Guide Your Study

1. "Values are private and should not be tampered with by school personnel." Defend or refute.
2. If values can be taught through persuasion and propaganda alone (e.g., television commercials), why bother emphasizing the processes of reflective thinking?
3. How may value indicators assist the teacher in teaching values?
4. Why must values teaching be personalized?

Based upon his own unique experiences, each individual develops guides to human behavior. These are called values. Values are continually being modified as experience accumulates. The teen-age years are characteristically a time of questing or searching for reliable guides to behavior. Values which were once accepted without question come into full critical analysis.

Every teacher is a purveyor of a value system. Even the most traditional teacher emphasizes certain facts over others by any number of gestures, incidental comments, and inflections in assigning a high or low value to certain ideas. The issue is whether students will develop values accidentally or whether they will be provided a learning atmosphere which lends direction and support to their efforts.

## FUNDAMENTAL PROPERTIES

Values exist at different levels of commitment. From a mere positive feeling about something one may develop a compelling urge to persuade others to his way of thinking. It becomes apparent then that values may be expressed in different ways. A number of value indicators may provide clues for value clarification and development.

### What Role Do Attitudes and Interests Play in the Acquisition of Values?

Attitudes are predispositions to behave in a prescribed manner. An individual may say he is for or against something as a result of impulse or observation of others. He may have given little thought or analysis to the attitude, however. An attitude may become a guide to behavior (value) in any number of ways. Ideally it should be carefully examined and re-examined in the presence of valid data. All too often, however, an attitude becomes fixed on the basis of erroneous assumptions and little or no data. Unfortunately, those values which are acquired illogically may be as difficult to dislodge as those which are the product of critical examination.

All individuals have passing interests which may be discussed or even pursued temporarily. In a sense, this is the manner in which one becomes informed about many things. Eventually, if the needed reinforcement is not provided, one interest will be replaced with another. The interests of teen-agers may vary considerably from one month to the next. Interests do provide clues or indicators of values, however.

### How Do Beliefs and Convictions Enter into Value Formation?

High school students freely express their beliefs and convictions. Generally such expressions represent an invitation for discussion and analysis. Essentially, this represents an individual's way of saying, "I would like to explore further in this area." Perhaps he senses the need for developing a stable value in the area. Thus a verbal expression of a belief may be no more than a mere indication of an emerging value. It provides an avenue through which a value may be developed as a result of careful examination.

### How Are Feelings Associated with Values?

Feelings or emotional reactions are closely associated with values. Values which are highly prized tend to create within the individual a certain amount of anxiety. Thus he may feel compelled to persuade others to his way of thinking. Feelings, however, do not necessarily reflect values. They are often of a temporary nature and are easily dissipated through reflection. Feelings represent a basic component of values, however. Accordingly, one can approach value teaching through either the affective or the cognitive dimension. There is considerable evidence suggesting that until feelings are examined little progress in value restructuring can be expected.

### How Persistent Are One's Values?

Values are the basic components of an individual's personality. As such they tend to change rather slowly over a period of time. Nevertheless, a teacher must bear in mind that values are products of experience. Since experience is continuous, values too are modifiable. If a value makes an individual unhappy, perhaps creating worries and problems, with appropriate guidance it may be altered. It has been observed that values per se are not so damaging as the tenacity with which they are held.

### What Are the Basic Ingredients of Values?

When an individual is asked to make a decision (a choice between alternatives) he is asked to think. When he is asked how he feels about that choice an appeal is made to his emotions. The process of valuing includes both domains.

In discussing the affective domain (see Chapter 2) Krathwohl concedes that the attainment of a cognitive goal may result in attainment of an affective goal as well.[1] He points out, however, that this process does not necessarily occur when he says that "the development of cognitive behaviors may actually destroy certain desired affective behaviors. . . . For example, it is quite possible that many literature courses at the high school and the college levels instill knowledge . . . while at the same time producing an aversion to . . . literary works."

# VALUE-FOCUSING PROCEDURES

Some people contend that teachers must indoctrinate students with the basic values of our democracy. Others are convinced that values cannot be taught at all—that they are somehow "caught" in the home, the church, and the school as individuals interact with others and with life in general. As a result, the schools have all too often steered clear of any systematized procedure for teaching values. This seems strangely at odds with the obvious needs of today's youth, who must cope with unprecedented value contradictions and complexities.

The teaching of values, like other instructional methods, involves a process of reflective thought. Since values are intimately associated with emotional responses (e.g., attitudes, interests, feelings, beliefs, etc.), unusual precautions are necessary. As Raths and his associates point out,[2] "we may raise questions but we cannot 'lay down the law' about what a child's values should be."

### How Are Value Problems Identified?

Value problems arise constantly, both incidentally as learners interact one with another and in connection with the content of every course of study. In either case one must look for value indicators in areas involving aspirations, purposes, attitudes, interests, beliefs, and so forth.

Value indicators of the incidental variety are usually statements such as the following:

1. Import duties should be enacted to protect our farmers.
2. The American Indian must be taken off the reservations.

---

[1] David R. Krathwohl et al., *Taxonomy of Educational Objectives: Affective Domain* (New York: David McKay Co., Inc., 1964), p. 20.

[2] Louis E. Raths, Merrill Harmin, and Sidney B. Simon, *Values and Teaching* (Columbus, O.: Charles E. Merrill Publishing Co., 1966), p. 37.

3. When I'm old enough I want to join the Navy.
4. I like to read poetry.

As the foregoing suggest, many such statements reveal what one stands for, what he supports, what he prefers to do, what his ambitions may be.

An appropriate problem for discussion, "What steps should be taken to minimize the air pollution in our industrial centers?" is clearly one involving values. In mathematics, the problem, "What procedures should be followed in switching from the English to the metric system?" is also one of values. The reader will note that the problem itself assumes a given value position. Thus a prior question might well concern itself with whether or not such action or policy changes are needed.

## How Are Value Problems Analyzed?

The initial phase of resolving problems usually takes one into a consideration of existing data or facts. Not only must the facts be recognized but they must be *evaluated* as well. Simon and Harmin contend that content material can and should be treated at three different levels: facts, concepts, and values.[3] To illustrate: What steps should be taken to make the U.S. Constitution functional in our own lives?

*Facts questions:*
1. What essentially is the subject of the constitution?
2. Who were the signers? What special interests did they represent?
3. How did it differ from the Articles of Confederation?
4. Why are the first ten amendments called the Bill of Rights?

*Concepts level:*
1. The constitution set the pattern for democratic forms of government.
2. The constitution provides for a system of checks and balances.
3. The Bill of Rights attempted to correct social injustices.
4. The constitution is an evolving concept, as reflected in amendments and Supreme Court decisions.

*Values questions:*
1. What rights and guarantees do you have in your family? In school?
2. Is your student government able to function democratically?
3. Should a student editorial board have the final say about what is printed in the school paper or the yearbook?
4. How can you initiate needed changes within the democratic framework?

It should be noted that value questions usually are of the "you" variety. They are designed to make content functional in the lives of the learner.

---

[3] Sidney B. Simon and Merrill Harmin, "Subject Matter with a Focus on Values," *Educational Leadership* 26 (October 1968): 34–39. Used with permission of the publisher.

### How Are Alternatives Evolved?

Following an analysis and evaluation of the existing state of affairs, possible alternatives are introduced and evaluated. Some alternatives are usually suggested or implied in text materials; others may be apparent from the data analysis. It is important, however, for the learner to advance beyond the obvious. He should be encouraged to apply his own creative imagination to the problem. Some creative and provocative solutions or alternatives relative to the foregoing problem might be: (1) rewriting the constitution, (2) passing certain constitutional amendments, (3) suspending the constitution for specific purposes.

Again, the values level of analysis would be employed to personalize the discussion. For example, "If you were rewriting the constitution what changes would you make?" "Should the president (or your school principal) ever be 'above the law'?" In each case the consequences must be carefully weighed.

### How Are Choices Affirmed?

A choice in the realm of values is held in high esteem if it is to become a true value. Unless one prizes, cherishes, or is happy with his choice, he is not willing to affirm his stand publicly. After a choice is finally reached, the learner must perceive ways of making his value functional in his own life. The teacher's role is to guide the student in discovering possible and practical applications. For example, "What immediate and specific steps in altering your student government rules may be taken?"

### What Activity Is Appropriate?

The logical conclusion to a values discussion is some form of action. Values, by definition, are guides to human behavior. Sometimes such action is ill advised simply because the learner does not fully understand the legitimate avenues of action open to him. A student strike, for example, initiated by the acts of a few can deny education to a majority. Less drastic forms of behavior may involve some reading on the subject, forming friendships or organizations designed to nourish the value(s), collecting and spending money for the cause, conducting a better writing campaign, floating petitions, and the like. The teacher will want to guide students in recognizing and evaluating possibilities for action relative to values.

## INSTRUCTIONAL TECHNIQUES

The teaching of values is not restricted to any one method. Rather, it may permeate every method if the right type of questions is asked. This is not meant to imply that values are easily developed or altered. Indeed the evidence suggests that value teaching has been woefully neglected and mishandled. All too often teachers have held up the "right" values for students to accept, providing few if any alternatives and almost no opportunity for the weighing and balancing processes which are necessary.

Many of the techniques described below have been recommended by Raths and his associates.[4] Value teaching basically is a *personalized* process. However, the influence of the peer group for an adolescent can be a powerful force in developing and altering values.

### How Is the Clarifying Response Technique Employed?

The clarifying response represents a way of responding to what a student has chosen, what he prizes, and/or what he is doing. Its purpose is to encourage the learner to think about and perhaps clarify his values. The technique is usually a brief verbal exchange between teacher and student and may occur at any time during an instructional experience.

The response seeks to raise questions in the mind of the learner by prodding him gently into examining his own ideas or activities. It is not designed to lead the student to the "right" answer, rather it leaves him hanging in the air. The teacher then moves on without moralizing.

Several criteria for an effective clarifying response are recommended by Raths[5] and his associates. Some have been briefly summarized below.

1. The response avoids moralizing, criticizing, giving values, or evaluating.
2. It puts the responsibility on the student to look at his behavior or his ideas and decide what *he* wants.
3. The clarifying response is permissive and stimulating but not insistent. One may choose *not* to examine his ideas or behavior.
4. The response is short, usually involving only two or three rounds of dialogue.
5. Such responses are usually individual in nature.
6. Clarifying responses operate in situations in which there are no "right" answers (e.g., feelings, attitudes, beliefs, or purposes).
7. The response must be used creatively. It must not follow a set formula.

Clarifying responses may take many forms. The illustrations are suggestive only.

> Tom: If the underprivileged are given a guaranteed annual wage they will lose all initiative.
> Teacher: How might this condition come about, Tom?
> Tom: Well, they will not need to work.
> Teacher: Can you give me an example?

> Joe: Last night I read a whole book on the life of Napoleon.
> Teacher: Do you enjoy reading about war heroes, Joe?

[4] Raths et al., *Values and Teaching*, pp. 51–162.
[5] Raths et al., *Values and Teaching*, pp. 53–54.

Joe: Yes, I certainly do.

Teacher: Do you see war as one acceptable solution to problems?

Joe: Not necessarily. I just enjoy the movement—the courage displayed by some military leaders.

## How Is the Values Sheet Used?

Unlike the clarifying response, the values sheet is designed as a group experience. The instrument begins with a stimulator. This can come from novels, essays, short stories, quotations, poetry, cartoons, and the like. This is followed with a few key questions designed to help the student clarify his thinking about the values problem raised by the stimulator. Since valuing is individualistic in nature, each student completes the values sheet on his own. Later, responses from different students may be shared in small or large group discussions.

The illustration was developed for use in a high school English class.

In Germany, first they came for the Communists, and I didn't speak up because I wasn't a Communist. Then they came for the Jews, and I didn't speak up because I wasn't a Jew. Then they came for the trade unionists, and I didn't speak up because I wasn't a trade unionist. Then they came for the Catholics, and I didn't speak up because I was a Protestant. Then they came for me—and by that time no one was left to speak up

—Pastor Martin Niemoller

1. What category are you in? When would they have come for you?
2. Is there something in your school, some "injustice" about which you might well speak out?
3. Why stick *your* neck out? Why not?
4. If you decide to speak up, how do you go about it? What are the best ways?
5. Some people say: "We need to value what we do and do something about what we value." Do you agree? If not, why? If so, what have you done lately?[6]

Values sheets have been especially fruitful in literature classes. They seem to provide an excellent way of bringing the academic concerns and the personal lives of students together.

## How Is the Value-Clarifying Discussion Developed?

The guided class discussion (described in Chapter 16) often does not provide an ideal setting for clarification of individual values. The reader will recall that the procedure calls for an evaluation of alternatives in terms of established criteria. Such criteria are usually evolved within a broad democratic

[6] Howard Kirshenbaum and Sidney B. Simon, "Teaching English with a Focus on Values," *English Journal* 58 (October 1969): 1071–76. Used by permission of the authors and the publisher. For a list of teacher workshops and materials on the values classification approach, contact: Values Associates, Box 591, North Amherst, Mass. 01002.

framework. They are frequently suggested from national policy and the like. They may not directly touch the individual values of students.

A value-clarifying discussion, on the other hand, is usually informal. It is usually initiated by some quotation, picture, scene from a play, provocative questions, etc. Frequently it is used as a follow-up of a values sheet, described earlier.

The values discussion does not end with a decision or even with a set of generalizations. Instead, the discussion may lead students to consider the next moves that may be taken. (Value clarification often leads to some form of action or activity.) The whole process usually involves a few thought-provoking, personalized questions, followed with some time for mulling over the ideas and comments. Those who want to clarify their thinking on the issue further will do this in private. There is a tendency to extend such a discussion beyond its usefulness. Really effective value discussions, however, may raise issues that will come up again and again as students ponder values that are important in their own lives.

### How Does Role Playing Contribute to the Acquisition of Values?

The sociodramatic method (described in Chapter 13) provides an ideal setting for the teaching of values. Students especially enjoy assuming new identities in a temporary and protected situation. To live briefly in the shoes of another offers a rare opportunity for insights into that person's feelings. Any kind of conflict situation in which actual feelings are often concealed in real life provides an opportunity for such an enactment.

### What Is the Place for the Incident Case in the Teaching of Values?

Somewhat related to the methods already described is the case method (treated in Chapter 14). With minor adjustments in the formulation of case questions, it can be used effectively as outlined. Again, liberal use of "you" questions should follow an analysis of feelings and relationships uncovered through a study of the case.

## VALUES

Values are of immediate concern to all high school students. They may not care as much for English, history, or science as we think they should, but they are keenly interested in developing clear, viable and sound values.

The teaching of values may be effected incidentally along with other instructional processes. Likewise, value teaching can be a powerful motivator for the teaching of content material.

A consideration of values in teaching can do much to close the so-called communication or generation gap. It provides an ideal means of making school relevant to the lives of students.

Since there are no "right" or "wrong" answers in the teaching of values, the procedure tends to promote increased tolerance among individuals and nations.

## LIMITATIONS AND PROBLEMS

Basic substantive values (e.g., one's feelings toward religion, politics and the family) are usually respected as private, personal affairs. One may raise questions, designed to provoke reflective thought, but he must not provide the "right" answers to such questions.

Teachers naturally hold values that are highly cherished. By word and deed they tend to reflect such values. Such activities can hamper effective instruction in the realm of values.

The teaching of facts, as a means of avoiding controversy, is safe. Even administrators have tended to prefer teachers who did not raise issues.

In a rapidly changing world one cannot be certain what values would be most appropriate for any individual. Indeed, values for each individual must grow and develop as life conditions change.

Some individuals are in greater need of value clarification than others. Although they are not readily indentifiable, Raths and his associates suggest a number of value-related behavior types which usually need immediate attention. These include individuals who are characteristically apathetic, flighty, uncertain, inconsistent, drifting, overconforming, negative, and those who tend to search for identity through pretending to be someone else.

## ILLUSTRATIONS FOR TEACHING VALUES

    I.   Useful in literature classes—on Shakespeare's *Hamlet*[7]

       *Values level questions*
         1.  King Claudius supposedly killed to get ahead. How far will you go to get what you want?
         2.  Laertes hears his father's advice, and it comes out a string of clichés. What kind of advice do you get which falls on *your* deaf ears?
         3.  Part of *Hamlet* is about the obligation of a son to seek revenge for his father. Where do you stand on that kind of act?
         4.  Death is a regular happening in *Hamlet*. How close have you ever come to death? What part of you responds to a news story of death on the highway, death in Vietnam?

[7] Simon and Harmin, *Subject Matter with a Focus on Values*, p. 37.

II. Useful in history or sociology classes—on war [8]

*Values level questions*
1. In *your* opinion, to what extent has the United States been justified in each of the wars she has fought? Which wars would you have considered "just"?
2. Should an individual be allowed to refuse to serve in the armed forces? For what reasons? Under what circumstances would *you* kill?
3. Have *you* ever done anything to promote world peace? What things might you do?
4. Have *you* ever been in a physical fight? What caused it? What were the results?
5. How are disputes settled in *your* family?
6. Where do you stand in the Vietnam war? Have you done anything to convince others of your point of view? Should you?

III. Useful in physics or general science classes—on Newton's Laws of Motion[9]

*Values level questions*
1. How, if at all, have the laws touched your own life?
2. Seat belts in cars stem from one of these laws. Do you use them in your own car? Explain.
3. What's the fastest you have ever driven a car? If you weren't driving, at what speed would you have insisted that the driver slow down?
4. Driving a car into a wall is like swinging a one-ton sledge hammer at a wall. Would you rather be the wall or the sledge hammer?

IV. Useful in biology or earth science—on the earth's crust[10]

*Values level questions*
1. Are you likely to become a rock hound some day?
2. Are the mountains a place where you really like to spend your vacations?
3. Where do you stand on oil companies getting a depletion allowance?
4. In some states, strip miners find it cheaper to pay the fine than to do the reforestation the law requires. What is your reaction to this?
5. Which, if any, of these worry you at all or more than others?
   a. Converting the Florida Everglades into housing for senior citizens.
   b. Bulldozing a mountain so a four-lane road can go by.
   c. The cities spreading out over the earth's surface, leaving less and less open space.
6. Grass is too hard to maintain in a city; cities should be all asphalt. Do you agree or disagree? Give your reasons.

[8] Merrill Harmin, Howard Kirschenbaum, and Sidney Simon, "Teaching History with a Focus on Values," *Social Education* 33 (May 1969): 568–70. Used by permission of the authors and the publisher. For a list of teacher workshops and materials on the values classification approach, contact: Values Associates, Box 591, North Amherst, Mass. 01002.
   [9] Merrill Harmin and others, "Teaching Science with a Focus on Values," *Science Teacher* 37 (January 1970): 16–20. Used by permission of the publisher.
   [10] Harmin et al., "Teaching Science," pp. 16–20.

V. Useful in American problems, sociology or psychology classes—on dogs[11]

*Values Sheet*

Dog owners spent $530 million on dog food last year, reports the *Wall Street Journal,* which adds that this is about 50 percent more than Americans spend on baby food.

Americans will spend $1.5 billion to acquire pets this year and in addition to the initial investment and the food bill, about $800 million will be spent this year on non-food items for pets. (For dogs: pajamas, cashmere sweaters, mink collars, Halloween costumes and Santa Claus suits; and cosmetics—color shampoo, creme rinses and hair dressing, perfumes, "shades of nail polish including lavender and green," a spray dentifrice, tranquilizers, etc.) Not to mention millions spent on veterinarian fees and boarding kennels. Pets are big business.[12]

1. If you are a dog owner should you feel badly about this report? Why? Why not?
2. If not a dog owner, might you spend money on something else which might be made to seem equally ridiculous? Explain.
3. Some people say: "What we spend our money on tells what we value, respect, hold dear, and cherish. If we really valued something else, would we not spend our money on that? Discuss.

VI. Useful in history, social studies, literature, or sociology classes—on patriotism[13]

*Values Sheet*

To me, patriotism is one's love or devotion to one's country. Having its root in religion, it includes respect for our leaders, honor for our heroes, belief in our ideals, and a stout defense of the integrity of America.

—J. Edgar Hoover

Many men have assumed that blind support of their country, "right" or "wrong" is the very essence of patriotism. But I agree with the view that "he who loves his country best who strives to make it best." Our schools will produce true patriots capable of saving this nation and all that makes it dear only if they turn out youngsters alert and alive to our country's shortcomings and weaknesses; only if they instill in our children a social conscience, a fervor for righting old wrongs, defying old fears, surmounting old prejudices, and banishing old social taboos.

—Carl T. Rowan, former head of the United States Information Agency

We love our country, in the final analysis, because it is *ours,* because it is an extension of ourselves, and because we love ourselves. . . . But the highest ethical command is to love others as we love ourselves. The basic patriotism, then, does not exclude and despise the foreigner, but gives him the love and respect to which all men are entitled.

—Steve Allen

To me, strong "national patriotism" is undesirable. What we need is devotion to self and all mankind. Rather than more persons blindly loyal to

[11] Merrill Harmin and Sidney Simon, "Values and Teaching: A Human Process," *Educational Leadership* 24 (March 1967): 517 ff. Used by permission of the publisher.

[12] Charles H. Wells, "Between the Lines," *Newsletter,* American Civil Liberties Union, September 15, 1964.

[13] Kirschenbaum and Simon, "Teaching English," 1075 ff. Statements on patriotism were taken from *NEA Journal* 56 (January 1967): 9–11.

a particular group, we need more persons who see that in this shrinking world all humans must share responsibility for each other's trouble and joy.

—Tamaji Harmin

1. Which of these four statements sounds like things you were taught about patriotism? Put an "O" (for old) or an "N" (for new) next to the statements which seem old or new to you.
2. If the world's people chose one of these statements rather than the others as its position on patriotism, which one or two statements, in your opinion, would lead to the best kind of world? Discuss fully.
3. According to the definition of patriotism which appeals to you most, are *you* a patriotic American? Discuss. (Here you might want to write down *your own* definition of patriotism if you think it more meaningful than any of the four above.)

VII. Useful in literature, social studies or sociology classes—on making choices (poem)[14]

*Values Sheet (Based upon "The Road Not Taken" by Robert Frost)*
1. What was the *most important choice* in *your* life that you have had to make between two divergent roads?
2. Which one was the "grassy" one that "wanted wear"?
3. In what way(s) has the choice made a "difference" in your life?
4. Are you proud of your choice? If yes, why? If not, why not?
5. Was there any adult who could have given you good advice at that time? Any of your friends?
6. Are you at or are you coming to any new forks in the road? How do you think you'll choose? What are the pros and cons of either choice?

[14]Kirschenbaum and Simon, "Teaching English," pp. 9–11. Used by permission of the authors and the publisher.

# CHAPTER 10

# Encouraging Creativity

## OVERVIEW

### Key Concepts

1. Creative teaching essentially provides a release from restrictions during the processes of reflective thinking.
2. All individuals are potentially creative; levels of creativity will vary with each individual.
3. Students who possess the highest ability for school work may not be the most creative.
4. Highly creative individuals tend to experience school and individual adjustment problems in conventional school settings.
5. Creativity, an individualized experience, may be cultivated in group (class) settings.
6. Deferred judgment (evaluation) is basic to creative processes.

### New Terms

1. **Convergent Thinking**—Emphasizes dependence on reproduction of existing data and the fitting of old responses to new situations in a more or less logical manner.
2. **Divergent Thinking**—Is characterized by flexibility and originality in the production of new ideas. Sometimes such thinking is featured by a sudden "flash" of insight.
3. **Detachment**—The ability to "back away" from an involved problem, enabling one to see it from the "outside"—in its totality.
4. **Incubation**—A period of little or no conscious effort relative to a problem, in which the subconscious apparently makes connections and associations which may be blocked out during periods of concentrated effort.

5. **Illumination**—A sudden flash of insight which may occur during or after a brainstorming session, after the problem has been put aside.
6. **Brainstorming**—A group process designed to amass as many solutions to a problem as possible in the absence of restraints or evaluation.
7. **Synetics**—The joining together of different and apparently irrelevant elements. Often used as an adjunct to the brainstorming procedure.

## Questions to Guide Your Study

1. Contrast creative problem solving and conventional problem solving processes.
2. What is the place of convergent thinking in creative endeavors?
3. Why is deferred judgment deemed essential to creative processes?
4. "Most conventional instructional methods tend to impede creative thinking." Defend or refute.
5. Why does the creative individual sometimes pose a threat to the classroom teacher?

Although the processes of creative or divergent thinking are still imperfectly understood, mounting evidence suggests that their behavioral manifestations are often stifled and criticized. Indeed Thomas A. Edison, one of the world's greatest inventors, was declared mentally "addled" by one of his early teachers. Thereupon, his mother withdrew Tom from school and taught him herself. Edison contributed numerous inventions even after he was eighty years old.

The precise relationship between creative imagination and problem solving presently is not fully understood. Most writers suggest, however, that too much emphasis on the formal structure of analytical thought processes is detrimental to creative (sometimes called intuitive) thought. Routinized activities of any sort seem to be detrimental to the process. Bruner, in stressing the complementary nature of the two, concedes that through "intuitive thinking the individual may arrive at solutions or problems which he would not achieve at all, or at best more slowly, through analytic thinking.[1] He points out, however, that ideas reached intuitively must be checked and refined by analytic methods. The procedure described in this chapter enables the learner to exercise considerable creativity within the broad framework of the problem-solving process.

The processes of creativity, like other modes of thought, are individualistic in nature. They are often prompted and developed, however, in group settings. Thus the technique of group brainstorming is emphasized in this chapter. Creativity can be furthered through any of the group methods treated in this book. *In many instances, however, it is not fully exploited, simply because the teacher is unaware of those factors which tend to block creative processes.* It is hoped that the insights gained may be applied to all instructional methods and strategies.

[1] Jerome Bruner, *The Process of Education* (Cambridge, Mass.: Harvard University Press, 1961), p. 58.

# FUNDAMENTAL PROPERTIES

An idea is creative when it possesses an element of novelty which can be applied to a given situation. The process includes the ability to change one's approach to a problem, to produce ideas which are both relevant and unusual, to see beyond the immediate situation, and to redefine the problem or some aspect of it.[2]

All individuals to some extent are creative. Some individuals, however, are much more creative than others. While a part of this difference may be of a hereditary nature, much of the difference likely results from the failure of many to express their creative potential. In fact, many essential attributes of creativity are all too often discouraged in the typical secondary school classroom.

## What Are the Basic Attributes of a Creative Person?

The attributes of a highly creative individual are not unique to such individuals. Their particular combination along with a high degree of development, however, seem to make such individuals "stand out" from their peers.

*Originality.* The ability to produce unusual ideas, to solve problems in unusual ways, and to use things or situations in an unusual manner is the essence of originality. Sometimes it is viewed as uncommonness of response—the ability to make remote or indirect connections. Such an individual, being skeptical of conventional ideas, is predisposed to the intellectual risks associated with creative discovery.

*Persistence.* A creative person is usually a persistent individual. He often displays a marked willingness to devote long hours to a given task, including a willingness to schedule his own time. Moreover, such an individual may display a willingness to withstand discomfort, often working under adverse conditions. Above all, the creative person displays a willingness to face failure. Frustrations seem to spur him on to greater effort.

*Independence.* The creative person is an independent thinker. He looks for the unusual, the unexpected. Indeed he notices things that other people do not, such as colors, textures, personal reactions. Frequently he may explore ideas for their own sake, toying with them to see where they may lead.

As opposed to the counterconformist who flouts convention because he feels a compulsion to be different, the independent thinker maintains a balance between that of the counterconformist and the conformist. Unlike the conformist, he is open to experience; unlike the counterconformist, he is different because of his greater perceptive ability. He has confidence in the worth of his ideas. Although the creative person is his own greatest critic, he has undying faith in his ideas.

---

[2] George F. Kneller, *The Art and Science of Creativity* (New York: Holt, Rinehart and Winston, Inc., 1965), p. 13.

*Involvement and Detachment.* Once a problem has been identified, the creative person quickly becomes immersed in the area. He reads, notes, discusses, explores. By finding out what others have done, the creator not only provides himself with materials with which to think, but also becomes acquainted with the difficulties and complexities of the problem.

Once such an individual has become fully immersed in his problem, he becomes detached enough to see the problem in its total perspective. By setting his work aside, the creative person gives his ideas freedom to develop. Thus involvement becomes a means of preparing him for his own creation.

*Deferment and Immediacy.* While allowing the problem to maintain its freshness, the creative person resists the tendency to judge too soon. He does not accept the first solution which appears but waits to see if a better one comes along. This tendency to defer judgment seems to be an attribute of an open-minded person, one who is unwilling to reach a decision prematurely.

*Incubation.* The aspect of the creative process which calls for little or no conscious effort is known as incubation. By putting the problem aside temporarily, the creative person allows the unconscious to take over, making various associations and connections which the conscious mind seems to impede.

The incubation period may be long or short, but it must be utilized. Sleep, above all, helps to encourage illumination. This "luring the muse" permits the mind to run free; it is a period of purposeful relaxation which may vary from a few minutes to several months.

*Illumination.* Intuitive thought processes are best characterized by a sudden flash of insight. Perhaps after a long period of frustrated effort the solution to a problem will suddenly appear, often at a time when least expected. This sudden flash of insight may be the fruits of unconscious effort in the form of inner tensions. It may be that the powers of association are enhanced when the mind runs freely on its own. At any rate, the flash usually occurs after a period of incubation when the individual is not actively pursuing his problem.

*Verification.* Although illumination provides the necessary impetus and direction for solving a problem, it must be checked and verified through conventional objective procedures. Sound judgment must complete the work that imagination has set in progress. Indeed a flash of insight may be partially if not totally unreliable. It may merely serve as a catalyst to liberate the creator from a restricted approach to his problem. Sometimes one flash of inspiration will set off a chain reaction to other such experiences during the process of verification.

## What Are the Differences Between Convergent and Divergent Thinking?

Convergent thinking is characterized by its dependence on reproduction of the already learned, and the fitting of old responses to new situations in a more or less mechanical way. Divergent thinking, on the other hand, involves fluency, flexibility and originality, and is essentially concerned with production of large numbers of new ideas.[3]

Both convergent and divergent thinking are essential to the problem-solving experience. When convergent thinking is applied during a divergent thinking phase of the problem-solving process, the latter may be seriously impeded. When students are casting about for solutions to a problem, for example, an evaluation of each idea *as it is presented* tends to minimize the flow of original ideas.

Most IQ tests measure convergent thinking almost exclusively. In essence, such tests require the student to apply what he has learned in the past to new problems or to abstract some rule from examples. Usually there is only one correct answer. Correctness is determined on the basis of logic, rules or laws. To illustrate:

> Which word is least like "new"?
>
> —old, big, shiny, satisfactory

The respondent is expected to notice that "new" denotes something's age. Thus the word is the opposite of "old" which also denotes age. The divergent thinker, however, could reason that "new" tells about some condition of an object and so does "old," "shiny," and "satisfactory." "Big," on the other hand, relates to size; thus it must be the right answer.

## What Are the Relative Merits of Individual and Group Creative Experiences?

Perhaps the most basic feature of creative endeavor is openness to experience. The tendency to "close" on a problem shuts off the flow of ideas which might produce unique and often better solutions to problems. This principle of "deferred judgment" is basic to both individual and group creativity.

Many have thought of creative thinking processes as purely individualistic in nature. Recognizing its inborn, developmental quality, little emphasis has been placed upon techniques for furthering and enhancing group creativity. Like all attributes of learning, however, it *can be developed through carefully selected class experiences*. Like other approaches to problem solving much individualized instruction is needed. Creative problem solving in carefully organized group situations is not only effective but economical of time as well. There is considerable evidence which suggests that the principle of *deferred judgment* is equally effective with individuals working *independently* on certain creative problem-solving tasks.[4] Thus *both* group and individual creativity

---

[3] A. J. Cropley, *Creativity* (London: Longmans, Green and Co., Ltd., 1967), p. 2.
[4] Sidney J. Parnes, "Do You Really Understand Brainstorming?" in Sidney J. Parnes and Harold F. Harding, *A Source Book For Creative Thinking* (New York: Charles Scribner's Sons, 1962), pp. 283–90.

should be emphasized. Emphasis in this chapter is placed upon the group approach to deferred judgment known as brainstorming.

## BRAINSTORMING AND RELATED TECHNIQUES

Brainstorming literally means using the *brain* to *storm* a problem. It is a technique by which a group attempts to find a solution to a specific problem by amassing all the ideas spontaneously contributed by its members. Brainstorming is a technique of applied imagination or creativity.

It should be noted that the essential aspects of brainstorming procedure which follow involve a careful combination of individual ideation and judgment as well as some group thinking. By far the greatest percentage of time is spent in individual ideation and judgment. In effect, the procedure introduces *additional* creative effort into conventional problem-solving procedures.

### How Is the Problem Identified?

In preparation for a brainstorming session the leader selects a *specific,* as opposed to a general, problem. The problem, "How can I write a better term paper?" is too broad. To narrow the problem two or three subproblems might be formulated: How can I improve my paragraph structure? How can I create and hold interest? How can I pinpoint major ideas?

When the problem has been reduced to its lowest common denominator, the selected subproblem(s) is posed as a concise, definite question. Questions of what, why, where, when, who, and how often serve to stimulate ideation on a problem. For example: Why is it needed? Where should it be done? Who should do it? How should it be done?

### How Is the Group Prepared?

New participants need to be conditioned for their initial session. A warm-up practice session on a simple problem will stimulate the production of ideas. For instance: "How could the classroom seating be improved?"

It seems profitable to supply the group with a background memo of not more than one page in length at least two days in advance of the session. The memo serves to orient the participants and to let them ponder over the problem in advance of the experience. Contained in the memo is a statement of the question or problem and a few examples of the type of ideas desired. An example follows:

> *Problem:* How can I pinpoint major ideas?
>    1. In the classroom
>        Write out my thought before expressing it.

2. In written papers
     Use short subheads.
3. In conversation with friends
     Enumerate my points with 1, 2, 3, etc., designations.
4. In my home
     Imagine that I am my own most interested listener.

Participants should not be permitted to read off their lists of ideas, however. Such lists should be handed to the leader in advance of the activity.

### What Is the Leader's Role in a Brainstorming Session?

In preparation for the actual brainstorming session, the leader explains and writes out four basic rules which must be faithfully followed:

1. *Criticism is ruled out.* Adverse judgment of ideas must be withheld until later.
2. *"Freewheeling" is welcomed.* The wilder the idea the better; it is easier to tame down than to think up.
3. *Quantity is wanted.* The greater the number of ideas, the more the likelihood of useful ideas.
4. *Combination and improvement are sought.* In addition to contributing ideas of their own, participants should suggest how ideas of others can be turned into *better* ideas; or how two or more ideas can be joined into still another idea.

Brainstorming must be kept informal, except for a recorder or two who keeps a written record of all ideas produced. Its function is idea-finding—not to deal with problems which primarily depend upon judgment.

The leader can develop his own list of suggested solutions to the problem. They are to be used, however, only for "pump priming," i.e., when the flow of ideas slows down. He should also be prepared to suggest leads by way of new categories or classifications which might open up new lines of thought.

The setting for brainstorming should be informal and relaxed. Following a short explanation of the problem, a list of the four basic rules (indicated in the first part of this section) is made plainly visible. The chairman explains that he will give a specified signal, like knocking on his desk, when a member violates any of the rules. Only one idea is offered at a time by any individual. The leader especially encourages ideas directly sparked by a previous idea. Perhaps a snap of the fingers can designate such association ideas. If several people desire to speak at once, the participants are encouraged to jot down ideas before they are forgotten. Because ideas tend to be contagious and many persons often desire to speak at once, groups of about ten to fifteen are best adapted to the technique. Much larger groups, however, have been effective under the direction of expert leaders.

The leader sometimes will want to repeat ideas as another spur to creative thinking. His objective is to "milk the group dry of ideas." In addition to opening up new channels of thought, he keeps prodding with, "What else?" "I cannot believe that you have expressed all your ideas?", etc. Short, silent periods are to be expected as participants cast about for ideas. It is usually in the later stage that the most unique and useful ideas emerge. Most ideation sessions will not exceed fifteen minutes. If the group is large and/or if more than one subproblem needs exploration, two or more subgroups may be utilized.

### How Are Afterthoughts Utilized?

In closing the ideation session it is interesting to ascertain the number of ideas produced. This serves to stimulate individuals to think further on the problem. The recorder(s) can quickly scan the ideas for categories. A glance at the full list usually indicates from five to ten classifications. The leader asks the participants to keep the problem on their minds until the next day, when they will be asked for afterthoughts. This can be made as a definite assignment. Such an incubation period sometimes produces some of the most valuable of all the ideas.

Sometimes referred to as the individual ideation or brainstorming session, the process can be further stimulated by offering "spurring" questions to elicit additional ideas. Thinking of one of the illustrated problems, "How can I pinpoint major ideas in writing term papers?" some or all of the following "spur" questions might be introduced. How can I:

| | |
|---|---|
| adapt? | substitute? |
| magnify? | rearrange? |
| modify? | reverse? |
| minify? | combine? |

—in a manner to better pinpoint ideas in writing term papers? Students have reported that what have turned out to be their most valuable ideas have often come as a flash of insight when they were making no conscious effort at ideation. Oddly enough, sleep seems to induce this sudden flash of illumination. Perhaps the idea will come during the middle of the night. It is extremely important that such ideas be recorded at the time or they may be forgotten entirely.

### How Are Ideas Processed?

After all ideas (including afterthoughts) have been assembled, they are screened, edited, and placed in appropriate categories. While this may be done by the entire group, it is usually preferable to utilize a committee of from three to five students. The teacher will usually want to assist in this process. It is usually desirable to establish a list of criteria for evaluation of ideas. One group established the following:

1. The idea must be concisely stated.
2. It should be feasible.
3. It should possess some element of the unusual, the novel.

The committee must exercise due caution in the elimination of ideas. Some of the "wildest ideas" may contain elements of imagination which will not be obvious at first glance. Sometimes it may even be desirable for the committee to brainstorm one or more of these "wild" ideas which hold a certain degree of fascination but are not readily understood by the group.

The deferred judgment characteristic of creative problem solving is culminated in this, the judgmental phase, of the process. Unique ideas which are generated during the brainstorming processes may be lost if imagination is not properly applied to the processing of ideas. By asking each individual to especially note any ideas which come to him as a flash of insight, his idea(s) can be amplified for the benefit of committee deliberations.

### How Are Ideas Implemented?

How a group uses the ideas of a brainstorming session is largely dependent upon its purpose. In most class settings such experiences are designated to suggest new and novel ideas for some necessary class activity. For example, the task may involve techniques of oral or written expression in art, literature, or music. It may involve novel ways of obtaining proper physical exercise, of memorizing, of doing some chore. It may even deal with certain aspects of human relations, such as how to maintain poise when one is made angry. Whatever the purpose may be, ideas must be implemented. This may be accomplished on an individual basis or in subgroups. Sometimes the fruits of various action programs may be shared with the class. On other occasions they may be of a private nature and may not be shared with anybody else except the instructor.

By way of illustration, "How can I pinpoint major ideas in writing term papers?" each student may be asked to write a paper employing one or more ideas generated earlier. Perhaps a short supplementary statement concerning his reactions to the new application would be appropriate. Several such experiences might be necessary for providing each individual with an opportunity to discover those techniques which might be most beneficial to him.

As a culminating experience, the group may draw generalizations, based upon various action programs. This enables all members to profit from the experiences of many. Certain experiences may set the stage for the enactment of one or more selected situations for further study and analysis. Sociodrama (described in a separate chapter) has been most useful in this connection.

## PLANNING FOR BRAINSTORMING

Although the ideation session is characterized by informality, the entire brainstorming experience must be carefully planned. The plan, illustrated below, indicates one way of stimulating a group to creative activity. Since the creative act is in itself a unique experience to the individual involved, the brainstorming method will take on many different dimensions, depending upon the purpose being served.

LESSON PLAN ILLUSTRATION (art class)

**Concept:** The expressive power of a linear statement is limited only to the artist's imagination.

**Problem:** What everyday sights can be expressed in terms of line?

**Goals:** After this lesson the student should further appreciate the role line plays in artistic creations, as evidenced by:
1. His production of ideas in the ideation session.
2. His use of these ideas in his own artistic creation.

*Lesson Approach:*

As has been previously pointed out, a line is defined as a point moving through space. Line is distinguishable from shape in that length is greater than breadth. Therefore, line tends to emphasize movement or direction. In the course of everyday experience we come across many beautiful and interesting expressions based on lines. Frequently, however, such experiences are so commonplace that they may go unnoticed. Have you ever thought of common visual experiences in terms of line and line alone? It is possible to project a line on, around, across, through, in, out, between, by, within, over, and under anything that we perceive visually or can perhaps imagine only. Today we will attempt to verbalize our visual or imagery experience in a series of descriptive phrases which point out the variety and moods of line. Such lines compose the structural essence of beauty as we perceive it in our everyday lives. The experience should set the stage for later production of our own creative artistic productions.

For the next few minutes we are going to "storm the brain" for ideas involving line. This is a "fun" type of experience if we abide by four simple rules. (Put on board.)
1. Criticism is ruled out.
2. "Freewheeling" is welcomed. (The wilder the idea the better.)
3. Quantity is desired.
4. Combination and improvement of ideas are sought.

(Appoint recorders from opposite sides of the room.)

I will knock on my desk when one of the rules seems to be violated. Just snap your fingers when you desire to express a "hitchhike" idea.

*Lesson Development:*

What everyday sights can be expressed in terms of line? Suggested categories (to be inserted as the flow of ideas diminishes):
1. Motion
   The line following the path of a football player as he tumbles through the air in a graceful inertia on a slow-motion TV camera shot.
2. Silhouette
   The scene of a distant horizon at sunset.
3. Flight
   The line formed by a spiraling eagle soaring high in the sky.
4. Sound (or heat) waves
   The line created by an auctioneer as he calls for bids.

UTILIZING AFTERTHOUGHTS:

Now that it seems as if our group is "dry" of ideas, let us determine how many have been produced in the last fifteen minutes. (Ask recorders to give the number and to suggest categories.) Do you suppose that we *could* produce even more ideas if we were really to try? That is just what I want you to do.

ASSIGNMENT:

Let us each write out our problem and the categories suggested by our recorders. Keep the problem in mind until tomorrow when I will call for your additional ideas. Just keep your mind open, jotting down ideas as they occur to you. Such afterthoughts may occur to you when least expected, so keep pencil and paper near you at all times.

PROCESSING IDEAS: (second day)

(Take up lists of additional ideas and pass along to the recorders.)

I am appointing a committee of five to screen, edit, and categorize your ideas of how line can be expressed. (Instructor will assist the committee as needed.) We will each receive a reproduced list of this master list.

IMPLEMENTING IDEAS: (third and fourth days)

Study our list of ideas and check two or three of these which you wish to use for an artistic expression of line.

ASSIGNMENT:

Your task is to produce at least one drawing from a suggested idea. Keep in mind that the idea may be expanded and altered as you apply your imagination. You should write out the original idea on the back of your drawing, however. We will then let the class try to relate our line production to our list of ideas.

*Deriving Generalizations:*

As a result of this experience a number of principles or ideas are evident, relative to line. Let us list some of these:

SUGGESTIVE IDEAS (to be derived by students):

1. Line expresses life.
2. Line exists in everything that we can visualize or perceive.
3. Line exists in infinite variety.
4. Perception of line may set the stage for artistic expression.

## How May Synetics Be Employed in the Ideation Process?

An ideational technique, somewhat related to brainstorming procedures, has been employed for many years by the Arthur D. Little Company, Cambridge, Massachusetts. Originally under the direction of William J. J. Gordon and sometimes known as the "Gordon Technique," the approach was designed to emulate the procedures that inventors apparently employ.[5] Synetics means

[5] For a thorough description of the technique, the reader should consult William J. J. Gordon, *Synetics* (New York: Harper and Brothers, Inc., 1961).

"the joining together of different and apparently irrelevant elements." Although utilized as a group technique, like brainstorming, its fundamental rules of operation are equally applicable to problem solving by an individual.

As an operational procedure, synetics depends heavily upon two mechanisms: making the strange familiar, and making the familiar strange. The objective is to rid one of conventional or habitual ways of viewing problems.

When confronted with a new problem the "strange may be made familiar" by searching for similarity. Is not this actually an old problem in disguise? Seeing even partial resemblances may lead to an application of familiar methods in solving the new problem. A new and difficult biological term, for example, usually contains elements of familiar terms.

Making the familiar strange is a way of eliminating preconceptions and habitual patterns of thought. In a speech class, for example, a conventional problem might be, "how can enunciation be improved?" An unusual, but perhaps equally fruitful, problem might be, "How can one communicate without enunciating?"

To attain the goals of making the familiar strange and the strange familiar, four main approaches have been employed: personal analogy, direct analogy, symbolic analogy, and fantasy. *Personal analogy* involves personal identification of oneself with an object, event, or thing. To illustrate: "If I were an automobile without wheels, how would I go from place to place?"

*Direct analogy* is perhaps best illustrated by Alexander Graham Bell's description of his invention of the telephone.

> It struck me that the bones of the human ear were very massive, indeed, as compared with the delicate thin membranes that operated them, and the thought occurred that if a membrane so delicate could move bones relatively so massive, why should not a thick and stouter piece of membrane move my piece of steel . . . and the telephone was conceived.

*Symbolic analogy,* as described by Gordon, is usually a visual image. He uses the following example: "How to invent a jacking mechanism to fit a box not bigger than four by four inches yet extend out and up three feet to support tons?" Thus the principle of the hydraulic jack was born.

*Fantasy* as used in synetics involves freeing the imagination from the bounds of a given word or concept. Specific physical laws are imagined not to apply. For example, "What would happen to a given land formation without the influence of the pull of gravity?"

It would appear as if the synetics technique might, on occasion, be used in conjunction with a brainstorming session when many novel ideas are sought. It is essentially a technique of freeing the individual from habitual and mundane ways of thinking.

## What Individualized Techniques Are Useful in Creative Endeavor?

Both brainstorming and synetics are useful solo experiences. In fact, originators of the techniques repeatedly emphasize the importance of individualized ideation practice. Although lacking the benefit of ideas sparked by others in an ideation session, solo practice can be employed informally when a problem arises.

It is estimated that tremendous creative potential is lost by inadequate planning. Although there is no established pattern for activating one's imagination, there are a number of guidelines which many creative minds have found effective, some of which follow.[6]

1. *Making a start.* Many individuals feel a vague urge to cope with a problem from time to time. Too often, however, a person defers action until he is "in the mood," or until he can "find the time." There is no substitute for getting started!
2. *Making notes.* Most really creative individuals carry a pencil and note pad with them at all times. Whenever they attend a lecture or meeting of any kind they take notes of ideas which are prompted.
3. *Setting deadlines and quotas.* In a sense this is a form of self-discipline. Deadlines and quotas intensify emotional power because we thereby make ourselves vulnerable to the fear of failure to meet our self-concepts. The pressure of deadlines tends to force one to become more efficient in daily routines which take time away from creative effort.
4. *Fixing a time and place.* We should take time for thinking up ideas! It has been suggested that this activity might well precede routines. By setting a time and place for such cognitive thought one may "lure the muse." Some people allow ideas to *incubate* by napping, listening to soft music, or by just sitting quietly in a dark corner. Of course, sudden illumination can come at *any* time, even in the middle of the night. Here again, a handy pencil and note pad ensures retention of an idea that might not be recalled otherwise.

The classroom teacher must assume responsibility for guiding youngsters into fruitful avenues of creativity. Although originality and creative imagination are private, individual virtues, guidance and training *can* substantially increase one's output, as in any other area of education. Too often the able, self-motivated person is permitted to shift for himself while attention is focused on the less able and less motivated student.

## How Can Creativity Be Fostered Informally in the Secondary School Classroom?

Although organized techniques such as brainstorming can do much to enhance the discovery of ideas, they are much more effective when creative processes are encouraged in all instructional activities. All instructional methods treated in this book involve some form of creative or reflective thinking. As such, they each involve skills of idea generation as the very core of the problem-solving process. If the stage is set for "bold guessing," each such experience will be more effective than might be expected when such acts are inhibited.

[6] Alex F. Osborn, *Applied Imagination,* 3rd Revised Edition (New York: Charles Scribner's Sons, 1963), ch. 15.

Experts on creativity repeatedly stress the importance of discovering *both* problems and solutions. Original ideas not only should be encouraged but should be actively sought. For example, a student who is to make an oral report might be encouraged to add his personal evaluation and to employ any unique techniques that he might conceive. Too often correct thinking—problems requiring one solution and one method—has been emphasized. Alternative solutions to a problem need not have been previously suggested by others to be viable. Indeed, alternatives should be solicited from the students that will not be found in any textbook.

Creativity can be encouraged by simply welcoming and reinforcing introduction of new ideas. Such ideas can be weighed on the basis of their own merits. It should be emphasized that most creative achievements seem revolutionary when first introduced.

> When John Kay invented the flying shuttle, it was considered such a threat to labor that weavers mobbed him and destroyed his mold. When Charles Newbold worked out the idea of a cast-iron plow, the farmers rejected it on the grounds that iron polluted the soil and encouraged weeds. In 1844, Doctor Horace Wells was the first to use gas on patients while pulling teeth. The medical profession scorned his new ideas as a humbug. When Samuel P. Langley built his first heavier-than-air machine—flown by steam—the newspapers dubbed it "Langley's folly" and scoffed at the whole idea of self-propelled planes.[7]

Rather than presenting fact or theory, the teacher might turn it into a problem for the class to solve. Rather than providing students with information, he can place them in situations where they are forced to seek out the information for themselves.

Above all, creativity involves self-direction. From time to time, students should be placed on their own to work on projects. Sometimes he must be permitted to make his own mistakes, to toy with ideas, and to follow up hunches which may not at first seem promising. Students, in turn, will be encouraged to evaluate for themselves the fruits of such endeavor. Curiosity acts as a spur to problems which others have taken for granted. By constantly probing with such questions as "What would happen if? . . . curiosity can be enhanced.

Perhaps the greatest deterrent to creativity is its effect upon the conventional teacher. Ideas tend to "pop up" at any moment, often catching the teacher by surprise. All too frequently such behavior may be mistaken for impertinence on the part of the student. An unexpected suggestion of a unique way of handling a problem or assignment, for example, can imply (to the teacher) that his own way of handling the situation is deemed to be inadequate. Actually, such a suggestion may merely reflect an individual's private "brainstorming" of an idea. Such brainstorming may be encouraged by permitting the individual (and the group which may be involved) to develop a plan for putting the idea to work.

[7] *Ibid.,* p. 54.

## VALUES

Applied imagination, through brainstorming, may open doors to truly creative individual effort.

The ideation session tends to minimize existing inhibitions which ordinarily tend to block creativity.

Brainstorming is useful in piling up alternatives to the resolution of problems. Effective problem solving is necessarily limited by the possible solutions perceived by the individual(s) involved.

The brainstorming experience tends to generate enthusiasm for learning. By capturing the imagination, most students progress at an accelerated rate.

## LIMITATIONS AND PROBLEMS

Despite the many values of group brainstorming, individual ideation is usually more valuable and can be just as productive. Actually the process incorporates both individual and group ideation in a threestage approach: individual ideation, group brainstorming, individual ideation.

The effectiveness of a brainstorming session is dependent upon the appropriateness of the problem employed. There is a decided tendency among teachers to select complex, as opposed to simple, problems.

Production of ideas through brainstorming is merely an initial phase of creativity. Analytical problem-solving techniques must complement production of ideas.

Brainstorming places the leader (teacher) in a new role. Instead of passing judgment and suggesting direction, he must develop an atmosphere of freedom from existing inhibitions. Some teachers (as well as students) experience difficulty in making such a transition.

## ILLUSTRATED BRAINSTORMING MEMOS

I.   Useful in history, government, art, and social studies classes

*Concept:* Man's history is recorded in his art.

*Problem:* How can man leave history for succeeding generations?

*Suggested categories:*
1.  In space
       Equip a special space capsule and put it in an earth orbit.
2.  In the earth
       Construct and equip a special cave with typical artifacts of our civilization.

        3.  In polar regions
              Construct a model city under the ice pack.

  II.  Useful in home economics, child development, sociology, and psychology classes

     *Concept:* Through play, the child develops an ability to create, to reason, and to talk.

     *Problem:* How may dolls contribute to growth and development?

     *Suggested categories:*
        1.  Role-playing
              Child may play roles of members of his immediate family.
        2.  Social development
              Child learns to share with other children.
        3.  Intellectual growth
              Child develops skill in communication.
        4.  Physical development
              Child learns to care for himself as he cares for play objects such as dolls.

  III.  Useful in English, speech, and drama classes

     *Concept:* Voice projection is a basic aspect of communication.

     *Problem:* In what ways may one project his voice?

     *Suggested categories:*
        1.  With facial expressions
              Exaggerate mouth formation of key words.
        2.  With the diaphragm
              Talk with the chest cavity.
        3.  With body expressions
              Use hands to support the uttered thought.

# CHAPTER 11

# Questioning Strategies

## OVERVIEW

### Key Concepts

1. The questioning level employed, in large measure, determines the level of thinking elicited.
2. Appropriately phrased problem questions (e.g., policy questions for class discussion) set the stage for use of high-order questions.
3. Through appropriate probing techniques the learner may be encouraged to indulge in the higher process of reflective thought.
4. Higher-order questions necessarily incorporate the lower levels of cognition.
5. Since evaluation questions call for personal reactions, they necessarily overlap with the affective domain.

### New Terms

1. **Recall Questions**—Questions which call for the recitation of specific facts, principles, or generalizations. Usually characterized by such words as *who, what, when,* and *where.*
2. **Comprehension Questions**—Questions which call for understandings, demanding manipulation of data through interpretation, summarization, example, and definition. Usually characterized by such key words as *how* or *why.*
3. **Analysis Questions**—Questions which call for taking apart data for the purpose of discovering hidden meaning, relationships, or basic structure. Characterized by using *established criteria* for discovering assumptions, motives, implications, issues, logical fallacies, and so forth.
4. **Evaluation Questions**—Questions which call for judgments, opinions, personal reactions, and criticisms, based upon the *learner's own cri-*

*teria.* Usually characterized by such key words as *should, could, would, in your opinion,* and so forth.

5. **Problem (Policy) Questions**—An open-ended type of question, often *preplanned* by the teacher, which forms the basis for an instructional experience. Often begins with the word *what* but sometimes may begin with such key words as *why* or *how.* The word *should* or *ought* is stated or implied in the question.

6. **Probing Techniques**—Asking intermediate questions, providing cues or hints, or asking for clarification after the student indicates his inability to respond effectively to an initial question. The technique is designed to lead the learner to the original question by capitalizing upon existing knowledge and understanding.

7. **Redirection**—Involving more than one student in the answer to a question. Such questions often involve several "reasons" or "factors," differences of opinion, and so forth.

### Questions to Guide Your Study

1. Review the cognitive, affective, and psychomotor domains of educational objectives (treated in Chapter 2). Why is the question taxonomy developed in this chapter based upon the cognitive domain only?
2. How would you judge the adequacy of responses to comprehension questions? Analysis? Evaluation?
3. "The bulk of any discussion should focus upon comprehension questions." Defend or refute.
4. Distinguish between probing and redirection. What factors will determine whether one will probe or redirect?

Questioning is the heart of teaching. It is involved in some way with every method and technique described in this book. Indeed one might say that a teacher is (or should be) a professional question maker. Asking questions is one of the most effective means of stimulating thinking and learning.

Analysis of classroom discourse (of both teacher and students) has revealed at least twelve areas of communication employed as one teaches. Most of these areas (such as defining, classifying, comparing, evaluating, etc.) involve the use of questions. The evidence indicates, however, that the average teacher is no more skillful in this vital aspect of teaching than his students or other laymen. Thus when instruction falls into logical or linguistic traps the teacher often is unable to handle the situation effectively. Accordingly, this chapter provides assistance in an area often neglected in instructional methods classes. Questioning techniques do not constitute a distinct instructional method; rather they constitute basic features of all methods.

## FUNDAMENTAL PROPERTIES

Each instructional method is developed within a framework of critical thinking processes. The classroom question constitutes the teacher's major tool for encouraging such thought processes. There are many different kinds of questions, each of which elicits different kinds of responses. If, for example, a teacher would emphasize the mere recall or memorization of facts, he will emphasize one type of question. If analysis and application are to be stressed, however, he will focus upon a different mode of questioning strategy. Fundamentally, the different kinds of questions parallel the different levels of cognition, described fully in Chapter 1.

## What Are the Properties of Recall Questions?

The process of critical thinking begins with data or facts. Factual questions often involve the key words of *who, what, when,* and *where.* There is but one correct answer. The student is merely required to recall or recognize information. The category includes recall of facts such as dates, events, persons, places. Also included is recall of basic principles and generalizations. It must be remembered, however, that unrelated facts are quickly forgotten. Moreover, memorized knowledge may not represent a very high level of understanding. Above all, concentrating on memory neglects other intellectual processes learned through practice. Solving problems is learned by actual practice rather than by memorizing the inductive conclusions derived by others.

Although a necessary starting point, the conscientious teacher is careful to avoid relying too heavily on such low intellectual level questions. In short, recall questions most appropriately serve as a means of guiding the learner into the higher intellectual processes of thinking. As the learning experience progresses, emphasis will tend to shift to higher order questions.

## What Are the Properties of Comprehension Questions?

After the learner gives evidence that he has the essential facts well in hand, questions to determine *understanding* are asked. Comprehension questions characteristically require the learner to *manipulate* information. He must relate facts, generalizations, definitions and the like by bringing in relationships between ideas. Key words in this category are *how* and *why.* Whereas recall questions call for remembering, comprehension questions call for manipulation and modification in some way. To illustrate:

1. What factors contributed to Mr. Nixon's presidential victory in 1972? (Involves recall of text materials.)
2. How were the campaigns of Mr. Nixon and Mr. McGovern related? Different? (Involves a comparison of the two campaigns.)

Although the foregoing illustrations appear to be characteristic of the two levels cited, the first question could be comprehensive in nature if the student must draw inferences from various media sources. If, however, the answer is to be found in the textbook or if the information has been previously presented in a lecture or report the question is merely one of recall. Likewise, the second question may be a memory item if the answer has been previously given to the student. Thus the *conditions of a question* must be known before it can be accurately classified. Question classification is merely a tool for recognizing the thought processes involved in answering them. For convenience, application-type questions are included as a form of comprehension. (See a summary of the Bloom taxonomy, pp. 23-24). The same kind of reasoning is involved except that the student is not informed relative to the specific idea or concept to be applied.

Comprehension questions may be subdivided into four groups: interpretation, summarization, example, definition. The first of these, illustrated above, asks the student to show relationships between facts or ideas. He may show likenesses, differences, cause-and-effect relationships, or comparisons. Summarization merely requires the student to restate ideas in his own words. Examples call for an illustration of the idea involved. Finally, the student may be expected to formulate his own definition of some idea. (It cannot be one that has already been given.)

A major element of questioning tactics is knowing when and how to introduce higher order questions. A comprehension question, for example, may elicit a recall response or perhaps a personal reaction. In such cases the teacher should probe for the analysis expected. Thus a series of questions may be initiated.

### What Are the Properties of Analysis Questions?

The process of analysis involves taking apart information and making relationships. The purpose is to clarify by discovering hidden meaning and basic structure. The student is able to read between the lines; to distinguish between fact and opinion; to assess degree of consistency or inconsistency. The science student, for example, is able to distinguish between relevant and extraneous materials or events. Likewise, the social science student is able to detect unstated assumptions.

Whereas comprehension questions emphasize *understanding,* analysis questions *involve seeking out underlying relationships and organizational patterns.* Certain key words suggest analysis. Among these are assumptions, motives, implications, identification of issues, logical fallacies, and processes of induction and deduction. Analysis questions ask the student to solve a problem by conscious observance of *established criteria.*

It should be emphasized that analysis questions follow questions of comprehension. The reader will recall the comprehension question cited earlier: "How were the campaigns of Nixon and McGovern different?" An analysis question could then be asked: "What *implications* can be drawn relative to Mr. McGovern's defeat?" (This assumes that the available implications have not been drawn by others.) As a general rule, analysis questions require the student to detect a logic or relationship between variables. The hidden motives, assumptions, implications, and the like are not the product of wild or even individual speculation, however. They follow established rules of logic and must be consistent with the known facts. The adequacy of responses is judged on the basis of their consistency with these views and conditions.

## What Are the Properties of Evaluation Questions?

It should be noted that the Bloom taxonomy makes two distinct categories that are here included under evaluation. These categories are labeled *synthesis* and *evaluation*. Synthesis is seen as a process of reassembly for new meaning. Thus the learner may develop new or creative ideas—ideas which were not apparent previous to this time. At this point in the critical thinking process he offers proposals for solving the problem under consideration. Closely followed is the related aspect of evaluation in which the learner critically examines the proposals offered through analysis. Evaluation may be deferred as in the case when the objective is to generate as many ideas as possible. Frequently, however, evaluation follows immediately after an idea is proposed. Often this is accomplished in a *single student response*. For this reason the processes of synthesis and evaluation are treated as a single aspect of questioning technique.

Evaluation questions call for comments involving judgments, opinions, personal reactions, and criticisms. Responses are judged on the basis of stated criteria. These criteria may be imposed by the questioner or they may be advanced by the respondent. Such questions usually include or imply such key words as *should, could,* or *would.* Questions as "In your opinion . . ."; "What is your personal relation . . ."; "How would you evaluate . . ."; "Do you think . . .", tend to call for evaluations. Unless otherwise indicated, the student should state his opinion and then provide a basis for such views. It becomes apparent that there is no one "right" or "wrong" answer to such questions. Answers are judged on the basis of how well the response was "defended." Sometimes a teacher may ask a student to state his views from a given frame of reference. In such cases the views are defended and judged on the basis of the given framework. "If a presidential election were held today *what do you think* would be the major issues?" In this case the student would be expected to *state and support* his views. The question could be stated in another way, however. "If a presidential election were held today, how would you evaluate the influence of militant groups on the outcome?" In this case the answer must be defended from a provided frame of reference.

Evaluation questions involve both the intellectual and the emotional. Accordingly, some responses will tend to be highly biased and opinionated. While this is to be expected on occasion, continued emphasis on acceptable criteria is needed.

## What Are the Properties of Problem Questions?

Although evaluation questions are considered to represent the highest order of complexity, some attention should be directed to those problem questions used as a starting point for most instructional methods. The various methods treated in subsequent chapters are developed within a broad framework of critical thinking or problem solving. Those which embody the entire problem-solving process are developed from broad problems of policy. A problem of policy is an open-ended question which implies a needed change from the status quo. It often begins with the word *what* but may begin with such key words as *why* or *how.* The words *should* or *ought* are also stated or implied in the question. For example, "What action should be taken to provide compensatory education for minority groups?" It is assumed (by the wording of the question) that some further action is needed.

A problem of policy is most effectively treated when certain definable steps are followed. Each instrumental method has its own unique problem-solving approach. Each level of questioning, previously described, usually will be employed. To illustrate from the above example:

1. What is meant by compensatory education? (Recall question)
2. Why is compensatory education needed? (Comprehension question)
3. What assumptions are made relative to the benefits of compensatory education and minority groups? (Analysis question)
4. In your judgment, should compensatory education be made available to adults and children alike? (Evaluation question)

It should be noted that several or even all of the questioning levels may be employed in each phase of the problem-solving process. Greater emphasis will be placed on certain questions at each level, however. For example, during the earlier part of a discussion recall questions will receive considerable emphasis.

*Problem questions must be carefully preplanned.* If such questions are ill-conceived, the subsequent problem-solving experience is of limited value. The most common error results from confusion between certain types of evaluation questions and questions of policy. An evaluation question, in effect, tends to deal with one possible solution to a problem, whereas a policy question opens the door to any number of possible solutions. In the foregoing illustration, for example, one possible solution could be to make compensatory education a pre-school requirement for all minorities. Sometimes the teacher, due to his own advance understanding and/or existing biases, may word the problem as an evaluation-type question. To illustrate: "Should compensatory education be made a preschool requirement for all minorities?" Under such conditions, discussion tends to be limited to the merits and limitations of the one proposal. Some issues of course may have developed to the point that the adoption or rejection of a proposed course of action is all that must be resolved. In this case a debate is in order. Such questions seldom provide an appropriate setting for discussion and related methods.

## QUESTIONING TECHNIQUES

An understanding of question levels is but a small part of the art of questioning. As previously indicated, questioning techniques are directly or indirectly associated with all the "logical areas" of communication. The techniques described in this section should be useful in establishing and maintaining a climate of continuous critical thinking whenever class questions are utilized.

## How Is the Quality of Student Responses Enhanced?

Probing for more adequate answers is a well known but often neglected technique. Socrates, who lived in the fourth century B.C., became famous for his skill in eliciting correct responses through probing procedures. Probing involves a question or a series of questions addressed to the *same* student. It is used when an initial response is inadequate. There are two principle types of probing: *prompting* and *clarification.*

Prompting involves the use of short hints or clues when the student is unable to give an answer or gives an incorrect answer to a question. Prior to the prompting sequence it may be desirable to rephrase the question to be assured that the student understands what is being sought. Prompting involves a series of questions designed to elicit those things the student knows relative to the original question. Thus the procedure usually involves a series of *recall* questions, designed to lead the student back to the original question. The procedure is used when the student is suspected of possessing the necessary background knowledge for handling the question. It is designed to guide him in the critical thinking processes. To illustrate:

T: How does the principle of immunization work?
S: I don't know.
T: Using a smallpox vaccination as an example, what happens if the vaccination "takes"? (A different question, recall in nature)
S: One usually gets sick. He runs a temperature.
T: Good. Are there any other symptoms? (Recall question)
S: He develops a lesion at the place of the vaccination.
T: Fine. Now what does this suggest to you about smallpox? (Comprehension question)
S: That the individual actually has a mild case of the disease, I guess.
T: Your answer is basically correct. Why is an individual made immune to the disease? (Analysis question)
S: His body would build up defenses against the disease.

As the illustration suggests the student is not told that his answer is wrong. Instead he is encouraged or reinforced at every step along the way. This tends to help him build confidence in himself. Generally one should avoid interpreting or rephrasing the student's response. All too often a teacher will inappropriately pass on to another student if an answer is not immediately forthcoming. This tends to cut such an individual out of the discussion. In some cases about 10 percent of a class may make 90 percent of the contribution.

Clarification is a probing technique which calls for a restatement or expansion of a response. It is usually sought when the response is not incorrect but still does not measure up to the teacher's expectations. Instead of giving hints, the student is asked to improve his response. Such comments as the following are often used: "Explain"; "Would you restate your answer in another way?"; "What else can you add?"; "Are there other reasons?"

T: What happens in the body when a person is immunized?
S: Well, we are usually immunized against such diseases as smallpox and whooping cough.
T: These are good examples but what actually happens in the body when we are immunized against such diseases?

It may be necessary to do some prompting if the student is unable to clarify his original response satisfactorily.

### What Practices Tend to Enhance Questioning Effectiveness?

Before asking a question which demands considerable thought the teacher can suggest that he does not want an *immediate* answer. This tends to discourage aggressive, hand-waving students from intimidating quieter students who, if given an opportunity to collect their thoughts, might make valuable contributions. To illustrate: "I want you to think quietly on this for a moment . . . then I will call on someone." By training himself to look for facial expressions (especially the faces of timid students), the teacher can learn to read such facial expressions as "I am thinking about the question" even though a hand is not waving for recognition.

Another technique for enhancing questioning effectiveness is the practice of calling on *nonvolunteers*. When students realize that they are not likely to be called upon unless their hands are raised, they are likely to keep their hands down. The few students who do raise their hands tend to monopolize the experience. They are usually those who have a good grasp of the problem and who like the reinforcement provided. The teacher, in turn, is reinforced by the apparent group progress suggested by his volunteer respondents. Nonvolunteers, however, most need the experience of active participation.

Student participation is enhanced when both volunteers and nonvolunteers are asked to respond. The teacher can simply announce that he will call upon individuals whether their hands are raised or not. Some teachers have made use of a class observer whose task is to record tally marks on a seating chart for each contribution. The technique serves as a constant reminder of the need for involving as many of the group as possible. It also enables the teacher to objectively evaluate the extent of participation for any given lesson.

Another way of enhancing questioning effectiveness is through *redirection*. Teacher talk can be minimized by asking questions which elicit several responses. This may involve a question in which several "reasons" or "factors" may be requested, or it may be one in which differences of opinion exist. Different students are thus expected to offer "reasons" or "opinions." It may be necessary to cue the group to what is expected by saying, "This question has many parts to it. Please give only one when you answer." Redirection has the added advantage of encouraging students to respond to each other. (All too often the pattern is teacher question-pupil response, etc.)

Another rather obvious technique is that of stating a question prior to calling upon the individual who is to respond. Not only should this practice be followed, but the teacher should pause for a few seconds after he asks the question and before he calls upon someone to provide an answer. If the teacher designates a respondent *prior* to the question, the rest of the class will tend to relax and may not even "hear" the question. By pausing, each student is given time to organize his thinking for a thorough answer. It should be pointed out that the higher level questions usually demand a few seconds for meditation. Furthermore, a teacher who habitually cuts a student off before he is finished tends to discourage the shy. Moreover, he should avoid interpreting a student's response to fit his own criterion of acceptability. The student who tends to experience difficulty in expressing his thoughts may be encouraged to write them out prior to expressing them verbally.

Too often neglected is the relationship of questions to individual differences. Although dull students can handle higher order questions, they cannot be expected to bring in the degree of association expected of bright students. Likewise, some students tend to be more adept at divergent thinking than others. By adapting questions to the individual, greater attention to different approaches to an issue can be gained.

## What Techniques Tend to Interfere with Effective Questioning Practices?

Sometimes one may fall into the habit of *repeating questions* before a student is asked to respond. The problem seems to be related to a certain lack of security residing with the teacher. Most individuals, for example, who talk excessively experience difficulty in expressing themselves effectively. Suspecting this, they keep talking, hoping to add clarity with more words. Unfortunately, the end result is often increased confusion. Such a person is likely to ask a question and then ask it a second time using slightly different wording prior to calling on a student. The practice of calling on nonvolunteers can contribute to the problem. A nonvolunteer may or may not be following the proceedings. By professing not to hear or understand the question, he "saves face" temporarily. In such instances, the teacher can immediately move to another student, without repeating the question. Thus the behavior is not reinforced; neither is teacher talk increased.

The practice of *answering one's own questions* is a particularly annoying habit which is unfortunately difficult to correct. It too seems to be tied to a basic psychological need of the questioner. By inviting student responses, a discussion, to some extent at least, becomes unpredictable. It is frequently impossible to complete a discussion as planned. Certain unexpected questions and/or responses tend to throw the discussion "off." And of course it is rather bothersome to probe for adequate answers. Nevertheless, the practice tends to be self-defeating since it definitely increases teacher talk and minimizes student volunteering. Moreover, students are likely to expend less effort in preparing for such experiences since the teacher will "answer his own questions anyhow." Students learn that if they wait long enough the teacher will do their work for them!

Perhaps the most common obstacle to effective questioning technique is the tendency to *repeat student response*. This may be considered appropriate for clarity or for more effective comprehension. Indeed, both are legitimate reasons and, on occasion, may render such a practice desirable. If student answers are repeated often enough, however, students will tend to be satisfied with incomplete answers. As indicated in a previous section, incomplete answers usually call for probing techniques. Responses which cannot be heard in all parts of the room should be *repeated by the respondent*. Thus such original responses are not reinforced.

Some teachers even develop the habit of not listening carefully to student responses. If a pupil drops a few key words or phrases the assumption is made that the question was answered satisfactorily. This can seriously interfere with the reflective process. By maintaining eye contact, asking for a brief rephrasing of the response, and probing when necessary, teachers can encourage students to clarify meaning. Sometimes students may be asked to write out their responses before answering. A closely related problem sometimes arises when an unexpected response is made. Such responses, all too frequently, are brushed aside when, if they were probed, they might contribute immensely to class discussion.

A teacher can easily check up on himself by taping one of his lessons occasionally. When one listens to himself in this manner, he is usually shocked to recognize a number of annoying techniques. If a tape recording is not possible, another technique might involve the use of one or more student recorders. Once the teacher becomes aware of a problem he can easily correct himself by use of self-prompts. A game might be played in which he attempts to reduce these practices with each succeeding lesson.

## What Are the Mechanics of Appropriate Questions?

Many leaders encounter difficulty in developing reflective thought because of the way they phrase their questions. A question which calls for a "yes" or "no" answer usually discourages discussion. For example, the question "Do you agree with the present United States foreign policy toward Red China?" demands a supplementary "Why?"

Questions which reflect a given point of view or bias of the teacher are all too common. The question, "Why should we withdraw our troops from Indochina?" begs the answer. It merely consists of support for a given point of view. A similar question, "Should we allow this appalling situation to continue?" builds in a bias. Beginning teachers have been observed to ask many "Don't you think . . ." questions.

The manner of asking a question has a tremendous influence on the response. Enthusiasm, coupled with a practical, common sense approach (as opposed to textbook language) tends to prompt responses in mind. Closely associated with this is the technique of handling student questions (or responses) which are not germane to the immediate point of issue. It is usually desirable to encourage the respondent, but it may be inappropriate to digress at the time the question is introduced. In this situation an effective technique is to accept the question as being a good one but defer the answer for a few moments. If so, an acceptable reason must be provided; one must be sure to come back to the point as promised.

It should be pointed out that questions tend to create considerable anxiety or fear among some students. Inadequate preparation may be an acceptable reason for not responding to a recall question, but it need not eliminate such an individual from expressing his views on the matter after a proper foundation has been laid. Thus the teacher might well say, "Now that we have discussed some of the facts what is your personal reaction to the suggestion that. . . ." Such a procedure is likely to make all students feel freer to respond as they realize that the recitation of textbook materials is not expected.

## How May Students Be Encouraged to Generate Their Own Questions?

Critical thinking is encouraged through the artful use of questioning techniques. The ultimate goal of all instruction, however, is an individual who can himself ask the right questions and then proceed to answer them effectively. Certain instructional methods (e.g., Processes of Inquiry, described in Chapter 18) are designed especially for this purpose. Student questions should be encouraged at all times, however. Unfortunately, a question session usually follows the pattern of teacher question–student response, teacher question–student response, etc. By asking questions with multiple answers, as described earlier, the pattern may be modified into teacher question–student response, student response, etc. A more desirable pattern might be teacher question–student response, student response, student question–student response, etc.

All teachers are aware of those relatively few occasions when students have carried a discussion themselves, almost forgetting the presence of the teacher for a time. Unfortunately, such experiences are relatively rare and are rather difficult to analyze. Rosinger has developed a technique which he has found effective for expanding thinking.[1] He sees great potential for the technique in eliciting student questions. The approach involves taking all student answers to a specific test question and pooling them for the class. He retains the student's language as much as possible, excluding only those comments which are clearly contradictory to the situation posed. The technique suggests different ways that one might have responded to an "open-ended" question. This tends to encourage divergent thinking as described more fully in the chapter on creative teaching. The technique could be readily adapted to any questioning session.

---

[1] Lawrence Rosinger, "The 'Class' Answer as a Teaching Device," *English Journal* 57 (October 1968): 1032–35.

### What Preplanning Is Needed?

As indicated in the illustrated lesson plan provided for each instructional method, anticipated key questions and key responses should be preplanned. Unfortunately, this is a "two-edged sword." On the one hand, the procedure tends to stultify a discussion, making it a "cut and dried" affair—leaving little room for creative imagination. On the other hand, it provides a structured sequence which contributes to realization of instructional goals. The most appropriate practice, then, seems to consist of developing preplanned question *samples.* Some may not be asked or may be asked by students. The preplanned questions are merely indicative of type and sequence anticipated.

Anticipated student responses are less often needed. Sometimes, however, an anticipated answer may serve as a reminder of a line of thought which can be developed. They serve other purposes as well, such as suggesting question level. Analysis questions especially should be followed with probable student answers, since they must be judged against established criteria. As a general rule, questions should not be read directly from a lesson plan, nor should one attempt to elicit those anticipated responses suggested in preplanned materials.

## VALUES

Questioning techniques apply to all instructional methods. The success of any given instructional experience is largely dependent upon how questions are handled.

Critical thinking is encouraged through the artful questioning above the recall level.

Appropriate questioning techniques tend to make the learner independent of the teacher. Such growth is identifiable by a questioning pattern of teacher question-pupil response, pupil response, pupil question-pupil response, etc.

Adequate probing techniques enable the learner to judge the adequacy of his own response.

Individual differences may be handled in questioning sessions by the effective teacher. Some students are capable of grappling with thought-provoking questions, while others may be more adept at recall and comprehension responses.

## LIMITATIONS AND PROBLEMS

The foremost problem associated with questioning techniques is the tendency to emphasize recall only.

There is a tendency for teachers to "rush" pupil responses and to expect answers which fit the teacher's preconceived notions.

A common problem among teachers is to involve relatively few pupils in the questioning process.

Many teachers encounter difficulty in developing reflective thought within pupils because of the way they phrase their questions. A question which calls for a "yes" or "no" answer usually discourages discussion.

Teacher behaviors of repeating questions, answering one's own questions, and repeating pupil responses tend to be major obstacles to effective questioning processes.

## QUESTIONING ILLUSTRATIONS

I. Useful in English, speech, and foreign language classes
   A. Comprehension questions
      1. Compare the merits of placing topic sentences at the beginning as opposed to the end of a paragraph.
      2. How do Jefferson's ideas of democracy compare with democracy in our time?
      3. Why do rules of parliamentary procedure sometimes prevent the democratic functioning of an organization?
      4. How does a study of Spanish contribute to an understanding of the Spanish culture?

   B. Analysis questions
      1. What are the implications of the letters RSVP on a formal invitation?
      2. What assumptions are suggested when the writer says, "Each person must do his own thing"?
      3. What support can one offer for a planned land use program adjacent to major metropolitan areas?
      4. What are some of the motives for the Mexican-American minority's insistence that some classes be conducted in Spanish in Southern Arizona and Texas?

   C. Evaluation questions
      1. What is your personal reaction to the suggestion that informal modes of communication be emphasized in English classes?
      2. What do you think of Langston Hughes' hip language style of poetic expression?
      3. In your opinion did the editorial hit upon the basic issue?
      4. Should Spanish be taught most appropriately by a person of Mexican heritage?

II. Useful in science and mathematics classes
   A. Comprehension questions
      1. Compare the moon, Mars, and Venus with respect to their atmospheric pressure and distance from the sun.
      2. Give an example which suggests that our mountains are in constant state of evolution.
      3. Why is there a move in this country to switch to the metric system?
      4. How would you define a quadratic equation?

B. Analysis questions
1. What techniques are being used to persuade young people to quit or not begin smoking?
2. How are common respiratory diseases related to weather conditions?
3. What are the implications of requiring algebra and geometry for college-bound students only?
4. What assumptions can you make relative to ratio and proportion?

C. Evaluation questions
1. Do you think that cloud-seeding is ethically desirable?
2. In your opinion should overage stands of timber be selectively harvested in the nation's wilderness areas?
3. What is your personal reaction to the contribution of modern math to general mathematics understanding?
4. How would you judge the plausibility of your answer to a problem on factoring?

III. Useful in social science and home economics classes

A. Comprehension questions
1. Give an example of the abuse of the electoral college system of electing a president in modern times.
2. In your own words, define the culturally disadvantaged.
3. Compare the adjustment problems of growing up in the inner city with those of the suburbs.
4. Could you summarize the major differences between the family of today and that of the nineteenth century?

B. Analysis questions
1. What were some of the motives which influenced our attempts to reestablish diplomatic contacts with Communist China?
2. What assumptions seem evident from pleas to withdraw our forces from Vietnam immediately?
3. What are some economic implications associated with floating the price of gold on the world market?
4. What are the logical fallacies to the argument that family size should be limited to the number that can be supported effectively?

C. Evaluation questions
1. In your opinion would the two-China policy in the United Nations General Assembly have been effective?
2. Should an avowed Communist be permitted to teach at a state university?
3. Do you think that the Supreme Court should be permitted to reinterpret the law?
4. What is your personal reaction to liberalized abortion laws?

IV. Useful in skills classes (physical education, art, music, and business)

A. Comprehension questions
1. How does a planned program of daily exercise affect the circulatory system?
2. How might one express personal emotions and feelings with color?

    3. Compare rock and western music with respect to tempo.

    4. Define, in your own words, John K. Galbraith's economic policy.

B. Analysis questions

    1. What are the assumptions associated with the plea for each person developing interest in some physical activity?

    2. What mood implications are apparent in Van Gogh's *The Orchard?*

    3. What are the motives behind the founders of rock music?

    4. How does an advertisement depicting a famous athlete using a special hair spray create a desire in men to purchase the product?

C. Evaluation questions

    1. Should a physically handicapped individual be exempted from physical education classes?

    2. What is your personal reaction to Paul Klee's *Girl with Jugs?*

    3. Who do you feel is the best contemporary musician in America today?

    4. Do you think that tobacco advertisements should be banned from magazines?

# CHAPTER 12

# Sociometric Techniques

## OVERVIEW

### Key Concepts

1. Through appropriate sociometric techniques, social problems may be identified.
2. Sociometric grouping is based upon the assumption that one works most effectively with his preferred associates.
3. An isolate or neglectee usually chooses one of the most popular individuals; such selections are usually most able (psychologically) to cope with the particular adjustment problems involved.
4. Sociometric grouping is merely a first step in helping boys and girls adjust to the dynamics of the peer group.

### New Terms

1. **Sociometrics**—Those techniques designed specifically for building and improving social relations.
2. **Isolate**—An individual who is not chosen by any other class member in response to a given sociometric criterion question.
3. **Neglectee**—An individual who is low (has only one or two choices) on a given sociometric criterion question.
4. **Sociometric Star**—An individual who is chosen by many of his classmates on a given criterion question.
5. **Criterion Question**—The specific question upon which teachers base sociometric techniques. Such questions should refer to a specific class situation which is anticipated.

6. **Matrix Table**—A table upon which both chooser and chosen patterns are recorded. Such an analysis is necessary for construction of a sociogram.
7. **Sociogram**—A "blank target" upon which sociometric data are depicted. As one moves from the outer edge toward the "bull's eye" he is able to note relative sociometric standing, ranging from low to high acceptability.

## Questions to Guide Your Study

1. Some teachers contend that sociometric grouping can be effectively simplified by letting students choose their groups directly. Evaluate this statement.
2. "Some isolates may not be true isolates." Defend or refute.
3. How might one develop a sociometric study around a situation that is considered "too hot to handle"? (Race relations, for example.)
4. Since sociometric status is subject to change, what impact does this have on the teacher who would group students accordingly?

Mr. Johnson had observed his social studies students for six weeks. He had permitted the students to select their own seats. In his own words, "For the first few weeks a youngster needs the security of his friends." Now he thought it was time to revise the seating arrangement. He was anxious to separate a few close friends and two or three tight cliques. Mr. Johnson believed that in this way the apparent social exclusiveness could be substantially reduced. This, in turn, should promote learning.

A few days after the new seating arrangement was effected Mr. Johnson again took stock of the situation. Things were not going as well as he had hoped. The group as a whole seemed to be restless. Someone seemed to be constantly giggling, shoving, or otherwise interrupting. Those who had been separated from close friends seemed to be looking for excuses to work together. Certain people who had formerly been trying to attract attention were still disturbing. In general, class atmosphere seemed to have deteriorated. Few seemed able to do better work, while some were making less progress than formerly.

Mr. Johnson's difficulties are little different from those encountered by thousands of beginning teachers every year. What are some of the aggravating causes of the problem? What is there about the social structure of a group that may build or destroy a desirable class atmosphere? Can a teacher somehow gain control of the interplay of forces going on in the social group? Fortunately, during the past two or three decades a great deal has been discovered about the interactions of the adolescent peer group. A more systematic approach to the building of good human relationships might have saved Mr. Johnson a lot of worry and frustration. This chapter offers a technique for recognizing and controlling the dynamics of the peer group which is frequently not fully understood by beginning teachers.

The word *sociometry* is derived from Latin and means literally *social or companion measurement*. The term has become closely identified with the *sociometric test,* originated and popularized by Jacob L. Moreno.[1] Actually it is not a test in the common sense of the word, but a technique or method. *The sociometric test (technique or inventory) is designed to evaluate the feelings of the group on the basis of a given situation.*

*Sociometry, then, would include all techniques for determining social status within a given group.* Some of these, such as various teacher-observation and pupil-reporting procedures, have long been used in the classroom. The emphasis here, however, is on more recent sociometric techniques which have contributed to a simple, yet highly satisfactory, approach to the improvement of social relationships.

# FUNDAMENTAL PROPERTIES

Sociometric techniques are based upon the premise that both social and academic learning are accelerated by recognizing and making use of friendship patterns and encouraging the development of others. An additional premise, supported by considerable research, is that teachers are often unable to determine social needs by observation alone. Thus sociometry may effectively supplement such techniques.

## What Is the Influence of Peer Relations on Learning?

One of the most compelling psychological needs is that of social acceptance. At adolescence this need comes into sharp focus as the teenager attempts to establish acceptable relations with his peers. Everything, including academic performance, takes second place to this continuing quest for acceptability.

Teachers have long recognized the influence of the peer group on almost all aspects of adolescent living from dress codes to morality. Oddly enough, however, the influence of the peer group on academic performance has frequently been completely disregarded. Indeed, teachers usually have attempted to break up friendship bonds (disturbing elements) as soon as they are detected. Sociometry, contrarily, is designed to cultivate and use friendship preferences as an instructional tool for effective learning.

## Why Is Sociometric Data Confidential in Nature?

Although secondary students are frequently less tactful than most adults, they are particularly sensitive to divulging their friendship preferences. Thus sociometric data must not be sought until rapport has been established. Even so, confidential nature of the data must be emphasized. (While some inferences can be made on the basis of new groupings, based upon sociometric data, such indirect knowledge is not particularly threatening.)

[1] Jacob L. Moreno, *Who Shall Survive?* (Washington, D.C.: Nervous and Mental Disease Publishing Co., 1934).

### How Are Sociometric Data Helpful to Isolates and Neglectees?

Basically sociometric techniques are designed to assist the identification of those individuals who are chosen by none of the group (isolates). The common practice of permitting students to sit by or work with whomever they prefer is an effective means of contributing to the social interaction of *those who are already accepted.* It does nothing for the isolate, however. Accordingly, the basic rule of sociometry is to place the isolate with his *first* choice. This rule should not be violated unless the isolate's first choice specifically rejects him.

A sociometric star is one who is selected by many individuals in the group. They provide actual or potential leadership for the group. The class isolates and neglectees (those who receive only one or two choices) usually choose a sociometric star as their first choices. This apparently is due to the fact that the sociometric star's popularity is a basic factor of his superior psychological adjustment. He does not usually find it necessary to deliberately hurt other, less popular, individuals. Accordingly, such an individual is likely to be most able to assist those who are experiencing difficulty in adjusting to the peer group.

### How Is Broadened Student Interaction Facilitated?

The school, sometimes referred to as a miniature society, provides an ideal testing ground for social interaction. Bias and prejudices, however, are acquired prior to the high school years. Consequently, they will be reflected through the nature of all interaction patterns and will merely be solidified if allowed to develop spontaneously.

As integration of minorities into the schools is accelerated, a systematic plan for integrating such persons into the social structure of the school must be effected. Accordingly, tight cliques, divulged through sociometric data, often should be broken up. This can be accomplished while at the same time honoring at least one friendship preference of each student. It has been observed that students who work together frequently develop friendship bonds where none originally existed.

### How Stable Are Friendship Patterns?

Friendship patterns of young children change from day to day and month to month. By the time they reach high school age, however, they become relatively stable. Changes do occur, as with adults, sometimes rather suddenly. Generally, a sociometric test and regrouping arrangement should be repeated every six to eight weeks. One can usually expect, within this time interval, the number of isolates to drop from about five to one, while the number of mutual choices will be increased from 25 to 35 or more. An individual who insists upon a sudden shift from one group to another should be accommodated. Experience indicates that such requests are seldom made, however.

# SOCIOMETRIC PROCEDURE

Sociometric data are extremely easy to obtain. The mere identification of social preferences, however, is merely a starting point. Thus emphasis in this section is placed upon the use of such data in building healthy relationships.

## What Constitutes an Appropriate Criterion Question?

Teachers frequently want to arrange students sociometrically for specific purposes, such as traveling companions on a school trip or for temporary buzz groups. Although such specific situations meet the necessary requirement of realism, they are of minimal value for diagnostic purposes. The most stable and generally useful results are obtained from a general criterion question. The above questions can be expanded as follows: What individuals would you prefer to be with while on school trips? Whom would you prefer to work with on committees?

Generally the criterion question must indicate the nature of the activity or situation to be applied. It should be one that is thoroughly familiar and realistic to students. It must be general enough to minimize the influence of transitory interests and should provide opportunity for mutual association and interaction.

Research generally has indicated that the main aspects of personal and social relationships are included in the general areas of seating, play, and work. Thus three criterion questions are needed if the entire range of class interaction is sought. Use of questions demanding psychological analysis should be avoided. For example, the criterion question "Which individuals make you feel most secure?" should *not* be used.

## How Are Sociometric Data Obtained?

The sociometric test (inventory) is a flexible procedure which can be administered in a matter of minutes. Directions may be oral, or a sociometric form may be constructed. In any event, the directions may be somewhat as follows:

> During the next three or four weeks we will be working in groups of five. Each group will have a selected problem to solve. This will involve a number of activities, such as making outlines and plans, reading books, interviewing people, collecting pictures and illustrations, and combining and evaluating the materials. Finally, each group will be responsible for presenting its findings to the rest of the class. These activities will involve a lot of teamwork. Some jobs will be hard; other jobs will be somewhat monotonous. It has occurred to your instructor that we might enjoy this work more and have better cooperation if we were permitted to work with our preferred choices. What do you think of the idea? (Responses are nearly always enthusiastic.)

Now, let us remember that if we are to accept the privilege of working with our preferences we must also accept the responsibilities which go with it. In other words, each person must do his share in helping his group and the entire class complete its job. This means that we must guard against wasting time discussing nonrelated topics; that we must work quietly enough to allow other groups to do their jobs too. One who, through his behavior, demonstrates his inability to accept these adult responsibilities will be deprived of this privilege.

Indicate on a sheet of paper the names of five people you would prefer to work with on committees such as this one. Indicate the order of preference of your choices. We will make every effort possible to place you with one or more of your choices when groups are formed. It is impossible to give everyone his first choice but each person will get at least one of his five choices. *Your choices will be kept strictly confidential.*

## How Are Sociometric Data Analyzed?

Sociometric test results from a class of thirty-five or more students can discourage the most conscientious teacher unless easy analysis of the data can be developed. Frequently the matrix table is used as the first step in such an analysis. This is merely a twofold table which shows the choices each person has given and received. The teacher who desires to make a thorough evaluation of interpersonal relationships will find the matrix table or some related graphic presentation a valuable tool.

Forms may be prepared and reproduced in quantity. The following steps are useful guidelines.

1. List names of students in alphabetical order. Then number consecutively from top to bottom.
2. Number consecutively across the top of the page.
3. Draw a diagonal line from the upper left to lower right corner of paper. This serves as a focal point for identifying mutual choices. It bisects the squares not used.
4. Provide for a "total" column at bottom of page.

Table 12–1 has been completed with the appropriate sociometric data included. Bill chose the following individuals: Clark, Howard, Otis, Mike, Virginia. His choices were recorded by entering, across from his name, number one in column five, indicating Clark. Number one is used in Clark's column because it was his first choice. Likewise, number two is used in column seven to indicate Howard as his second choice. Accordingly, the numbers three, four and five are placed in Otis's, Mike's, and Virginia's columns respectively to indicate his third, fourth, and fifth choices.

After all choices are recorded it becomes apparent that choices given go across the table, whereas choices received go down the table. Mutual choices

**TABLE 12–1.** Matrix table

PUPILS CHOSEN

| Chooser | | 1 | 2 | 3 | 4 | 5 | 6 | 7 | 8 | 9 | 10 | 11 | 12 | 13 | 14 | 15 | 16 | 17 | 18 | 19 | 20 | 21 | 22 | 23 | 24 | 25 | 26 | 27 | 28 | 29 |
|---|---|---|---|---|---|---|---|---|---|---|---|---|---|---|---|---|---|---|---|---|---|---|---|---|---|---|---|---|---|---|
| Bill | 1 | | | | 1 | | 2 | | | | 4 | | | | 3 | | | | | | | | | | | | | | | 5 |
| Ben | 2 | | | 1 | 2 | | | | | | 4 | | (3) | | 5 | | | | | | | | | | | | | | | |
| Dick | 3 | | 5 | | 4 | (1) | | | 2 | 3 | | | | | | | | | | | | | | | | | | | | |
| Chris | 4 | | | | | (2) | | | | | | | | (3) | (1) | | | | | | | 4 | | | | | | (5) | | |
| Clark | 5 | | (2) | (3) | | | 4 | | (1) | | | | | | | | | | | | | | 5 | | | | | | | |
| Gam | 6 | 5 | | | 3 | | | | | (1) | | | 2 | 4 | | | | | | | | | | | 5 | | | | | |
| Howard | 7 | | | | | | | | 4 | | | | 1 | 3 | | | | | | 2 | | | | | 5 | | | | | |
| Lucky | 8 | | | | (2) | | | | | | | | | | | 1 | (3) | | | | | 4 | | | | | | 5 | | |
| Mack | 9 | | | 1 | 4 | (5) | | | | | | | | 3 | | | | | | (2) | | | | | | | | | | |
| Mike | 10 | | | 2 | 1 | 4 | | | | | | | | 3 | | | | | | 5 | | | | | | | | | | |
| Mitchell | 11 | | | | | | 3 | 4 | | 2 | | | | 1 | | | | | | 5 | | | | | | | | | | |
| Morris | 12 | | (3) | | | | | | 1 | | | | | 2 | | | | | | | 4 | | | | 5 | | | | | |
| Mund | 13 | | 5 | | (1) | | | | | | | | | | | | | | | (4) | | (3) | | | | | | (2) | | |
| Nagy | 14 | | | 5 | (3) | | | | | | | | | | | 4 | | | | | | (2) | | | | | | (1) | | |
| Otis | 15 | | | 3 | | 1 | | | | | | | | 2 | | | | | | | | 5 | | | | | | 4 | | |
| Paul | 16 | 5 | | | 1 | | | | | | | | | 3 | | | | | 2 | | | | | | | | | 4 | | |
| Porkey | 17 | | | | | | | | (4) | 5 | | | | 2 | | | 3 | (1) | | | | | | | | | | | | |
| Tommy | 18 | | | 5 | 2 | 4 | | | | | | 3 | | | | | | | (1) | | | | | | | | | | | |
| Tonky | 19 | | | | | | | | | | (1) | | | (2) | 3 | 5 | 4 | | | | | | | | | | | | | |
| Wes | 20 | | | | | 2 | | 4 | | | | | | | 1 | | | | | | | 3 | | | | | | 5 | | |
| Grace | 21 | | | | | 3 | | | | | | | | | | | | | | | | | (4) | | 2 | (1) | | 5 | | |
| Lucy | 22 | | | | | | | | | | | | 5 | (2) | (3) | | | | | | | | | | | (4) | | (1) | | |
| Linda | 23 | | | | | | | | | | | | | | | | | | | | | (5) | 2 | | | (4) | | (1) | (3) | |
| Rana | 24 | 3 | | | | | | | | | | | | | | | | | | | | 4 | | | | 2 | (5) | | | (1) |
| Rachell | 25 | | | | 4 | | | | | | | | | | | | | | | | | (1) | (5) | | | | | 3 | | (2) |
| Sally | 26 | | | | | | | | 2 | | | | | | | | | | | | | (1) | | | 5 | (3) | | 4 | | |
| Sonya | 27 | | | | (4) | | | | | | | | | (5) | (2) | | | | | | | (1) | (3) | | | | | | | |
| Tam | 28 | | | | | | | | | | | | | | | | | 1 | | | | | 2 | (4) | | | | 3 | | 5 |
| Virginia | 29 | | | | | | | | | | | | | | | | | | | | 5 | | 4 | 2 | (3) | (1) | | | | |
| TOTAL | | 3 | 4 | 4 | 12 | 8 | 5 | 2 | 8 | 4 | 4 | 0 | 4 | 11 | 7 | 5 | 1 | 3 | 3 | 4 | 3 | 2 | 12 | 7 | 2 | 7 | 2 | 12 | 2 | 4 |

may be identified and circled. This can be readily accomplished by using the diagonal as a focal point to find the vertical column indicating those who chose a given pupil. Mack, for example, chose Chris, Clark, Gam, Nagy, and Tonky. By following the vertical line of number nine (Mack's number) it is seen that Mack was chosen by Dick, Gam, and Tonky. Two of these individuals, Tonky and Gam, were also chosen by Mack. Thus mutual choices have been circled in *both* horizontal and vertical columns.

Finally, the choices received are totaled at the bottom of the page. The teacher is now able to determine the sociometric status of individual pupils, but before he can arrange appropriate groups he must make use of a *sociogram* (see Figure 12–1).

The *sociogram* is designed to portray the indicated group social structure. It is a blank target. Each circle except the outer one is an equal distance apart. The vertical line through the center of the diagram is to separate the sexes, as there tends to be a sex cleavage at all ages. The numbers along the line below each

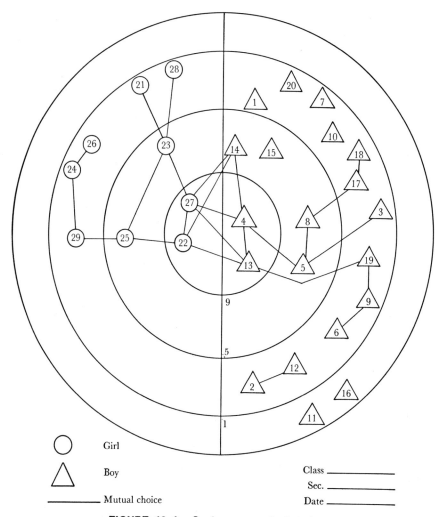

**FIGURE 12–1.**  Sociogram—mutual choices

circle indicate the choice levels for each of the circles. The numbers are based on Bronfenbrenner's fixed frame of reference.[2]

Pupils receiving one or no choices would be placed in the outer ring of the diagram; those receiving between 1 and 5 would be placed in the next ring and so forth. The sociogram may be plotted easily by beginning with the least chosen students and moving toward the most chosen students.

It will be noted that mutual choices only have been indicated. This provides a clear picture of the indicated group social structure with a minimum of

---

[2] N. L. Northway, "A Method for Depicting Social Relationships Obtained by Sociometric Testing," and U. Bronfenbrenner, "The Graphic Presentation of Sociometric Data," from Norman E. Gronlund, *Sociometry in the Classroom* (New York: Harper and Row, Publishers, 1959), p. 69.

effort. When it is desirable to ascertain one-way choices the matrix table may be reviewed. The resourceful teacher usually has a number of blank sociogram "targets" duplicated and ready for use.

Sometimes teachers may desire a simplified method of grouping students sociometrically. For the purpose of expediency only, the matrix table may be bypassed. In such cases the papers (indicating student choices) may be sorted into groups by casual inspection. In most cases there are three or four ill-defined groups indicated. The next step is to pick out the most highly chosen individuals of each group in preparation for the construction of a sociogram. The sociogram may consist of symbols with lines and arrows to indicate mutual and one-way choices. Three choices can be readily plotted in this manner; this will produce the data needed and can be completed very quickly. After some experience, the author was able to complete such an analysis in about twenty minutes with groups ranging from thirty-five to forty in number.

## How Are Groups Rearranged Sociometrically?

After sociometric data have been analyzed, the first step in improving social relations is that of putting student choices into effect. Sociometric information should not be considered the sole basis for the rearrangement of groups but a valuable guide. The teacher attempts to develop more satisfying social relationships as well as a cohesive group structure. The following steps are recommended for sociometric grouping:

1. Decide the size of the groups to be formed. Work groups of five are often satisfactory.
2. Give unchosen pupils (isolates) their highest choices. Honor their first two choices if possible, but avoid placing two isolates in the same group whenever possible. Never place more than two isolates in a single group.
3. Consider those who received only one choice (neglectees). If the choice should be reciprocated, put him with the other person involved, regardless of the level of choice.
4. Continue to work from the least chosen to the most chosen individuals. In each case attempt to satisfy mutual choices first.

A number of other considerations should be taken into account when groups are being formed:

1. When more than two choices are possible, attempt to give them to isolates and neglectees.
2. When group cleavages exist it is often desirable to formulate groups with a view of minimizing them. Some such cleavages may be socioeconomic, sex, race, rural-urban, and the like. There should be a minimum of two from such subgroups to provide additional security to those involved.
3. Sometimes it is desirable to break up tight cliques. A typical work group, thus formulated, may have one or two isolates or neglectees, one highly chosen individual, and about two pupils of average choice status. Variations can be expected, of course.

## What Follow-up Techniques Are Recommended?

The mere process of organizing sociometric groups is no guarantee of successful interaction, especially for isolates and neglectees. Such individuals hold low social status for some reason(s) that they are unable to understand or correct. Thus careful observation of these persons is essential. Gronlund[3] offers some guidelines which should prove helpful in analyzing and understanding such students:

1. Does the pupil voluntarily withdraw from social interaction or does he attempt to establish social contacts with other pupils?
2. Are there any obvious reasons for the pupil's social isolation (e.g., physical handicap, inadequate attention to cleanliness, lack of social skill)?
3. Does the isolated pupil enjoy constructive, individual activities, or does he appear unhappy in his position of isolation?
4. Does the pupil reflect a need and desire for social acceptance by making excessive efforts to obtain the approval of the teacher?
5. Do any of the class members initiate social interaction with the isolated pupil? How does he react to their efforts?
6. How do the class members react to the isolated pupil's attempts to initiate social interaction with them?
7. What type of social contacts does the isolated pupil seem to have outside the classroom? Does he play alone on the playground? Does he walk home alone? Does he have friends in other classes?
8. Is there anything notable in the isolated pupil's social behavior that can be used as a basis for helping him build better social relationships?

Following a period of careful observation a conference or conferences with pupils becomes essential. The nondirective approach usually is preferred in such cases. The teacher usually desires to find out how the pupil feels about his peers, himself, and his social acceptance. The pupil should not be informed of his low social status. Emphasis is placed on his attitudes and feelings and the degree to which his social aspirations are consistent with his social reality.

Low social status may be a normal phenomenon with the child. Some people, by preference, enjoy pursuing individual interests. If so, little need be done. Other individuals withdraw from social contacts because they lack self-confidence. They are generally unhappy people. Such individuals need social acceptance. There also is the aggressive person who tends to be rejected by his peers. This student needs guidance into more socially acceptable behavior. Finally, there is the cultural isolate. In this case emphasis probably should be placed on altering group attitudes toward cultural and racial differences.

There are any number of additional techniques which may be utilized to help the unpopular student gain acceptance. One of the most valuable approaches involves the use of sociodramatic experience which will be described in the following chapter. Another approach involves helping such pupils attract favorable recognition from their peers. Many times situations can be arranged which afford an opportunity for one to demonstrate a skill which is highly

[3] Gronlund, *Sociometry in the Classroom,* pp. 273–74.

valued by the group. Collections, special knowledge, and the like fall into this category. As previously indicated, sociometric regroupings must be done every six to eight weeks.

## VALUES

Sociometric techniques help the teacher identify students who need assistance in social relationships.

Likewise, sociometry discloses potential social leaders (referred to as stars). With secondary students especially, development of social sensitivity is most effectively accomplished indirectly through social leaders.

Sociometric procedures reveal the existence of existing group cleavages, such as social cliques, minority groups, religious and cultural minorities, and the like.

Sociometric techniques provide a necessary starting point for developing adequate social interaction patterns.

## LIMITATIONS AND PROBLEMS

Use of unrealistic criterion situations (e.g., "Whom would you like to travel with to the North Pole?") may seriously limit the value of sociometric results.

Validity of sociometric choices is dependent upon rapport established in the class situation.

Some isolates or neglectees may not be "true" isolates or neglectees. Their preferred choices may just happen to be in other classes.

A low sociometric rating does not necessarily indicate social difficulties. An occasional isolate, for example, may be alone by choice.

## SOCIOMETRIC ILLUSTRATIONS

I.  Seating Arrangements

One of the most common applications of sociometric data is a revised seating pattern. This is especially useful when the chairs (and tables) are movable and when considerable seat work is anticipated. It has been observed that the "natural" pattern of seating produces a definite hierarchical structure. The most competent and articulate students are easily detected as a group just as its counterpart stands out. Usually near the back of the room, the isolates and rejects come together—not because they really want to be together but because this seems to be their only place. By placing a highly chosen student at each table (of five or six) those low in sociometric status may be helped in their quest for social acceptability.

II.  Forming Subgroups

This is probably the most frequent use made of sociometric results. Subgroups of about five are ideal for maximum interaction. Some variation in size may be necessary, however, in adjusting to sociometric preferences. Generally one or two highly chosen students will be grouped with one or two isolates or neglectees. The remaining numbers may consist of those who fall between the two extremes.

If some systematic plan for subgrouping within a class for academic purposes is planned (as described in Chapter 6), students still can be temporarily grouped sociometrically for specific purposes. (Seating arrangements *within the basic subgroups* also can be worked out.)

III.  Social Roles Testing

Although emphasis in this chapter has been placed upon choices based upon a specific criterion question, there are times when it is desirable to obtain a more generalized type of personal-social assessment. One such technique is a social roles test, designed for the purpose of obtaining an indication of those who are best in group-approved social activities. (By inference, those at the other extreme can be easily identified.)

The instrument consists of four or five key questions such as the following:

1.  Which individuals are best at sharing their experiences with others?
2.  Which ones tend to make the best contributions to class discussion?
3.  Which ones are best at helping you with class assignments?
4.  Which ones usually have something interesting to tell about outside of the classroom?

Such an instrument provides information needed in helping individuals improve their social functioning. It has the advantage of providing a more comprehensive picture of one's social adjustment than is provided through use of a specific criterion question.

IV.  Working with Stars

Although one's first concern in sociometry must be with the class isolates and neglectees, some attention should be given to class stars. Often a star will need some encouragement in assuming desirable leadership roles. Although popularity alone does not indicate leadership ability, such potential usually can be found among the highly chosen individuals. Leadership potential can be developed. Furthermore, repeated sociometric testing sometimes reveals that a star suddenly loses his status. Such sudden drops in popularity must be investigated and assistance rendered.

# CHAPTER 13

# The Sociodramatic Method

## OVERVIEW

### Key Concepts

1. A simulation of reality may be superior to reality itself for instructional purposes.
2. Role-playing is merely a vehicle for portraying a selected life situation.
3. Sociodramatic problems must be immediate to the lives of those involved; one does not play his own life role, however.
4. "Success" or lack of success in the dramatization has no bearing on the usefulness of the experience for class analysis.
5. Analysis of the dramatized situation emphasizes factors which contributed to actual feeling reactions.

### New Terms

1. **Sociodrama**—A spontaneously enacted situation (usually five to ten minutes long), depicting an actual life problem which is used for study and analysis.
2. **Role-playing**—The enactment phase of a sociodrama, sometimes referred to as a skit.
3. **Verbal and Nonverbal Cues**—Subtle hints which suggest emotional reactions to events during the dramatization.

### Questions to Guide Your Study

1. How might one develop a sociodramatic situation around an issue that is considered "too hot to handle"?

2. "Students should select their own sociodramatic situations." Defend or refute.
3. "Sometimes a student might be selected for the dramatized situation." Defend or refute.
4. Under what conditions should an enactment be stopped?

In sociodrama, role-playing is used as a vehicle to portray a situation for study and analysis. It involves the spontaneous enactment of a realistic life problem in the realm of interpersonal relationships. When used effectively it may enable the learner to improve his response to a situation, to increase his repertoire of responses, and to increase his sensitivity to the feelings of others.

## FUNDAMENTAL PROPERTIES

Any meaningful portrayal of a selected life experience depends upon its immediacy and relevancy to the lives of those involved. Almost any concept can be related to problems of everyday living so long as the learner is able to project himself into the situation. The properties which follow seem essential to a realistic setting.

### How Is Student Readiness Determined?

When the learner recognizes inadequacies of previous behaviors, he is challenged to seek new ways of coping with situations. Various techniques can be used to create an awareness of inadequate understanding of a concept. In a family living class, for example, the following concept may be involved: Empathic ability aids in the resolution of different points of view. To test readiness or determine present level of understanding, the learner may be shown a film and asked to cite evidence of empathy or lack of it and to identify factors that appeared to block the empathic process. Other techniques might include a case analysis, written examples from past experience, or an open-ended problem situation. The learner may be asked to indicate how he would react to a problem situation and then asked to designate those behaviors which show empathic ability. Such experiences help the learner realize his need for expanding his understanding of the concept and for improving his skill in applying appropriate principles in the area.

### What Affective Considerations Are Important?

Problems of interaction are usually associated with man's inability to understand the impact of human emotions. Thus a dramatized situation is usually structured around a conflict situation, the resolution of which demands some insight into basic needs of the other person. The basic objective is to determine the impact of specific events upon feeling reactions of those involved.

### What Constitutes a Realistic Situation?

A situation, close to the lives of the students, is a basic essential of the sociodramatic experience. Unlike drama, which often re-creates scenes far removed from student experiences, the sociodramatic situation is developed from the everyday lives of those involved. For example, one does not play a role of George Washington, of the Queen of England, or even of some local adult figure. An adolescent plays roles which are within the realm of his personal experience. He does not play an identifiable life role which may, in effect, subject his own inadequacies to public display.

### Why Must the Situation Be Simple?

Although human interaction varies from the simple to the complex, analysis is greatly facilitated when the situation is kept as simple as possible. Situations involving two students are usually preferred. Additional players not only complicate the analysis but also may place one member of the cast on the defensive unnecessarily. There seems to be a tendency to "gang up" on the underdog. Sometimes additional players may be added if the situation is replayed.

### Why Must the Situation Be Spontaneously Enacted?

The situation for enactment is not rehearsed. Indeed, the participants are selected immediately after the situation has been developed. After one has been projected into his role, the way it is played is not a critical issue. The individual is instructed to react to the situation as he feels at the time. If certain comments or inferences have a positive reaction, for example, he will reflect this through his own behavior just as any individual might behave. Likewise, feelings of indifference or even negative reactions are reflected through various behaviors. One makes no effort to telescope such feelings, however. They are allowed to develop in as natural a manner as possible.

## SOCIODRAMA PROCEDURE

Sociodrama should be conceived as a series of steps with each step necessary to a successful learning experience. Inasmuch as the method focuses upon human emotions, careful planning is essential if a sound psychological climate is to be maintained.

### How Is the Problem Identified?

From his identified concept, the teacher formulates a problem to be solved. After students are made aware of their present inadequacies in the area, the problem is placed on the board for all to see. From the concept, *Empathic ability aids in the resolution of different points of view*, the following problem might be evolved: "How can we further appreciate another person's point of view?" In this manner, students are made aware of the concept to be learned in language that they can understand.

Sometimes the course content will appear less directly related to the lives of students than is evident in the preceding illustration. A World History class, for example, could take up the following problem: "How should the United States assist the emerging nations to become economically independent?" It is necessary to help students become aware of the extensions of such a problem to their own lives. One extension of such a problem could be: "How does a paternal relationship make others feel?" The more immediate problem is used as a basis for development of the sociodramatic experience.

### How Is the Situation Developed and How Are the Players Prepared?

The specific situation for enactment is based upon the felt needs of the learner. For example, the teacher may ask, "What instances can you call from your own lives which illustrate lack of empathy?" He then suggests that one of these be acted out through a skit. The broad situation may be developed by students (with teacher guidance), or it may be preplanned by the teacher. If the broad situation is preplanned by the teacher, students should assist in developing details of the situation. In conventional fifty-minute class periods the teacher may want to define the broad situation so that the experience can be completed within a single class period.

To illustrate, using the problem of empathy: Someone (or the teacher) may suggest a situation where the daughter is serious about a boy and her parents disapprove of him. The broad situation is then placed upon the board.

> Susie, a high school senior, has been dating Tom for more than a year.
> He is in college.
> They would like to become pinned, with the possibility of marriage within a year.
> Susie decides to discuss the matter with her parents.

At this point, students fill in some details of the situation, such as where and when the discussion takes place, Susie's age, something of Tom's character, ambitions, professional plans, and possibly some characteristics of his parents.

After assuring the group that one's acting ability is not to be evaluated, a volunteer cast is selected. Susie (the one who is to lead the conversation) is then asked to leave the room while the class adds additional points relative to the situation as seen by the parents. These would be factors and feelings that would definitely influence the situation but would not be fully appreciated or understood by Susie. For example: They have never taken Susie's romance seriously. They consider him a fine fellow but not for her. While they would prefer that she finish college, they would not object to her marriage within a year or two. For Susie, they would like an ambitious fellow who would fit in well with the rest of the family.

### How Is the Class Prepared for Observation and Analysis?

The class is asked to watch for clues which are indicative of the situation as it develops. What questions or comments seem to contribute to or detract from the development of empathy? What clues are (or are not) pursued? What behaviors indicate that Susie (or her parents) did or did not understand each other's feelings? Why did you identify with either Susie or her parents? How else might the situation be handled to show empathy?

### What Factors Are Important During the Enactment?

Prior to the return of the leading character, the teacher helps the other players identify their roles. He may briefly summarize the situation or he may merely ask two or three leading questions. To illustrate: What do you think of Tom? What plans do you have for Susie's education? What type of person do you want her to marry?

(Susie is called into the room.) The teacher then prepares Susie for the role she is to play. How old are you? How long have you been dating Tom? How well has he been doing in college? How ambitious is he?

The players are instructed to react to their role situations just as the events make them feel. The drama continues uninterrupted for some five or ten minutes. Action is cut when enough of the scene has been portrayed to enable the audience to analyze the situation.

### How Is the Situation Analyzed and Discussed?

When the drama is stopped, the teacher will want to ask three or four key questions designed to draw attention to the situation. The following are suggested:

1. Might this situation actually have occurred? (A "yes" answer is expected.)
2. (To those reacting to the situation) How did you feel as the situation developed?
3. (To the leader of the situation) Did you feel as if you were making progress?
4. (To the class) What clues did we get which may account for these feelings?

The class then recalls comments and nonverbal expressions which reflected changes in feeling reactions. The players are used as resources to substantiate various forms of the analysis. Attention is continually directed to the processes of interaction; criticism of how the roles were played is forbidden.

Finally, after the enacted situation has been thoroughly analyzed, some attention is directed toward other approaches which might have been employed. It is sometimes desirable to replay the situation.

### How Is the Situation Expanded to Related Situations?

Following the analysis, students must be made aware of the variety of similar situations which could have been selected for analysis. Thus they recognize the generalizability of the concept. Empathic ability, for example, is needed in a wide variety of interaction situations. These include other adult groups, other adolescent situations, and contacts with younger children.

### How Are Generalizations Derived?

As a culminating activity, students are asked to formulate generalizations from the experience. Generalizations should apply equally well to any number of related situations. Students may be asked to perform this task individually by writing them out, or they may do it jointly through class discussion. In any event, generalizations represent the basic learnings which result from the sociodramatic experience.

To illustrate:

1. Empathic ability is increased when one attempts to reflect the feelings of the other person(s) involved.
2. Communication channels are opened when the other person(s) is given an opportunity to talk freely.
3. Words, phrases, or facial expressions sometimes reveal hidden feelings.
4. An apparent willingness to compromise may open the door to greater understanding.

## PLANNING FOR SOCIODRAMA

The illustrated plan is designed to clarify further the essential steps of employing the sociodramatic method of teaching. Although each teacher will eventually develop his own techniques in the area, none of the steps included in the "Lesson Development" can be safely omitted.

LESSON PLAN ILLUSTRATION (family living class)

*Concept:* Empathic ability aids in the resolution of different points of view.

*Problem:* How can we further appreciate another person's point of view?

**Goals:** After this lesson the student should have increased his sensitivity to the feelings of others, as evidenced by:
1. His ability to detect clues to hidden feelings.
2. His ability to identify specific comments or nonverbal behaviors which influence empathy.
3. His ability to derive valid generalizations as a result of the experience.

## Lesson Approach:

In our study of empathy as a process of interaction, we saw a need for increased understanding of how empathy operates in a real-life situation. Perhaps we can take a problem-situation, act it out, and then analyze it in relation to the use of empathy. What situation would you like to take? (Students) Let's take a situation in the family where the daughter is serious about a boy and her parents disapprove of him. (Other students give approval.) Fine. We will develop the situation that follows.

## Lesson Development:

BROAD SITUATION:

Susie, a high school senior, has been dating Tom for more than a year.

He is in college.

They would like to become pinned, with the possibility of marriage within a year.

Susie decides to discuss the matter with her parents.

DETAILS OF THE SITUATION: (Class develop.)

Concentrate on general aspects of all parties involved, e.g., Susie, Tom, her parents.

THREAT REDUCTION

In this type of experience no one is to be criticized on his acting ability. There is no right or wrong way of doing this.

SELECTION OF PLAYERS:

Volunteers (One should not be permitted to play his real-life role.)

SEND LEADING CHARACTER FROM THE ROOM.

FILL IN ADDITIONAL DETAILS: (By class)

Why do Susie's parents object to the marriage?
What elements of social status are involved?

PREPARATION OF CLASS FOR OBSERVATION AND ANALYSIS:
1. Jot down key words and phrases that seem to affect feelings—either positively or negatively.
2. Note expressions on students' faces.

WARM UP THE PLAYERS:
1. Who are you?
2. What time of day is it?

DRAMA (No more than ten minutes)

ANALYSIS OF THE SITUATION:
1. How did the drama come out?
2. How did you feel? (To each of the players in turn)

3. What clues did we get which may have accounted for these feelings?

RELATED SITUATIONS:

What similar situations can you recall which illustrated empathy or a lack of it?

*Deriving Generalizations:*

What generalizations can we draw from this experience which might also apply to many other related situations?

EXAMPLES:

1. Empathic ability is increased when one attempts to reflect the feelings of the other person(s) involved.
2. Communication channels are opened when the other person(s) is given an opportunity to talk freely.

## VALUES

Sociodrama provides the learner with new insights into possible responses to social situations.

The method increases one's sensitivity to the feelings of others in conflict situations.

Through sociodrama, an individual is able to project himself into the shoes of another. Realism is maintained without the usual threat to one's personality which characterizes analysis of actual life situations.

The enactment of selected situations provides a rare opportunity for discussion of actual feeling reactions.

CONCRETIZES THE ABSTRACT

## LIMITATIONS AND PROBLEMS

The sociodramatic experience demands meticulous planning of a series of steps. A breakdown at any point may block the learner's ability to portray a realistic situation.

The problem must be of immediate concern to those involved. In some subject areas realistic parallels are difficult to visualize.

Discussion analysis must focus on the situation at all times. When rapport in the situation is not effectively established, there may be a tendency to criticize the players.

Role-playing, as employed in the sociodramatic experience, is merely a tool for developing understanding. Therapy—emphasizing the motives behind the roles played—has no place in the classroom. The tendency of some teachers to select a role for the purpose of "putting somebody in his place" should be avoided.

# ILLUSTRATED SOCIODRAMATIC SITUATIONS

I. Useful in history, government, and social studies classes

*Unit:*    Economic Assistance Programs

*Concept:* Economic aid, as charity, is seldom appreciated.

*Broad Situation:*

> The junior-senior prom traditionally has been a formal occasion. The expense of formal attire in the past has prevented some students from attending this memorable event. A committee of students, representative of different economic levels, has been appointed to develop a plan so that all may attend. (The desirability of holding this as a formal event is not under consideration.)

*Concept:* When individuals (or nations) have basic rights violated, they can be expected to rebel.

*Broad Situation:*

> A committee of students attempts to impose formal attire upon those who attend the junior-senior banquet. They realize that some of the students cannot afford this style of dress. The committee is discussing the matter with a representative of the group which opposes such a mode of dress.

II. Useful in home economics, group guidance, sociology, and psychology classes

*Unit:*    Family Finances

*Concept:* Budgeting procedures demand a definite plan of action.

*Broad Situation:*

> Two seventeen-year-old girls meet at local soda fountain. Both have about the same amount of income of approximately seventeen dollars per week. Betty wants to know why the other (Kathy) always has money and could Kathy help her.

III. Useful in speech, general communications, and social studies classes

*Unit:*    Sharing Ideas with Others

*Concept:* Encouragement from the peer group may help one overcome withdrawing tendencies.

*Broad Situation:*

> Sue, a shy, quiet girl, is disturbed because of a student council ruling. John, her student council representative, learns of her distress and wonders why she failed to voice her feelings when he asked for them from the class. Sue states that she was afraid to do this in front of the class.

IV. Useful in American or English literature, history, and sociology classes

*Unit:*    Conflict

*Concept:* Traditional behavior must be viewed in terms of the times; as times change, so should customs.

*Broad Situation:*

A boy's organization is holding its annual freshman initiation. Being a selective club, the initiates traditionally have been subjected to considerable discomfort. It is a tradition that one boy, selected at random, is to be singled out for extreme measures. This year Tom's assignment is to steal a car. He is discussing his feelings with the initiation committee.

*Unit:* Ambition

*Concept:* Insincere persuasion or flattery is often misleading.
(Based on *Julius Caesar,* Act I, Scene II, by William Shakespeare)

*Broad Situation:*

Two seniors, Mike and Paul, are members of the student senate. Mike is the leader of a small group of students who want to get an unpopular bill through the senate. Mike wants to make sure that Paul is on his side and approaches him for support.

V. Useful in home economics classes

*Unit:* The Family

*Concept:* Emotional family stress can break down family ties.

*Broad Situation:*

Ted Smith has just spent two days in the hospital. His parents have just brought him home. Ted knows his parents are upset and have been placed in an awkward position. He decides to discuss how he feels about the inconvenience to his parents.

# CHAPTER 14

# The Case Method

## OVERVIEW

### Key Concepts

1. The case method may be used for resolution of problems and/or derivation of principles.
2. By emphasizing feeling reactions in the situation, the case analysis closely parallels reality.
3. The short, incident case (structured around a simple conflict situation) is most effective for secondary school use.
4. Case analysis focuses upon three dimensions: Facts, feelings, and relationships.
5. The incident case, based upon a single unit concept, is most appropriately developed by the user.

### New Terms

1. **Incident Case**—A short (three to five paragraph) account of a situation, used for study and analysis.
2. **Case Types (Styles)**—Manner of presentation of case data. Includes such approaches as the vignette, historical narrative, documents, and research data.
3. **Case Questions**—Questions which immediately follow case materials. Designed to stimulate independent thought. Such questions may or may not be utilized in the actual case analysis.

## Questions to Guide Your Study

1.  What are the psychological advantages associated with the case method?
2.  Why is the short incident case preferred for secondary use?
3.  "Students should be given the actual solution to a case after they have completed their own analysis." Defend or refute.
4.  Why are teachers urged to develop their own cases?

Clarence Earl Gideon, a fifty-three-year-old drifter and ex-convict, sat slumped over a half pint of vodka in a dingy bar on Florida's Gulf Coast. He thinks it was a "pretty day" when he was arrested at 12:30 A.M., but that's about all he can remember.

Arrested for the burglary of a poolroom on skid row, Gideon stoutly denied his guilt because as he said, "I've never done anything drunk that I didn't remember when sober." Nevertheless, as someone had reported seeing Gideon prowling inside the establishment early that June morning, his denials carried little weight, especially since he had spent most of his adult life in jail.

Gideon asked the court to provide him with a lawyer but was refused. Under Florida law he was not entitled to one! Serving as his own lawyer, the man was tried and convicted by a six-man jury. A maximum sentence of five years was imposed.

Gideon did not particularly mind the jail sentence since prison was more or less his "home" anyhow, but for once he actually believed he was innocent. Furthermore, he thought that a fair trial should have entitled him to the services of a lawyer. After the Florida Supreme Court denied Gideon's petition for a writ of habeas corpus, he decided to appeal to the United States Supreme Court. Although handwritten, and poorly spelled, his petition fell upon fertile soil. The Court ruled that he, in fact, did have the right to counsel. A new trial was ordered. This time, with the services of legal assistance, Gideon was set free.

What are the historical roots of basic liberties in this country? Why is the Supreme Court able to upset the state court decisions, as in the Gideon case? Why would a "poor risk" like Gideon be permitted to go free—at the risk of endangering life and property of the community at large? What basic civil liberties are involved?

The foregoing is an illustration of a *case* which might be used in a general business class. In all probability the reader developed immediate interest in Gideon's problem. Indeed most readers probably caught themselves pondering the key questions posed in the fifth paragraph. Why is this? Why do we, after reading an account of less than 200 words, want to assist in the analysis of the problem? The answer, of course, is that Gideon's problem is real—one that many have faced in some way at one time or another. Furthermore, it involves the common emotions and values encountered in our daily existence. The element of human interest captures our imagination.

The case method is not new. Indeed, it dates back many centuries and has been used by such outstanding teachers as Jesus (parables), Aesop (fables), and Grimm (fairy tales). Oddly enough, however, it has only recently received attention as a useful instructional procedure in the secondary schools.

A case is an account of an actual problem or situation which has been experienced by an individual or a group. It includes facts available to those facing the problem, along with a description of perceptions and attitudes of those who are confronted with the problem. Thus the learner is placed in the unique position of having to resolve a real problem in his area of interest or endeavor.

## FUNDAMENTAL PROPERTIES

Since a case is merely a slice of reality, any one of several different types may be utilized, depending upon the purpose involved. Likewise, the complexity of a case will vary according to the maturity level of students. Generally, however, short, relatively simple cases are preferred for secondary use. In fact, Pigors and Pigors recommend the incident case technique for adults.[1]

### What Are Some Case Types (Styles)?

The case study can serve many instructional functions. As Newmann and Oliver point out, there is no one case approach to teaching. Not only are there many different types or styles of case materials, but there are different uses to which they may be put.[2] The prevalent assumption of *the* case, according to Newmann and Oliver, has led to much confusion and ambiguity. They believe that the common characteristics are outweighed by important differences.

Case types or styles include the familiar story or novel approach which portrays specific events, human behavior, dialogue and feelings. It presents an episode, having characters and a plot. The story style, according to Newmann and Oliver, is especially effective for involving students emotionally. Closely related to the story is the vignette, a short excerpt or slice of human experience with no completed plot.

Another case type is the *historical narrative* told as a news story. Such a presentation of events makes no effort to build a plot or characterization. It may be a point-by-point description or it may be an eyewitness account of an event.

*Documents,* another case style, include court opinions, speeches, letters, diaries, transcripts of trials, laws, and the like. Court opinions and briefs are typically used in the teaching of law. As an official judgment, a law case is to be learned and heeded as precedent.

Still another case style or type is *research data,* sometimes used for developing skills in statistical analysis from which valid generalizations can be derived. As opposed to the primary, raw data offered in research, there is the

[1] Paul Pigors and Faith Pigors, *Case Method in Human Relations: The Incident Process* (New York: McGraw-Hill Book Co., 1961), pp. 139–58.
[2] Fred M. Newmann and Donald W. Oliver, "Case Study Approaches in Social Sciences," *Social Education* 31 (February 1967): 108–13.

text type of case. In describing public movements, organizations, or different groups of people, for example, a textbook writer may use the case approach to illustrate generalizations.

### For What General Purposes Are Cases Used?

Cases are used for two general purposes: (1) to illustrate foregone conclusions, or (2) to provoke controversy and debate on issues for which definite conclusions do not exist. On the one hand, the issue has been resolved, while on the other the issue remains open-ended. Both categories permit the study of descriptive issues (factual material) *and* prescriptive issues (what ought to be).

In those cases which deal with foregone conclusions, specific facts, definitions, or concepts may be presented in the form of an exciting narrative. This may be in the form of historical narratives, stories, or hearings. In a similar manner, the teacher may want students to "discover" a set of basic generalizations. Finally, cases may be used to lend support to certain prescriptive conclusions or moral lessons. Thus it is seen that cases *inappropriately may be used* to support predetermined "answers," dogmatism, and rigid indoctrination.

As a method for stimulating inquiry on unresolved problems, the case approach probably has no equal. The object of such inquiry is not to have the student learn or discover the correct answer. Rather it is to provide a basis for reaching a decision on the basis of a specific situation. The student analyzes the facts available, takes responsibility for determining a course of action, and finally accepts the responsibility for consequences of the proposed action. Quality of performance is based upon reasonable justifications for the position taken, rather than mastery of the facts.

### What Are the Essentials of the Method?

Although there are many different approaches to cases, the emphasis in this chapter is upon its approach to problem solving. As a device for promoting critical thinking, the case is superior to most methods.

The case method is characterized by its usefulness in teaching students to think in the presence of new situations. Case problems, taken from real life experiences, are probably as close to reality as possible in the absence of the experience itself. The learner, placed in the role of a major participant, is able to visualize concrete, specific, personal contact of the situation. Thus a great deal of interest is developed.

A case is structured around a conflict situation. If used for the discovery of important generalizations only, the conflict is of a general nature. If, however, an immediate decision is to be reached, the conflict situation must be specific, involving an impending decision. In either case, certain basic elements are emphasized.

*Facts.* Basic background facts must be identified. It is especially important to recognize those facts that apply to the different parties involved. Although some teachers prefer to introduce extraneous facts and conditions for the purpose of making cases more realistic, most secondary teachers limit their cases to the essentials.

*Feelings.* An especially important aspect of a case analysis is consideration of important feelings involved. It is recognized that many instructional methods and techniques tend to disregard basic emotions associated with human interaction. The case method is uniquely suited to a consideration of *feelings as facts.* The prevailing sentiments and emotions of each of the parties involved must be portrayed as clearly as the objective facts.

*Relationships.* Basic to every case are important human relationships. A desired course of action frequently cannot be taken, due to conflicting interactions between important parties to a conflict. Sometimes a teen-ager feels he must be dishonest, for example, in order to protect his relations with the peer group. This is precisely why the case is such a useful technique. It captures important relationships which are frequently ignored by those who are not actual parties to the situation. Such relationships must be clarified in the case materials.

## CASE PROCEDURE

As with other teaching procedures, the case method must be integrated with other methods. Its use presupposes a fundamental background in the area. Thus it will be used to supplement textbook materials. Furthermore, it should be prepared in such a manner as to integrate previous learnings so that the student can see the correlation of different content areas. Banking, in a general business class, for example, can become much more meaningful if supplemented with a case problem dealing with the borrowing of money. The procedure which follows is suggestive only.

### How Is the Problem Identified?

After the teacher has clearly identified the basic concept to be taught, he selects an instructional method or technique which seems most appropriate for concept attainment. The case method is especially useful when affective considerations are paramount. A realistic case must direct attention to a problem of immediate concern to adolescents. Generally, the basic concept is first approached through textbook materials. It is then extended and applied to the learner's own life with the introduction and analysis of case materials. To illustrate from biology: A study of microorganisms suggests the following concept: Each person has a public responsibility for controlling infectious diseases. From this basic idea, Case III (last section of this chapter) was developed. Thus students are able to feel the emotions involved in a problem related to their own lives.

## How Are Cases Prepared?

Case materials abound in every area of human interaction. Preparation of cases is an easy process if a few simple rules are followed. Although existing cases are sometimes adaptable to class use, they seldom apply fully to the specific concept one wishes to emphasize. The best cases are based upon actual experience. Any teacher can quickly prepare a short, incident case by following the procedure outlined below.

First, he must identify the unit concept to be portrayed. As indicated in Chapter 1, the concept will incorporate or imply a real life application. The case is a mere portrayal of this life application. It attempts to capture human emotions in a conflict situation.

The first paragraph or two includes a brief description of the individual or individuals with which one is to identify. Included will be background material (both facts and feelings) and the current situation. An occasional quote, designed to dramatize feelings, provides an added touch of realism.

The next paragraph or two will include a brief description of the opposing individual or individuals involved in the situation. Again, the writer will attempt to provide background information, along with the current situation. He will attempt to portray basic feelings and relationships.

Finally, a paragraph or two will be devoted to the basic problem of the case. This will clearly portray clashes, differences of opinion, or issues which are provoking the problem. Immediate facts, feelings, and relationships will dramatize the conflicting conditions. This will be culminated with a final statement or paragraph designed to portray an impending decision.

The case material usually ends with three or four case questions, designed to provoke reflective thinking prior to the actual case analysis. As illustrated earlier, they usually will emphasize the higher levels of cognition.

In teaching case writing techniques to prospective teachers, the writer has effectively utilized selected photosituations. Through use of overhead projection, students can prepare cases directly in class. Some students can complete two such cases within a single class period. After a careful analysis of each case, the prospective teacher is usually able to develop his own cases with little difficulty. Most of the case illustrations were developed by prospective teachers.

## How Is the Case Presented?

Case materials are usually presented to students prior to analysis. This enables them to do essential background reading in the area. It also provides them with an opportunity to ponder over the issues prior to the class experience. It may be desirable to read the case aloud just prior to analysis. This tends to refocus events and relationships, even though students have advance access to case materials.

## How Is the Case Problem Analyzed?

The discussion analysis is initiated when the teacher asks, in some manner, "What is the issue or problem in this case?" It is essential that students know precisely what the difficulty is. In complex cases, there may be three or four minor "problems," but usually it is relatively easy to identify the basic issue upon which the other difficulties rest.

The second step is the analysis of the facts in the situation. *Here the emphasis is upon what actually happened rather than personal opinion of the facts.* The purpose of this phase of the discussion is to get the case facts into the open, making sure that insignificant, but sometimes important, bits of information are not disregarded. Some teachers find it desirable to put these points on the chalkboard for all to see. If the case is somewhat complex, it may be desirable to ask each student to prepare a written analysis prior to the experience. Such a technique tends to promote an atmosphere of free and uninhibited discussion.

Indications of the *why* of behavior can be gained by quoting from what case participants actually said. Key phrases also may be jotted down for future reference.

Next, the discussion might turn to the *relations* between the people involved. To whom is the party responsible? Is there evidence of a hidden allegiance? What are the established channels of communication?

A third step in the analysis may be conceived as *sentiments and beliefs.* Here expressed feelings or attitudes are considered. A word of caution is in order, however. It is important to distinguish between attitudes and feelings expressed in the case and those inferred by students who are participating in the case analysis.

## How Are Hypotheses Derived?

After case activities, relations, and sentiments and beliefs have been thoroughly explored and evaluated, attention is turned to decision making. "What needs to be decided, and done, right now?" It is helpful to consider decision or action in terms of *each party* to the conflict. This usually results in more than one proposal. Pigors and Pigors suggest a technique which they have found most effective.[3] First, each member of the group (working independently) jots down his own decision and outlines his reasoning. He signs his paper and presents it to the discussion leader. Next, the class is assembled in separate opinion groups for the purpose of comparing notes and consolidating reasoning. The strongest possible argument for a given decision is prepared. Then, a spokesman is selected to present and argue this case briefly before the entire class.

[3] Pigors, *Case Method,* p. 144.

(Sometimes the various decisions may be role-played.) Thus tentative decisions are tested from the standpoint of each party to the conflict. Sometimes it becomes apparent that more than one decision is best, depending on the frame of reference accepted and the basic assumptions made.

## How Are Generalizations Derived?

As a culminating activity, students are encouraged to derive generalizations from the experience. These are the basic ideas which they are expected to transfer to related situations. As Pigors and Pigors so aptly express the process, it involves *looking back, looking up, looking about, and finally looking ahead.*[4] Reflecting on the case as a whole (along with other cases previously studied), the student once again assumes a position "outside" of the case. He examines the fundamental issue explored, reflecting upon those behaviors which appeared to be highly effective (or ineffective) in the situation. For example, the teacher might ask, "How might this conflict have been prevented?" "How might more have been accomplished?" This process naturally leads to *looking up* to the level of general ideas and principles. Thus the teacher might ask. "What guiding concepts can be distilled from our case analysis?" This, in turn, leads to *looking about* for other situations which contain commonalities with the present one. "How well do the general ideas which stand out in this case also apply to other cases?" Finally, the basic concepts are *thrust forward* to problems which might be reasonably anticipated. It must be emphasized that the basic assumption underlying use of the case method is that the fundamental concepts derived from particular cases are applicable to a variety of other, similar situations. The teacher must assist the learner in this knowledge expansion process. In psychological terminology, "Transfer of learning is enhanced when the student is taught to transfer."

## What Role Does the Teacher Play?

The heart of the case method is discussion analysis. As in a problem-solving discussion, the teacher must set an atmosphere conducive to *student* analysis. This forces the teacher to play many roles and to change roles frequently. He asks questions, restates problems and issues, and voices his own opinions and draws upon his own knowledge of fact. The appropriate combination of these can be acquired from direct experience only.

The instructor often opens case analysis by asking for identification of the basic problem posed. He may or may not refer directly to the four or five questions which often accompany a case report. The written questions which accompany a case report are designed to provoke thinking *in advance* of the discussion analysis.

Perhaps the most basic principle of case discussion is cooperative leader-

[4] Pigors, *Case Method*, p. 145.

ship. In the mutual search for ways of solving selected case problems, both teacher and student must recognize that wise decisions are sometimes based on personal and social values as much as factual information. The leader must recognize that his own hunch as to the best solution may not stand the test of critical analysis.

A critical aspect of productive leadership is the necessity of keeping the discussion focused. At any given moment, for example, the entire group should be centering its attention on the same dimension of the case. Furthermore, all members should attempt to stick with a given level of abstraction at any one time. As a case in point, the student who proceeds into the realm of general ideas while others are discussing specific facts should be asked to cite specific illustrations of his point of view.

The leader must resist the urge to supply his own solution to the problem. On the other hand, he must not withhold knowledge or points of view which are needed in the situation. It occasionally may be important, for example, to suggest alternative proposals, not because they are better than those suggested by the group but because they will further stimulate productive thinking of the group. Above all, he must help the group to make decisions on the basis of evidence, rather than merely to sit in judgment of the people in the case.

# PLANNING FOR CASE ANALYSIS

In addition to preparation of case materials, a lesson plan must be developed. Major emphasis will be directed to the essential steps of a case analysis. The illustrated plan involves a problem-solving approach. It features key questions which may be used to develop thinking along appropriate channels.

LESSON PLAN ILLUSTRATION (biology class)

*Problem:* How can each of us assist in the control of microorganisms?

*Concept:* Adequate health safeguards are responsibilities of all the people.

*Goals:*    After this lesson in microbe diseases, the student should have furthered his understanding of the problems involved in the prevention of disease, as evidenced by:
1. His distinguishing between fact and opinion in case materials.
2. His discussion analysis of aids against diseases and their importance.
3. His ability to justify case decisions from given points of view.

*Lesson Approach:*

Following preliminary investigation of the basic essentials of microbe diseases as provided in textbook materials, students will be provided individual copies of the case entitled *The Inoculation.* (See Case III, pp. 218-19.)

Students will be asked the question, "Have you ever seen a person who is dying of lockjaw? Let me briefly tell you what it is like." Then they will be told a brief story of a person dying of lockjaw. Students will be asked to read, underline, and/or take notes on the case materials. They will be asked to reflect briefly on the key questions which follow the case report.

*Lesson Development:*

INITIATING THE DISCUSSION:

What is the basic problem of this case?
What might be done to inform Jeff of the necessity of this inoculation?

ANALYZING THE PROBLEM:

What are the facts of the situation?
What is the importance of a tetanus shot?
What is the relationship of Jeff to Bill?
How does Bill feel about Jeff's actions?

WEIGHING ALTERNATIVES:

Now in view of the facts, relationships and feelings just discussed, what action, if any, should Bill take?
What might be the consequences of such action? (Each of the possible solutions will be discussed until alternatives are reduced to two or three likely courses of action.)
At this point let us jot down our own preferred course of action, along with specific reasons supporting this action.
*Buzz groups:* We will now divide into discussion groups, corresponding to different decisions reached. Have a representative prepare the best possible case for your proposed course of action.
*Reassemble:* Now each spokesman in the group will present and briefly debate his group's case for the class. Questions may be interjected by others as needed.

*Deriving Generalizations:*

What similar situations have you encountered?
What general principles seem to apply? Examples might include:

1. Discussing value questions with others who have had wider experiences in the area.
2. If possible, create opportunities to discuss similar problems with friends in your own age group.
3. Communicate (indirectly at least) with your family doctor.

# VALUES

The case method is realistic. Analyzing an actual slice of reality is about as close to the real thing as possible.

By treating human emotion and feelings, the case approach captures the interest and imagination of the learner.

The case method holds an advantage over other simulated techniques (e.g., sociodrama and role-playing) in that it can deal with a larger slice of reality. For example, factors leading up to a conflict and the interrelated aspects of conflict can be readily analyzed.

Case analysis treats feelings as facts. Some instructional approaches (e.g., discussion methods) tend to strip cognitive facts from their affective components.

By capturing and analyzing real problems, the student is able to bridge the gap between school and real-life experiences.

## LIMITATIONS AND PROBLEMS

Although the case method is realistic, it is *not* actual reality. Actual decisions are sometimes reached on the basis of intangibles which cannot be captured in a case incident.

The case method tends to collapse time and space dimensions. Consequently, it tends to emphasize positive action. Sometimes in real-life situations, action may not be justified. A solution may not be feasible.

The case approach is time-consuming. If used extensively, it will definitely limit the content material which can be covered.

Preparation of cases is an art which must be learned. Use of already prepared, fictional cases may limit the realism of case situations.

## CASE ILLUSTRATIONS

I.   Useful in history, government, and social studies classes

*Concept:* A man is innocent under the law until proved guilty.

Jack Phillips grew up in a wealthy section of Chicago. Even though his parents provided him with toys and games during his childhood, he began to steal comic books and candy from the local stores. As soon as he reached the age of sixteen, with his parents' reluctant consent he quit school and began to work as a stock boy in a local sporting-goods store. In addition to his earnings from his job, he received an allowance from his parents. This enabled him to flaunt his wealth and, as a result, he had few, if any, friends.

During the first few months of his job he found it easy to steal sports equipment and to sell it for his own personal profit. However, his boss, beginning to notice that certain items were missing from stock, notified the police. After watching Phillips for a number of days, the police entered his home, searched it, and, after finding some sports equipment there, arrested him. He was sent to jail to await trial.

Jack's family, sparing no expense, immediately contacted a prominent lawyer, who agreed to defend their son. After examining his client's case, the lawyer claimed that several of Jack's constitutional rights had been violated and that he should be released from jail.

*Questions:*

1.   From the description of this case, what rights do you feel might have been violated?

2. The events described all occurred before Jack Phillips appeared before a jury for trial. Do you feel that the case should come to trial?
3. In view of the wealth of the Phillips family and the fact that they spent money on their son, how might you explain Jack's desire to steal?
4. Do you feel that Jack's family has any *legal* responsibility for his actions?

II. Useful in home economics, group guidance, sociology, and psychology classes

*Concept:* Empathy is essential to a successful marriage.

Jane and her husband, Bill, live in a middle-class suburb. They have three small children, all under school age. Bill is not a college graduate but is capable and ambitious. Jane indicates that she values these traits in her husband. He is a salesman for a large company, but his work is largely confined to his home state. Sometimes he is away for two or three days and he often gets home late at night. Occasionally his work interferes with their weekends.

Lately Jane has been complaining about his being away so much and getting home so late. Bill explained that he had made several contacts which he considered good prospects for a sale and that it was difficult to break up his conferences to come home at a regular hour. Besides, he sometimes had book work to do when he got back to the office. Bill feels that she should appreciate his efforts for the family. Jane said that he was always about to make a sale, which usually fell through, and that he should spend more time with his family. Moreover, financial support, she says, is not the only kind she needs. She would like help with the children.

*Questions:*
1. What is the problem?
2. What are the incidents which show lack of empathy?
3. What are some understandings about Jane's feelings that Bill needs in order to empathize, and vice versa?
4. What are some specific ways in which Jane and Bill can develop empathy?
5. If the present relationship continues, what type of family life will they likely have? Give the principles that explain your answer.

III. Useful in biology, general science, health, and physical education classes

*Concept:* Adequate health safeguards are responsibilities of all the people.

Jeff Jones is a sophomore at West High School. He participates in school athletics and has a hobby of working on automobiles during the weekend. He comes from an average-income family—including one brother and one sister—of which he is the eldest child. During his freshman year in high school, Jeff became injury-prone in athletics and, as a result of his injuries, he was hospitalized twice. Jeff hates to have anyone give him shots and, if at all possible, he will avoid inoculations at all cost.

At West High School it is a policy that all athletes receive a tetanus booster at least once a year. Dr. Adams, the school doctor, gives the athletes their tetanus shot when he gives them physical examinations at the beginning of each sport season. The only student cost involved is a twenty-five cent fee to cover the antitoxin and syringe. If the student cannot afford the twenty-five cents, the doctor will give it to him free; the only way an athlete can avoid the shot is by presenting a waiver form signed by his parents stating that their son has received a shot within the last three months.

Bill Smith, Jeff's best friend, has known Jeff since first grade. They live a block away from each other and Bill participates in the same sports as Jeff. When Jeff found out about the tetanus shot, he asked Bill to forge his mother's name on the waiver. Bill refused, so Jeff decided he would forge his mother's signature.

Bill is the type that usually lets a person do as he wishes, and this is especially true when it comes to Jeff. On the other hand, Bill takes pride in the fact that he has, on several occasions, gone against Jeff's will for Jeff's own protection.

On the way to school, a week before physicals for football, Jeff tells Bill that he forged his mother's name on the waiver. Bill seems to be disturbed by Jeff's action and doesn't immediately say anything to Jeff.

*Questions:*

1. What is the major problem in this case?
2. What are the issues involved?
3. What action would you take if you were Bill?

IV. Useful in speech and social studies classes

*Concept:* Each group member must contribute to group progress.

Ron Powell, a sophomore at East High, lives with his divorced mother. He is the only child, lonely, and has little opportunity to participate in small-group activity. However, Ron is liked by his classmates and is likewise very fond of them. This is his first year as student council representative for his homeroom.

Ken Goodwin is also a member of student council. He is the oldest child in his family of six. He is usually quite tactful in his relationships with others but does have a hot temper.

Every September at East High the student council holds a workshop, and the representatives break into committees to discuss problems and plans for the coming semester. This year the workshop is held in the gymnasium, and the committees are seated in groups about the room. Several faculty advisers are also present. When the committees are formed, Ken, Ron, Bob—a close friend of Ron's—and two others are assigned to the group discussing dress regulations. Ken, a senior and discussion leader, is trying his best to establish some rules that will be acceptable to both the students and faculty. Ron keeps trying to tell the group about his week at summer camp. They listen reluctantly, only wanting to continue with their business. Ken tries again to get some ideas from the group when Ron cuts in and begins to tell about his dog. Ron continues to monopolize the conversation, talking on completely irrelevant subjects.

*Questions:*
1. What is the major problem in this case?
2. What are the issues involved?
3. What action would you take if you were a member of the group?

V. Useful in American problems, history, and sociology classes

*Concept:* Behavior relates to one's past experiences.

Marquette Frye had grown up in a small coal-mining town in Wyoming until early 1957, when the mine had shut down and his father had moved the family to Los Angeles. From a friendly, integrated community high in the Rockies, he plunged into the black world of southeast Los Angeles. The first day after the family's arrival, Marquette was picked up by the truant officer.

Marquette soon learned that he was an outsider because of his attitudes and speech. Rapidly losing his former interest in school, in his senior year at Fremont he dropped out completely. When he was seventeen, it was a very bad year as the police arrested him for the third time and the judge sent him to a forestry camp for two years. For two years after he got out, he stayed out of trouble and got off probation in July, 1965. Although he felt free for the first time in years, he still had his problems—his arrest record prevented him from getting most jobs and his girl had just told him that she was pregnant.

Officer Lee Minikus of the California Highway Patrol was riding his cycle looking for speeders on the night of August 11, 1965. He had joined the patrol to escape an office job that he had gotten after he finished his hitch in the service. Now married, with three children, he had been on the patrol for over ten years. As he pulled up to Avalon Boulevard, a black truck driver called to him, telling him he thought that the driver of a Buick that just went by was a bit drunk. Minikus saluted in acknowledgment and began to chase down the Buick.

Inside the Buick, Marquette Frye and his brother Ronald had had a few drinks apiece and now were speeding down Avalon at 65 within sight of their apartment house. Ronald saw the cycle and they stopped. Marquette Frye got out, confident that if he treated the officer right he wouldn't get a ticket.

He had misplaced his license and told Minikus this and yes, he had been drinking but he was only a block from home and wasn't drunk. According to regulations, Minikus ordered Frye through a series of coordination tests to see if he was drunk, while a crowd of local residents gathered to watch. After relaying his decision to his control that Frye was drunk, Minikus returned to him and began filling out a ticket, asking Frye the information relating to birth date, address, color of eyes, hair color, etc. Frye replied, while doing a jig, "It's black, man, all over. Can't you see?" Minikus replied good-humoredly, "You're a real comedian, aren't you, Marquette?" Then Minikus's partner arrived with a transportation car to take Frye to jail. As the police consulted, Frye had walked toward his car. He began to argue with his mother, who had just gotten there within the crowd of over a hundred. "Momma, I'm not going to jail." Minikus and his partner saw him in the crowd, called to him, "Marquette, get over here." Frye replied, "You sonofabitchin' white cops, you're not taking me anywhere!" The crowd growled its approval.

*Questions:*
1. What is the immediate problem?
2. What are some issues involved, or by what criteria may we judge a solution?
3. What are some facts and feelings involved in this case?

VI. Useful in health, American problems and sociology classes

*Concept:* Each individual has the responsibility of establishing and living by an acceptable code of conduct.

Andy is a junior at Central High, where he is an excellent student. He is active in student government, the drama club, Future Teachers of America club, and the athletic club. Andy has an exciting personality and is well liked by everyone in school, including the teachers. Andy tries to hold himself responsible for all his actions. To Andy what a person thinks of himself is very important. He plans to attend the State University upon completion of high school. Andy is from a middle-class family, his father being an instructor at the city's junior college. Andy and his sister have their separate rooms in their new house in the suburbs. Andy also has a used car which he uses to drive to and from school. Neither of Andy's parents drink, and they express their wishes that their children refrain from picking up the habit.

One day after school when Andy was giving Frank a ride home as usual, Frank asked Andy to pull off to the side road. When the car came to a stop, Frank pulled out a pint of gin from under his jacket. Frank stated that he stole the gin from his father because, as he put it, "I want to see which one of us is the bettter man." Andy was reluctant and did not accept Frank's offer or challenge. Frank then told Andy that he had nothing to worry about because everyone was drinking and it was the thing to do. Also Frank said that if Andy refused to take a drink, he was chicken and a sissy.

*Questions:*
1. What is the major problem in this case?
2. What are the issues involved?
3. What action would you take if you were Andy?

VII. Useful in industrial arts and vocational agriculture classes

*Concept:* Safety precautions are group, as well as individual, responsibilities.

Mr. Wilson is a woodworking instructor at Valley High School, where he teaches classes in beginning woods, advanced woods, and cabinet making. He is a good instructor and holds the respect of almost every student in his classes. It is a well-known fact to his students and fellow teachers that he is a "real stickler" on safety practices in his shop. His strictness partially stems from the fact that he had nearly been sued by the parents of a boy who had cut his hand in Mr. Wilson's shop two years ago.

Ron Perkins is one of Mr. Wilson's better students in advanced wood-working class. He has great respect for Mr. Wilson and tries to obey all of the shop rules.

Bill Jacobs is another of Mr. Wilson's students in this same class. He is quite an independent individual and often expresses resentment of Mr. Wilson's rules to his classmates.

On this particular day, Bill has set up the circular saw to make a rather difficult cut. Because of the nature of the cut, he needs to have both hands on his piece of wood at all times to avoid ruining the wood or hurting himself. Mr. Wilson is busy on the other side of the room and has his back turned to Bill. Being impatient, Bill calls Ron and tells him to turn on the saw for him. (One of the safety rules states that a person should turn on his own machine so that he will have control of the situation at all times.)

*Questions:*

1. If Ron turned the saw on, would his knowledge of the safety rules make him equally guilty? What if someone got hurt?
2. Is it Ron's responsibility to help Bill?
3. How should Ron handle the situation?

VIII.  Useful in music classes

*Concept:* Restrictions, when faced honestly and fairly, are usually modifiable.

Jonathan Wright is seventeen years old and a top student in Centerville's only high school. He is the son of a self-made man who, through hard labor, sweat, and calluses, has risen to the head of a business and earned the respect and admiration of his community. Mr. Wright married a talented violinist who had been given every possible advantage that a small community could offer musically. Her promising career ended with the birth of their only son, Jonathan.

Through the years his mother devoted her life to the development of the musical talent that was so apparent in her young son. She guided his musical education through what he termed "good" music. While other children were reading comic books, Jonathan was becoming intimately acquainted with such masters as Corelli, Vivaldi, Bach, Handel, Rameau, Mozart, and other composers of Baroque, Classical, and Romantic periods of music history. Jonathan found extreme pleasure in experimenting in combining musical techniques of different masters into little creations of his own. This often brought frowns from his mother, who felt that "good" music should not be tampered with.

By the time Jonathan had entered high school, he was already noted throughout the state as an accomplished violinist. The high school music instructor was delighted to have the son of one of his former students in his class in Music History. But within a very short time the teacher became aware that the contents of his class were not really a challenge to Jon; in fact, the teacher felt that Jon was capable of teaching the class himself should the need arise. He decided to take the matter up with a new teacher who was experimenting with a new class in 20th Century Composition. Together they approached Jonathan with the suggestion of transferring into this other class.

The idea intrigued Jon, but he knew of his mother's dislike for some of contemporary music. He finally decided that there was no real need in anyone knowing, so he would give it a try.

This class soon became the center of Jon's musical education and endeavors. He wås fascinated with the sounds created in the 20th century style. He created new arrangements for the up and coming "bop" combo, the "Dynamics" of Centerville High.

The music teachers felt that Jon ought to try his hand at original composing and suggested that he pursue the statewide contest on contemporary music. They felt confident that he had a good chance of winning. This was a definite temptation to Jon, but it was completely against the value, indoctrinated for years by his mother, of his pursuit of only "good" music and not current "trash." What should he do?

*Questions:*

1.  What is the major problem?
2.  What are the issues?
3.  What action should be taken?

IX.  Useful in business classes

*Concept:* Secretarial responsibilities must be ordered along established lines of responsibility.

Miss Cindy Jansen is a new (two weeks) receptionist for the main office of an expanding company. Miss Jansen is an attractive nineteen-year-old who had one semester of junior college but then found it necessary to go to work. She is from a smaller town, where she knew just about everyone because her parents owned the main grocery store. From this type of upbringing Cindy had a ready smile, pleasant personality, and willingness to be helpful. This was the type of person Mr. Oak, the personnel manager, was looking for to fill the position. He knew that she was young and needed to build up her self-confidence, but he also knew that everyone needs a start and believed that she would be a good receptionist.

The main office housed the president, vice presidents (two), treasurer, accountant, attorney, transportation manager, personnel manager, and mining engineer. Much of the time these men would be out of their offices for meetings, out-of-town appointments, etc. It was a job just to keep track of the people so that they would get their telephone calls and messages. Everyone liked Cindy and thought that she was doing a fine job, especially since she had worked only one day with the previous receptionist and there was much to learn. Everyone helped Cindy when they could when it came to names to remember and who to associate the name with, what department should receive questions that would arise, etc. The only problem seemed to be the President's secretary, who more or less kept her own hours—based on luncheon dates, hairdresser's appointments, and shopping—and sometimes did not come in when her boss was out of town.

Mr. Jones, president, was a self-made millionaire. He had started in agriculture on his father's farm and now had expanded into mining, lumber, livestock, and frozen-food processing throughout the West, Midwest, Northeast, and Southwest. He was a big, gruff man but had twinkling blue eyes. His manners were rough, but his intentions were kind. However, when he was upset, the fur would fly and the fact that he was upset was no secret to anyone in the office.

The Monday of Cindy's third week began very well. When Mr. Oak came in, he greeted her with "good morning" and complimented her on her new dress. Then Mr. Dahl brought some quarterly reports to be typed (original and five copies) by 1:00 for the bank. This was usually the job of Jan, the president's secretary; but today was one of those days when she hadn't shown up because Mr. Jones was not expected back until Tuesday. Then about 10:30 Mr. Jones came in—the whole office jumped. The telephones started ringing; the other men in the office wanted to see Mr. Jones just as soon as he was through with Mr. Dahl. However, when Mr. Dahl came out, Mr. Jones asked Cindy to call Mr. Hansen in New York City. That was all the information she was given. Cindy finally got Mr. Hansen on the phone, but, meanwhile, Cindy, asking Mr. Hansen to hold on, went to find Mr. Jones. By the time Mr. Jones got to the phone, Mr. Hansen had hung up. When Cindy got back to her desk, her phones were ringing; people were waiting to see Mr. Jones; Mr. Oak asked about the reports which are due at 1:00; and just then Mr. Jones stepped out of his office and shouted, "There is no one on line 3. Now get Mr. Hansen on that phone immediately! Can't you even make a simple call?"

*Questions:*
1. What is the major problem?
2. What are the issues?
3. What action should be taken?

[Many of the foregoing cases were prepared by preservice teachers, under the direction of the writer.]

# CHAPTER 15

# Developmental Reading Techniques

## OVERVIEW

### Key Concepts

1. Reading development is a continuous process; most young people need guidance throughout their public school experience.
2. The language of every content area is unique and must be taught.
3. Reading rate varies with the purpose. Without assistance, the typical student approaches all reading assignments in a line-by-line and page-by-page manner.
4. Comprehension is enhanced through a systematized study technique (SQ4R).
5. An individual's reading habits become engrained as he matures. Thus a specific program of exercises must be employed if poor reading habits are to be corrected.
6. All assignments that involve reading should call attention to needed reading skills and techniques.

### New Terms

1. **Readability Level**—The general reading level of a book or other printed matter. It is based upon sentence length and word syllables and is usually interpreted in terms of grade level.
2. **"Stopper" Words**—Words in an assignment that will tend to stop or block the reader's comprehension or train of thought.

3. **Context Clues**—Clues to word meaning that may be derived from the way a word is used.
4. **Indicator or "Flag" Words**—Words, usually italicized or boldfaced, that alert the reader to specific information. Such words are essential to effective scanning.
5. **SQ4R**—A systematic study technique. It includes the following: survey, question, read, recite, "rite," and review.
6. **Skimming**—A form of rapid reading useful in gaining a general impression or main ideas.
7. **Scanning**—A second form of rapid reading useful for acquiring specific information such as dates and word definitions.

### Questions to Guide Your Study

1. Why has it been said that every content area has its own special language?
2. Most students enthusiastically receive instruction designed to help them improve their reading skills. Relatively few, however, employ such techniques unless specific assignments are provided. Why is this?
3. How is the SQ4R technique employed?
4. The question "What is your reading rate?" is unanswerable. Why?
5. "Whenever an individual encounters a new word he should consult the dictionary." Defend or refute.

Benjamin Harrison Smith was a troubled high school senior. Now that graduation was only a few months away, he realized that his chances of success in college were practically nil simply because he could not cope with the written language. "It's too late now," Ben thought, "to go back and learn what I should have learned in my early years of school."

Reflecting back, Ben knew that his problems began early in his elementary school experience and had become progresively worse as he advanced through junior and senior high schools. From an early reading indifference he had developed an intense dislike for the written word, avoiding written assignments whenever possible. Fortunately he was capable enough to make average grades in most classes on the strength of his verbal ability and "practical intelligence." He suspected that some of his teachers had been totally unaware of his reading problem.

When the guidance counselor asked Mr. Tompkins if Ben had experienced reading difficulty in Senior Science class he replied, "No more than many other of my students. Many students either cannot or will not read directions. They read science assignments only if forced." When asked what action had been taken to help students cope with the language of the subject he retorted, "Look! My job is to teach science. Students are supposed to learn to read in elementary school. I realize that the job is often not very well done but I simply do not have time to teach reading *and* science."

Literally thousands of high school students, like Ben, are "academically crippled" as a result of reading deficiencies to some degree. The reason may be a lack of ability or interest, a bilingual home, an impoverished home environment, an inadequate elementary school experience when reading was emphasized, or any combination of a dozen or more other reasons. Whatever the source of the difficulty, an effective high school teacher cannot afford *not* to take the necessary time to help students cope with the language of his subject area. ~~Fortunately, the language of his subject area.~~ Fortunately, the task is relatively simple and over a period of time may result in a net savings of instructional time. This chapter offers techniques and procedures that can be used effectively by every secondary teacher. The first section of the chapter emphasizes fundamental considerations that must be taken into account. This is followed by those basic techniques and procedures that can be readily applied. Finally, problems and principles of an effective program are treated.

# FUNDAMENTAL PROPERTIES

Ability to cope with the language of various school subjects comprises a complex of skills that must be developed by every student. Some students, quite naturally, employ fairly adequate techniques that they have developed intuitively from past experiences. Most students, however, flounder, wasting needless hours of study time as they attempt to adjust to strange words and new approaches to learning. In a study involving 1500 freshmen at Harvard, for example, it was found that after twenty-two minutes of a two-hour study allocation of an assigned chapter only 150 of the group had done *any* exploring beyond the pages they were reading. Just 15 of the 1500 could give a general view of the chapter content.[1] The fundamental properties that follow, in many cases, are associated with erroneous assumptions of teachers.

### What Individual Reading Differences Are Important?

Students vary tremendously in their abilities to cope with the language of different subjects. Some are barely able to comprehend the vocabulary at fourth or fifth grade level. Others typically read all materials at the same rate. Few indeed are acquainted with appropriate overview techniques essential to efficient utilization of study time. As the foregoing suggests, the all too common question, "What is his reading rate?" can be extremely misleading. The rate should vary with the nature of the material to be read.

Each subject area has its own special reading requirements. Reading adequately in one subject area does *not* assure adequacy in another. The teacher does more than introduce new terms and expressions in his subject area. More importantly, he *teaches* the necessary skills that will lead to self-mastery. All students need such instruction as a basis for effective learning. As in any teaching-learning context, some students will need more help than others. Entry reading deficiencies merely complicate the problem further.

---

[1] William G. Perry, Jr., "Students' Use and Misuse of Reading Skills: A Report to a Faculty," *Harvard Education Review* 29 (Summer 1959): 193–200.

## What Characterizes a Flexible Reader?

Unfortunately, most students, some of their teachers, and the public generally think of reading rate as a unitary factor. Students often ask, "How fast should I read?", implying that there is a single optimum speed at which all readers should read all kinds of materials for all purposes. Moreover, many silent reading tests provide a single measure of reading speed based on a single type of material. Actually the good reader varies his reading rate constantly as his reading purpose varies.

Persistent reports of individuals who read at fantastic speeds are misleading. It has been claimed, for example, that a few individuals can read an entire page at a single glance. Such claims are usually made in support of speed reading programs. For purposes of skimming and scanning for main ideas a fantastic reading speed is possible and desirable. It should be noted, however, that for other purposes the reader must read slowly, reflecting as he moves along. Even the best reader, moving from sentence to sentence with adequate comprehension, can seldom read more than 700 to 800 words a minute. Even 500 words a minute is somewhat unusual.

## How Do Restricting Habits Interfere with Reading Improvement Programs?

A poor reader has subconsciously developed a series of reading habits that interfere with his reading effectiveness. If asked, he would likely admit their ineffectiveness. Nevertheless, like all human beings, he is a creature of habit. The mere exploration of new techniques is not enough. Even though he may intellectually accept different approaches to reading, the must be "forced" into new patterns of behavior through specific, in-class exercises. This, in turn, must be followed with repeated assignments that have a bearing on the problem. In short, assignments must incorporate desirable reading techniques and be followed through by the teacher.

## What Bearing Does Vocabulary Have on Reading Efficiency?

One of the most obvious fundamentals of reading is vocabulary and word attack skills. Strangely enough, however, vocabulary building is frequently neglected by teachers in content areas. The assumption is often made that words which students can use in some contexts will be automatically understood in all other contexts. Although vocabulary drill has its place, comprehension can be blocked if the learner continually attempts to apply literal word meanings.

Poor readers tend to "slide over" new words. Sometimes prefixes and suffixes and root words within a new word are sufficient for adequate comprehension. On other occasions a dictionary must be consulted. In the absence of some notion of the intended meaning, however, the dictionary may be more confusing than helpful. *Webster's New International Dictionary,* for example, provides sixteen meanings for "book."

## What Is the Role of Comprehension in Reading?

The concept of rate of comprehension is much more useful than the notion of rate of reading. Speed without comprehension is worthless! While it is true that rate of reading and comprehension tend to be closely associated, this does not mean that comprehension will improve by speeding up one's reading. Indeed the evidence indicates that reading rate adjustments that are severe enough to disturb one's normal thought processes will result in decreased comprehension.

Comprehension itself is a complex concept. At its lowest level it is a process of *translating* the writer's thought into one's own words. Meaningful interpretation or reproduction demands a basic understanding of grammar and the structure of language. The teacher facilitates this process by calling attention to titles, key words in context, sentence structure, and the like.

From translation the process of comprehension proceeds to *interpretation* of implied meaning, sometimes referred to as "reading between the lines." Words are mere abstractions of reality; they do not say all. Instead, the reader is expected to make his own inferences and deductions. For example, such expressions as "buying time," "cold war," "hot dog," cannot be interpreted from the literal meaning of the words but only through their contexts.

Comprehension at its highest level involves "reading beyond the lines" in making *generalizations and drawing conclusions*. Thus the reader must grasp a thought in its totality and reflect upon related possibilities. In essence he goes beyond the lines as he evaluates arguments, deductions, inferences, and the like. Eventually he draws his own conclusions as he critically evaluates what he reads.

## At What Point Can Reading Skills Be Considered Independent of the Teacher?

For years it was assumed that mastery of the "three Rs" was the basic function of the elementary school. Upon leaving elementary school all such instruction ceased. Today, however, it has become apparent that some students do *not* achieve proficiency in the basic skills. Indeed growth in reading is a *continuous process* that can be assured only through the organization of sound developmental reading programs. Studies have shown that the student whose reading instruction was terminated at the end of elementary school was no better a reader at the end of his senior year than when he entered high school. Wide reading alone does not necessarily result in reading improvement.[2]

---

[2] Willare J. Massey and Virginia D. Moore, *Helping High School Students to Read Better* (New York: Holt, Rinehart & Winston, Inc., 1965), p. 6.

Ultimately, learning must become self-directed. The elementary student normally learns to cope with the written word. As he begins to expand his reading into specialized subject areas, however, specific techniques of coping with the language are needed. These cannot be fully developed during the elementary school years. Even the best reader can profit from specialized developmental reading instruction.

# DEVELOPMENTAL READING SKILLS AND TECHNIQUES

Many schools employ a reading specialist whose primary responsibility is to work with poor and "reluctant" readers. For such students remedial reading classes may be established. Essential to the success of the program is a close working relationship with classroom teachers. Teachers are informed and advised relative to techniques of helping remedial reading students cope with the language of regular classes.

Although some attention may be given to developmental reading for all students, the regular student is often left entirely in the hands of a classroom teacher who may not be adequately prepared for the task. This section is designed to prepare the teacher for coping with the developmental reading needs of regular students.

### How May a Preliminary Survey of Textbook Aids
### Contribute to Effective Learning?

Many high school students (and some college students) often complain of their inability to derive meaning from printed materials. The all too familiar quote, "I've read and reread the chapter but can't remember anything it says," suggests a need for more effective study skills. Fast and slow readers alike may experience such difficulties if they fail to make effective use of textbook aids.

Effective textbook use involves a methodology that bears much resemblance to the various instructional methods of the classroom teacher. Just as the lecturer foreshadows his main points in his initial summary, the textbook writer attempts to provide learner readiness through his table of contents, preface, and various chapter headings.

By making the preliminary survey of textbook aids *prior to reading,* the student is able to establish *purpose.* Purpose determines *how* one will read. Finding answers to questions, understanding main ideas, determining the conclusions of the writer, and reading for specific detail are but a few of the many purposes of reading. Each demands a different style of study.

The *table of contents* enables the reader to gain an overall perspective of the entire book. As Karlin[3] points out, one generally expects to find the answers to the following questions:

[3] Robert Karlin, *Reading for Achievement* (New York: Harcourt, Brace and World, Inc., 1961), p. 4.

1. What is the general organization of the book? Is the book divided into large divisions and then subdivided into chapters? Are chapters, in turn, subdivided?
2. What do the headings reveal relative to content? Is the scope of the book limited to a narrow area? What general emphasis is evident?
3. What special resource materials and instructional aids are provided? Are there maps, charts, and pictures? Does the author provide chapter summaries, study guide questions, chapter bibliographies? (By taking a quick look at some of these the reader can evaluate their usefulness for later study.)
4. What type of organization is employed? Is it chronological? General to specific? Topical? How much overlapping is evident?

A survey of the *preface* (introduction or prologue) enables the reader to determine the author's purposes, the limitations of the book, and its intended audience. In addition the writer may indicate his point of view toward the subject and suggest how the book may be used.

The preliminary survey, finally, involves a *preview of individual chapters.* This usually involves various chapter instructional aids. Some of these may include the chapter overview or introduction, study questions, chapter headings, summaries, pictures, tables, or charts. When surveying the entire book, the chapter-by-chapter preview will be much more superficial than when one is preparing to study a particular chapter.

## How Is the Readability Level of a Book Assessed?

A book that is far above (or below) the readability level of the student produces extreme frustration and discouragement. Usually a basic text is provided for an entire class or at least a considerable number of the students. Textbooks, often written by college professors, may be appealing to the teacher but too difficult for the student. Fortunately, Fry[4] has developed a technique for quickly assessing the readability level of a textbook. As he points out, the technique correlates highly with most other, more laborious, techniques of readability.[5]

Use of the Readability Graph involves the following directions:[6]

1. Select three one-hundred-word passages from near the beginning, middle, and end of the book. Skip all proper nouns.
2. Count the total number of sentences in each hundred-word passage (estimating to the nearest sentence). Average these three numbers.
3. Count the total number of syllables in each hundred-word sample. There is a syllable for each vowel sound; for example: cat(1), blackbird(2), continental(4). Don't be fooled by word size; for example: polio(3),

[4] Edward Fry, "A Readability Formula that Saves Time," *Journal of Reading* 11 (April 1968): 513–16.

[5] Concerning the use of the technique Fry reports that The Readability Graph is not copyrighted. Anyone may reproduce it in quantity, but the author and the publisher would appreciate it if this source were cited.

[6] Fry, *op. cit.,* p. 514.

through(1). Endings such as -y, -ed, -el, or -le usually make a syllable; for example: ready(2), bottle(2). I find it convenient to count every syllable over one in each word and add 100. Average the total number of syllables for the three samples.

4. Plot on the graph the average number of sentences per hundred words and the average number of syllables per hundred words. Most plot points fall near the heavy curved lines. Perpendicular lines mark off approximate grade level areas.

For example:

|  | Sentences per 100 words | Syllables per 100 words |
|---|---|---|
| 100-word sample, page 5 | 9.1 | 122 |
| 100-word sample, page 89 | 8.5 | 140 |
| 100-word sample, page 160 | 7.0 | 129 |
|  | 3)24.6 | 3)391 |
|  | 8.2 | 130 |

Plotting these averages on the graph, we find that they fall in the fifth grade area; hence the book is about fifth grade difficulty level. If great variability is encountered either in sentence length or in the syllable count for the three sections, then randomly select several more passages and average them in before plotting.

**TABLE 15–1.** Graph for estimating readability
(Edward Fry, Rutgers University Reading Center, New Jersey)

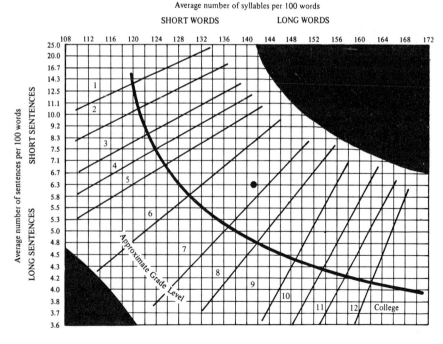

DIRECTIONS:  Randomly select three 100-word passages from a book or an article. Plot average number of syllables and average number of sentences per 100 words on graph to determine the grade level of the material. Choose more passages per book if great variability is observed and conclude that the book has uneven readability. Few books will fall in gray area, but when they do, grade level scores are invalid.

| EXAMPLE: | | *Syllables* | *Sentences* |
|---|---|---|---|
| | 1st Hundred Words | 124 | 6.6 |
| | 2nd Hundred Words | 141 | 5.5 |
| | 3rd Hundred Words | 158 | 6.8 |
| | AVERAGE | 141 | 6.3 |

READABILITY 7th GRADE (see dot plotted on graph)

For further information and validity data see the April 1968 *Journal of Reading* and the March 1969 Reading Teacher.

## How May Context Clues Aid Students in Vocabulary Development?[7]

It has been estimated that over 75 percent of all that is learned at the secondary school level is acquired through reading.[8] Yet students are continually frustrated as they encounter words that have little or no meaning to them. Frequently they will continue to read right past unfamiliar words, making absolutely no effort to understand the unknown. The cumulative effect of such practices is self-defeating.

In most cases the meaning of an unfamiliar word can be acquired through the manner in which it is used, i.e., through the context. When students become aware of specific clues they are often able to reason out strange word meanings.

*Through direct explanation.* Frequently the writer, realizing he has introduced an unfamiliar term, will clarify his meaning directly. For example, he may use words in apposition, setting them off with a comma or with an "o":

A politician, a public servant, is expected to represent the will of the majority of his constituents.

A similar technique involving a direct explanation is the use of clarifying phrases, usually introduced by the words "that is" (i.e.) or "for example" (e.g.):

For all practical purposes the man was dead upon arrival at the hospital, i.e., his heart had stopped beating.

There was a dearth of information on the subject. Several researchers, for example, had pointed out a need for investigation in the area.

---

[7] The sections that follow rely heavily on the materials in Ellen Lamar Thomas and H. Alan Robinson, *Improving Reading in Every Class* (Boston: Allyn and Bacon, Inc., 1972). Used by permission of the publisher.

[8] Leo C. Foy, *Reading in the High School* (National Educational Association. "What Research Says to the Teacher," No. 11, 1956), p. 10.

Occasionally the writer offers an explanation in a sentence or two *prior to* his introduction of a new word; then he *summarizes* his meaning with the word:

> The football team seemed to have trouble getting off the ground. Tackles were slow and uncertain. Some players were even observed to confuse key plays. In short, the team was *lethargic.*

*Through experience or mood.* Often one's own practical life experience will provide the necessary clue to understanding. At other times the author sets the mood, allowing the reader to deduce an approximate meaning:

> As the soldier crouched in his bunker on the lonely ridgeline, expecting an attack that never came, he became painfully aware of the frightening sounds of the heavy artillery in the distance. Finally, as the minutes and hours dragged by, his thoughts turned to home and family. A feeling of *nostalgia* swept over him.

In the foregoing illustration the mood or tone clue, along with the experience clue, were employed. The reader knows, for example, that *frightening* is merely a continuation of the feeling of gloom or despair, whereas *nostalgia* relates to an urge to be with friends and loved ones.

*Through Comparison, Contrast, or Inference.* Through comparison (or contrast) the reader may deduce a new word's meaning by relating it to a word or idea with which he is familiar:

> Time after time the young athlete attempted to surmount the obstacle. Once he barely made it, but the coach made him try again for greater precision. To him, the task was *stupendous.*

> Unlike the calm waters of Lake Pleasant, the waters of Lake Mead were generally *turbulent.*

Sometimes the reader can *infer* the meaning of a word from the general context:

> For days he had been wandering around in the desert, trying to save his dwindling supply of water. His thoughts, his dreams, his hopes were constantly focused on water. Looking out over the sandy ridges he suddenly saw a rather large lake. For a moment he had a compelling urge to dash toward it, but reason finally prevailed. It was only a *mirage.*

### How May Root Words and Origins Assist the Student to Cope with New Words?

Most polysyllable words can be broken down into monosyllable words. The words *polysyllable* and *monosyllable* themselves may be sources of difficulty until a few common Latin and Greek word parts are emphasized. *Poly-,* for example, means many, whereas *mono-* denotes one.

Often there are easy-to-spot root words within a word, i.e., inter*change*able.

By actually "seeing" word parts, aided by context clues, long, imposing words frequently can be easily mastered.

Common prefixes and suffixes often provide much needed clues to meaning. Think of the number of words that begin with the prefix *Pre-*, which means before, or *re-*, which stands for again or back.

New words, of course, are being evolved constantly as the need arises. While such words may offer few direct clues to meaning, their interesting origins can permanently fix meaning. During the Civil War, for example, a General Burnside distinguished himself by letting his facial hair grow to a point well below his earlobes. Thus the word *sideburn* was coined from the name Burnside. Likewise, during Governor Gerry's term of office (Massachusetts) an election district was drawn up that was actually shaped like a salamander. Thus the term *gerrymander* was born.

Many students may simply pass over new words unless word attack techniques are taught and made a vital part of assignments. By preteaching "stopper" words many obstacles to learning are removed. Such preteaching activities eventually may be no more than calling attention to already familiar techniques of word attack skills. Learner independence is the goal desired.

## What Study Techniques Will Enhance Learning of Textbook Materials?

Seldom, if ever, do students receive help in developing an efficient approach to textbook reading. An untold number of precious study hours are wasted. It has been repeatedly demonstrated that even the best students tend to attack their reading assignment page by page, plodding along until they finish the reading assignment.

Fortunately, a systematic pattern of study has been developed by reading specialists that can reduce study time by as much as 25 percent without reducing comprehension.[9] This technique, described by Smith[10] as the *SQ4R Method*, can be readily employed by the classroom teacher. It involves a sequence of events that includes survey, question, read, recite, "rite," and review.

A chapter is *surveyed* for the purpose of determining the author's outline or guideposts. This is the skeleton upon which details and illustrations rest. First read and think about the chapter title. Then read the chapter overview or introduction. Next, look at the chapter's major and minor headings. Finally, turn to the chapter summary. It is also useful to glance at charts, diagrams, and pictures along the way. For those books that do not afford such instructional aids, Smith[11] suggests a modified procedure of reading the first and last paragraphs, followed by reading the first sentence of every third paragraph. A chapter survey can be completed in five or six minutes.

[9] Thomas and Robinson, *op. cit.*, p. 119.

[10] Donald E. P. Smith, gen. ed., *Learning to Learn* (New York: Harcourt, Brace and World, Inc., 1961), pp. 15–50.

[11] *Ibid.*, p. 20.

Next, the effective reader develops a series of *questions before he reads the chapter.* Such a technique arouses a state of curiosity or need to know and serves to provide focus to study activities. The author sometimes provides questions in his chapter overview; more often questions for study and discussion appear at the end of the chapter. The reader will want to develop his own questions also. Titles, subheadings, italicized words, and new terms can be easily reworded as questions. Smith suggests that one should try to *guess* the answer prior to reading to find the answer. This, he suggests, has the effect of creating an emotional reaction that enhances learning.

The third step in the SQ4R sequence is *reading.* Rather than reading the chapter line by line and page by page, one reads *selectively.* He first skims through a section, reading a few words here and there. Then he attempts to focus upon that material which bears upon his questions. This is accomplished by looking for signal phrases, such as "'the first reason,' 'my next point,' and so on. After skipping to each signal phrase briefly (usually marked by separate paragraphs), he then moves back and reads more carefully the supporting material for each of the "reasons."

When one has found the answer to one of his questions, he should *stop* and then *recite* the answer in his own words. This thinking through process, unlike underlining in the textbook, results in real learning. It may be necessary to check back to the text briefly until all points are clearly understood.

The reciting process is followed immediately by *writing* key words that serve as cues to answers. One or two words consisting of *cues to one's own recitation* provide the most meaningful connection for later recall of the complete answers. The questions and cue words constitute one's permanent study notes.

The last step in the SQ4R process involves *review.* This consists of concentrating on the questions formulated earlier. For those that cannot be answered, a brief look at one's cue words should be sufficient. This process should immediately follow completion of the assignment. It should be repeated at least once a week to minimize the effects of forgetting.

It is seen from the foregoing that the SQ4R method involves a systematized approach to textbook study. It involves reflective thinking processes just as do all other instructional methods. These are skills that must be taught if effective study is to be assured.

### How Is a Flexible Reading Rate Developed?

Reading speed should vary according to the nature and purpose of the material being presented. Unfamiliar terms, difficulty concepts, technical material, detailed directions, and the like require the reader to reduce his reading rate. On the other hand, simple materials, illustrations that are not necessary for understanding, restatement of ideas, and materials where the important facts only are desired can be read rapidly. Although speed in many situations is desirable, constant speed is not a characteristic of a highly skilled, purposeful reader.[12]

The skillful reader is an expert at *skimming* for the purpose of grasping the general drift of a passage. When skimming, the student reads selectively. If, for example, his source is an entire book he looks at the table of contents, preface, and introduction to gain a general idea of the book's content. Then he turns to the chapters that bear directly on his problem or purpose. He glances at the headings and subheadings. In addition, he reads introductions and summaries. Finally, he focuses upon paragraphs for main ideas.

Each paragraph is skimmed for the purpose of locating the main idea, often contained in a single sentence, called a *topic sentence*. A topic sentence often appears as the first or last sentence of the paragraph. It may appear, however, near the middle of the paragraph. Sometimes it appears in no one sentence and thus must be deduced from the entire paragraph. In any event, the process is simplified if one looks for word signals such as "in the first place," "nevertheless," or "moreover."

*Scanning* is another form of rapid reading employed when looking for specific information such as dates and word definitions. After finding his general informational source through appropriate skimming processes, the reader quickly runs his eyes down a page, looking for indicator words, such as italics, capitalized words, and figures.

According to Thomas and Robinson,[13] there are three levels of scanning.

*Level I:* The least complex, this level merely involves scanning for a specific point that stands out easily. A history student, for example, may need to find the date of an important battle or event. The reader sweeps down the page looking for dates in the form of numerals or italicized words. When he finds the information he slows down, carefully checking to make sure that he has found the needed information.

*Level II:* This level of scanning involves looking for an answer to a specific question. It is still easy and rapid, though not quite as simple as Level I. The reader, for example, may want to know the average annual rainfall in Phoenix, Arizona. Before he begins his search he asks himself what indicator words might help him find the information. Some of these indicators might be climate, temperature, rainfall, or seasons. Again, he concentrates on the indicator words constantly as he runs down the page, expecting them to stand out from the rest. Once he finds his information he reads very carefully for the purpose of verifying and expanding his answer.

*Level III:* At this most complex level of scanning the reader looks for information that will not appear as a simple answer to his question. He may need to know, for example, why August is the "wet" month in Phoenix, Arizona. He again makes use of indicator words, but this time he is less certain of where to find the information. Thus he usually must enlarge his list, e.g., thermal lows, humidity, desert monsoons, prevailing Westerlies, cloud formations. He proceeds

[12] Thomas and Robinson, *op. cit.*, p. 188.
[13] Thomas and Robinson, *op. cit.*, p. 209.

as before but must move at a slower pace, since he is looking for a specific fact that may appear under a larger heading. When he finds his information he reads very carefully as he checks out the details.

The key to efficient scanning is fixing in mind precisely what one is searching for and then glancing swiftly down the page for words that call attention to the information sought. This is followed by careful reading for the purpose of verification.

### How Are Students Prepared for Reading Assignments?

The all too familiar assignment, "Read the next chapter," has probably caused more frustration and resentment among students than any other aspect of today's education. Even if all students were competent readers such an assignment would be woefully inadequate. Is one to read for main ideas? Is he expected to pick out specific facts or bits of information? Is considerable reflection necessary?

In addition to capturing student interest and providing the learner with a valid purpose, the wise teacher preteaches "stopper" words. Moreover, he guides the learner in *how* to read most efficiently for accomplishing his purpose.

"Stopper" words should be pulled out of the reading assignment and examined for meaning. As previously discussed, root words, Latin or Greek origins, syllables, and appropriate pronunciation guides should be noted. This tends to remove the fear of the unknown and to reduce any obstacles or barriers that new words create.

As the assignment is made a few minutes can be devoted to the best method of reading it. It may be desirable to provide a few moments of guided practice by way of illustration. This is one reason for beginning most assignments during the class period. If, for example, general background information is all that is needed, the teacher should make this point. He might suggest, "Read this section rapidly for a general impression, just to catch the mood without remembering the details."

If high speed scanning is in order the teacher should either include appropriate questions or guide students in developing such questions. He may say, "Scan the material rapidly, looking for flag words, until you think you have found the needed information. Then slow way down to determine if you have really located the needed information."

Many times close, intensive reading is necessary. The teacher calls attention to this by suggesting that the learner stop and reflect on each sentence and paragraph. He might forewarn him that the two or three pages of assigned reading are equivalent to fifty or more pages of a novel. Sometimes carefully worded analysis or evaluation questions can be useful in serving such a purpose.

Variable reading rates often are necessary *within* a given assignment. Thus a vital part of every reading assignment involves calling attention to specific parts and how they are to be read. As previously indicated, the SQ4R method is ideal for increasing retention of specific information. Since reading habits are deeply engrained, students need considerable practice under close supervision in adopting more efficient techniques.

### How Is the Dictionary Used Most Effectively?

Some students turn to the dictionary for assistance each time they come across a new word. Others seldom, if ever, consult a dictionary. Each extreme is undesirable. A dictionary offers little help unless the general context of word usage is perceived. Since the dictionary provides an unlimited number of word definitions, it is left to the user to select the meaning that is closest to his "word in context."

Most students can profit from a few simple pointers on dictionary use. Word meaning cannot be derived unless the word can be located. Guide words appear at the top of every page. The word that appears at the top of the first column of a page is the first entry word on that page. The guide word at the top of the second column of the page indicates the last entry on that page.

The dictionary also offers assistance in pronouncing words. The student must know the phonic respelling system of the dictionary he is using, however. This information is offered in the dictionary guide, located in the front or in the back of the dictionary. The student must be taught to look at the phonetic respelling of the word and to refer to the key word for each vowel sound as an aid in pronouncing the word by syllable. In pronouncing the entire word he must note the accented syllable or syllables.

The dictionary should be used *after* various context clues have been employed. It is sometimes an essential tool in confirming word meaning and is certainly useful when context clues are not very helpful. By referring to synonyms (designated by SYN in the word entry) the reader can sometimes gain a clue to word meaning when all other clues fail. The dictionary may be the only source of correct pronunciation open to an individual doing a home assignment.

## VALUES

All students can profit from some guidance in developmental reading techniques. A few simple suggestions frequently can make the best students even better students.

Poor readers must have constant help in coping with the language of technical subjects. Even though they "know better," such students are likely to lapse into their old habits unless constant guidance is available.

Reading speed varies between and within given assignments. Key questions, attention to "stopper" words, and the like are essential to effective assignments.

Calling attention to prefixes, suffixes, root words, and derivations is especially useful in helping the learner cope with new words.

Since words and word meanings are constantly changing, attention to word context provides a most valuable clue to meaning.

Use of the dictionary as a valuable (last) source of help in ascertaining word meaning must be emphasized.

## LIMITATIONS AND PROBLEMS

Poor readers subconsciously employ inappropriate reading habits. Since such habits vary from student to student, often involving a system of thought processes only, systematic analysis is difficult. Observations of lip movement, erratic eye movement, along with exercises for reading aloud, are useful diagnostic techniques.

Teachers frequently claim that there is insufficient time to "teach reading." Since reading skills are *prerequisite* to adequate coping with the language of a subject, one teaches reading *as he teaches content.*

Many teachers feel incompetent in the area. As this chapter implies, however, *developmental* reading techniques are quite simple. Rather than teaching reading, the teacher is merely helping the learner cope with specific reading problems in given content fields.

Students, and some teachers, often labor under the misconception of a single reading rate. Rate must vary with the nature of the assignment. Such expressions as "you will want to skim this," or "read this for detail," provide necessary clues for effective teaching.

## ILLUSTRATED TECHNIQUES

   I.  Preliminary textbook survey

     Within the first week of the semester it is desirable to guide students in a preliminary textbook survey. (If multiple texts are used, different students can be asked to survey them.) It is a good idea to ask each student to write out comments for each point of the survey. (See pp. 230–31 of this chapter for details.)

     A.  Organization of the book
     B.  Headings relative to content
     C.  Instructional materials and aids
     D.  Type of organization
     E.  Preface
     F.  Preview of individual chapters

     The survey is probably best accomplished in steps, followed by a brief discussion of each step prior to moving to the succeeding step. The ultimate objective is to set the stage for a self-initiated survey of *any* text that may be used.

II. Assessing textbook readability level (A task for the teacher)

One to five or six books frequently are selected as basic texts for most high school subjects. Usually at least one of the books will be considered easy enough for the poorest readers in class. Judgments often are based upon content material only, despite the fact that the vocabulary may be beyond the comprehension level of poor readers. Until recently, many basic high school texts were written at a college reading level—well beyond the reading level of most high school students. Thus it behooves every teacher to assess the readability level of each textbook that is to be used extensively. The procedure, described on pp. 231–33 of this chapter, can be easily applied.

III. Context clues

A mere discussion of context clues is inadequate for most students. Poor readers especially have developed the self-defeating habit of reading right past unfamiliar words. The first step in breaking such undesirable habits is to conduct a class assignment in which each student is asked to find specific context clues, write them out, and then share them with the rest of the class. Context clues, as described on pp. 233–34 of the chapter, include:

A. Direct explanation (flag words and symbols: i.e., e.g., to summarize, in short)
B. Experience or mood (often characterized by a moving anecdote)
C. Comparison, contrast, or inference

This experience should be repeated frequently. Some teachers use this as a readiness technique for each teaching unit.

IV. Root words and origins

Words with several syllables often are "skipped" by most students. Sometimes these are called "stopper" words because they tend to block or impede meaning. Most courses have a number of "stopper" words that are unique to a particular subject. Although special lessons on general terminology are sometimes appropriate, it is usually most efficient to concentrate on prefixes, suffixes, and word origins.

A useful approach is to ask students to write out all prefixes and suffixes from selected reading assignments. Root word meanings (through use of the dictionary or glossary of terms) can be discussed and if necessary memorized. This can be followed by introduction of new words in the subject field that employ such root words.

V. SQ4R method

It has been demonstrated that study time can be reduced by as much as 25 percent (without reducing comprehension) if a systematic pattern is followed. Known as the SQ4R method, the technique involves the following:

S—*Surveying* a chapter to determine the author's outline
Q—Developing *questions* (often accomplished by developing topic headings into questions)
R—*Reading.* Rather than a line-by-line reading, the learner looks for

"signal" or "flag" words. (To illustrate: "the first reason," "my next point," etc.)

R—*Reciting.* When an answer has been found, the learner *stops* and *recites* the answer *in his own words.*

R—*Writing* key words (permanent study notes) that serve as cues to answers.

R—*Reviewing,* by concentrating on one's original key questions. Cue words (from study notes) should be used in areas of difficulty. Review immediately following completion of the assignment and repeat at least once weekly to minimize the effects of forgetting.

The SQ4R method is *not* likely to be used extensively unless specific study assignments incorporate the method. Such structured assignments should be repeated frequently and followed up with a class discussion of problems encountered.

VI.   Skimming and scanning

A flexible reading rate is basic to effective study. One *skims* for main ideas. By looking at the table of contents, preface, and introduction the learner quickly assesses a book's content. Likewise, chapter headings and subheadings, introductions, summaries, and paragraph topic sentences are noted in order to quickly grasp the general drift of the contents. (Five minutes are adequate for the task.)

Scanning (the first of the 4Rs described in item V) involves rapidly looking for details by noting "flag" or "indicator" words. (See p. 237 for the different levels.)

A few specific assignments involving skimming and scanning are definitely in order. These should be timed, as the emphasis is upon rapid reading.

VII.   Use of the dictionary

A dictionary can be helpful for developing word meaning *after* (and only after) general context is perceived. A few simple pointers on dictionary usage are helpful at intervals throughout a course. One might concentrate on the following (see p. 239 for details):

A.   Guide words (left column guide word denotes the first entry on the page; right column guide word denotes the last entry).

B.   Phonetic respelling (for assistance in pronunciation). Note the accented syllables.

C.   Synonyms (designated by SYN).

D.   Others that seem appropriate.

## SELECTED BIBLIOGRAPHY

Adams, Dennis M. *Simulation Games: An Approach to Learning* (Worthington, N.J.: Beacon House, Inc., 1973).

Beckman, M. D. "Evaluating the Case Method." *Educational Forum* 36 (May 1972): 489–97.

Berman, Mark L., ed. *Motivation and Learning* (Englewood Cliffs, N.J.: Educational Technology Publications, 1971).

Blanton, William E., et al., eds. *Measuring Reading Performance* (Newark, Del.: International Reading Association, 1974).

Bloom, Benjamin S., ed. *Taxonomy of Educational Objectives—Handbook I: Cognitive Domain* (New York: David McKay Co., Inc., 1956).

Carin, Arthur, and Sund, Robert B. *Developing Questioning Techniques* (Columbus: Charles E. Merrill Publishing Co., 1971). Chs. 4 and 5.

Carter, Ronald D. *Help! These Kids Are Driving Me Crazy* (Oshkosh, Wisc.: Research Press, 1972).

Clarizio, Harvey F. *Toward Positive Classroom Discipline* (New York: John Wiley and Sons, Inc., 1971).

Cofer, Charles S. *Motivation and Emotion* (New York: Scott, Foresman and Co., 1972).

*Educational Technology* (September 1972). Entire issue devoted to various types of learning activity packages.

Feder, B. "Case Studies: A Flexible Approach to Knowledge Building," *The Social Studies* 64 (April 1973): 171–78.

Glasser, William. *Reality Therapy Approach* (New York: Harper and Row, Publishers, 1965).

Gnagey, William J., et al. *Learning Environments: Readings in Educational Psychology* (New York: Holt, Rinehart and Winston, Inc., 1972).

Gordon, Thomas. *Teacher Effectiveness Training* (New York: Wyden, Inc., 1975).

Gray, Jenny. *The Teacher's Survival Guide* (Palo Alto, Calif.: Fearon Publishers, 1967).

———. *Teaching Without Tears: Your First Year in the Secondary School* (Palo Alto, Calif.: Fearon Publishers, 1968).

Gronlund, Norman E. *Sociometry in the Classroom* (New York: Harper and Row, Publishers, 1959).

Haring, Norris G., and Phillips, E. Lakin. *Analysis and Modification of Classroom Behavior* (Englewood Cliffs, N.J.: Prentice-Hall, Inc., 1973).

Herndon, James. *The Way It Sposed to Be* (New York: Simon and Schuster, Inc., 1968).

Inbar, Michael, and Stoll, Clarice S. *Simulation and Gaming in Social Studies* (New York: The Free Press, 1972).

Hyman, Ronald T. *Ways of Teaching.* Rev. ed., Part III (Philadelphia: J. B. Lippincott Co., 1970).

*Journal of Reading.* A reading periodical directed to high school teachers. Suitable for supplementary reading.

Kennedy, Eddie C. *Methods in Teaching Developmental Reading* (Itasca, Ill.: F. E. Peacock Publishers, Inc., 1974).

Kenworthy, L. S. "Role-Playing in Teacher Education." *The Social Studies* 64 (November 1973): 243–46.

Kravitz, B. "Analysis of Decision Making in the Study of United States History." *The Social Studies* 65 (February 1973): 60–63.

Ladas, H., and Osti, L. "Asking Questions: A Strategy for Teachers." *The Home Economics Journal* 56 (January 1973): 174–89.

Madsen, Charles H., Jr., and Madsen, Clifford K. *Teaching/Discipline.* 2d ed. (Boston: Allyn and Bacon, Inc., 1974).

O'Conner, Kathleen. *Learning: An Introduction* (Glenview, Ill.: Scott, Foresman and Co., 1971).

Olson, Richard D., et al. *Learning in the Classroom: Theory and Application* (Berkeley, Calif.: McCuhran Publishing Co., 1971).

Sanders, Norris. *Classroom Questions: What Kinds?* (New York: Harper and Row, Publishers, 1966).

Shaver, James P., and Larkins, A. Guy. "The Case Method and the Study of International Affairs." *National Council for the Social Studies Yearbook* 38 (1968): 215–36.

*Sociometry* (a journal of interpersonal relations). Quarterly. (Beacon, N.Y.: Beacon House, Inc.).

Steinback, Susan B., and Steinback, William C. *Classroom Discipline: A Positive Approach* (Springfield, Ill.: Charles C. Thomas Publisher, 1974).

Thomas, Ellen Lamar, and Robinson, H. Alan. *Improving Reading in Every Class* (Boston: Allyn and Bacon, Inc., 1972).

Weinberger, Robert A. *Perspectives in Individualized Learning* (Itasca, Ill.: F. E. Peacock Publishers, Inc., 1971).

Williams, Robert L., and Anandam, Kamala. *Cooperative Classroom Management* (Columbus: Charles E. Merrill Publishing Co., 1973).

## ANNOTATED FILM LIST

*Case Method of Instruction,* Parts I, II, III
    16 mm films; 19, 23, 19 minutes
    Treats the principles, applications, and values of the case method of teaching.
    U.S. National Audiovisual Center
    National Archives and Records Service
    Washington, D.C. 20408

*Individual Differences*
    16 mm film; 28 minutes
    Treats the nature of individual differences in evaluating classroom marks.
    From the *Nursing Effective Evaluation* Series
    University of Nebraska Television Council
    University of Nebraska
    1800 N. 33rd
    Lincoln, Nebr. 68503

*Questioning Skills,* Cluster II. Divergent Questioning
16 mm film; 8 minutes
Illustrates use of open-ended questions that require students to think creatively. From the *Teaching Skills for Secondary School Teachers* Series. General Learning Corp.
250 James St.
Morristown, N.J. 10022

*Questioning Skills,* Cluster II. Fluency in Answering Questions
16 mm film; 7 minutes
Depicts how to increase pupil talk while reducing teacher talk.
Same source as above.

*Questioning Skills,* Cluster II. Higher Order Questions
16 mm film; 8 minutes
Illustrates questions that require student reflection.
Same source as above.

*Questioning Skills,* Cluster II. Probing Questions
16 mm film; 7 minutes
Illustrates techniques of taking students beyond superficial responses.
Same source as above.

*Questions for Thinking*
16 mm film; 28 minutes
Explores what can be done to encourage students to think.
Media Five Film Distributors
1011 N. Cole Ave.
Hollywood, Calif. 90038.

## SELECTED FILMSTRIPS

*Asking Questions*
Filmstrip
Suggests the need for and the proper framing of class questions.
AVI Associates, Inc.
825 Third Ave.
New York, N.Y. 10022

*Motivation in Teaching and Learning*
Sound filmstrip
Summarizes recent research on motivation in teaching.
National Education Association
1201 16th St., N.W.
Washington, D.C. 20036

*Systematic Instructional Decision-Making*
Sound filmstrip
Offers an instructional model for selecting instructional activities in a teaching sequence.
Vimcit Associates
P.O. Box 24714
Los Angeles, Calif. 90024

*The Teaching of Discipline*
    Filmstrip
    Indicates how to improve student behavior in the school.
    Educational Filmstrips
    Box 1401
    1409 19th St.
    Huntsville, Texas 77340

*The Teaching of Reading*
    Sound filmstrip
    Provides techniques for teaching and evaluating developmental reading techniques.
    Vimcit Associates
    P.O. Box 24714
    Los Angeles, Calif. 90024

# SELECTED OVERHEAD TRANSPARENCIES

*Simulation*—A Series
    Transparencies
    Offers fundamentals and applications of simulation.
    Langford Publishing Co.
    P.O. Box 8711
    1088 Lincoln Ave.
    San Jose, Calif. 95155

*The Social Interaction Perspective*
    8 x 10 prepared transparency
    Same source as above.

*Student Interest and the Learning Process*
    10 x 10 prepared transparency
    Same source as above.

# FREE AND INEXPENSIVE LEARNING MATERIALS

*Controlling Classroom Misbehavior.* No. 387-11862.
    50 cents
    *What Research Says to the Teacher* Series.
    National Education Association
    1201 16th St., N.W.
    Washington, D.C. 20016

*The Encyclopedia: A Resource for Creative Teaching and Independent Learning.* No. SA 2611.
    50 cents
    Offers creative ways of using the dictionary at all school levels.
    Field Enterprise, Education Corp.
    The Merchandise Mart
    Chicago, Ill. 60654

*How to Plan and Manage Minicourses*
$1.00
National Science Teachers Association
1201 16th St., N.W.
Washington, D.C. 20016

*Motivation in Teaching and Learning.* No. 387-11866.
50 cents
*What Research Says to the Teacher* Series
National Education Association
Same as first item above.

*Simulation in the Classroom*
$1.95
Penguin Books, Inc.
7110 Ambassador Rd.
Baltimore, Md. 21207

# Methods with a Focus on the Group

| | |
|---|---|
| Discussion Methods | Drill and Practice |
| Debate | Procedures |
| Processes of Inquiry | Measurement and Evaluation |
| Small-Group Techniques | Techniques and Devices |
| Group Processes | Evaluation and Reporting |
| Lecture Method | Procedures |
| Review Method | |

*Education for all the people is dependent on effective instructional groups. Students universally are assigned to groups, both large and small. While there is indeed some merit in the tutorial relationship, costs involved are prohibitive. Groups, however, are much more than necessary evils. They represent life at its best. Man is a social animal. His very existence is dependent on the cooperative effort of all the people. In today's age of space exploration traditional boundaries are becoming less important, as man finds it necessary to rely more and more upon all the peoples of the world.*

*The class group does much more than provide a setting for instruction. It lends support and offers direction to those involved. It permits the emergence of leadership, realistic group problem solving, and the application of democratic principles to everyday living.*

*The instructional methods and techniques described in the chapters of this unit have one important common characteristic: They utilize a group structure to enhance learning. The organization and sequence of the chapters is a logical one, proceeding from an emphasis on relatively small, short-lived subgroups to utilization of the class group as a whole. This is not to imply, however, that one will rely wholly on small group discussion and debate groups or on the larger, purely democratic group approaches. As indicated throughout, an integration of instructional procedures is essential if the broad range of student needs is to be met.*

*Chapters 16 and 17 offer systematic approaches to three closely related techniques: guided class discussion, and debate. Perhaps the most widely used instructional approach today is class discussion in some form. It is known that students will indulge in serious reflection only to the extent that the group setting is conducive to such reflection. While groups of thirty* to forty students admittedly are not of optimum size for class discussion, the technique can be far more effective than it typically is. A much less used, but often more effective, instructional tool is the closely related technique of panel discussion. Again, the misuse of panel discussion groups frequently has produced results that have been disappointing. In these chapters, panel discussion, designed to facilitate the problem-solving pursuits of the entire class group, is emphasized. Debate as a major class activity is also described. In the normal process of events discussion is followed with debate whenever group decisions fail to materialize. Debaters utilize all their powers of persuasion in presenting opposing arguments on highly controversial issues. By abiding by the rules of the game, students can weigh highly emotional matters through the processes of debate in an atmosphere conducive to learning.

Approaches to classroom utilization of democratic processes at their best are described in Chapters 18, 19, and 20. Overall problem-solving activities under such conditions are planned and directed by the class group. The instructor, instead of assuming a traditional role of taskmaster, director, and evaluator, works cooperatively with students. As indicated in Chapter 18, he assumes joint responsibility with students for planning and directing learning activities. In purely group approaches to learning, described in Chapter 20, he becomes even less a central figure.

A technique that provides for considerable learner independence is the small group, treated in Chapter 19. It is noted that such groups can be short- or long-lived. They feature students working together in groups of from three to six for a specific purpose. In such situations the teacher's role is relegated to that of a participating guide.

As a technique for realistically extending learning, review has no equal. Extensive psychological research, for example, supports the value of review in bringing out important relationships. By taking a new look at previous learnings, important associations and insights can be disclosed. The technique illustrated in Chapter 22 thus differs from traditional review procedures, which too often involve mere repetition of events. Current misuse of review procedures can serve only to underscore the urgent need for a thorough understanding of this basic instructional tool. Drill and practice procedures, treated in Chapter 23, are somewhat related to but distinctly different from review techniques.

Measurement and evaluation techniques have been recognized as the weakest aspect of the instructional process. Some parents, and indeed a number of educators, recently have made a plea for the abolition of tests and grades. They point to the general poor quality of many teacher-made tests and the all too frequent arbitrary, capricious use of grades. Testing devices and techniques, however, need not be of poor quality. When used appropriately, they become an indispensable aspect of the instructional process.

When instruction is based upon basic unit concepts and predicted behavioral outcomes, measurement and evaluation become an integral part of the instructional process. Reflective thinking, as emphasized throughout this book, becomes the basis for assessment experiences. Indeed, multiple-choice and essay test items can be so constructed as to involve the learner in similar processes of reflection.

CHAPTER **16**

# Discussion Methods

## OVERVIEW

### Key Concepts

1. Controversial issues provide a sound basis for discussion; accordingly, the intent is not so much the resolution of a problem as it is the weighing of evidence and proposals.
2. Open-ended problems (policy problems) are most appropriate for discussion.
3. Discussion follows a more-or-less logical sequence of development.
4. In discussion, student questions usually are reflected back for class analysis.
5. Problem analysis, followed with a consideration of alternatives, are minimum essentials of the discussion process.
6. Students themselves may appropriately participate in evaluation of a panel discussion.

### New Terms

1. **Problem of Policy**—An open-ended type of question, often *preplanned* by the teacher, which forms the basis for class and panel discussion. Often begins with the word *what* but sometimes may begin with such key words as *why* or *how*. The word *should* or *ought* is stated or implied in the question.
2. **Problem of Advocacy**—A proposed solution to a problem, usually beginning with the word *should* or *ought*. Such questions enter into discussion especially when hypotheses are being considered.
3. **Panel Discussion**—A discussion which is led and directed by students themselves, usually consisting of five to seven individuals.

4. **Enlightenment Discussion**—A discussion (usually panel) dealing with clarification of facts. Not usually appropriate unless the facts themselves are confusing and somewhat contradictory in nature.
5. **Follow-through Discussion**—A teacher-led discussion which follows a panel discussion (or related instructional technique). Purpose is to clarify issues, derive generalizations and the like.

## Questions to Guide Your Study

1. Why is enlightenment discussion sometimes appropriate for panel discussion but considered generally inappropriate for class discussion?
2. "Students should evolve their own discussion problems." Defend or refute.
3. Why is guided class discussion sometimes referred to as *pseudo* discussion?
4. What are the advantages and disadvantages attributed to the problem-type discussion treated in this chapter?
5. It has been contended that discussion *process* is more important than the end product. Why?

The students were gathered around a table drinking coffee. They were discussing the important aspects of the farm problem. The discussion was characterized by individual opinions, many of which dealt with personalities.

Professor Burton was talking to his class about seventeenth-century aristocracies. He outlined the relevant facts, brought in important relationships, and drew certain conclusions. Finally, during the last ten minutes of the hour he entertained questions from the group.

Miss Killinger was questioning her biology students on their assigned readings. Most of the questions dealt with definitions and facts presented. Occasionally a student asked about important relationships, which Miss Killinger was only too happy to enlarge upon.

Mr. Buell was using the factual materials of an assigned lesson to help students make relationships and conclusions. It soon became obvious that few students had read the materials. Their responses, for the most part, consisted of value judgments, many of which were not related to the facts of the case.

While the above illustrations represent discussion in a broad sense, none of them characterize the guided class discussion technique described in this chapter. The college professor is *not* conducting a guided discussion. His method of teaching, whether it be lecture, demonstration, or something else, may be appropriate, but it does not qualify as guided class discussion. Nor does the method of having students recite materials from their texts constitute a true class discussion. The rather questionable classroom practice of discussing anything and everything which just happens to evolve—often called "bull sessions" by the participants—certainly does not qualify as a guided discussion. *The guided class discussion is designed to develop group agreement through talk and reflective thinking.* It aims to stimulate analysis, encourage interpretations, develop or change attitudes. In other words, the individual is guided in some sort of *reflection* on a problem which involves "weighing" the evidence before a decision or opinion can be reached. Through appropriate leadership, evidence is brought to bear on the crucial issues of a problem; the evidence is analyzed and evaluated *by the group;* and certain generalizations are reached.

When individuals engage in discussion, they ponder or meditate; they think critically. The discusser *reflects* upon his ideas along with those of his colleagues. He is a searcher, an inquirer. In effect, he says, "Here are my ideas. How do they relate to your opinions and the facts of the situation?" He is willing to alter views which seem inadequate under the scrutiny of thoughtful analysis. He does not change his views, however, on the basis of peer pressure or emotion. If the objective evidence seems to warrant reassessments of tentative ideas and assumptions, he is ever ready to adjust accordingly.

Discussion is most appropriate when basic areas of controversy exist. Although a rather poor means of disseminating information, the method is ideal for evolving, sorting, and sifting facts and values essential for the resolution of problems. Discussion is ideally suited for attainment of the higher cognitive goals; it is also useful for attainment of affective goals.

## FUNDAMENTAL PROPERTIES

Discussion essentially embodies the basic properties of the democratic process. It is based upon the assumption that individuals, when sufficiently informed on an issue, are capable of decision making in an atmosphere characterized by a free interchange of ideas and expressions. Whether the leader is a teacher or a student, his role is essentially one of creating an appropriate environment for open reflection.

### Why Must the Discusser Be Open Minded?

The discussant is receptive to new ideas. He examines or ponders new ideas alongside his own notions, making objective comparisons and contrasts. Above all, he must cultivate the ability to look at himself and his ideas objectively and dispassionately. First of all, he seeks to identify his own biases and prejudices. He must seek to avoid either-or thinking, recognizing the possibility of middle ground. This does not mean, of course, that he must change his attitudes. It does suggest, however, that each participant probably will see his own notions as not quite as good and the ideas of others as not quite as bad as he had originally seen them.

### Why Is Flexibility Important?

As implied in the foregoing, the discussant is willing to change his mind on the basis of logical, objective evidence. He does not necessarily do so, however. If, on the basis of his considered judgment, other ideas must be rejected, he stands his ground. When other discussants likewise must take opposing stands, the stage is set for debate (treated in the chapter following).

Even when discussion evolves into opposing camps, the discussant must be flexible enough to understand other views from the frame of reference of those involved. He must be able to say honestly, "I understand why you take the position you do but cannot accept your conclusions." In rare instances a discussion group may merely agree to disagree.

### What Role Does Objectivity Play?

Although the spirit and life of a discussion is projected through basic human emotion, intellectual processes of objectivity are emphasized. Ideas advanced by others are accepted on their own merits. Sources of information are frequently cited; evidence which might discredit certain facts or evaluations is brought into the open forum of reflection. Emotionalism, through persuasive language and gestures, is definitely discouraged. Even in a teacher-led discussion, contributions or inferences by the leader must be open to careful scrutiny.

### What Is the Reflective Process?

The basic purpose of discussion is to reflect upon information and ideas which lead to the resolution of a stated problem. Accordingly, there are no speeches in a discussion. One makes his point, contributes a bit of information, or asks a question and then waits for somebody else to react to his contribution. The discussion leader reflects questions back to the group for analysis. Even in teacher-led discussion the leader must be viewed as one of a panel of equals. In attempting to accomplish this "impossible" task, he usually restricts himself to skillful questions designed to encourage penetrating analysis and evaluation of ideas.

### What Are the Important Problem Types?

Discussion often breaks down because of the wording of the discussion problem. Four major types or kinds of questions have been identified. All may become involved during the discussion process. The *policy* question, however, is basic to the problem-solving type of discussion emphasized in this chapter. It should serve as a major problem for discussion. The four kinds of problems that lend themselves to varying degrees of reflective thinking are described.

*Fact.* Problems of fact are concerned with the discovery and evaluation of factual information. They are emphasized during the analysis of the problem when facts are introduced and clarified. For example: "What U.S. goods, if any, are being traded to Communist China?"

*Value.* Problems of value are concerned with matters relative to value judgments. They call for the application of accepted standards in determining the appropriateness, rightness, or effectiveness of an issue. Examples: "How well is our trade policy being administered?" "Is our trade policy interfering with efforts to keep the peace?" Questions of value arise frequently during the early phases of a discussion. They are related to the *evaluation* of facts.

Problems of fact and problems of value usually can be identified by the presence of some form of the verb *to be.* Indeed they are sometimes referred to as *is* or *are* questions.

*Advocacy.* Problems of advocacy, as the term implies, focus upon specific solutions. Such a question encourages argument rather than discussion. Advocacy questions most often emerge when hypotheses or tentative solutions to a problem are being evaluated. It is for this reason that establishment of accepted criteria should be developed prior to weighing the alternatives. To illustrate the type of question: "Should trade with Communist China be increased?" The question can be answered by yes or no. Wording of the question precludes consideration of other alternatives. This is the type of problem used in debate, illustrated in the chapter following. Such questions usually begin with the word *should* or *ought.*

*Policy.* Problems of policy deal with matters necessitating decisions or action. Implied in the problem is the importance of exploring all possible solutions. Policy questions often begin with the words *What, How,* or *Why.* The words "should" or "ought" are also stated or implied in the question. For example: "What should be the U.S. trade policy with Communist China?"

In resolving a problem of policy, questions of *fact, value,* and *advocacy* will be involved. The reverse does not follow, however. In formulating problems for discussion, teachers often confuse policy with advocacy questions. Advocacy immediately directs attention to concern for one particular solution. Furthermore, it tends to divide a group into opposing camps.

# DISCUSSION PROCEDURE

When people associate with each other, they usually discuss. Individuals often find solutions to their daily problems by talking them over with others. Ask your neighbor what he thinks of the slate of candidates for the school board and he will probably respond with, "I don't know; what do you think?" After some discussion it is quite likely that both you and your neighbor will have clarified your views on the problem. Such informal discussion goes on continually in and out of the classroom. Indeed it is basic to the democratic process.

To be most effective as an instructional method, however, discussion must be carefully planned and executed. Although there are a number of variations and interesting modifications, the basic aims of discussion are to stimulate analysis, to encourage interpretations, and to develop or change attitudes. In this section a technique which embodies all of these aims is described. Through appropriate leadership, evidence is brought to bear on the crucial aspects of a selected problem; the evidence is evaluated and analyzed by *the group;* certain proposed solutions are introduced and evaluated; and finally generalizations are derived from the experience.

## How Is the Problem Identified?

In nurturing the basic skills of critical thinking, problem discovery and formulation must be considered of basic importance. The individual must somehow become aware of a problem or difficulty. Perhaps inconsistencies between related facts are noted. Sometimes incomplete data or puzzling events raise problems. Often there are questions of application involved.

This basic aspect of critical thinking has all too often been handled exclusively by the teacher. In a mathematics class, for example, the problems are carefully developed in the text or by the teacher. Likewise, in science classes "experiments" are commonly defined and delineated for the student. Problem identification is indeed a difficult task—sometimes even for the teacher. Nevertheless, students should have some experience in identifying problems for themselves. This "set" toward problem discovery which characterizes the creative person is an essential aspect of democratic processes.

Certainly during the early stages of a course, the teacher may want to identify and state problems carefully for the benefit of students. Later, he may want to shift much of this responsibility to students themselves. Generally, discussion problems should be related to current issues of the day. They will involve some life application as closely related to the lives of the students as possible. As indicated in the foregoing topic, problems of policy are most appropriate for class discussion. Many teachers favor the practice of writing the problem on the board as a springboard to effective discussion.

Students (and indeed many teachers) experience difficulty in formulating problems in a meaningful way. The problem must be so worded as to point up the crucial issues to be resolved and in such a way as to avoid a misleading set. After students have been guided in problem development, they should be assisted in developing the issues into one of policy, *prior* to its exploration and analysis.

## How Is the Problem Analyzed?

As a preliminary step in decision making, the various components of a problem must be introduced and evaluated. The process leads the learner from definition of important terms to an inspection of important facts and circumstances associated with the problem. In this phase of discussion the seriousness of the problem is examined.

A discussion is offered for the problem, "What steps should be taken to minimize the use of LSD among teen-agers?"

1. What is LSD?
2. How widespread is its use among teen-agers?
3. What are its effects?
4. What evidence indicates the problem is likely to persist? Are there evidences to the contrary?

## How Are Hypotheses Established?

After reviewing and evaluating the related facts and ideas relative to the problem, possibilities for solving the problem must be introduced. Sometimes referred to as the "idea generation" phase, this is the very heart of the problem-solving process. It is at this point that the teacher refers the group to the original question and poses the big question, "What should be done?" Students are invited to offer possibilities for solving the problem. Some such possibilities may be entirely new and may seem a bit "wild" when first introduced as is typical of much creative thinking.

Each proposed solution can be followed with a brief discussion of advantages and disadvantages which seem apparent. An alternative procedure and one preferred by those who would emphasize creativity in teaching involves a listing of possible solutions *prior* to any sort of evaluation. Sometimes a fifteen to twenty minute brainstorming session may be in order to this point.

## How Are Ideas Tested?

In many relatively simple problems a brief analysis of advantages and disadvantages of the alternatives is all that is needed. Through this process, appropriate action becomes obvious. Other issues are not so easily handled, however. A "best" solution often appears best because of the particular needs or frame of reference of the individual involved.

In such cases the group must develop a set of standards or criteria for evaluating proposals. This may become rather difficult if the problem is close to the lives of students. If the problem is one of national or international policy, the process will be less difficult (for students) but essential if the issue is to be examined from as many angles as possible. To illustrate: "What should be the U.S. trade policy with Communist China?" The problem might be viewed from the standpoint of national security; it may be treated on purely humanitarian grounds; or it may be seen in relation to its effects on the trade balance with other Asiatic nations. Sometimes a priority system must be established.

## How Are Generalizations Derived?

Sometimes the outcome of a problem-solving discussion is a definite plan of action. Thus by weighing each of the suggested hypotheses some decision relative to one or more preferred courses of action may emerge. In most classes, however, the scope of the problem will be too broad to achieve such an end.

Most class discussion experiences culminate with the derivation of generalizations which emerge from the experience. To illustrate:

1. LSD users may incur permanent brain damage.
2. While under the influence of LSD, a person loses his ability to distinguish between reality and fantasy.
3. Use of LSD may render an individual emotionally dependent upon the drug.

## What Is the Role of the Teacher as Discussion Leader?

Basic to effective class discussion is appropriate use of questions. Both student and teacher questions must be clearly and impartially stated. It is relatively easy for a biased leader to influence the discussion process by interjecting slanted questions from time to time. The question, "Why is the use of LSD dangerous?" for example, merely calls for support for a preconceived point of view. A better question might be, "What are the effects of LSD?"

An effective discussion leader must know how to handle nonrelated or remotely related questions. In the spontaneous interplay of individual reactions to issues, a variety of questions tends to emerge. The leader must continually make quick decisions as to the desirability of pursuing given questions. To push the group too forcibly can impede or even block group reflection, while to entertain any and all questions can lead to a myriad of blind alleys, resulting in little or no progress. Sometimes the wise leader may simply ask the questioner, "Would you clarify for us how your point relates to our problem?" Some leaders practice putting both the problem and key questions on the board *in advance* of the discussion; this practice tends to keep the issue constantly before the group.

In class discussion, student questions are usually redirected to the group. It can be assumed that the teacher has a fairly good understanding of the discussion problem when the discussion begins. His purpose, then, is to provide an opportunity for the group to develop an understanding by discussing the problem through to a conclusion. The act of answering questions tends to emphasize his role as an "expert." Few individuals do their best thinking when they are constantly reminded that the leader already "knows" the answers. Under such conditions they are inclined merely to let this person think for them. Redirection of student questions tends to bring out new relationships and interpretations. If a question is vague, the redirecting of it to the person doing the asking is sometimes appropriate. A rephrasing of a question will be in order at other times.

Skillful teachers generally adopt an air of acceptance when dealing with pupil responses to questions. If, however, a response obviously is in error, students themselves can handle the situation if adequate time for reflection is provided. Inaccurate responses may stimulate further questions and analysis designed to evoke reappraisal of the issue. Undue pupil embarrassment should be carefully avoided, however, if reflection is to continue. A teacher sometimes accepts an inaccurate response temporarily, simply by calling for other ideas pertaining to the issue. Usually subsequent responses will clarify the inaccuracy. (Occasionally the matter may have to be clarified before the group is permitted to advance to the next point.)

Reflection demands time! The glib person can impede such thinking. The leader can inadvertently encourage glibness by rushing responses unnecessarily. The pressure of time, especially in large classes, frequently contributes to this problem. As one student expressed it, "He doesn't care what you say so long as you say it in a hurry." There are times, however, when through a sudden insight an individual needs to make a quick response. This is usually evidenced by the unusual eagerness of the respondent.

# PANEL PROCEDURE

Panel discussion involves a group of five to eight people who are seeking agreement on a problem of concern to themselves and to an audience. Like class discussion, it is usually structured around a problem of policy. Occasionally a panel may be formed for the purpose of exploring problems of fact if the evidence is highly controversial and/or contradictory. Such an *enlightenment* discussion, however, must be followed with an appropriate policy problem if the higher cognitive goals are to be achieved. Panel discussion contains many of the elements of freedom characteristic of democratic decision making. The threat of manipulation toward predetermined ends is minimized in panel discussion.

### How Is the Problem Identified?

Sometimes appropriate problems for panel discussion evolve from ongoing class activity. Recognizing the inadequacies of existing policy, for example, students may express a desire to explore other ways of resolving a difficulty. One group of science students, for example, who was studying game management regulations wondered if the policy could not be improved to give both the sportsmen and the game a "better break." For the discussion, the teacher assisted the group in formulating the problem: "What steps should be taken to improve game management policies on federal lands?"

Frequently, panel discussion is anticipated and preplanned by the teacher. It is a relatively simple matter to identify those areas of greatest controversy within a given unit. It is essential, however, that students fully recognize such areas themselves before panel groups are established. They must accept the problem as their own if enthusiasm is to be assured.

After a problem area has been identified, the teacher must assist the panel group to formulate the problem into one of policy. If left to their own resources, students are likely to suggest a definite proposal. For example, "Should federal park lands be opened to hunting?" Although such a discussion may be fruitful, the problem tends to eliminate other worthwhile proposals that warrant consideration. Furthermore, it tends to divide a discussion group into opposing camps. Such an attitude is not conducive to the open-mindedness normally associated with discussion.

### How Are Panel Groups Selected and Organized?

The panel group is usually selected on the basis of expressed interest. A ten to fifteen minute initial planning session is necessary for the selection of a panel leader and division of labor if the problem is a complex one. The most enthusiastic, able, and tolerant student should be selected leader. Some groups may need help with this task. The problem is then subdivided into subtopics for individual research if the problem is complex. (The leader will study all subtopics so that he may acquire a much needed overall view of the problem.) For example, the problem "What steps should be taken to improve game management policies on federal lands?" might be subdivided as follows:

1. Forest lands
2. Park lands
3. Wildlife refuges
4. Wilderness areas
5. Bird and animal sanctuaries

Under optimum conditions each person is equally qualified in all aspects of the problem. Time limitations and complexities of many problems, however, often render some division of labor desirable. Each member should have at least a workable knowledge of all aspects of the problem. Such background information is often attained from assigned textbook readings.

For most panel problems a group will need about a week's preparation time. The teacher will work closely with the discussion leader. After the group has completed its investigation of the problem, it should meet briefly to discuss the major aspects of the problem to be explored. The discussion should not be rehearsed, however. Many teachers limit such discussion to a period of fifteen minutes. Formulation of specific questions should be avoided.

### What Are the Responsibilities of the Panelists?

The panel leader provides a liaison between the instructor and the other panelists. He generally guides and directs students in their background reading efforts. In preparation for the discussion experience, he prepares a list of guide questions. The guide questions will remind him of the scope and sequence of the problem. They also provide a handy reference when discussion drags or bogs down. Most of his prepared questions will be posed by different panelists as they introduce and probe various issues. The discussion guide will be very similar to the key questions posed in the illustrated plan for class discussion.

## What Are the Responsibilities of the Audience?

Although the panelists discuss the problem among themselves, the experience is designed for the benefit of other class members also. Contributions must be audible to all. As discussion proceeds, the other class members are expected to participate vicariously in the reflective process. Questions and points which need further clarification are jotted down for use during the question period which follows the presentation. They also may participate in a panel evaluation as described later in this chapter. Note-taking during the actual panel discussion process is discouraged.

## What Are the Responsibilities of the Teacher?

The instructor must see that all members of the class follow the presentation fully. By establishing a few signals with the leader, he can encourage members to raise their voices, provide guidance for moving from one part of the discussion to another, and the like. He will usually want to guide the learner in bringing the discussion to a close. A question period of from five to ten minutes is essential.

## How Is the Panel Evaluated?

If students are to receive a mark for panel discussion, carefully constructed rating scales must be developed. The "Panel Discussion Evaluation Form" (see Figure 16–1) is one way of accomplishing this goal.

Inasmuch as students are discouraged from taking notes during a panel presentation, it may be desirable to let them assist in the evaluation. Each contribution is tallied in the appropriate column, e.g., major, minor, or doubtful contributions. (In case of doubt, the contribution is tallied in the minor contribution column.) Then immediately following the question period, the individual rating scales are employed. A student is identified by a number on each rating scale if he seemed to "stand out" in one direction or the other. For example, if Paul's voice quality and stress were especially strong, a number 1 would be entered to the left along the line for this scale. If he did not speak clearly, his number would be entered toward the right end of the scale. If he failed to impress the evaluator in this respect, *no mark* would be entered. Relatively few individual marks would be appropriate for most such experiences, as most panelists would rank in the "average" categories on most of the scales. The leader (who is not marked on this basis) can be assigned the task of deriving total points for each person, based upon established criteria.

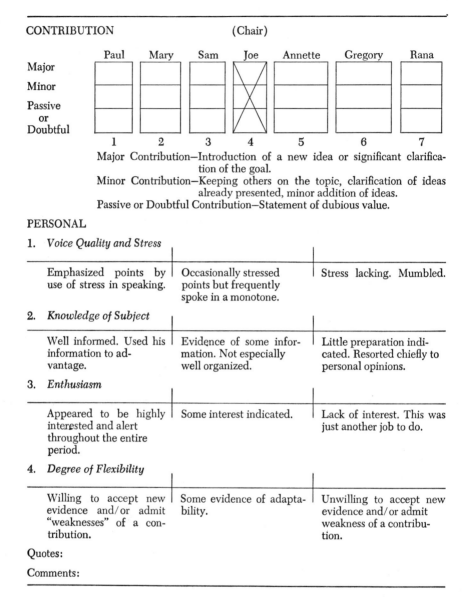

CONTRIBUTION                    (Chair)

|  | Paul | Mary | Sam | Joe | Annette | Gregory | Rana |
|---|---|---|---|---|---|---|---|
| Major |  |  |  |  |  |  |  |
| Minor |  |  |  |  |  |  |  |
| Passive or Doubtful |  |  |  |  |  |  |  |
|  | 1 | 2 | 3 | 4 | 5 | 6 | 7 |

Major Contribution—Introduction of a new idea or significant clarification of the goal.

Minor Contribution—Keeping others on the topic, clarification of ideas already presented, minor addition of ideas.

Passive or Doubtful Contribution—Statement of dubious value.

PERSONAL

1. *Voice Quality and Stress*

| Emphasized points by use of stress in speaking. | Occasionally stressed points but frequently spoke in a monotone. | Stress lacking. Mumbled. |
|---|---|---|

2. *Knowledge of Subject*

| Well informed. Used his information to advantage. | Evidence of some information. Not especially well organized. | Little preparation indicated. Resorted chiefly to personal opinions. |
|---|---|---|

3. *Enthusiasm*

| Appeared to be highly interested and alert throughout the entire period. | Some interest indicated. | Lack of interest. This was just another job to do. |
|---|---|---|

4. *Degree of Flexibility*

| Willing to accept new evidence and/or admit "weaknesses" of a contribution. | Some evidence of adaptability. | Unwilling to accept new evidence and/or admit weakness of a contribution. |
|---|---|---|

Quotes:

Comments:

**FIGURE 16–1.** Panel discussion evaluation form[1]

Panelists can evaluate each other (including the leader), but they will need a slightly different set of criteria. The form "Evaluation of Panel Participants" (Figure 16–2) has been used effectively with secondary school students.

[1] The top portion of this figure is adapted from R. Murray Thomas, *Judging Student Progress,* 2nd ed. (New York: David McKay Co., Inc., 1960), p. 268.

You have worked with these people so are probably better informed on many of these points than anybody else. What happened behind the scenes?

DIRECTIONS: Rate all other participants on the panel, *including the chairman.* Assign each participant a rating for *each* criterion. Several persons may be assigned the same rating on any one point. (Your rating, to be done in private, will be held strictly confidential.)

| | | |
|---|---|---|
| 5 Superior | 2 Below Average |
| 4 Above Average | 1 Poor |
| 3 Average | |

|   | #1 | #2 | #3 | #4 | #5 | #6 | #7 |
|---|----|----|----|----|----|----|----|
| 1. *Preparatory Activities* | ___ | ___ | ___ | ___ | ___ | ___ | ___ |

   Attended and contributed in pre-liminary planning sessions. Did his share of reading in the area.

| 2. *Contribution to Panel Progress* | ___ | ___ | ___ | ___ | ___ | ___ | ___ |

   Facilitated panel progress by ad-hering to discussion pattern, ask-ing thought-provoking questions, and assisting others make key points.

| 3. *Value of Contributions* | ___ | ___ | ___ | ___ | ___ | ___ | ___ |

   Depth of understanding; authori-tative support for comments; reasoning ability.

| 4. *Discussion Attitude* | ___ | ___ | ___ | ___ | ___ | ___ | ___ |

   Objectivity-open-mindedness; goodwill toward others; contrib-uted to "groupness."

| 5. *Communication Skills* | ___ | ___ | ___ | ___ | ___ | ___ | ___ |

   Listened to others; effective voice control; courteous to others.

Total

Key to Identification:
(Names)

1. _____       5. _____
2. _____       6. _____
3. _____       7. _____
4. _____

**FIGURE 16–2.** Evaluation of panel participants

A panelist should not evaluate himself. His evaluation is kept confidential. The instructor can take his rating and average with the other two ratings for a most reliable mark. The whole process can be completed in five minutes if forms are available and if the leader assists as indicated.

### What Functions Does the Follow-through Discussion Serve?

Following the brief question period, the teacher leads the group in a follow-through discussion. In conventional class schedules this is usually the period following the panel presentation. At this point students are expected to derive key generalizations from the experience. Most of the generalizations should come from the members of the audience. Clarification and expansion of basic points are often needed. Thus the panelists become useful resource personnel. The teacher may also want to expand or introduce neglected points.

It is usually desirable to take a look at the panel experience if other groups are to follow. Could all members be heard? Was there enough probing? Was proper balance achieved? The instructor usually jots down key questions in this area as the discussion progresses.

Preparation for the follow-through discussion is facilitated when the teacher jots down key points for later reference. (He should also identify the student who makes each point.) In essence this becomes a useful guide for the follow-through experience.

## PLANNING FOR DISCUSSION

Discussion often breaks down as a result of inadequate preplanning by the teacher. Although students themselves often suggest the need for a class discussion by the questions they ask, the teacher usually assumes responsibility for formulating the problem for discussion. Furthermore, he must develop a structured discussion guide which incorporates the essential dimensions of the discussion process. The lesson plan illustrated below is suggestive only.

LESSON PLAN ILLUSTRATION (health class)

*Concept:* Use of drugs may permanently damage an individual's health.

*Problem:* What steps should be taken to minimize the use of LSD among teen-agers?

*Goals:* After this lesson the student should have furthered his understanding of the principal effects of LSD on physical and mental processes, as evidenced by:
1. His contributions during the discussion process.
2. His ability to draw generalizations from the experience.

*Lesson Approach:*

Show a ten-minute film: *The Use of LSD.* Ask students to jot down questions immediately following the film presentation.

*Lesson Development:*

ANALYSIS OF THE PROBLEM:

What is LSD?
How widespread is its use?
What are its effects on the physical and mental processes?
What factors contribute to its use among teen-agers?
Is the problem likely to continue? Why or why not?

PROPOSING ALTERNATIVES:

Now in view of our analysis of this problem, what steps should be taken to minimize the use of LSD among teen-agers?
Types of solutions which may be offered:

1. Launch an educational program designed to inform all teen-agers of the specific facts associated with its use.
2. Impose stricter penalties upon those who use it.

(Advantages and disadvantages of each proposal will be treated fully.)

*Establishing Criteria:*

Before weighing possible solutions to this issue we must establish some standards. For example, one might be, "Any action taken should protect the basic rights of the accused" (e.g., the right to counsel, a fair trial, etc.). What other standards seem important?

EXAMPLES:

1. Preventative measures should be given top priority.
2. Remedial action should not unnecessarily jeopardize a young person's future employment potentialities.

*Deriving Generalizations:*

From our discussion, what important generalizations seem apparent? Examples of points which may be advanced:

1. LSD users may incur permanent brain damage.
2. While under the influence of LSD an individual may commit almost any crime with complete emotional detachment.

# VALUES

Group discussion involves the processes of give and take essential to a democratic system.

Prejudices and biases are frequently modified when subjected to the scrutiny of the peer group.

The combined critical thinking of a group is much more likely to correct deficiences in evidence and reasoning than an individual might.

The processes of discussion involve cooperation and group sharing of ideas. Thus judgments tend to improve.

The technique tends to render the learner progressively less dependent upon the teacher.

## LIMITATIONS AND PROBLEMS

Discussion presupposes adequate preparation. It is impossible to reflect effectively upon facts and concepts which are unknown or incompletely understood.

The permissive characteristic of discussion tends to encourage digression.

The discussion leader may be unable to maintain an open mind.

Even when carefully organized, class discussion is unpredictable.

Group agreement or consensus does not insure accomplishment.

## ILLUSTRATED DISCUSSION OUTLINES

I. Useful in biology, general science, and health classes

*Unit:* Microorganisms

*Concept:* Respiratory diseases are transmitted in many ways.

*Problem:* How can the transmission of respiratory diseases be minimized?

*Sample Analysis Questions:*
1. What are some common respiratory diseases?
2. What are airborne microorganisms?
3. How are they transmitted?
4. Why is the problem more important today than in the past?

*Some Possible Solutions to Consider:*
1. Pass strict laws on air pollution
2. Require inoculations against disease
3. Require medical checkups
4. Require regular chest X-rays

II. Useful in United States history, government, American problems, and sociology classes

*Unit:* The Beginnings of the American Tradition

*Concept:* Thomas Jefferson's political ideals provided the foundation of American democracy.

*Problem:* How can we best apply Thomas Jefferson's ideals of democracy to today's democracy?

*Sample Analysis Questions:*
1. What were some of Jefferson's ideas of democracy?
2. How did he define aristocracy?
3. What did he mean by a "natural aristocrat"?
4. How do ———— and ———— as present American leaders fit that definition?

*Some Possible Solutions to Consider:*
1. Tests designed to classify public candidates for office
2. Limit campaign funds

3. Investigate family and background
4. Consider leadership potential

III. Useful in American history, government, American problems, and sociology classes

*Unit:* Birth of Democracy

*Concept:* The check and balance system is an integral part of all forms of democratic life.

*Problem:* What steps should be taken to change the method of electing a United States president?

*Sample Analysis Questions:*

1. What is the electoral college? Why was it established?
2. What purposes does it presently serve?
3. What difficulties have been experienced relative to its use?
4. What hazards are involved in its continued use?

*Some Possible Solutions to Consider:*

1. Electoral college votes based on a percentage of popular vote in each state
2. Abandon, using percentage of popular vote only
3. States vote only
4. One electoral vote for each congressional district, plus two for every state

IV. Useful in home economics and sociology classes

*Unit:* Marriage

*Concept:* There are many valid reasons why couples may or may not marry.

*Problem:* What factors should be considered in selecting a mate?

*Sample Analysis Questions:*

1. What are some of the sources of mutual attraction?
2. What is meant by the phrase "love is blind"?
3. What is the purpose of the engagement period?

*Some Possible Solutions to Consider:*

1. Age, religion, and cultural background
2. Values
3. Life goals
4. Physical features

V. Useful in art and home economics classes

*Unit:* Color Relations

*Concept:* An individual can control color when he has the ability to analyze color relationships.

*Problem:* How might one use color in creating a work of art?

*Sample Analysis Questions:*

1. What are the essential properties of color?

2. How did Albrecht Dürer use color in his painting "Young Hare"?
3. How did Paul Klee use color in his painting "Around the Fish"? "Girl with Jugs"?
4. How did Van Gogh use color in "The Orchard"?

*Some Possible Solutions to Consider:*
1. To give spatial quality to the pictorial field
2. To create mood and symbolize ideas
3. To express personal emotions and feelings
4. To attract and direct attention as a means of giving organization and composition

VI.   Useful in earth science, biology, and general science classes

**Unit:**      Our Dynamic Earth and Its Materials

**Concept:** The sequential order of events enables us to reconstruct the earth's history.

**Problem:** What procedures should one follow in interpreting geologic history?

*Sample Analysis Questions:*
1. How are "first events" identified in the earth's crust? later events?
2. What does the angle of beds mean in the history of rocks?
3. How does pressure contribute to the ordering of events?

*Some Possible Solutions to Consider:*
1. Submergence and disposition
2. Emergence and erosion
3. Igneous activity, dikes, and stocks

# CHAPTER 17

# Debate

## OVERVIEW

### Key Concepts

1. When discussion breaks down, debate is necessary.
2. Debate focuses on the merits and problems associated with one proposed solution to a problem.
3. The affirmative debate team has the burden of proof.
4. Every debate deals with three stock issues: Need, plan, and desirability of the plan. All three issues must be effectively supported by the affirmative team.
5. The negative team supports the *status quo* (conditions as they are) or (rarely) supports a counterplan.
6. Debate makes full use of the persuasive appeal, psychological traps, and the like.

### New Terms

1. **Debate Proposition**—A problem of advocacy (defined in previous chapter) stated as a proposed course of action.
2. **Stock (Key) Issues**—The basic structure of every debate, as follows:
   a. Is there a need?
   b. Is the plan of the affirmative sufficient to solve the need?
   c. Is the plan workable and desirable?
3. **Affirmative Team**—The debate team which supports the debate proposition as stated. Advocates a change from the *status quo.*
4. **Negative Team**—The debate team which supports the *status quo.*
5. **Burden of Proof**—Likened to a court of law in which a man is considered innocent until proven guilty. Assumed by the affirmative team.

6. **Debate Strategy**—Techniques used to keep the opposing team "off balance."
7. **Rebuttal**—Probing weaknesses of opponent's case. Usually involves considerable indirect clash.

### Questions to Guide Your Study

1. "Since the debater is not supposed to change his mind, the whole process is futile." Develop a refutation for such a statement.
2. Why does the affirmative debate team have the burden of proof?
3. Why is it necessary for the negative team to destroy only one of the stock issues?
4. How do the constructive speeches differ from the rebuttal speeches?
5. "Only the first affirmative speaker may present a previously prepared (canned) speech." Defend or refute.

Debate is the process of advocacy. The advocates argue for or against a proposed course of action. Generally speaking, the purpose is to influence an audience for or against a proposition. Although the dual approach is common, it does not preclude the presentation of more than two points of view. Like discussion, debate involves reflective thought. The debater weighs, ponders, thinks carefully. Unlike a discussant, however, the debater has moved from an attitude of searching with others for the best solution to one of conviction that he has found the best solution. Thus his mission is viewed as that of convincing others to accept his point of view. Where discussion is cooperative, debate is competitive. Where the discussant explores and inquires, the debater advocates and persuades.

## FUNDAMENTAL PROPERTIES

Debate often occurs when the processes of ordinary discussion break down. When two opposing factions have been formed, the need for orderly processes of debate is present. Each of the parties (or groups), unable to resolve differences, attempts to "sell" its proposal to others. In doing so, however, each of the advocates must adhere to democratic principles of fair play. The fundamental properties, described below, must be used within such a framework.

### What Is the Role of Emotional Appeal?

Debate makes full use of feeling reactions. Whereas many instructional methods emphasize objective inquiry, sometimes almost to the exclusion of emotion, debate provides a legitimate outlet for feelings. Although the debater obtains all the objective evidence available, his presentation is cloaked within a carefully prepared persuasive appeal. By appealing to existing emotions, biases, and prejudices of his listeners, the debater seeks to persuade an audience to accept his point of view.

Although the debater is expected to exploit the emotional appeal fully, he does not attempt to destroy the worth and dignity of his opponent. Although wrong, his opponents are not made to appear wickedly wrong. Rather, they are usually pictured as uninformed, misguided, or lacking in an overall perspective of the problem under consideration.

## What Function Does Debate Strategy Serve?

In most arguments individuals will attempt to gain advantages over the opposition. This bit of finesse usually exists in some degree whether the occasion be in a court of law, some social organization, or the usual type of classroom debate. Strategy in debate is closely associated with surprise. If the participants thoroughly understand the reasonable limits of strategy, they can contribute decidedly to the general interest of all concerned. Five strategic approaches have been recognized:

1. Use of an unexpected plan or counterproposal.
2. Presentation of an unexpected advantage or disadvantage.
3. Acceptance of the negative counterproposal, in the middle of the debate, as a part of the affirmative case.
4. Use of various kinds of traps.
5. Use of operational psychology.

In most classroom debates the degree of strategy will usually be limited. However, the degree of creative imagination which students apply to a debate proposition is often most impressive. Bright students especially enjoy pitting their wits against others. The use of maps, charts, and diagrams is encouraged by some teachers. Sometimes a direct question of the opposition early in the debate will result in a later inconsistency. Any team, of course, which can bring out unexpected advantages or proposals has gained a decided advantage.

## Why Is Spontaneity Necessary?

Debate demands extensive and meticulous preparation and planning. Except for the first presentation, however, speakers must adjust to conditions of the moment. Each speaker must be prepared for any contingency, calling upon extensive notes and knowledge as the case demands. Utilizing notes and questions prompted by previous presentations, the debater puts together a convincing argument each time he faces an audience. He must know when and how to agree with or take over the substance of an opponent's argument, just as he must know when and how to reject an argument, inference, or train of thought.

## Why is an Either-Or Proposition Appropriate for Debate?

The debate method has been severely criticized by its critics. The heart of such criticism is usually focused on its two-sided appeal. The critics point out that there are usually an unlimited number of possible courses of action to any conflict; that debate tends to create an artificial dichotomy.

While it is true that debate tends to be two-sided (with certain notable exceptions), the method logically follows the processes of discussion. When problems cannot be resolved through the orderly processes of discussion, two or more opposing camps tend to emerge. At this point, discussion becomes inoperative. Parties to the dispute will try merely to make a case for given points of view. Debate provides an orderly democratic process for achieving this end. Frequently a debate proposition is selected by the leader prior to class discussion. This is a defensible practice if the issue has been discussed (and perhaps even debated) at length by the larger society.

The purpose of a class debate is to provide students with opposing and often extreme points of view so that the middle ground may become more readily apparent. In essence, then, a class debate merely sets the stage for the resolution of an emotionally laden issue.

## Why Must the Affirmative Assume the Burden of Proof?

In a debate, the party that advocates a change from existing conditions (the affirmative) assumes the burden of proof. This might be likened to a court of law which assumes that a defendant is innocent until proven guilty. In short, the *status quo*, with all its problems, is preferable to any new, untried plan until proven otherwise.

The burden of proof concept is fundamental to many problems and situations common to the life of a teen-ager. Rumors that may threaten one's reputation, guilt by association, and objections to school policy are but a few of the situations which may demand a full understanding of this basic democratic concept.

## What Time Limitations Are Imposed?

Each party to a debate must be provided an equitable amount of time for presentation of arguments. To do otherwise provides an unfair advantage. As each debater (there are usually four) usually speaks twice, a strict time limitation must be imposed. When university-style debate is used in conventional fifty-minute classes, each person usually has one seven-minute and one four-minute presentation. If time permits, speeches of ten and five minutes are preferred.

# DEBATE PROCEDURE

Debate can take many forms. It can occur informally between two individuals, or it may be organized as an activity involving opposing teams who present their cases for the benefit of an audience. About the only requirements are that (1) some proposal or plan of action be advanced, and (2) advocates of both sides be allowed equal time for a presentation of their cases. Informal debate, however, is usually inappropriate for classroom use.

There are also a number of formalized debate procedures, all of which may be useful to the classroom teacher. Among the most popular is the cross-question and the university-style debate. The cross-question style debate provides opportunities for each debater to question members of the opposing team directly. The university-style debate has no such provision but does permit a more indirect form of questioning through alternating presentations. For class use, the university-style debate is preferred by most teachers. Accordingly, this debate form is treated in the pages which follow.

## What Constitutes an Appropriate Selection and Statement of the Problem?

Once an area of controversy has been identified, a proposed course of action is advanced. This can be reached through preliminary discussion in which division arises on an issue. Sometimes ready-made debate situations are provided through some current issue of controversy at the national, state, local, or school level. In recent years such timely topics as the following have been debated at length in many sections of the nation. (Each has been stated in the form of a proposition for action.)

*Resolved,* That the federal courts should accept the pupil-placement plan of school integration.

*Resolved,* That a stronger labor law is essential to the security of the United States.

*Resolved,* That management-labor differences should be settled by compulsory arbitration.

*Resolved,* That the states should ratify the "Women's Equal Rights Amendment" to the Constitution.

*Resolved,* That the local community should assume full financial obligations for private schools.

*Resolved,* That a course in sex education should be added to the secondary school curriculum.

As illustrated in the foregoing, a problem for debate usually is stated in the form of a resolution. Since the resolution usually represents some form of proposed action, it is customarily called a proposition. The classroom debate proposition usually is stated as indicated above. Sometimes, however, it may be made in the form of a bill or motion, if the class is so organized. Occasionally a debate proposition may be implied without the necessity of a formal resolution or proposition, as in the case of the discussion which evolves into a question of advocacy.

## How Are Debate Teams Selected?

Due to the very nature of debate, clash of opinions is inevitable. Some students are secure enough to accept such a challenge without difficulty; others will need guidance and assistance. In any event, debate affords a unique opposition. Some of the important considerations are as follows:

1. The participants must feel strongly (really believe) on the issue to be debated.
2. They must be willing and able workers. Debate demands careful and exacting preparation.
3. Those directly involved need some skill in organization and analysis.
4. The participants must be able to "give and take" in the emotional appeals and clash of views which are so vital a part of debate.
5. It is essential that the two teams be as evenly matched as possible. The effect of a strong debate team on one of limited ability can be little short of disastrous. Generally speaking, debate is more appropriate for bright students than for those of more limited ability. Creative imagination, social finesse, and verbal facility are all important assets in debate activities.

It has been established that preparation and defense of a given point of view tends to have a permanent effect upon the debater's attitudes. Accordingly, debaters probably should be asked to argue that case most nearly opposed to existing convictions. This not only results in a less extreme position but also may contribute to greater tolerance for those who hold opposing points of view.

## How Are the Cases Organized?

Each team is composed of two individuals. Those on the affirmative side advocate adoption of the proposition, whereas those on the negative side are opposed to such action. For example, the proposition "*Resolved,* That the minimum voting age should be uniformly lowered to eighteen years of age" would be supported by the affirmative team; the negative team, on the other hand, would oppose the proposition.

There are three major issues in a debate. They are usually stated as questions:

1. Is the proposed course of action necessary?
2. Will the proposal remedy the existing state of affairs?
3. Is the proposal feasible or desirable?

The affirmative team must effectively prove all three points. The negative team, however, need only discredit one of the major issues, although it may concentrate its efforts on all three issues.

In planning overall strategy, members of the affirmative must propose and be prepared to defend a definite and feasible plan of action. There is always some doubt as to how detailed and involved the plan must be. Generally speaking, two or three main points will suffice, depending on the scope of the topic.

The negative team, being unable to know the exact strategy of the affirmative, must base much of its strategy upon prediction. If possible, it must be prepared for any eventuality. The best debaters often concentrate their efforts on the weakest point(s) of the affirmative case. Such strategy demands thorough preparation, coupled with on-the-spot analysis.

## What Factors Are Important in Collecting Evidence?

Thorough preparation for debate is of primary importance. Without it, the procedure can be little more than opinionated bickering. Adolescents often tend to interchange facts and opinions, distort, or otherwise misrepresent supporting data. Sometimes questionable authorities may be quoted for expediency alone. With a minimum of guidance, however, evidence can be used effectively. Some systematic filing of references is usually desirable. Index cards, of the 5″ by 7″ size, have been used effectively for this purpose. Sometimes a two- or three-statement annotation may be sufficient, while on other occasions a more detailed record is needed. Most arguments are more effective when occasionally supported by authoritative sources. This is an especially important factor in debate. Sometimes the strength of opposing arguments must be measured by the relative value of the different sources of evidence. Debate affords an excellent opportunity for a group of youngsters to evaluate different and opposing sources of information.

As in panel discussion and other similar methods, the debate participants must have adequate time for preparation. For most students at least a week is needed for the typical classroom debate. Although a preliminary meeting of the teams may be desirable, most participants prefer to keep their strategy a secret until the day of the presentation.

## How Is the Class Prepared for the Debate?

Seldom is a classroom debate conducted for purely academic or theoretical reasons. Quite often the entire class group is vitally concerned with the issue. As such, students are frequently more or less emotionally involved before the actual debate begins. Naturally, many are eager to hear arguments which may support previously held positions. The purpose of a classroom debate, however, is not to prove or disprove an issue. Instead, it is designed to provide important concepts for and against an issue. A teacher can help students make such an appraisal by having them enter main points of each case in opposite columns. A code may be developed for indicating how well each point was defended or refuted. Students also may be instructed to make notes of unanswered questions.

## What Are the Responsibilities of Each Debater?

The presentation customarily is divided into two parts: the constructive speeches and the rebuttal presentations. For the most part, the constructive phase emphasizes building of the cases (affirmative and negative). Rebuttal speeches are primarily concerned with attacking weaknesses of opponents' arguments and strengthening one's own case more directly than is usually possible in constructive arguments.

A number of procedures have been used in intercollegiate debating. Many of these have been modified or discarded through experience. In any event, presentations must focus on the three major issues discussed earlier, i.e., the need for the proposed course of action, the specific plan of the affirmative for solving the problem, and the desirability or feasibility of the plan. The first affirmative speaker attempts to establish the need, while the second accepts the responsibility for presenting the proposed plan and showing why it is desirable or feasible. Likewise, the negative speakers talk against any or all of the major issues.

Each person normally speaks twice, alternating between the teams. Constructive speeches usually are about seven minutes long; the rebuttal speeches normally are about four minutes long. The most effective speakers usually follow techniques of effective public address.

## What Types of Strategy May Be Employed?

The crux of any debate rests with how well each speaker is able to withstand the arguments, inferences, and allegations of his opponents. He refutes (denies or wards off) the arguments of his opponents and at the same time attacks (rebuts) the case of his opponents. This process begins early in the debate and reaches its climax in the second set of speeches. One's ability to discount or minimize the importance of key aspects of an opponent's argument demands skillful and coordinated analysis. His strategy is to lead the opposition into traps, inconsistencies, or absurdities. The trap is sprung in the rebuttal speeches!

## What Can Be Accomplished by Leading the Follow-through Analysis and Review?

A debate presentation usually affords an ideal basis for a follow-through analysis. An opportunity to hear considered arguments for and against a definite proposal, in effect, prepares a group for further analysis. Each major point will be discussed in terms of its validity with respect to the major issue. Usually a group must be guided into the realization that opposing arguments each have their merits and problems; that a more likely solution is probably some point between the two extremes. Major points will be extended and modified into important concepts (generalizations) relative to the issue.

In almost every debate a number of relationships are suggested or implied which may need further exploration. By following a review procedure somewhat consistent with suggestions made in the chapter on review, students may be able to make additional associations and relationships. To illustrate the various aspects of the follow-through analysis and review, let us refer to the proposition: *Resolved,* That a stronger labor law is essential to the security of the United States. A follow-through discussion might proceed as follows:

1. What were the major points made during this debate?
2. How well did each of these withstand the arguments of the opposition?
3. What generalizations seem apparent as a result of this experience?
4. What are some related problems which might bear investigation? To illustrate: Should school teachers be denied the right to strike? Should some disputes be settled by compulsory arbitration?

The foregoing are only a few of any number of similar questions which can be more intelligently discussed following an effective debate. The reader will observe that, in the main, the last set of questions are of advocacy, i.e., debate problems stated in question form. Such problems are fully appropriate when used to extend associations through review, but, as indicated earlier, they can be inappropriate if attempted prior to a thorough debate or some other type of analysis.

A follow-through discussion also affords a sound basis for helping a group analyze various techniques of persuasion. Some of the following may have become evident:

1. The effects of emotional appeals.
2. Distortion of facts or evidence.
3. Use of loaded words or question-begging terms. For example, some debaters have been asked such questions, "Are we going to allow this terrible situation to continue?"
4. Use of questionable evidence.
5. Incidences of glossing over.
6. Use of high-order generalizations as a technique of avoiding real issues.
7. The impact of traps, psychological devices, and the like.
8. The use of inferences.
9. The art of capitalizing on existing biases of a group.

Some consideration of each of these might be of real value in helping a student cope with the ever-growing pressures of mass media in our society. Debate can be a very useful basis for such an analysis.

## How Is the Debate Evaluated?

Debate evaluation can be handled in a variety of ways. For the most part, however, teachers prefer a simple instrument which takes into account a number of factors and which can be easily applied. Evaluation is complicated by the number of speeches, all of which serve somewhat different functions. The form illustrated in Figure 17–1, "Debate Evaluation Form," is probably the most com-

### 1st Affirmative

| 9 | 8 | 7 | 6 | 5 | 4 | 3 | 2 | 1 | |
|---|---|---|---|---|---|---|---|---|---|
| | | | | | | | | | Analysis |
| | | | | | | | | | Organization |
| | | | | | | | | | Knowledge & use of supporting facts |
| | | | | | | | | | Refutation-rebuttal |
| | | | | | | | | | Language persuasiveness |
| | | | | | | | | | Delivery |
| | | | | | | | | | General impression |

(average stanine)

7 ⟌‾‾‾‾ ←Total points

### 2nd Affirmative

| 9 | 8 | 7 | 6 | 5 | 4 | 3 | 2 | 1 | |
|---|---|---|---|---|---|---|---|---|---|
| | | | | | | | | | Analysis |
| | | | | | | | | | Organization |
| | | | | | | | | | Knowledge & use of supporting facts |
| | | | | | | | | | Refutation-rebuttal |
| | | | | | | | | | Language persuasiveness |
| | | | | | | | | | Delivery |
| | | | | | | | | | General impression |

(average stanine)

7 ⟌‾‾‾‾ ←Total points

**Analysis:** Debate proposition thoroughly understood: vital issues clearly defined.

**Organization:** Sequence of points easy to follow, characterized by previews, summaries, smooth transitions, visual aids, etc.

**Knowledge & Use of Supporting Facts:** Source apparently substantial and reliable. Arguments highly consistent.

**Refutation-rebuttal:** Meets opposing arguments; responds to important questions and poses ones of his own—especially in rebuttal speech.

**Language Persuasiveness:** Vocab. adapted to the listeners; choice of words creates vivid mental images; appeals to one's feelings.

**Delivery:** Gestures, eye contact, voice control, etc., are appropriate.

### 1st Negative

| 9 | 8 | 7 | 6 | 5 | 4 | 3 | 2 | 1 | |
|---|---|---|---|---|---|---|---|---|---|
| | | | | | | | | | Analysis |
| | | | | | | | | | Organization |
| | | | | | | | | | Knowledge & use of supporting facts |
| | | | | | | | | | Refutation-rebuttal |
| | | | | | | | | | Language persuasiveness |
| | | | | | | | | | Delivery |
| | | | | | | | | | General impression |

(average stanine)

7 ⟌‾‾‾‾ ←Total points

### 2nd Negative

| 9 | 8 | 7 | 6 | 5 | 4 | 3 | 2 | 1 | |
|---|---|---|---|---|---|---|---|---|---|
| | | | | | | | | | Analysis |
| | | | | | | | | | Organization |
| | | | | | | | | | Knowledge & use of supporting facts |
| | | | | | | | | | Refutation-rebuttal |
| | | | | | | | | | Language persuasiveness |
| | | | | | | | | | Delivery |
| | | | | | | | | | General impression |

(average stanine)

7 ⟌‾‾‾‾ ←Total points

**FIGURE 17–1.** Debate evaluation form

mon one.[1] This form is limited by the lack of specific description of each factor measured. Some teachers prepare a supplementary page with a more thorough description of points, for the benefit of those involved. Debate, unlike discussion, is designed to present cases for and against a proposal. This may make it desirable for students to take notes of important points and issues. As a consequence, they usually are not involved in the formal evaluation as readily as might be the case in panel discussion. Sometimes it is appropriate to have each debater evaluate the other participating members on the same type of scale suggested in the form illustrated.

The reader will probably recall that in intercollegiate debating societies one team is usually declared a winner. This practice is definitely discouraged for class debate. The evaluational technique described in this section is used for individual evaluation. It should be pointed out, however, that the combined assessment of individual ratings cannot be interpreted in a win or lose manner. The total impact of a debate is frequently greater (or less) than the sum of its parts.

## PLANNING FOR THE DEBATE

Each debate team must develop a well-integrated case, based upon the three major issues: need, plan, and desirability of the plan. This is often referred to as a debate brief. Patterned somewhat after a lawyer's brief, most debate manuals and textbooks offer detailed and sometimes complicated illustrations. Although careful planning is essential, the debate brief, designed for class use, need not be elaborate. The illustration which follows will probably suffice in most cases.

*Debate Proposition: Resolved,* That wildlife refuges should be established in every state.

  I.  Need

    A.  Population growth
    B.  Increased leisure time
    C.  Some wildlife species threatened with extinction
    D.  Encroachment of civilization

  II.  Plan

    A.  Congressional Amendment to be enacted by Congress
    B.  Ratified by two-thirds of the states
    C.  Private property owners to be reimbursed at a fair and just rate

  III.  Feasibility and desirability of the plan

    A.  People favor establishing additional wildlife refuges
    B.  Our society can support such a plan

[1] Adapted from Waldo W. Braden and Ernest Brandenburg, *Oral Decision Making: Principles of Discussion and Debate* (New York: Harper & Row, Publishers, 1955), pp. 522–23.

    C.  Some wildlife refuges currently in existence
    D.  Natural resources contained within current refuges not readily marketable
    E.  Wildlife refuges make natural resources available to all the people

Although the illustrated brief is designed specifically for the affirmative team, the negative team would develop a similar brief, defending the *status quo*. It would have as major issues: no need; existing plan works; desirability of existing plan. Each speaker, of course, must document and cite appropriate examples and illustrations in support of each point. At the same time, he is responsible for adjusting to the arguments of the opposing team. In short, he cannot write out a speech in detail prior to the debate experience.

## VALUES

Debate is one of the few teaching methods which provide a legitimate outlet for persuasive techniques. In this respect it resembles persuasive speaking; it also provides for a certain amount of indirect clash.

Issues which are to "hot" to handle through class discussion are most appropriate for debate.

For the able student who "thinks well on his feet," debate probably has no equal. Balanced teams are desirable.

Debate provides a unique opportunity for the inspection of propaganda and bandwagon techniques of persuasion.

The very nature of debate focuses upon human interests. It is controversial, dramatic, spirited, thereby providing a basis for motivation.

## LIMITATIONS AND PROBLEMS

The less able or the emotionally disturbed student may find actual debate participation a frustrating experience.

Except for the actual participants, debate is ineffective in altering value-attitudes with respect to an issue.

Due to the nature of the technique, individual emotions may become extreme unless carefully supervised.

Debate, in the absence of adequate preparation, is a waste of time.

Debate presupposes a restricted number of solutions to a problem.

In some communities where public feeling is exceedingly strong, certain issues may evoke criticism if proper public relations groundwork has not been prepared.

# ILLUSTRATED DEBATE BRIEFS

I. Useful in social science, American problems, sociology, and psychology classes

   *Concept:* Cruel and unusual punishment is inconsistent with democratic ideals.

   *Debate Proposition: Resolved,* That capital punishment should be abolished.

   *Need:*
   1. Any sane individual can be rehabilitated.
   2. A mentally ill person is not responsible for his acts.
   3. Legal processes may continue indefinitely.
   4. Wealthy, influential citizens who commit a crime are rarely executed.

   *Plan:*
   1. Life imprisonment, without parole, should be mandatory until criminals are fully rehabilitated.
   2. Rehabilitation specialists will be employed to work with criminals.
   3. Carefully selected, qualified review boards will review each case periodically.
   4. Released, rehabilitated criminals will receive continued guidance as long as needed.

   *Feasibility and Desirability of Plan:*
   1. Most people favor abolishing capital punishment.
   2. Most developed nations have already abolished capital punishment.
   3. Systematic rehabilitation programs would be no more costly than current practices.
   4. Extreme cruelty (now imposed by an execution date often delayed for many years) would be abolished.

II. Useful in science and mathematics classes

   *Concept:* The metric system of measuring is simpler and more efficient than our existing measuring system.

   *Debate Proposition: Resolved,* That the metric system should be adopted in this country.

   *Need:*
   1. The metric system is simpler than the English system now in use.
   2. The metric system is the most precise measuring system yet invented.
   3. The metric system is easier taught than the present system in use.

   *Plan:*
   1. The metric system would replace the existing system in all public and private school curricula.

2. For a period of time (perhaps ten to twenty years) the current system would be taught as a second system of measure.
3. For some ten to twenty years both metric and English systems of measure would be available to the public (side by side).
4. After a reasonable transition period (ten to twenty years), the metric system would replace the current system entirely.

*Feasibility and Desirability of Plan:*
1. Most nations have already adopted the metric system.
2. Other nations have switched systems.
3. The metric system is in current use in scientific fields in this country.
4. More than 90 percent of the people are literate. Thus the school program would apply to practically every boy and girl in the United States.

III. Useful in earth science, history, and sociology classes

*Concept:* Many scenic and geologic wonders are in mountainous country, developed by the erosive activities of centuries.

*Debate Proposition: Resolved,* That reclamation projects should be prohibited in areas of unusual scenic and geologic interest.

*Need:*
1. Historical artifacts provide valuable clues to life in the distant past.
2. Water erosion has created some of the most scenic and unusual formations in existence.
3. The unspoiled beauty of nature must be preserved for future generations.

*Plan:*
1. Proposed reclamation projects may be appealed by the states involved.
2. A national review board will attempt to adjust plans to meet opposing interests.
3. When national interests are deemed more important than state and local interests, a reasonable period of time must be provided for necessary anthropological exploration.

*Feasibility and Desirability of Plan:*
1. The interests and purposes of all the people must be considered in a democratic system.
2. Some scenic areas are unique.
3. Reclamation projects are often massive enough to permit adjustments which might satisfy conflicting interests.
4. The people of a state should have some control over how their natural resources will be utilized.

IV. Useful in home economics, sociology, and psychology classes

*Concept:* The health and security of both parent and child must be protected.

*Debate Proposition: Resolved,* That the United States's abortion laws should be liberalized.

*Need:*

1. More than one million illegal abortions are performed annually.
2. Illegal abortions seriously endanger the health of both mother and child.
3. Unwanted children often lead to broken homes, suicides, and murder.

*Plan:*

1. Abortion would be legalized in cases where the mental and physical health of the mother is threatened.
2. A panel of medical specialists would be available to decide the merits of each case.
3. Abortions would be limited to qualified doctors in medically approved hospitals.

*Feasibility and Desirability of Plan:*

1. The majority of childbearing females favors liberalized abortion laws.
2. Marriage in today's world is postponed far beyond the age of physical maturity.
3. Many church groups favor liberalized abortion laws.
4. Most members of the medical profession favor such a plan.
5. The plan merely legalizes and establishes acceptable standards for current practice.

V. Useful in English and literature classes

*Concept:* Verbal expression often differs markedly from written language.

*Debate Proposition: Resolved,* That common conversational English should replace formal English structure.

*Need:*

1. Both verbal and written expression are designed for communication of ideas.
2. It is through verbal expression that new words, innovations, and word combinations originate.
3. The spoken word is having an increased impact today with the widespread availability of radio, television, and tape recorders.

*Plan:*

1. Language of each locale would receive emphasis in the schools. (The hip language of the culturally disadvantaged, for example would find its way into the classroom.)
2. Formal expression would be taught along with informal language structure.
3. Idioms and other elements of the vernacular would be employed whenever practical.

*Feasibility and Desirability of Plan:*

1. Most individuals, both old and young, commonly use informal language in most social interaction.
2. Language should change as peoples change.
3. Informal language facilitates communication, especially among culturally disadvantaged groups.

# CHAPTER 18

# Processes of Inquiry

## OVERVIEW

### Key Concepts

1. Inquiry techniques are designed specifically for independence in problem solving.
2. A set for inquiry is established when the student is guided into asking questions for which he has no logical answers.
3. Inquiry processes may range in length from one or two class periods to two or three weeks.
4. Inquiry processes may be structured around several unit concepts.
5. The teacher's role may vary from one of guidance to one of "devil's advocate."

### New Terms

1. **Inquiry Processes**—An approach to learning which emphasizes student initiative and direction of his own learning experiences.
2. **Pupil-teacher Planning**—An older term used to describe inquiry processes. As the term implies, student and teacher often work cooperatively in planning and directing the experience.
3. **Discovery Lesson (Episode)**—A short (often initiatory) experience designed to provoke a set for learning by "offending the learner's imagination," or otherwise prompting questions.

### Questions to Guide Your Study

1. What characteristics of inquiry probably account for the author's description as "the cooperative experience"?

2. What areas of this approach do you anticipate as the most difficult to apply? Why?
3. Extended inquiry processes differ in basic purpose from the "discovery episode." Defend or refute.
4. "Certain critics have contended that inquiry techniques lead to a de-emphasis of 'content learning.' " How would you respond to such an argument?

"What do you people see here on the table?"

"Two beakers of water." The class members at their places view these beakers at the teacher's demonstration table.

"What would happen if I put ice cubes in the beakers?"

"They would float."

The teacher then places an ice cube in each beaker. In one beaker it floats, and in the other it sinks. The excitement generated by this "anti-intuitive" event is at once apparent by the excited murmur through the room.

"What's wrong?" the teacher asks.

"One of those beakers contains some pretty silly water."

"One ice cube is heavier than the other."

"The cube that sank is not ice."

The responses of all the students are directly related to the nature of the materials that are viewed. They are mildly frustrated by being unable to touch and handle the materials. This kind of reaction is generally true of student response to demonstrations of any kind.

"What can I do that will allow you to check some of your ideas?" The teacher asks the question only after he is sure that the students have exhausted a good supply of possible explanations.

"Switch the cubes," one student challenges to a chorus of approval from his peers.

The teacher switches the cubes and the results are the same. The cube sinks in the same liquid in which it had sunk previously and floats in the same liquid in which it had floated before.

"I told you it was silly water," said the student who originally proposed this notion.

"Well, we *proved* it couldn't be the cubes," said others.

"Since you people have worked with calculating the densities of different materials, can you make some kind of a statement about the densities of these things we are viewing?"

After a bit of discussion, the students decide that they can rank the density order of liquids on the basis of ice. The liquid in which the ice floats is denser than ice, and the liquid in which it sank is less dense than ice. The teacher writes these relationships on the board.

"Okay, here's your assignment: Using these liquids, which are, by the way, water and rubbing alcohol, you will measure the density of an ice cube. You will need scales, beakers and the liquids. Go to it."

From this point on, the teacher's role is to act as director of inquiry who turns student questions back to the results of the demonstration, their knowledge of the technique of measuring density, and their own ideas of how the problem might be solved. Several groups decide on different ways of solving the problem; they are concerned at first about the differences in their approach. The teacher tells them that they should try what they proposed and evaluate the results. There is not, he assures them, an *only* way to reach the solution.

**286**

Throughout these multiple approaches, the students "discover" the variables that might affect their results, such as the melting of ice in the alcohol-water solution mentioned by our first teacher. They also become aware of the change in volume of the ice while the mass is being measured on the scales. The materials themselves guarantee that these variables will bcome apparent.[1]

The foregoing is a discovery lesson which might be used in a science class. The demonstration developed immediate interest and curiosity. Why? Before reading further, stop to analyze what specific instructional techniques are apparent.

Actually the demonstration offended the student's intuition. It created a situation that was not readily acceptable, forcing him to find his way out of an intellectual maze established for him.

Viewing learning as a process of exploring and discovering personal meaning suggests the need for jointly planned classroom procedures. Cooperative teacher-pupil planning and direction of learning activities occur in a variety of ways at various levels of abstraction. Indeed, they are utilized to some degree in all group work, as illustrated in the preceding chapters. The present chapter and the one which follows, however, deal with cooperative approaches to teaching which employ democratic processes to their fullest degree.

The new emphasis upon processes of "inquiry," or "discovery," or "inductive" teaching has created considerable confusion among teachers. Although often referred to as "a method," a perusal of the recent literature suggests many interpretations of meaning. The basic process of inquiry, it is generally agreed, is synonymous with Dewey's steps of "reflective thinking," first published around the turn of the century.[2] (They are illustrated in the problem which follows.) The "new" emphasis focuses upon student self-direction as an outgrowth of a carefully planned situation. *How* a situation may be structured and *how* student self-direction may be structured provides most of the apparent confusion over methodology, suggesting not one but many approaches to the problem.

The essence of inquiry, according to Romey consists of interpretation, generalization, and conclusion.[3] He contends that *interpretation* is best accomplished in group discussion, based upon a problem designed to encourage students to argue. The teacher, as a discussion leader, plays the role of devil's advocate. The class as a group develops its own chain of reasoning as it seeks to *generalize* from the data provided. *Conclusions* are an outgrowth of student analysis.

An apparently different point of view holds that the goals of inquiry or investigation-oriented teaching are designed to reach the student as an individual learner rather than as a member of a large group. Each individual has

---

[1] Robert E. Samples, "Death of an Investigation," *Journal of Geological Education* 5 (April 1966): 69–72. Used by permission of the publisher. For an interesting contrast of an authoritarian approach with the open-ended discussion, the reader is urged to read the entire article by Samples.

[2] John Dewey, *How We Think*, rev. ed. (Boston: D. C. Heath and Co., 1933).

[3] William D. Romey, *Inquiry Techniques for Science* (New York: Prentice-Hall, Inc., 1968). For detailed instructions on how to conduct a large number of "invitations to inquiry" in biological science, consult Joseph J. Schwab, *The Biology Teacher's Handbook* (New York: John Wiley and Sons, Inc., 1963).

some topic, problem, or question to investigate that has high interest appeal and about which he is curious. Findings, of course, are shared and evaluated by the entire class group.[4]

The illustrated model provided in a later section of this chapter emphasizes the latter approach. Although the two *can* be incorporated as a single approach if the teacher desires, it should be noted that there are other equally valid approaches to "inquiry" teaching. The major requirement seems to be that of a cooperative experience involving student-teacher planning, discussion, conjecture, and attempts at generalization of findings.

## FUNDAMENTAL PROPERTIES

Like most other instructional approaches, the processes of inquiry approach is representative of systematized problem-solving. Unlike some other approaches, however, this technique is based upon current student needs and interests rather than upon organized bodies of subject matter as a starting point. Indeed, the processes of reflective thought are applied by the entire group. The topics which follow represent essential conditions necessary for effective application of the method.

### Why Is a Democratic Framework Important?

Inquiry experiences are conceived within a framework which may be new to both student and teacher. Teacher-imposed activities and assignments are replaced by problems and projects often suggested by students themselves. A competitive class climate is replaced with a climate of cooperative group interaction as students pursue different aspects of a complex problem. All legitimate areas of choice must be identified (by either or both student and teacher) and then resolved by the class group. The teacher's role is relegated to that of a participating guide. His task is that of guiding students in their objective consideration of issues; sometimes acting as a resource person; sometimes discouraging or even rejecting suggested actions which would carry students beyond the particular problem under investigation; sometimes offering suggestions and advice of his own. The basic objective is that of supplying guidance, assistance, and support at every step of the way *without* unnecessarily imposing his wishes or authority upon the group.

### Why Are Immediate Applications Important?

In selecting an appropriate topic for inquiry, attention must be directed to the immediate concerns of adolescents. Some areas of school work are more directly related to the group than are others. There are areas within almost

[4] K. B. Cummings, "Discovery Learning with Illustrations," *High School Journal* 53 (February 1970): 281–97.

all subject fields, however, in which immediate parallels can be found. If such parallels can be made apparent to students, *prior to a thorough investigation of the topic,* such an experience may be effective.

## Why Is Flexibility Important?

Adolescents feel real concerns in many areas of their daily existence. If the inquiry (inductive) experience successfully touches their lives, the quantity and quality of questions will be almost overwhelming. Textbook units will no longer seem adequate, as questions tend to cut across topical areas. Some questions may seem more directly related to courses other than the one under consideration. The answers to other questions will be difficult to find. A few questions may be embarrassing or even appear to go beyond the realm of prudence acceptable to school authorities.

Both teacher and students must be flexible in such matters. The teacher must be willing to revise his thinking with respect to units and courses, recognizing that conventional lines are often extremely arbitrary. Questions which seem inappropriate for class consideration frequently can be reworded to incorporate the basic idea in a more acceptable form. Biology students who are studying reproduction, for example, may want to know the "safe" days during the menstrual cycle when conception cannot occur. A more appropriate question might be, "What are the factors which may influence the ovulation period?" Thus by inference the student understands the basic idea or concept involved. Sometimes a teacher will find it necessary to exclude questions which more appropriately may be treated in a different context or which are remotely related to the area or subject. An explanation of such matters is desirable.

## What Resource Materials Are Needed?

The diversity of questions will usually render textbooks inadequate. One must search through journals, encyclopedias, yearbooks, and the like. Frequently, personal interviews with individuals knowledgeable in the area is appropriate; sometimes school trips and individual experimentation are needed. The teacher, anticipating such needs, must make preliminary arrangements for study groups in a variety of settings. Key books must be placed on study reserve; potential resource people must be contacted. If resources are limited, it may be desirable to restrict the experience to one class group at a time. Since students will be working somewhat independently of the teacher, expected rules of conduct must be clearly established.

## What Are the Time Requirements of the Method?

The processes of planning, researching, and reporting take time. Developing questions, establishing study groups, and researching a given area usually necessitates a time span of at least one and a half weeks. Reporting, review, and evaluational activities will likely involve another one and a half weeks. On the other hand, most teachers have found that three and a half or four weeks' duration is about the maximum time that interest in a given problem area can be maintained. (When used for the purpose of developing a "set" for inquiry, the experience may merely involve a few minutes of a single class period.)

## INQUIRY PROCEDURES

The processes of inquiry generally follow a logical sequence of problem solving. The basic objective is to guide the learner in his exploration at every step along the way. Above all, the learner must anticipate each phase of the experience well in advance of the activity and plan accordingly. The procedure which follows is suggestive only.

### How Is the Problem Identified?

With inquiry processes, as here conceived, the teacher identifies the problem *area.* He then attempts to develop interest in the area. This may be accomplished in a variety of ways, including such techniques as a short lecture, discussion, film, resource speaker, or oral report. For purposes of illustration, a specific example from high school biology is employed. Let us assume that the unit is entitled "The Human Body" and the particular topic *which the teacher has selected* is the circulatory system.

> Teacher: Our next topic for exploration is the circulatory system. Let us read ——— books for an overview or broad picture of the problem. Then we will let Bill give us a ten-minute report on "The Heart and You."

The reading is designed to acquaint the students with the general area, while Bill's report will open up definite avenues of interest. He is directed to touch upon such aspects as heart diseases, disorders, and malfunctions. Such an activity is designed to provoke student thought in the area.

### How Are the Issues Clarified?

Once the proper foundation has been established, students are urged to formulate questions which they would like answered. Emphasis is placed upon realistic, practical problems, rather than upon questions which they think the teacher wants them to ask.

> Teacher: From our general inspection of the circulatory system what subheadings or divisions seem appropriate? For example, Bill sug-

gested many diseases which may affect the circulatory system. What are some other areas which might be worthy of exploration?

The class then suggests five or six groupings. Some of them might be:

1. Organs of the circulatory system
2. Diseases
3. Disorders or malfunctions
4. Conditions which affect the heart
5. First aid in relation to the heart

Teacher: Now, as an assignment, you will be provided an opportunity to list specific questions which you would like to have answered as we study the circulatory system. Your questions will determine what we will study, so make sure they represent what you really want to know. You might want to work with others on this assignment. It is not necessary that you submit questions, nor are there any specific number requested. If there are no questions, just write me a note to this effect. To assist us in organizing our thoughts, we will refer to the general areas listed. Some may develop questions in each area, while others may be interested primarily in only one area.

The next day questions are grouped and refined. To save time, it may be desirable to appoint a committee for this purpose. When the list of questions has been compiled, the teacher should make copies available to each person.

## How Are the Learning Activities Planned and Developed?

Students at this point are assigned to subgroups, usually on the basis of choice. Subgroups of five are preferred. Each subgroup is expected to select a leader and a recorder and to develop a study plan. Each subgroup considers informational sources, along with methods of investigation, reporting and evaluation. Students should give some consideration to all phases of the project so that they can more fully grasp the total task ahead. The teacher moves from group to group, to guide and direct as necessary. For example, students may need guidance in rephrasing and expanding some of the questions. "Why do we want to know about the diseases which affect the circulatory system? How can we use the information in our daily lives?" The teacher may find it necessary to assist some groups to develop an appropriate division of labor. Does each person know his specific responsibility? Are the tasks appropriate for the individuals involved?

At the outset the teacher will want to suggest the amount of time available for the project. Time allotments for each group report must be established early. By providing for some flexibility in this respect, students are encouraged to use their own imagination relative to unique and creative ways of reporting to the class. They will then need assistance in carrying out such plans.

### How Are the Data Collected?

The instructor, well in advance of need, should have placed key library references on reserve, made arrangements for some of the class in the library schedule each day, and looked into the possibilities of field trips and other resources.

While investigating a variety of problems, the groups will have different resource needs. These require careful supervision, a great deal of trust in students, and a cooperative attitude on the part of other teachers and administrators. The wise teacher will set the stage carefully. The first five minutes of every work period might well be devoted to brief progress reports and plans for the day's activities. Copies of the reports should list problems needing attention. The teacher quickly determines which problems need immediate attention. A short class discussion on how to find information may be in order, especially for groups inexperienced in the procedure.

If a project is to have a two-week duration, four class periods may be devoted to collection of data. A major portion of another period likely will be needed for specific preparation of the reporting procedures to be employed.

### What Reporting Procedures Are Employed?

Although a group may have accomplished a great deal in planning and research activities, the value to the class group depends on how well findings are shared with others. Somewhere in the process the entire class might profitably set up standards for this phase of the project. Each group can be asked to consider the problem before planning its specific method of reporting. A master list is then distributed to the chairman of each group. One class listed eight points essential to an appropriate presentation:

1. Material presented should relate to the goals established.
2. Presentations should involve all members of the group in some way.
3. Presentations will be brief, preferably not exceeding fifteen minutes.
4. Presentations should not be read.
5. Other class members should be allotted time for questions. If a key question cannot be answered, some member of the group should be designated to find the answer.
6. As a general rule, technical material should be omitted from presentations. When it is necessary, however, it should be reproduced for the class.
7. Sources of information should be available.
8. Contradictory evidence should be presented as impartially as possible.

Following each presentation the teacher may lead the class in a general review for the purpose of expanding, clarifying, or correcting important points. It is seldom possible to have more than two group presentations in one class period of fifty-five to sixty minutes. Sometimes keen interest may be indicated, suggesting the desirability of extending discussion to a full class period.

## How Are Generalizations Derived?

As a culminating activity the teacher will want to conduct a review of the entire project. This will involve recalling the major concepts and procedures employed and expanding to related areas. (See Chapter 22, "Review Method.") The activity, usually extending over a period of some two class periods, serves the important function of organizing and clarifying basic ideas which have been developed gradually over a period of several class periods.

## How Is the Experience Evaluated?

Early in the cooperative experience, students are asked to give some consideration to evaluational techniques. As indicated previously, they assist in establishing standards of reporting. They may want to participate in some sort of group evaluation. Perhaps a group mark, derived by students, may be combined with an individual mark administered by the teacher. Whatever procedure is employed should be developed jointly by teacher and students.

# PLANNING FOR THE INQUIRY EXPERIENCE

A detailed lesson plan is needed if the teacher-pupil planned project is to develop smoothly. The illustration which follows incorporates the essential steps of the procedure. It is designed to serve for the entire project.

LESSON PLAN ILLUSTRATION (biology class)

*Concepts:* 1. The circulatory system influences all body functions.
2. Many serious diseases are associated with the circulatory system.
3. Our living habits directly influence the health and function of the circulatory system.

*Problem:* How can we better understand the intricacies of the circulatory system?

*Goals:* After this experience the student should have furthered his understanding of the influence of the circulatory system upon an individual's health, as evidenced by:
1. The questions he asks in a discussion of these problems.
2. His planning an appropriate schedule of activities for himself necessary for a healthy circulatory system.
3. His analysis of diseases, disorders, and other conditions which may affect the circulatory system.
4. His ability to apply concepts developed in class to related problems.
After this class the student should have furthered his skill in independent and semi-independent study, as evidenced by:
1. His ability to find needed resource materials.
2. His ability to function effectively in committee activities.

**293**

*Lesson Approach:*

Our next topic is the circulatory system. Let us read ——— books for an overview or broad picture of the problem. Then we will let Bill give a ten-minute report on "The Heart and You." Make a note of any questions which occur to you.

*Lesson Development:*

TEACHER: From our general inspection of the circulatory system what subheadings or divisions seem appropriate? For example, Bill suggested many diseases which may affect the circulatory system. What are some other areas which might be worthy of exploration?

The class then suggests five or six groupings. Some of them might be:
1. Organs of the circulatory system
2. Diseases
3. Disorders or malfunctions
4. Conditions which affect the heart
5. First aid in relation to the heart

TEACHER: Now, as an assignment, you will be provided an opportunity to list specific questions which you would like to have answered as we study the circulatory system. Your questions will determine what we will study, so make sure they represent what you really want to know. You might want to work with others on this assignment. It is not necessary that you submit questions, nor are there any specific number requested. If there are no questions, just write me a note to this effect. To assist us in organizing our thoughts, we will refer to the general areas listed. Some may develop questions in each area, while others may be interested primarily in only one area.

(Reproduce question list for each student. Add two or three questions if this seems necessary for accomplishment of major objectives.)

FORMULATION OF BUZZ GROUPS:

At this time we will form a separate buzz group for each identified area of our problem for the purpose of correlating our questions. (Ask for volunteers.)

Select a leader and a recorder. List and rework questions, cutting out duplications. *Then* add other questions which are prompted during this activity.

Reproduce question list for each student. Add two or three questions if this seems necessary for accomplishment of major objectives.

*Development of Learning Activities:*

Now that you have studied the list of questions in each area, you see the task before us. We will ask for an indication of preference for committees to be formed for each area.

COMMITTEE BUZZ GROUPS:

Our task is to find the answers to our list of questions and somehow to provide the class with these answers. What are some possible sources of information? (List on chalkboard.)

EXAMPLES:

1. Books

2. Magazines
3. Resource people

Now let us move into our committees and organize for action, selecting a leader and a recorder. Work out an appropriate division of labor. I will visit each group for the purpose of answering questions.

COLLECTING DATA:

At the conclusion of each day's activities I want you to indicate progress for that day and to suggest problems (if any). Recorder should submit this report after each work period.

LOOKING AHEAD—ANTICIPATING REPORTING TECHNIQUES:

Now that we have had an opportunity to work on our projects for two or three class periods, let's turn our attention to reporting techniques. What are some possibilities? (List.)

EXAMPLES:

1. Oral reports
2. Skits
3. Panel discussion

STANDARDS:

What standards should we establish for the presentations? (List.)

EXAMPLES:

1. Not to be read.
2. Limit to twenty minutes long. (Teacher suggests this one.)
3. Separate findings from your own opinions.

ORGANIZE FOR REPORTING:

At this time you should decide upon a technique(s) for group presentations. Leaders will discuss plans with your instructor, pending final approval.

EVALUATION:

How should the presentations be evaluated? Let us list some possibilities. (List.)

EXAMPLES:

1. Rating scales
2. Group evaluation of individuals; class evaluation of groups
3. Written tests

From this list (as groups) decide upon preferences. (Reporters meet with instructor to resolve differences.)

CLASS PRESENTATIONS:

Each individual should list questions as they arise. (Ask during question periods.)

## Deriving Generalizations:

Now, as a result of our experiences, let us formulate major ideas or concepts which have emerged from these experiences. (List.)

EXAMPLES:

1. The heart is similar to a machine. If kept in good working condition, it may function appropriately for many years.

2. Circulatory disorders or malfunctions are usually reflected in the state of one's health.
3. There are numerous myths associated with the circulatory system.

## VALUES

Inquiry teaching is democratically conceived, resulting in increased pupil independence in his own learning activities.

The self-imposed tasks inherent in the procedure result in intrinsic motivation. Indeed discipline problems are rare if real choices are provided.

The procedure emphasizes *processes* as much as *products* or learning. Thus *discovery* of new ideas and concepts is sought as a *means* of giving meaning to further performance.

Cooperation between student and student and between student and teacher is emphasized. Competition tends to shift from individuals to small groups and self-imposed standards.

The instructional approach emphasizes an active student. Indeed the method has often been called "project work," calling attention to the inherent nature of the activities involved.

Development of creativity is encouraged, since the learner must assume responsibility for solving problems in his own way.

## LIMITATIONS AND PROBLEMS

In some areas it is difficult to find legitimate areas of choice. Especially in skill areas, a minimum of opportunity for such activities may be available.

Sometimes individual students are not prepared to accept the freedoms essential for self-direction. The break from conformity in learning teacher-imposed tasks may, on occasion, create anxieties and tensions. These, in turn, may be reflected in class misbehavior. A pattern of gradually increased responsibilities is usually preferred.

Teachers sometimes lack the ability to relinquish control necessitated by teacher-pupil planning. Indeed this seems to be the greatest single deterrent to democratically conceived classes. Although one is, to a marked degree, a victim of his own school experiences, the cycle can be broken by a process of gradually increased pupil involvement.

A criticism, occasionally voiced by experienced teachers, is the time required for such experiences. Unfortunately, the necessity of "covering the text or subject" is often implicitly assumed to be the teacher's basic task. Today, however, the advancement of knowledge is expanding at a geometric rate. Facts soon become outdated. An implicit assumption associated with the democratic classroom is the importance of ideas and concepts in an orderly process of exploration and discovery.

# INQUIRY ILLUSTRATIONS

I. Useful in biology and general science classes

*Unit:* Similarities and Variation

*Concepts:*
1. Mutations are sudden, unexpected changes.
2. Inherited lethal or handicapping conditions are fairly common.
3. Abnormal chromosome number influences health.
4. Drugs and radiation are growing problems associated with heredity.

*Problem:* What hereditary maladies and conditions might be explored?

*Possible Areas of Interest:*
1. Inherited deficiencies and conditions
2. Inherited disease tendencies
3. Chromosome number maladies
4. Influence of drugs
5. Influence of radiation

II. Useful in world history and literature classes

*Unit:* Imperialism

*Concepts:*
1. Religious ideas of predetermination influenced Indian and Oriental habits and customs.
2. Southwest Asia has served as a commercial "crossroads" between India and China.
3. China has tended to visualize herself as somewhat self-sufficient.
4. Japanese culture shows evidence of much adaptation from other civilizations.

*Problem:* How might we enhance our understanding of the influence of imperialistic policies on nations of the Far East?

*Possible Areas of Interest:*
1. Religion
2. Political systems
3. Trade and industry
4. Type of economy
5. Population distribution

III. Useful in home economics, sociology, and psychology classes

*Unit:* Marriage

*Concepts:*
1. There are many valid reasons why people may or may not marry.
2. The engagement period has both hazards and advantages.
3. For a satisfying marriage, each partner must be flexible in his thinking and actions.

*Problem:* What factors about marriage should be explored?

*Possible Areas of Interest:*
1. Engagement
2. Love
3. Courtship
4. Marriage customs
5. Dating
6. Sex

IV. Useful in English literature, sociology, and world history classes

*Unit:* The Aspiring Mind

*Concepts:*
1. The emancipation of restricted classes provided new opportunities for the individual in every aspect of Elizabethan life.
2. Elizabethan society flourished in all areas of life and raised the aspirations of its citizens during the Renaissance.

*Problem:* What aspects of Elizabethan life might we explore in considerable depth?

*Possible Areas of Interest:*
1. Rebirth of interest in literature and the arts
2. Democratic society and theater development
3. Influence of religious change
4. Emergence of Great Britain as a leading nation

CHAPTER **19**

# Small-Group Techniques

## OVERVIEW

### Key Concepts

1. The optimum small-group size is usually placed at five. (Effective small-group work, however, may be accomplished in groups ranging up to twelve or eighteen students.)
2. The small group may be used as a testing ground for effective group interaction.
3. Small-group experience is an ideal means of increasing student participation.
4. Small-group experiences may be short- or long-lived, depending upon the nature of the activity involved.
5. Small-group techniques are frequently used in connection with other instructional methods.

### New Terms

1. **Short- and Long-lived Groups**—A short-lived group may function ten or fifteen minutes for a class period or two. Long-lived groups (sometimes called committees) on the other hand may extend for a week or more.
2. **Learning Styles**—Habits employed by the individual learner in processing information. Some students, for example, seem to learn more effectively through verbal discourse; others tend to learn more effectively by listening to others.
3. **Group Therapy**—Use of the group as a means of altering personality. This technique is inappropriate when not under the control of a specialist.
4. **Task (Committee) Groups**—Usually long-lived groups that carry a task to its conclusion. The entire reflective process is involved.
5. **Buzz Groups**—Usually short-lived groups which often focus upon one aspect of a problem only.

6. **Fishbowl Technique**—A training technique whereby group roles are assigned, played, and reflected upon in a controlled setting. Designed to develop group cohesion and awareness of the influence of various individual roles (treated in Chapter 20).

### Questions to Guide Your Study

1. What are the relative merits of short- and long-lived groups?
2. "The creation of small groups in itself tends to minimize teacher-domination." Defend or refute.
3. Why should group therapy (including sensitivity training) be carefully avoided by the classroom teacher?
4. What implications do different learning styles have upon the formation of small groups?

In addition to the properties of a group, described in Chapter 20, a *small* group is characterized by a face-to-face relationship. Each person in a small group must have a distinct impression of *each other person,* enabling him to react, at any time, to other members as individuals. In actual numbers a group of up to twenty members is usually considered by sociologists to be "small." The optimum small-group size is usually placed at about five. Essentially a small group must be large enough for development of a sense of "groupness" or unity but small enough to discourage group cleavages or factions.

## FUNDAMENTAL PROPERTIES

The small group is often viewed as a microcosm of a larger group. As such, it is characterized by all the group forces which are necessary for group dynamics. In addition, there are a number of other properties which render it one of the most viable methods of teaching.

### Why Is Freedom from Restraint Desirable?

When an individual is grouped with five to eight other students in an intellectual encounter he feels increased responsibility to participate orally. The usual inhibitions which characterize conventional-sized classes are missing. A teacher can hardly lecture to a group of this size, nor can one or two members readily "carry" the discussion. Active participation generates a feeling of independence and responsibility as one assesses the immediate impact of his contribution on others.

### Why Is Idea Testing Important?

The intimacy of the small group provides a testing ground for ideas. Like the family, a small group provides a "private" audience for determining how well a "brilliant" idea can stand up under the full force of intellectual logic. Because of the very nature of the group, criticism tends to be sincere as well as constructive. No longer is one motivated to talk merely for the purpose of impressing others. In fact, the atmosphere is one which almost compels one to listen as well as contribute. This is a rather unique experience for some.

### What Are the Relative Merits of Long- and Short-Lived Groups?

Small-group experiences can be short- or long-lived, depending upon the purpose(s) to be served. In conventional classes the well-known committee assignment may extend over a period of several days. At other times groups may not extend beyond a single class period. When associated with flexible scheduling, small groups are usually short-lived, serving as a transition between large-group instruction and independent study.

Short-lived groups demand much less structure than do long-lived groups. Although the same forces of group structure exist, each session must be treated as a separate unit. In Chapter 20, for example, it is emphasized that group cohesion tends to develop slowly over a period of a week or more. Group cohesion in short-lived groups is desirable but is seldom attained unless some preliminary training is provided. The evidence suggests that most teachers are inadequately prepared for short-lived, small-group instruction.

Perhaps in response to such a need, some schools are currently emphasizing in-service education in sensitivity training (sometimes called T-Group experiences). The objective is to increase the learner's sensitivity to the needs and interests of others. Such techniques actually incorporate some elements of group therapy which, in the hands of an improperly trained person, can create more problems than they can solve.

### What Learning Styles Are Important?

Through small-group activity an individual may discover and develop his own best cognitive style of learning. Styles of learning may be defined as information processing habits that function generally with the individual. Differences among individuals in perceiving, cognizing, and conceptualizing are probably as real as are differences in ability levels. Individuals tend to display differences in seeing, hearing, and handling things during the learning process. Although this phenomenon is as yet imperfectly understood the work of Frymier and his associates suggests at least three different personality dimensions which have a bearing on one's style of learning.[1]

*Internal-External.* Learning is a combination of internal and external forces. Equally motivated individuals, however, apparently differ markedly with

[1] Jack R. Frymier, "Motivating Students to Learn," *NEA Journal* 57 (February 1968): 37–39.

respect to the relative influence of these forces. Some positively (or negatively) motivated students, for example, seem to draw heavily upon internal forces. The novel and the new excite them. Ambiguity and uncertainty provide a basis for their quest for problem resolution. Other students, equally motivated, appear to be influenced more by the quantity and quality of external stimuli. Exciting class activities (e.g., fascinating movies, interesting methods, and vivid illustrations) seem to stimulate learning behaviors.

*Intake-Output.* Some students are basically consumers of the world around them. They are avid readers, thoughtful listeners, and generally information seekers. "Intake" class activities have a strong appeal for such individuals. Other students, who are equally motivated, might be classified as "output" individuals. They learn readily when production activities are stressed, such as writing, talking, doing.

*Approach-Avoidance.* Teacher approval, class marks, social acceptance, and the like have a strong appeal to some positively (or negatively) motivated students. Others who are positively motivated, however, tend to avoid such activities. They find such activities distasteful.

If Frymier's conclusions are correct, the task of activating the desire to learn becomes much more complex than most teachers suspect. Class activities which appeal to two equally motivated students should be varied on the basis of personality structure.

Recently Kagan has discovered still another learning style that has a direct bearing on the reflective processes of individual learning.[2]

*Reflection-Impulsivity.* Some students, according to Kagan, tend to reflect over alternatives to problems while others tend to group data on a rapid global inference basis. This learning style is seen as touching the problem-solving experience at three points: When one initially verbalizes and comprehends the available data; when he selects hypotheses; and when he evaluates the accuracy of the final solution. Both Frymier and Kagan believe that learning should capitalize upon the learner's habits of information-processing while at the same time seeking to improve or alter styles with a view of increasing productivity.

## How Do Small Instructional Groups Differ from Group Therapy?

Group therapy is currently one of the most widely used methods of helping individuals adjust to their problems. Its most fundamental value can be expressed in the adage that "misery loves company." All people, especially those with severe emotional problems, seem to feel better when they realize that their problems are shared by others.

Group therapy essentially uses the group to change personality. The group is controlled by the therapist, although he typically employs a permissive attitude as a means of encouraging communication. He must always be ready and willing to protect any group member from excessive threat, however.

[2] J. Kagan and others, "Conceptual Impulsivity and Inductive Reasoning," *Child Development* 37 (1966): 583–94.

Group interaction provides the therapist with a valuable source of diagnostic information. This diagnosis can then be fed back to the individual in the group or in a private conference. There is no basic task goal. The individual does not surrender his identity but rather reinforces it through group interaction. The therapist uses the situational events of a group to enable the patient to discover the source of his tensions and maladjustments. The therapist interprets behavior in terms of the individual involved.

A small group in education, on the other hand, emphasizes task goals. The individual is expected to subordinate his personal goals to those of the group. He becomes a part of the group, surrendering a part of his own identity as he interacts with his peers in the resolution of a task problem. As in group therapy, interaction is important and should be evaluated. In task groups, however, interaction is analyzed from the standpoint of communication and progress toward the stated goal. While students may reflect upon the impact of certain contributions to group progress, *they should not discuss individual feelings or attempt to analyze the personal behaviors of one of the members.*

Group therapy techniques are dangerous in the hands of the untrained person. Thus teachers should not only prevent students from using the small group as a therapy session but should themselves carefully avoid such diagnosis. It is recognized that through group interaction certain tensions will be minimized and certain minor personality adjustments may be made, supplying important concomitants to the process. Deep-seated problems, however, demand more intensive professional treatment than the classroom setting can provide. When such difficulties become apparent during small-group interaction, the school psychiatrist should be consulted.

## SMALL-GROUP APPLICATIONS

The small group is ideally suited to processes of reflective thinking. It is *not* an appropriate setting for covering content, but it *is* an appropriate setting for reflecting on issues related to teacher-dominated presentations. In such a microcosm students can easily reflect on practical applications of important issues. Since the small group can be used in many different ways, the applications which follow must be considered as suggestive only.

### How Are Task Groups Organized?

A task (committee) group sets out to solve a problem. Basically it follows the same general procedures as those outlined in Chapter 16 for class and panel discussion. In size it usually ranges from four to seven or eight members. Unlike other types of discussion, however, each member is actively involved in reflective processes. The task must be clearly defined and understood by all; roles and individual assignments must be clearly understood; needed resources must be made available. In addition, a realistic time schedule must be developed with appropriate progress reports at designated points. Finally, some type of feedback to the entire class must be arranged. Such activities may be short- or long-lived depending upon the nature of the task. Students themselves should be provided considerable latitude in decision making—at least with options along the way.

Since the task group often represents an initial departure from purely teacher-dominated activities, students often flounder in their attempts to work on their own. Indeed this is to be expected until necessary skills are mastered. The discussion guide which follows represents the sort of *initial* guidance which may be necessary. As students gain experience each small group can be given the responsibility for developing its own problem. The problem may be appropriate for a social science, English class, or a safety education class, depending upon the nature of the unit involved.

***Issue:*** *What protection should a youth offender have under the law?*

A.  Analysis of the Problem

1.  What basic assumptions are associated with special treatment of youth offenders in the courts? Are these assumptions valid?
2.  What are the consequences of giving a youth offender "the breaks" after he has committed one or more serious crimes? In many states the judge may permit the offender to be tried in regular criminal court. Do you approve of this practice? Why or why not?
3.  As a legal institution the juvenile court does not possess the procedural safeguards of other courts. For example, a child may be required to testify against himself; he may be denied the right to hear the evidence against him; he may not be permitted representation by an attorney or the right to appeal his case. What are the advantages and disadvantages of such a system? What changes, if any, would you suggest?
4.  How long are the police justified in holding a youth for investigation? What techniques of eliciting information are admissible?

B.  Weighing Alternatives

1.  For minor offenses a youth may be released to the custody of his parents without a court hearing or legal disposition of the case. Police often exercise unauthorized "voluntary" supervision over the child, sometimes collecting money in order to make restitution for damages done by the child. Some oppose such an arrangement, claiming that police officers are seldom trained for such supervision. How would you evaluate this practice?
2.  In some states youth offenders are not photographed or fingerprinted, since many employers check police records as a condition of employment. Some states, however, defend such procedures as a means of assisting them to solve future crimes. How would you evaluate such a practice?
3.  Truancy is a school problem up to a certain point. Nevertheless, it is usually specified as an act of delinquency, making the juvenile courts available for the enforcement of school attendance laws.

Generally, there is no clear-cut line between the school's responsibility and the court's responsibility in the matter. What recommendations do you have in this situation?

4. What other solutions or innovations have been tried in combatting juvenile crime? [In this connection you should investigate especially Work (Forestry) Camps, Psychiatric Treatment Centers, and Guided Group Interaction programs.]

5. Study the California Youth Authority's success in rehabilitating the juvenile offender. Would you recommend such an approach for the nation as a whole? Why or why not?

6. Visit a juvenile court or talk with a juvenile-court judge. What impressions did you receive? What improvements, if any, would you recommend?

7. Talk with individuals who have run afoul of the law. Do they seem to feel that they received adequate treatment by the police or the courts? Why or why not?

Although problem-solving groups can work on any of three levels—fact, value, and policy—most small-group discussions should grapple with all three problems. It should be noted that a problem of policy (illustrated above) includes problems of fact and value. Thus we say that the first two levels are "nested" in the third. In problem-solving discussion, it is necessary that the group consciously pass through the necessary steps. Thus it is inappropriate to jump immediately from problem identification to problem solution.

## How Are Buzz Groups Employed?

Frequently it is appropriate to subdivide a class group into groups of four to six individuals. This is considered about the optimum size for most effective interaction. Small *buzz* groups are usually short-lived. After interacting for fifteen to twenty minutes they "report" to the main group.

Buzz groups have been used effectively in developing group cohesion, for encouraging the timid person to speak, for developing plans germane to the total group, and for providing additional opportunities for leadership. Perhaps the most important function of such groups is to provide expanded opportunities for participation in problem-solving discussions.

Whatever the purpose, buzz groups must be sufficiently oriented to the task at hand. If the task is that of providing expanded opportunities for problem solving, each group must have access to a discussion guide. If each group is assigned a separate phase of the problem for discussion, it must clearly understand its limits and responsibilities for presenting results of the deliberations to the main group. If each buzz group reflects upon a different problem it must "walk" the total group through a brief recapitulation of its own experience.

Buzz group reporting can be handled in a number of ways. Sometimes one member from each group may serve on a panel of representatives to treat the essential issues raised. Occasionally individual members may be asked to present brief, informal reports on group findings. An interesting derivation of the oral report is to provide opportunities for each group to list major ideas and findings on the chalkboard. The class is then provided an opportunity to raise questions relative to these points. Thelen[3] recommends the group interview as an interesting reporting technique. Selected buzz group reporters are asked questions by a designated *class interviewer*. His questions are designed to elicit the basic issues, problems, and conclusions derived from the experience.

Since small-group work is usually limited to one or not more than two sessions, class buzz group reports must be brief. They will seldom continue for longer than ten minutes. Informality is encouraged.

Although buzz groups have been used effectively in both small and large classes, they sometimes may lead to the development of undesirable factions. This is especially true when the same students are assigned repeatedly to the same buzz groups. Furthermore, it is more difficult for the teacher to detect the introduction of undesirable games. His responsibility is to move from one group to another, offering assistance as needed. He must carefully resist tendencies to provide answers for the discussants.

### What Functions May Be Served Through Tutorial Teaching Groups?

Even when "homogeneously grouped," students vary tremendously in a variety of ways. Teacher-led discussion of an entire class is essential for certain purposes. Real meaning, however, may not be achieved until students are provided opportunities to "talk it over" in small groups.

By employing appropriate diagnostic techniques, students with common problems can be identified and grouped accordingly. The teacher (along with teacher aides and/or able students) can then move from group to group for the purpose of remedial assistance. The mere process of sitting down and discussing problems with a small group of students seems to enhance learning.

Sometimes students with different problems can be paired off for the purpose of helping each other. A fellow student who "speaks the language" of the adolescent frequently is more valuable than the regular teacher for such purposes. A modification of this procedure has been employed by foreign language teachers who have arranged student teams to listen to the pronunciation and enunciation of new language expressions. Students "teaching" each other is a concept that has been neglected in instructional situations.

### What Training Techniques Are Effective?

Most *teachers and students* are ineffective in small-group experiences simply because they are unable to interact effectively with one another. Potentially destructive roles, described in Chapter 16, tend to divide and isolate members from

---

[3] Herbert A. Thelen, *Dynamics of Groups at Work* (Chicago: University of Chicago Press, 1963), pp. 215–16.

each other. It must be recognized that such roles represent expressions of needs on the part of the individuals using them. The dominator, for example, is expressing his need for leadership, just as the blocker wants to be seen as a thoughtful intellectual. In like manner the aggressor may be merely trying to get action started while the playboy desires to demonstrate his humor and superiority. Until some group cohesion is established, however, such behaviors not only fail to satisfy the needs of the user, but they tend to render group work ineffective.

As a means of helping students develop effective group skills of participation and observation, the "fishbowl" technique is recommended.[4] While it is ideally suited to small groups, it also may be effective in groups of up to thirty-five or forty students.

The teacher divides the class into three equal groups (designated as A, B, and C). Chairs are arranged in three concentric circles. Members of Group A (in the inner circle) are paired with members of Group B. Group B members, in the middle circle, position themselves so that the faces of their partners can be observed. Group C takes the outer circle in no particular order.

Members of Group A, the task group, discuss a selected problem for twenty minutes while their Group B partners observe. Each observer partner jots down points which will enable him to reflect or mirror the participant's behavior. His comments will be in the form of "As I saw you, you . . ." and designed to help the participant think through his own group behavior.

In exactly twenty minutes the teacher stops the action and allows ten minutes for each pair from Groups A and B to confer. Meanwhile, Group C members will meet with the teacher to discuss the interacting pattern of the *whole* group. This group will have been instructed to note who speaks most and least, who the leaders seem to be and what behaviors produce group action, satisfaction, or dissatisfaction. They also will note whether the interaction group has cohesion or not and what seemed to be responsible for this phenomenon.

Following the ten minute critique, the groups reassemble as previously noted and continue until five minutes before the close of the class period. Thereupon, each student is asked to write out his reactions to the experience.

At the beginning of the second session the teacher may wish to comment on some of the written reactions. He then shifts Group B to the interaction group. (Group A becomes the general observer group and Group C takes its place as partner observers.) The above process is repeated. The third session proceeds in like manner with Group C becoming the interacting group.

Session four is devoted to general class reaction to the experience. By the fifth session the class should be ready to function as a cohesive group. Although destructive roles will likely emerge from time to time the group is at least prepared to cope with them in a constructive manner.

Although flexible scheduling involves students in small-group work a mere

---

[4] This technique has been described in considerable detail by Alfred H. Gorman, *Teachers and Learners: The Interactive Process* (Boston: Allyn and Bacon, Inc., 1969), pp. 64–70, and Dorothy J. Mail, "The Fishbowl: Design for Discussion," *Today's Education* 57 (September 1968): 27–29.

20 percent of the time, the flexibility of the program can be readily adjusted to cope with special needs as they arise. It should be emphasized that the effectiveness of independent and semi-independent study activities are largely dependent upon the effectiveness of small-group experiences. The fishbowl technique may be followed with other such experiences as needed. Gorman describes eleven such experiences.

### How Are Small Groups Organized?

The aim of small-group processes is to provide an appropriate environment for student reflection with members of the peer group. Just as a large group inhibits free expression of ideas so does a teacher-led discussion inhibit free interaction. Accordingly, the small class group is often organized with a student leader, recorder, and one or more process observers. Brown,[5] in treating the group as an independent study support activity, recommends the following task roles: questioner-leader, negative critic, positive critic, and the analyzer who sums up the discussions. Responsibilities of each are defined and described in Chapter 20. The instructor may or may not assume the role of participant and/or process observer. Generally, he will want to minimize his influence as much as possible.

Each student should probably have an opportunity to serve in all service capacities. Some training in these areas is usually needed. Leadership is an especially critical area. Role-playing has been found to be singularly effective for this purpose. Sometimes sociodrama is useful in helping students develop empathy for the responsibilities of the various roles. Sociodrama is treated in Chapter 13.

As in other discussion situations, reasonably balanced participation is preferred. Verbose individuals must learn to listen effectively. Sometimes they may be encouraged to write out their comments prior to making them. The quiet person must not be overly critical of his own ideas. It is not his prerogative to decide his ideas are not worthwhile. Such a decision is legitimately left to the group. Attention to a quiet person's nods, facial expressions and hand gestures can be useful in drawing such a person into the discussion.

### How Are Small-Group Processes Evaluated?

The major function of process observers is to evaluate and feed back their observations. They are primarily interested in group cohesion and its influence on group progress. A thorough treatment of this function is presented on pp. 324–25. Although individual contributions (as described on pp. 326–27) also may be evaluated, the process described in Chapter 20 is not usually recommended

---

[5] B. Frank Brown, *Education by Appointment: New Approaches to Independent Study* (West Nyack, N.Y.: Parker Publishing Co., 1968), p. 134.

in small groups. Such behavior tends to inhibit group interaction in face-to-face groups.

Conventional evaluation (emphasizing use of teacher-made tests) is possible. The nature of these experiences when used in connection with small groups, however, will be altered substantially. Teachers have been accustomed to testing for the acquisition of knowledge, along with some application of concepts. Since the basic function of small-group processes is to provide experiences in group reflection or problem solving, it follows that teacher-made tests must be constructed for this purpose. The major aspects of critical thinking which can be tested have been identified in the Thirty-fifth Yearbook of the National Council for the Social Studies. They include identification of critical issues, recognition of underlying assumptions, the evaluation of evidence, and the drawing of warranted conclusions. Chausow[6] provides a number of test item illustrations for measuring these important dimensions of problem solving. He develops multiple-choice items from selected case or anecdotal materials.

Small-group processes bridge the gap between teacher-led presentations and independent study activities. Much independent study features small groups of students working on a common problem. Thus it is imperative that small-group activities emphasize the essentials of group interaction. These include the communication of ideas, listening activities, group participation, and the process of facilitating participation of others.

The group evaluation sheet shown in Table 19–1 is an effective device for evaluating group interaction.[7]

**TABLE 19–1.** Instruction sheet

GROUP MEMBER RATINGS

STUDENT DIRECTIONS: Rate each group member, including yourself, on all four questions. Rate all members on one question before going on to the next question. To make your ratings: read the descriptions, A, B, and C for each question. Then choose and record the appropriate number from the following scale:

| A | B | C |
|---|---|---|
| IF THE PERSON IS MORE LIKE *A* THAN *B* RECORD: | IF THE PERSON IS MORE LIKE *B* THAN LIKE *A* OR *C* RECORD: | IF THE PERSON IS MORE LIKE *C* THAN *B* RECORD: |
| Much More / Somewhat More / Slightly More | Almost Like A / Between A and B / Almost Like B | Slightly More / Somewhat More / Much More |
| ⑨ ⑧ ⑦ | ⑥ ⑤ ④ | ③ ② ① |

[6] Hymen M. Chausow, "Evaluation of Critical Thinking in the Social Studies," from Harry D. Berg, editor, *Evaluation in Social Studies*, 35th Yearbook. (Washington, D.C.: The National Council for the Social Studies, 1965), pp. 86–89.
[7] The rating device was prepared by Dr. Gerald Moulton, Associate Professor of Education, Arizona State University. (Used by permission.)

**TABLE 19–1.** (Cont.)

1. *HOW CLEARLY DOES HE/SHE COMMUNICATE IDEAS, INFORMATION AND/OR SUGGESTIONS?*

*A.* This person is extremely easy to understand. He/she gets to the point and is neither too detailed nor too general. An outstanding communicator.

*B.* This person is, generally, an adequate and satisfactory communicator.

*C.* This person is often hard to understand. It is because he/she often speaks in generalities—or rambles—or assumes too much—or gives too many confusing details. A poor communicator.

2. *HOW ACTIVELY DOES HE/SHE TRY TO UNDERSTAND THE IDEAS AND SUGGESTIONS OF OTHERS?*

*A.* This person really tries to find out what others mean and how they see a situation whether he agrees or disagrees with them. An active and superior listener.

*B.* This person is, generally, an adequate and satisfactory listener.

*C.* This person makes little effort to understand what others mean. Seldom checks how well he understands what another has said. It may be because he is indifferent to others' ideas or because he assumes that he understands. He is often formulating own remarks rather than listening. A poor listener.

3. *HOW ACTIVELY AND EFFECTIVELY DOES HE/SHE PARTICIPATE IN THE GROUP'S WORK?*

*A.* This person actively and enthusiastically prepares for and participates in the work of the group. He often initiates, proposes, and analyzes group tasks and goals. An excellent group participant.

*B.* This person usually prepares for and participates in an adequate and satisfactory manner.

*C.* This person seldom offers his/her resources to the group. He often appears silent, listless, or bored. Seldom prepares, initiates, or helps group to define or solve problems. An ineffective and passive group participant.

4. *HOW EFFECTIVELY DOES HE/SHE ENCOURAGE AND SUPPORT THE PARTICIPATION OF OTHERS?*

*A.* This person makes it quite easy for others to actively participate by encouraging members to speak freely and by supplying warm and supporting comments. An excellent facilitator.

*B.* Usually, this person adequately facilitates and encourages the participation of other group members.

*C.* This person makes it difficult for others to feel free to share; seldom supports others; seldom yields; doesn't seem to value others' contributions. A poor facilitator.

Name _____

Group member names

| | | | | | | | | | | | | | | | Average |
|---|---|---|---|---|---|---|---|---|---|---|---|---|---|---|---|---|
| 1. Communicates his ideas | | | | | | | | | | | | | | | | |
| 2. Listens to ideas of others | | | | | | | | | | | | | | | | |
| 3. Participates in group work | | | | | | | | | | | | | | | | |
| 4. Facilitates participation of others | | | | | | | | | | | | | | | | |

*Student Directions*
1. Using the foregoing instruction sheet as a guide, rate each member of your group, including yourself.
2. Enter your name on a second Summary Rating Form. Permit each group member to record his ratings of your performance.
3. Enter your average rating for each of the four criteria.

**FIGURE 19–1.** Group member rating summary

## How Are Small Groups Used as an Independent Study Support Activity?

Emphasis is placed upon the small group as a transition between large group instruction and independent study. Preparatory activities for independent study are discussed fully.

The small group, however, serves still another role in such a program. *After* students have become involved in independent and semi-independent study activities, they frequently need to meet in small groups for the purpose of sharing ideas and problems with others. Such groups (sometimes referred to as seminar groups) are necessary to the orderly functioning of independent study programs. Brown, in discussing the functions of study seminars *before and after* independent study, lists the following:

1. Seminars for discussing the possibilities of independent study in a particular discipline.
2. Seminars to discuss the objectives and techniques for tackling independent study in a particular discipline.
3. Seminars to discuss the implication of contemporary issues for independent study in a particular discipline.

4. The all-important seminars where students report their findings in independent study and submit to questioning from other students and faculty members.[8]

He points out that while such a use of the small group does not employ the classic rules of small-group discussion, it is a form of group activity that is extremely valuable.

## VALUES

The small group provides each member with an opportunity to participate and thereby influences decision making.

Such face-to-face learning situations promote an atmosphere of cooperation and empathy seldom achieved in other learning situations.

Empathy does not mean uncritical acceptance of ideas, but rather the ability to "feel" why people believe as they do.

A basic strength of small-group techniques is its contribution to open-mindedness. Many secondary students especially are prone to extreme positions and to jump to conclusions. Some experience difficulty in listening to other points of view. Small groups thus contribute to patience, tolerance, and eventually to modification of one's stand if it cannot withstand the test of scrutiny.

Small-group techniques necessitate attention to skills in communication. Since advocacy is not a goal, ideas are not attacked. Opposing views are better expressed as questions, the right to full self-expression is assured, and differences are reconciled as nearly as possible. Consequently, clarity of expression is encouraged, as well as the art of listening—actually hearing what the other fellow has to say.

## LIMITATIONS AND PROBLEMS

Small-group techniques relegate the instructor's role to one of a recorder-observer. When used as a vehicle for problem solving, it forces the teacher to accept problem solutions which may be different from his own. Some teachers experience difficulty in withholding judgment pertaining to matters of extreme controversy.

There is the danger of overcooperation. Thus each member may become so solicitous of the feelings of others that direct action is avoided for fear of offending someone.

Sometimes there is a tendency for individual members to play destructive group roles. Such roles have been identified as blocker, special interest peddler, aggressor. Such roles may originate from one's failure to maintain an open mind.

[8] Brown, *Education by Appointment*, p. 136.

Small-group techniques assume adequate time and resources for extensive investigation of issues. They presuppose adequate preparation and background. Too little or too much structuring may be destructive to this instructional approach.

Appropriate evaluation of small-group processes is extremely difficult. This especially applies to buzz-group procedures. The intrusion of any sort of individual evaluation while students are interacting in a buzz-group situation is likely to have undesirable effects on the outcome.

Teachers must avoid group therapy since this is the task of a specialist. Small-class group procedures emphasize task goals (i.e., problem-solving), whereas the therapy group directs attention to individual feelings and attitudes as they relate to self-concepts.

## ILLUSTRATED SMALL-GROUP EXPERIENCES

I. Useful in business classes[9]

*Business Letter Writing*

Group students into five-member committees. Each committee selects a chairman and a recorder.

A. Assignment: Invite a panel of speakers to present a topic to the class or to a school business club.
B. Committee decides upon its approach, the details of the investigation, development of the message, and the final composition.
C. Recorder types the letter.
D. Letters are exchanged and each committee assumes a role of the invited panel of speakers. A reply must be prepared.
E. Acceptance depends upon the committee's reaction to the unit. Was the invitation courteous? Was it concretely and definitely extended? Were details clearly defined?
F. In addition, a short critique of letter invitations and replies is prepared by each committee.
G. Class discussion, using overhead projections of committee letters, follows.

Since the project was recommended as a learning experience, no letter grades were given. As a follow-up activity individual letters of invitation and reply were prepared and marked.

II. Useful in English classes[10]

*Novel Study (The Scarlet Letter)*

Objective was to have students grapple with the book themselves in order to acquire meaning of significance in their own lives.

[9] Based upon Gayle Sobolik, "Let's Move . . . to Appoint Committees," *Business Education Forum* 23 (November 1968): 20. Used by permission of the National Business Education Association.

[10] David M. Litsey, "Small-Group Training and the English Classroom," *English Journal* 58 (September 1969): 920–27. Used by permission of the author and the publisher.

    A.  Teacher prepares three penetrating questions for each group (of four or five each) to discuss for one or two class periods.

    B.  Questions:

       1.  Why, after the group has tried and condemned Hester Prynne, but at the same time left her free to come and go as she pleases, does Hester in fact decide to stay?

       2.  Why and under what altered circumstances does she at a later date settle on a plan of flight?

       3.  And finally, why does not the flight materialize, or rather to phrase the question more in keeping with the novel's suggestions at this point, why is the scheme foredoomed even before it is tried?

    C.  Teacher acts as a resource person.

    D.  Use of student observers or video tape is employed.

Although the writer did not so indicate, a general class discussion, emphasizing different group responses, may provide a fruitful follow-up experience.

III.  Useful in science classes[11]

    A.  Since the results of research often require years of study, high students may be grouped in pairs for the purpose of science research.

    B.  Each pair of students consists of the researcher and his understudy.

    C.  The researcher is responsible for the project and the understudy will move into the researcher's role when he graduates.

    D.  The understudy, therefore, should be a year or two younger than the researcher in order that he can move into the position of researcher when the researcher graduates.

This gives a continuity to research. When students pursue long-range problems, they will be working with the same kind of advance research as that of scientists.

IV.  Useful in any class[12]

An autolecture is essentially a synchronized coupling of a cassette tape recorder, a wide-range amplifier, a high-fidelity loudspeaker, and an overhead projector, all capable of filling a room with a clear sound and a wall with a brilliant image, even with room lights on.

    A.  Makes use of programmed materials.

    B.  Follow with a seminar group discussion, based upon questions raised by the autolecture.

The technique has the advantage of combining many facets of instruction and all the senses in learning. The teacher need not be present during the autolecture. It is normally run by a teacher aide. He may or may not be present during the seminar experience.

[11] Brown, *Education by Appointment*, p. 142.

[12] Arthur J. Bergman, "Seminar/Autolecture," *Today's Education* 57 (December 1968): 33–36. Used by permission of the author and the publisher.

# CHAPTER 20

# Group Processes

## OVERVIEW

### Key Concepts

1. A functional group posesses a "personality dimension" which differs from the individual members.
2. Group interaction develops slowly as members develop independence from teacher domination.
3. A fully functioning group defines its own problems, directs its own activities, and develops its own evaluational experiences.
4. Group processes are based upon the assumption that individual input is essential to effective group output.
5. The basic operational pattern of group processes is the "round table" discussion.
6. The teacher's role in group processes is relegated to that of a resourceful guide.

### New Terms

1. **Group Dynamics**—Those forces which influence the behavior of a group.
2. **Group Processes**—The steps followed by a group engaged in its own problem-solving processes.
3. **Social Access**—"Nearness" of one member of the group to another. Includes both physical and psychological factors, such as seating arrangements and the presence or absence of restraints.
4. **Group Leader**—The individual to which the group turns for guidance. This may or may not be an appointed or elected leader.

5. **Process Observers**—Individuals who observe, record, and report both individual and group behavior.
6. **Recorder**—An individual designated to record major ideas (concepts) and problems faced by the group.
7. **Steering Committee**—Designated individuals who offer suggestions for solving ongoing problems faced by the group.
8. **Group Roles**—Various roles played by individuals in the group. These range from task to group maintenance and destructive roles.

### Questions to Guide Your Study

1. Compare the three basic social components of authority, goal orientation, and social access.
2. Educational critics sometimes have linked "group-centered" instructional practices with "poor," "inefficient," or "lazy" teachers. Yet, teachers who have applied such procedures appropriately consider them the most difficult of all. What seems to account for these opposing views?
3. Perhaps the most difficult problem associated with the creation of functional group processes is insecurity. Both teacher and students find themselves in unfamiliar roles. What specific action might rebuild needed security as quickly and efficiently as possible?
4. "Students should practice playing different roles, as a means of increasing group sensitivity." Defend or refute.

When individuals work together to satisfy common goals, a state of "groupness" may be identified. Individual needs and wants become *subordinate* to general group functions. As the group begins to "move" (called dynamics), it takes on all the properties of a *superstructure* which is greater than its component parts. It becomes a vehicle through which individual goals are met, through which individual problems are resolved.

The term *group processes* refers to the steps or methods employed by a group in exploring, investigating, and planning in problem-solving situations. The definition embodies procedural devices used, discussion techniques employed, and consideration of the roles played by the members. The term is frequently used interchangeably with *group dynamics*. In this chapter, however, *group dynamics* will be conceived as those forces which influence the behavior of a group. As such, then, group dynamics is not a method, i.e., something that is done to groups. Every group *has* its own dynamics, just as every person has his own dynamic personality. Group processes as an instructional approach is dependent on appropriate analysis and control of the dynamics of the group.

Group process, as an instructional approach, differs from teacher-pupil planning processes in at least two respects: (1) Essentially, it relegates the role of the teacher to that of an equal group participant. In essence, the approach is teacher-pupil planning with a capital "P" for the pupil. (2) Replacing the traditional role of the teacher is a *group structure* which, in essence, controls the various behaviors of individual members.

# FUNDAMENTAL PROPERTIES

Effective group processes are dependent upon a cooperative group atmosphere in which each member feels responsible to the group. Each individual must, to some degree, subordinate his needs to that of the total group. Individual contributions (input) are the essential ingredients for the realization of worthwhile goals (output). A dynamic group possesses a number of identifiable properties.

## What Constitutes a Democratic Framework?

The group-centered approach represents democracy par excellence. It features a permissive atmosphere in which students make their own assignments, develop their own methods of grappling with problems, and finally evaluate progress toward goals. The instructor, after identifying the major objectives, broad content areas, and general class and school policies, accepts his role as another member of an organized team of coworkers. Basic democratic principles are generally applied. All problems relative to both content and procedure are resolved by the group through appropriate committees. Final decisions rest with the total group.

## What Group Forces Are Important?

Once a class begins to function effectively as a group, a recognizable cohesive force becomes apparent. This force is evident when teachers wonder why one class seems to exhibit a better atmosphere than another. The group-process approach relies heavily upon a high degree of cohesiveness.

A favorable group atmosphere is a product of a variety of forces and conditions, some of which are reflected through various behavior patterns. By promoting a more flexible pattern of responses, a teacher may substantially enhance the dynamics of a group.

*Communication Structure.* The question of who talks to whom and under what conditions is known as communication structure. It contains a number of properties, some of which are listed below.

1. *Highs* tend to initiate more communications than do *lows*.[1]
2. *Highs* tend to address their comments to the group as a whole, whereas *lows* are prone to address their comments to specific individuals.
3. Communication tends to be directed to one who disagrees with the group view until the group decides that his views cannot be reconciled with the group view. As the deviate's view is rejected or as it moves toward the majority position, communication addressed to him tends to decrease rapidly.

[1] For an excellent treatment of group interaction the reader is referred to Halbert E. Gulley, *Discussion, Conference and Group Process* (New York: Holt, Rinehart and Winston, Inc., 1960), ch. 5.

4. *Highs* are more likely to make direct influence efforts, whereas *averages* and *lows* tend to make nondirective influence efforts. For example, *highs* tend to say, "Let's do this." *Averages* and *lows*, on the other hand, tend to say, "Do you think we might consider this possibility? Some people have used this approach."
5. Both *highs* and *lows* tend to prefer high-status over low-status members.
6. *Lows* are more likely than *highs* to contribute task-irrelevant remarks.
7. Minority views are more likely to be expressed if the leader encourages (reinforces) those expressing them.
8. As group size increases, restraints against communication seem to develop. Furthermore, there is some evidence that, as groups become excessively large, the emergence of "discussion cliques" tends to become evident. The optimum size for maximum group interaction is dependent on many variables. Groups of more than five and less than twenty are most often suggested, however. It is possible, nevertheless, that as average size of classes increases, techniques which are effective for larger groups will receive increased attention. Therefore the suggested model offered in the second part of this chapter emphasizes such arrangements.

*Authority Structure.* The authority or leadership of a teacher constitutes a major source of social pressure experienced by the members. The teacher as an authority symbol determines the behaviors of all other members of the group. If he exerts too much authority, he forces all members into low-status positions in the authority (leadership) structure. Students will tend to remain passive. On the other hand, activities which distribute responsibilities facilitate differentiation within the authority or leadership structure. In establishing a dynamic group, students must assist in establishing goals and techniques for the coordination of the processes of inquiry. The changed pattern of authority requires time and patience.

*Goal Orientation.* Every cohesive group must have a clearly defined purpose. The most critical stage in the development of such a group is when the goal is first introduced and clarified. As with the structure of authority, there will be individual differences at any given moment with respect to goal orientation. Accordingly, continuous goal clarification is desirable for maximum group cohesiveness.

*Social Access.* Both physical and psychological factors are important determiners of social access. Physical factors include seating arrangements, group size, and freedom of movement. Psychological factors involve the presence or absence of restraints affecting communication.

A circular seating arrangement can do much to increase total social access. Groups in excess of twenty severely limit the influence of any individual member. A few stronger personalities will tend to pick up followers, resulting in two or more cliques. So long as individual members can be heard and so long as they can communicate face to face, democratic leadership can be maintained in long-lived groups. It may be desirable to encourage students to shift their seats each day after they have become fully acquainted. In this manner, power cliques are discouraged.

Social access is increased in small, "buzz" group activities. Subgroups of five each tend to be especially effective during the early stages of development.

This tends to break down individual inhibitions and anxieties and to create a feeling of responsibility to the total group.

## Interaction Patterns

As group members interact with each other, they tend to develop recognizable communication patterns. Each individual pattern tends to elicit certain responses from others. In fact, communication patterns and their concomitant responses lead to certain expectancies (predictable behaviors) in communication. Berne refers to such behaviors as games. A game, according to Berne, is a "series of moves with a snare, or 'gimmick'."[2] Each game has an ulterior motive and has a dramatic "payoff." He contends that every game is basically dishonest. The word *game* should not be misleading. It does not necessarily imply fun. Indeed the most serious behaviors in life are here classified as games. War and suicide are grim game payoffs.

Group communication can be interpreted as a complex of games, some of which may be constructive, others destructive. A game begins with a standard statement (move) by some member of the group. If another member responds as expected, the game is usually played to its conclusion. Constructive games result in progress; destructive games will cause a group to bog down.

Although an infinite number of games or roles are possible, some are used more frequently than others. An understanding of these may facilitate the processes of interaction. Typical constructive games or roles, as described by Benne and Sheets,[3] are:

*The Encourager.* He agrees with and accepts contributions of others. He indicates a warmth and solidarity toward others. In various ways he indicates understanding and acceptance of other points of view, ideas, and suggestions.

*The Harmonizer.* This individual mediates differences, attempts to reconcile disagreements, relieves tension in conflict situations through jesting or pouring oil on troubled waters, etc.

*The Gate-Keeper or Expediter.* Such an individual attempts to keep communication channels open by encouraging or facilitating participation of others ("We haven't got the ideas of Mr. X yet."), or by proposing regulation of the flow of communication ("Why don't we limit the length of our contributions so that everyone will have a chance to contribute?").

*The Standard Setter or Ego Ideal.* This person expresses standards for the group or applies standards in evaluating the quality of group processes.

*The Follower.* He goes along with the group, more or less passively accepting ideas, serving as an audience in group discussion and decision.

Other games or roles can deter a group from its purpose. A functional group disciplines its members. It is essential to know what is happening, however, before effective remedial action can be taken. Generally, the person who remains

---

[2] Eric Berne, *Games People Play* (New York: Grove Press, Inc., 1964), p. 48.
[3] Kenneth D. Benne and Paul Sheets, "Functional Roles of Group Members," *Journal of Social Issues* 4 (Spring 1948): 41–49.

*individually oriented* tends to impede group progress. He may be vaguely aware of his role or he can be using it deliberately. Many of these roles are readily apparent before interaction is evident.[4]

*The Aggressor.* This person works in many ways—deflating the status of others, expressing disapproval of the values, acts, or feelings of others, attacking the group or the problem it is working on, joking aggressively, showing envy toward another's contribution by trying to take credit for it, etc.

*The Blocker.* He tends to be negativistic and stubbornly resistant, disagreeing and opposing without or "beyond reason" and attempting to maintain or bring back an issue after the group has rejected or bypassed it.

*The Recognition-Seeker.* This individual calls attention to himself, whether through boasting, reporting on personal achievements, acting in unusual ways, struggling to prevent his being placed in an "inferior" position, etc.

*The Self-Confessor.* This person uses the audience to express personal, nongroup-oriented "feeling," "insight," "ideology," etc.

*The Playboy.* Making a display of his lack of involvement in the group's processes, this individual may utilize cynicism, horseplay, and other more or less studied forms of "out of field" behavior.

*The Dominator.* This individual tries to assert authority or superiority in manipulating the group or certain members of the group. This domination may take the form of flattery, of asserting a superior status or right to attention, giving directions authoritatively, interrupting the contributions of others, etc.

*The Help-Seeker.* This person attempts to call forth "sympathy" response from others or from the whole group, whether through expressions of insecurity, personal confusion, or depreciation of himself beyond "reason."

*The Special-Interest Peddler.* Such an individual speaks for the "small businessman," the "grass roots" community, the "housewife," "labor," etc., usually cloaking his prejudices or biases in the stereotype which best fits his individual needs.

## What Time Factors Must Be Considered?

Development of a dynamic group takes considerable time. Not only must those involved understand group processes generally, but they must also become fully aware of the new relationships essential to the procedure. Progress will at first seem slow indeed. After a period of a week or ten days, however, dynamic group forces should begin to emerge. When full momentum is reached (usually after some two or three weeks), progress often exceeds that of conventional class groups.

Although the method may be employed for one unit of work only, it tends to be most effective over an extended period of time. Some teachers have utilized the approach as a basic methods framework for an entire semester. It is sometimes difficult to revert to highly teacher-centered methods after group processes have become fully operative.

[4] Benne and Sheets, "Functional Roles of Group Members," pp. 44–45.

# GROUP PROCEDURES

Effective group interaction is more than mere happenstance. One class, for example, may be "alive" or respond well to group methods while another may be lethargic or hard to manage. Such conditions reflect the numerous forces of interaction present in all class groups. These forces can be controlled for the benefit of those involved. The procedures outlined in this section serve such a purpose. Other approaches may serve equally well.

### How Is Student Readiness Established?

Let us suppose that a teacher desires to initiate a group approach in world history. The unit involves history at the time of the French Revolution and the Napoleonic era. Some of the unit goals which relate directly to this era of history may be as follows:

After this unit the student should:

1. Further appreciate the impact of the French Revolution on the westward expansion and economic development of the United States.
2. Further understand the consequences of too much reform at one time.
3. Further appreciate those forces which tend to undermine civil liberties.
4. Understand the historical implications of France's current foreign policies.

How can a class of about thirty-five to forty students be guided into assuming full responsibility for directing their own learnings in this area of investigation? In the first place, the general goals (illustrated above) are in some manner brought to the attention of the group. The instructor then can approach the problem somewhat as follows:

For several years now, much of your formal education has been controlled and directed by your teachers. In general, you have read the materials, followed methods and techniques, reported, and taken tests which have all been made by your teachers. In short, you have followed teacher-assigned tasks or been "told what to do."
Such a practice has tended to emphasize competition. You have competed with each other in many ways—often for grades. In our democracy we do believe in the spirit of competition, but, more important, we believe in cooperation. Let us take our basketball team as an example. There may be a great deal of competition for a place on the team, but after one has made the team he is expected to cooperate. What happens to the individual who thinks only of himself and how many points he can score? He becomes a liability to the team, of course! The most valuable player places the good of his team above his own wants and desires. Each member *cooperates* as a team to *compete* successfully with other teams. Some teachers have wondered if students are not capable of directing their own learning. Is it not possible that we—this class—could work together as a team and accomplish far more than is possible through individual competition? Dick, let us suppose you

could complete eight different references on this era of history. If we could all do as much, through cooperation we might receive the advantage of 38 x 8, or 304 sources. This is far more than any one person could accomplish! The only requirement of the school is that the unit goals or purposes be realized within the next four to five weeks. Your instructor generally will play a role of consultant and participating guide. To facilitate the team or group approach we will need to organize our group with a leader, recorder, and four observers. We will arrange our chairs in a big circle so that we can work better as a team.

When the organization is completed and duties explained, the group usually wants to know "how to start," but the instructor reflects such questions back to the group. Some members of the group usually suggest preliminary reading so that the nature of the unit may be better understood. Such a practice tends to give members an overview of the subject. Someone may want the group to think of sources and methods of finding information. Directing the group is a student; the instructor assumes the role of a participating member. A teacher must be extremely careful not to dominate the group. In the early sessions he will offer few suggestions, educating the group to develop reliance on its own resources.

When the group is first formed, difficulties inevitably will become apparent. In all probability group discussion will be unnecessarily vague and disorganized. Students experiencing extreme anxiety at this point usually welcome subtle suggestions for systematic organization of content and activities. The process of directing and redirecting learning behaviors is continuous. As problems of group process are encountered, they are resolved by the group. The problem of evaluation arises early. By assisting in both group and individual evaluation (to be described later) the usual anxiety associated with "threat of grades" can be reduced substantially.

### How Are Problems Identified?

In a group-oriented situation especially, students are encouraged to use factual materials as a basis for solving problems. The problems of a dynamic class group, however, are not always defined in specific terms. Using the foregoing illustrations from world history as an example, the group might first decide to explore those events in the United States that were influenced by the Napoleonic era. Thus, along with a study of Napoleon's policies as Emperor of France, a discussion of the circumstances associated with the Louisiana Purchase and the Embargo Act under Jefferson's administration would be in order.

Other problems are identified by the group as it moves along. Perhaps the adoption of the Bill of Rights under the Madison administration could be discussed in relation to the reform movement in France at the same time. This would logically lead to a discussion of civil liberties as interpreted in the United States today. Thus the group evolves its own problems through the discussive process. Problems may or may not be stated in explicit terms that characterize other instructional approaches.

## How Is the Group Organized?

In a class of twenty-five to thirty-five students, five members are selected to accept clearly defined service roles: leader, recorder, three observers. (The instructor may serve as a fourth observer.) The instructor may appoint the first group of service personnel; subsequent groups are usually selected by the group. As a means of insuring group stability, each group of service personnel usually serves for a period of four or five class periods.

## What Are the Responsibilities of the Group Leader?

The leader is responsible for getting the discussion started. He sets the stage for a meeting of minds by encouraging full participation. There may be times when the verbose individual must be ignored, to allow a shy individual to make a contribution. Occasionally a quiet individual can be encouraged by asking, "Johnny, do you have something to add to Paul's remarks?" His is the task of keeping the group on the topic and reducing needless repetition. Occasional summaries may be of assistance here. The discussion leader, above all, plays the role of a harmonizer-compromiser. A discussable topic, of necessity involves differences of opinion. There is a point, however, when discussion becomes purely argumentative. Emotionally held ideas usually are difficult to support merely on the basis of experimental research. Sometimes a quiet "John, what research do you have which would tend to support your statement?" may accomplish a great deal. As members become accustomed to group processes, others tend to share more and more of the harmonizer-compromiser role.

To facilitate group progress the leader needs to be the best-informed member of the group. Usually he develops a broad outline of the problem under discussion. The outline may serve more for his own clarification of the issues, however, than as a goal to be accomplished. The group may choose to follow its own outline. Any outline, however, should be consistent with the steps of problem solving which are pertinent to discussion. (See Chapter 16, "Discussion Methods.") Group deliberation is slow and sometimes painful to the bright student, but it is indicative of a basic premise of democratic process. The leader will ask questions, but they more often will be asked *for the purpose of* clarification or for the introduction of· new ideas. In an efficiently functional group the leader tends to become the quietest of the participating members.

Major responsibilities of the leader are as follows:

1. Getting the discussion going.
2. Mediating arguments.
3. Keeping the discussion on the topic. Sometimes he may ask the recorder to summarize for the group.
4. Keeping the group from bogging down. An observer might be requested to give reasons.
5. Recognizing and utilizing all individuals within the group.
6. Making certain that a permissive atmosphere is maintained.

7. Devoting time to periodic summaries. He should take time to ask, "Where are we? What have we been doing? Do we have an answer?"

## What Are the Responsibilities of the Recorder?

The recorder keeps a record of discussion content. He, in effect, records the points just as a person might record in a more traditional setting. His function is not to act merely as a stenographer or secretary but also to make a record of the important aspects of the discussion—the major concepts reviewed or developed. One of his major responsibilities is to report to the group when requested. Many groups have found that a five-minute summary of the last discussion, given at the beginning of the period, offers an excellent basis for beginning the current discussion.

The usefulness of a recorder sometimes is not fully realized if efforts have not been made to organize major points. In some instances a well-organized report is of little value when given orally. Sometimes the recorder can elect to have notes reproduced for class use. This, if done consistently throughout the experience, provides each member with a valuable record of group accomplishments.

Benne and Muntyan offer a guide for the group recorder:

1. Keep track of major contributions to the discussion:
   a. Points on which group agreed or on which formal action was taken;
   b. Points on which there was cleavage of opinion in the group;
   c. Points where the recorder is not sure of the group opinions;
   d. Points mentioned but not discussed, which the group may wish to consider later.
2. Report to the group—what was discussed and concluded rather than merely what the discussion was *about.*
3. Be ready to report at any time and to make an inclusive report at the end of the session.
4. Ask for suggestions from the group as to how the recorder's work may be made more helpful.[5]

## What Are the Functions of Observers?

The observers have a dual responsibility. First, they are interested in group progress. How well are the participants contributing to progress? What effect does the leader have on the group? Was discussion lopsided? Why or why not? Did the group stick to the point and actually analyze situations? Or was it satisfied with superficial analysis? Was there evidence that participants were listening to each other?

Very closely allied to interest in group process is observers' concern with *quality* of *individual* contributions. Unless an individual's contributions are con-

[5] Kenneth D. Benne and Bozidar Muntyan, eds., *Human Relations in Curriculum Change* (New York: Holt, Rinehart and Winston, Inc., 1951), p. 158.

sidered, there is real danger that he will become submerged within the group. Consequently, some scheme is needed which may be applied to each individual. The observers are given time at the end of each session to offer evaluations of group progress. Continued usefulness of observers depends on the tactfulness displayed in summary statements of evaluation. An observer may have noticed some personality clashes, but it is usually best to keep such knowledge to oneself for a while. Observers frequently introduce their evaluative comments with something like "I wondered about . . ." or "Could it have been done . . . ?" In short, *do not judge; be supportive!* Start with an area of observation that is least personal, such as participation.

A helpful checklist for observers is suggested.

1. He tries to observe what goes on in an objective manner.
2. He makes notes as he goes along for his summary statement.
3. He checks to see that the leader does what he is supposed to do.
4. He identifies the role(s) which each member of the group is playing.
5. He does not talk down to the group when he makes his report.
6. He is ready to report to the group at any time.
7. He remembers he is part of the leadership team—consisting of the group leader, recorder, consultant, and himself—which is dedicated to improving the group.

## What Role Does the Teacher Play?

In the final analysis the instructor can make or break the group situation. In actual practice he cannot create a desirable group operation; he can merely provide a setting and atmosphere in which such attitudes and behaviors may develop. Careful encouragement and direction is needed constantly. If he is to dominate, the whole business can become a farce—another authoritarian class operation. Students are quick to detect symptoms of domination. Conversely, the instructor must avoid a laissez faire attitude. His role is *not* merely that of letting the learners do what they please. The instructor's energies are used for creating and maintaining a mutual feeling of responsibility to achieve group goals. These goals, of course, must be within the framework of the general course goals. Indeed, the general goals must always be determined by the teacher, and group goals must fall within this framework.

The instructor himself may experience many anxieties and insecurities. He realizes his responsibility for learning. Since he already "knows" most of the answers, he may lack patience in the deliberations of the group. He is responsible for contributing specific information when needed or for prodding the group to a deeper analysis. This often "opens the door" to excessive contributions, which can be recognized by the "silent periods" which follow. There are times when neither the leader nor any group member seems capable of analyzing a point under consideration; these are times when groups get bogged down. Sometimes some member of the group may request help from the instructor. At other times a timely question or contribution may be in order without such a request. The teacher must bear in mind that he is a participating member of the group and, as such, has definite obligations and responsibilities to the group. A few guidelines may assist the instructor in assuming his proper role:

1. *Speaks only after being recognized by the leader.* It is the leader's responsibility to call upon any person who evidences a sudden insight or desire to speak.
2. *Reserves five to ten minutes at the end of the day for his "two-cents worth."* Because of his greater understanding of the issues and greater experiential background, the teacher is in an ideal position to clarify and expand difficult points. Many teachers have found it preferable to withhold comments until the end of the period.
3. *Encourages observers to evaluate the impact of the teacher on the discussion.* In a permissive atmosphere observers will do this!
4. *In case of doubt, he does not talk.* This encourages groups to solve their own problems.
5. *Is an observer at all times.* This not only gives the instructor an added responsibility in observing group processes at work, but it also preoccupies him so that he cannot become overly dominant.
6. *Observes the frequency with which members (subconsciously or otherwise) direct questions to the instructor.* If the teacher finds he is assuming a leadership role, chances are he should "bite his tongue a bit harder."
7. *In a final written group evaluation, he has students express opinions as to whether the teacher's role was too central or too permissive.* This may serve as a guideline for the next class.

## What Are the Responsibilities of Participating Members?

The backbone of group process rests with all the participating members—both instructor and students. Service roles, including that of the instructor, are created to help the participating members do their job. What do they do? How can they best contribute to group progress?

The participant, above all, should contribute. Regardless of how much he may be gaining from the group, he is not fulfilling his full measure of responsibility unless he "gives a little" too. On the other hand, he is duty-bound not to dominate or monopolize discussion. Effective group work presupposes adequate preparation and the formulation of questions which might be raised at the next discussion. In this manner one may experience individual growth through group work.

A participating member who tends to talk more than others can train himself to pass over minor points—emphasizing a few selected issues. Perhaps the most useful member is the individual who is fair to other points of view. At times he acts as a spokesman for minority views. The sincere individual readily challenges views which he cannot accept. He does not let the group pass over important points before they are clarified. Unfamiliar terms must be understood. Others can profit from and appreciate the individual who tries to keep the discussion meaningful to all. As a round-table discussion of this sort emphasizes reflective, logical thinking, hidden assumptions frequently need reviewing. One who is able to help the group see the middle ground tends to gain respect from his peers. The basic purpose of any discussion is to utilize a variety of views to create an improved solution. Hence, basic differences should not be superficially treated; they need clarification if basic issues are to be resolved. It takes time to think. Sometimes a silent period is needed.

If the group seems to be too agreeable when discussing a controversial issue, a more penetrating analysis probably is in order. Sometimes the discussion may be too generalized. The astute observer may improve the situation by calling for, or presenting, a specific example. This tends to bring the discussion back to basic reality. Occasionally apparent agreement or disagreement may be attributed to semantic difficulties. Specific illustrations again may be helpful. Each individual is superior to other individuals in at least one respect, while the experience of all is superior to the experience of any single person.

## How Are Procedural Problems Solved?

One essential of the group-centered approach is group planning. The group must continually direct and redirect its efforts toward major course goals. There are problems of method, problems of evaluation, and problems of discipline with which the group must continually grapple. Procedural problems often impede group progress; yet they must be resolved if the group is to continue to function effectively.

The use of a *steering committee* can greatly expedite group planning. The teacher can select, or the group can elect, three to five members to serve in this capacity. The committee should meet periodically to cope with anticipated and actual difficulties. Each class member should bring his grievances or suggestions to a member of the committee who, in turn, would place it on the committee agenda. The function of a steering committee is to meet and solve problems for the group. Members then share the results of their efforts with the entire group when a business meeting is called. The group may accept, modify, or reject the steering committee's recommendations. If the problems have been given due consideration, a group is likely to accept many of its proposals. Such a procedure can add immeasurably to the workings of the group. If the instructor is to serve on this committee, however, he must not use it as a "smoke screen" for furthering his own purposes.

## How Are Group Processes Evaluated?

In a dynamic group both group and individual evaluation are the direct responsibility of observers. One basic principle of good teaching is that of continuous evaluation. The nature of *group* evaluation was discussed under the duties of the process observers. With the present emphasis on *individual* evaluation in the schools, it seems appropriate also to introduce *continuous individual evaluation.* Although each group will develop its own evaluative criteria, the following may be useful in giving direction to those involved.

A seating chart, as appears in Figure 20–1 as the "Individual Evaluation

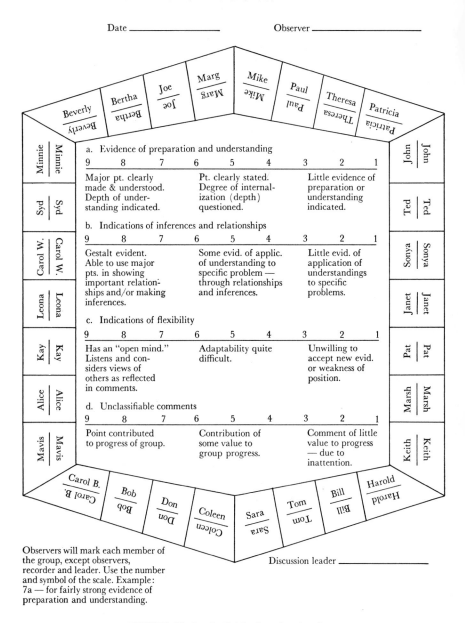

Date _____ Observer _____

a. Evidence of preparation and understanding

| 9 | 8 | 7 | 6 | 5 | 4 | 3 | 2 | 1 |
|---|---|---|---|---|---|---|---|---|

Major pt. clearly made & understood. Depth of understanding indicated.

Pt. clearly stated. Degree of internalization (depth) questioned.

Little evidence of preparation or understanding indicated.

b. Indications of inferences and relationships

| 9 | 8 | 7 | 6 | 5 | 4 | 3 | 2 | 1 |
|---|---|---|---|---|---|---|---|---|

Gestalt evident. Able to use major pts. in showing important relationships and/or making inferences.

Some evid. of applic. of understanding to specific problem — through relationships and inferences.

Little evid. of application of understandings to specific problems.

c. Indications of flexibility

| 9 | 8 | 7 | 6 | 5 | 4 | 3 | 2 | 1 |
|---|---|---|---|---|---|---|---|---|

Has an "open mind." Listens and considers views of others as reflected in comments.

Adaptability quite difficult.

Unwilling to accept new evid. or weakness of position.

d. Unclassifiable comments

| 9 | 8 | 7 | 6 | 5 | 4 | 3 | 2 | 1 |
|---|---|---|---|---|---|---|---|---|

Point contributed to progress of group.

Contribution of some value to group progress.

Comment of little value to progress — due to inattention.

Observers will mark each member of the group, except observers, recorder and leader. Use the number and symbol of the scale. Example: 7a — for fairly strong evidence of preparation and understanding.

Discussion leader _____

**FIGURE 20–1.** Individual evaluation form

Form," is prepared. The group establishes criteria for individual evaluation of each contribution. Although some modifications are to be expected, criteria that have been utilized effectively are the following:

1. Evidence of preparation and understanding
2. Indications of inferences and relationships

3. Indications of flexibility
4. Unclassifiable contributions

As indicated in the evaluation form, contributions are averaged by each of the four observers for administering daily marks. Service personnel usually are marked on a different basis.

As problems arise, various modifications will need to be introduced. Again, problems are resolved by the group itself. For example, one problem is the tendency of certain individuals to form "closed conversational patterns." To correct the difficulty one group introduced a flow chart, designed to reveal direction of conversational flow. Excessive attention to individuals as opposed to the group as a whole warranted a penalty. The problem was quickly resolved.

## VALUES

The group provides its own motivation and directs its own activities.
Full participation in round-table discussion is assured. Imbalanced participation or lack of it soon becomes a major concern of the group.
The role of the instructor as an equal participant tends to minimize restraint in group discussion.
Critical evaluation of data is featured. As the group progresses, members show increased ability to listen.

## LIMITATIONS AND PROBLEMS

Group processes proceed as fast as the slowest members of the group. Consequently, until individuals begin to feel responsible for others, group progress may appear to be painfully slow. After the group begins to move, however, accelerated progress is evident.
The method, initially, is highly frustrating to both instructor and students. Students must learn to rely upon their own resources.
Unless democratic processes are thoroughly understood by all parties concerned, the approach may hopelessly flounder.
Since group dynamics is most effective in areas where demonstrable answers are *not* available, it has broader application in some subject areas than in others.
The method can become unwieldy in large classes (over forty to fifty students). It is more efficient with groups of twenty-five or less.

## ILLUSTRATED PROBLEM AREAS

I.  Useful in history, government, social studies, and literature classes

   *Unit:* Roots of American Democracy

*Concepts:*
1. Our democratic system was based upon Greek foundations.
2. The desire for religious freedom provided a favorable environment for establishing democratic principles.
3. Basic freedoms were not available to all.
4. The Bill of Rights provides a basis for the basic freedoms.

II. Useful in home economics, group guidance, sociology, and psychology classes

*Unit:* Family: Basic Institution of Society

*Concepts:*
1. The family provides security to its members.
2. The family represents group living at its best.
3. Family living is dependent upon adequate communication.
4. Family roles are learned through the family organization.

III. Useful in biology, general science, health, and physical education classes

*Unit:* The Human Body

*Concepts:*
1. A healthy body provides its own defenses against disease.
2. Malfunctions of one organ tend to influence all body systems.
3. Body deficiencies are reflected in appearance and behavior.
4. Early diagnosis and treatment of disease are essential.

IV. Useful in speech and communications classes

*Unit:* Parliamentary Procedures

*Concepts:*
1. Rules of procedure are designed to expedite the democratic process of groups.
2. Democratic procedures may be thwarted unless each member understands the basic rules of procedure.
3. The freedom of dissent is essential to a functional democratic group.

The reader will note that the foregoing illustrations are the least structured of the illustrations provided in this book. Group processes, by their very nature, leave further analysis to the group itself.

# CHAPTER 21

# Lecture Method

## OVERVIEW

### Key Concepts

1. The lecture method for many years has been both overused and misused in the secondary school.
2. The informal lecture (lecturette) is basically a means of clarifying or expanding information; other supplementary methods must be employed to complete the reflective process.
3. The lecturette is short, usually extending for less than thirty minutes.
4. The lecture essentially involves "telling them what you are going to tell them," "telling them," and "telling them what you have told them," e.g., the initial summary, detailed information, and final summary.
5. The lecture is usually more effective when hearing is supplemented with visual experiences.

### New Terms

1. **Formal Lecture**—A presentation extending for a whole class period, designed to offer information and solve problems *for* the learner. (When used in flexible scheduling, it is designed to set the stage for small group activities and independent study.)
2. **Informal Lecture** (lecturette)—A short presentation designed to inform or clarify points which may be temporarily blocking the processes of reflective thinking.
3. **Initial Summary**—The technique of foreshadowing major points for the learner.

## Questions to Guide Your Study

1. Why is extensive use of the formal (college-type) lecture considered inappropriate for use in conventional secondary school classes?
2. "The lecture method is an easy method to employ." Defend or refute.
3. "Reflective thinking processes are at a minimum level during a lecture." Defend or refute.
4. What techniques for improving listening do you consider most practical?
5. What are the functions of questions and discussion following an informal lecture?

Strictly speaking, there is no single lecture method. Rather, the term encompasses several allied techniques. Those teacher-centered techniques which are designed to inform others by telling, explaining, or showing are classified as lecture procedures. The traditional (formal) lecture method, first popularized in the medieval university, was designed as the basic instructional approach for a school system which emphasized knowledge as an instructional end. As emphasis shifted from the acquisition of knowledge for its own sake to the *use* of knowledge to solve meaningful life problems, the formal lecture fell into disrepute.

The informal lecture (hereafter called the lecturette) basically is designed to expedite student problem-solving activities. It may be employed for varying lengths of time at any point in the learning process when it becomes obvious that students can profit from outside assistance. Lecturettes are frequently used to provide students with essential background information for subsequent learning experiences. The procedure frequently will involve use of certain films, demonstrations, or oral reports.

Large-group lectures (groups of three hundred or more have been utilized) are currently popular in those schools which have been adapted to flexible scheduling arrangements. Nevertheless, they serve the same basic function as the lecturette by providing basic background information or enrichment materials needed in subsequent small-group and independent study activities.

## FUNDAMENTAL PROPERTIES

There is nothing sacred per se about the size of a class group in which a student learns. Learning results in a combination of listening, viewing, reading, and talking activities. The size of a group is most appropriately determined by the purposes or objectives being sought. Likewise, choice of instructional method will depend upon what must be accomplished. It has been assumed throughout this book that the bulk of major learning activities should be so organized as to accommodate critical thinking. The fundamental properties of the lecture method are treated within this general framework.

## Why Is Objectivity Important?

In evaluating evidence the learner must have access to the pertinent facts. Since the lecturer may represent the major source of information, an objective, unbiased presentation is essential. The lecturer (demonstrator, or reporter) must clearly label private opinions if they must be stated. He will state his knowledge sources and indeed will encourage further investigation when controversy is evident. Whenever possible, the lecture is avoided in highly controversial areas.

## Why Are Visual Aids Desirable Along with a Lecture?

Oral presentations are difficult to understand and to remember unless supplemented liberally with visual aids. Use of the chalkboard, pictures, color transparencies, diagrams, and the like can greatly enhance effectiveness of oral presentations. An effective lecturer, for example, frequently outlines his major points on the chalkboard and then proceeds to develop each point by offering numerous illustrations and examples. By outlining the major points as the lecture develops, the student is provided adequate time for necessary note-taking activities.

## Why Is Repetition Deemed Essential?

Repetition provides another useful means of supplementing the spoken word. It is characterized by an initial summary, periodic summaries along the way (if the lecture is of considerable length), and a final summary. A speech teacher once expressed the idea in these words: "Tell your listeners what you plan to say, tell them, and then tell them what you have said." Such planned repetition seems more vivid, thereby providing a much needed structure for retention of major points.

## What Role Does Feedback Play?

Feedback is an essential aspect of the instructional process. Teachers quite naturally accept and sometimes elicit questions during difficult explanations. Lecturettes, student oral reports, and demonstrations are usually short, providing opportunities for clarifications immediately after the experiences. Sometimes the question period may even exceed the length of the original presentation. Large-group lectures wisely provide for student questions immediately following each presentation. It is only through such feedback that the lecturer is able to discover blocks to communication and learning.

## Why Are Supplementary Instructional Techniques Needed?

When learning is conceived as a process of critical thinking, it is obvious that the lecture cannot stand alone. While some college lectures are defended on the grounds that the learner may solve problems vicariously through the lecturer, there is ample evidence to the contrary. Psychologists have emphasized repeatedly the importance of an overtly active learner. Whenever the lecture is employed, it merely serves the function of providing data and background information needed for resolution of an important problem. Thus the lecture must be supplemented with additional learning activities germane to a given problem.

### What Time Limitations Are Imposed?

The secondary school age is an active one. The adolescent usually experiences difficulty in concentrating on a problem for long. He needs to move about, to ask questions, to express himself frequently. Thus oral presentations are usually limited to a period of not more than twenty minutes. Large-group lectures may consist of two modules of twenty minutes each. Even so, they must be interspersed with extended periods of activity. In conventional class settings an extended lecture should be broken into two time periods, separated with a lively question-and-answer session.

## LECTURE PROCEDURE

As has been indicated, lecture procedures vary somewhat from one situation to another. A lecture, for example, may vary from one or two minutes of spontaneous explanation to an entire class period. The frame of reference utilized in this section is the preplanned presentation (by the teacher or by the student) which usually ranges from ten to thirty minutes. Generally the procedure will incorporate the essentials of large-group lecture, the lecturette, demonstration, and reporting procedures. Important differences in these techniques are noted.

### How Is the Problem Identified?

The lecture problem is usually formulated as a question of fact. Such problems are characterized as *is* or *are* questions. A biology student, for example, might be asked to prepare an oral report on the American buffalo. When formulated as a question of fact, the problem might be: "What factors contributed to the virtual extinction of the American buffalo (bison)?" Although oral reports are often assigned as topics, students limit and clarify problems by formulating specific factual-type questions.

Problems of a highly controversial nature are usually not handled as oral reports. Sometimes a teacher will find it necessary to lecture on such a problem, but he must present different points of view as objectively as possible. In pointing out the weaknesses of the United Nations, for example, the history teacher must show how such weaknesses may be considered strengths in the eyes of those who live in small, underdeveloped nations. He might also point out the "facts" as might be viewed by members of the Communist states.

## How Is the Lecture Organized?

Oral techniques are usually ineffective unless the speaker captures the imagination of the listeners. He can do this by beginning his presentation with an unusual or startling statement. One student, for example, who was reporting the effects of fluoridation on teeth began his presentation with, "I hate dental appointments."

When the topic is of considerable interest to the group, one may go into it directly. This is usually best accomplished by reference to the main theme or purpose. The teacher, for example, who finds it necessary to interrupt other class activities to give a needed explanation usually will plunge directly into the points to be clarified. Many times, however, the group will not be especially concerned with the subject. They may not understand how a presentation relates to the ongoing class activities. Most reports and demonstrations fall into this category. In addition to a catch title, designed to arouse curiosity, an *attention-getting* opening is needed. A startling statement, question, or unusual illustration at the very beginning can gain immediate attention. The student who was to present a report on the effects of fluoridation on teeth might open his talk with these words:

Your teeth are as old as a forty-year-old man. A man who has lived forty years has lived almost two-thirds of his life; a tooth which has lived sixteen years has lived approximately two-thirds of its life. But with the help of fluoridation the average tooth may chew well for you. . . .

The speaker cited above made an unusual comparison. Then, while attention was high, he indicated how his information could be of value to his listeners.

The attention and needs stages set the stage for that which is to follow. Usually three or four statements will suffice. The speaker must carefully avoid extending this part of his presentation beyond its usefulness.

It is in the *satisfaction* phase of a presentation that one states his references and presents the main points of his talk. The individual can greatly increase the effectiveness of this phase of his presentation by adhering to a simple outline.

1.  *Initial Summary.* This consists of a brief enumeration of the main points to be made. For adolescents especially, it is desirable to write these points on the chalkboard.
2.  *Detailed Information.* Here the speaker brings in supporting facts, examples, and illustrations to clarify the issues. Usually it is desirable to show the relationship between the major points.
    Some individuals have difficulty in determining what the main points will be. The reporter can consider breaking his topic into such

categories as time sequence (past, present, future), cause-and-effect relationships, interested parties involved, anticipated problems and their solutions, and topical arrangement.

The speaker completes his discussion of a point before proceeding to the next one. By referring to the original points listed on the chalkboard, he is able to move from one area to another without losing his listeners.

3. *Final Summary.* The speaker concludes by restating his main points and important conclusions which have been developed.

The writer who reported on the effects of fluoridation on teeth broke his presentation into three parts: causes of tooth decay; effects of fluoridation; permanence of fluoridation treatment. After placing his main points on the board for the benefit of the class, he presented facts and examples designed to clarify each of the main points.

### How Is Listening Improved?

One of the most difficult problems facing a teacher involves ways and means of educating a group to listen effectively. It is easy enough to spot the student who is overtly disturbing, but much of the time it is practically impossible to detect the individual who has let his mind wander to more pleasing avenues of thought. On the other hand, some individuals who attempt to listen carefully have difficulty forming the mental images essential for comprehension.

In many life situations, listening is voluntary or purposeful. This is often not the case in ordinary classroom situations. Many times members of the audience are captive listeners. (In most states, youngsters are required to attend school until age sixteen; they are required to take many courses in which they have no genuine interest.) Attention, however, is enhanced *when the listener realizes that he is to become directly involved in subsequent activities.* To illustrate:

"I want you to pay especially close attention for the next few minutes because I am going to ask you to describe what you see."

The day before an examination a teacher summarized what he considered to be the highlights of the course.

A teacher explained an algebra problem involving principles necessary for doing the assignment.

The class leader issued final instructions before the start of an extended field trip.

Mary gave a report on the mountain rattlesnake which the group was likely to encouter on a science excursion.

The physical education teacher demonstrated techniques of artificial respiration prior to practice by each student.

Listening is also enhanced when the speaker is sincerely interested in what he is saying. Speakers who share themselves (tell of personal experiences) often get through to their audiences better than do those speakers who remain aloof. In an oral report, for example, a student who sees his task as more than just a job to be done will provide anecdotes, sometimes making his presentation almost a life-or-death matter.

Students listen better when a presentation appeals to basic motives. All people have certain basic physical and psychological drives or desires. It has been established that the need for social approval, self-preservation, affection, integrity, sex, pleasure, and the like exist in varying degrees within all human beings. The reporter or lecturer is more likely to interest his audience if he identifies his subject with one or more of these needs. To accomplish this end, however, he must project himself into the shoes of his listeners. At some point in the process the speaker replaces his own motives with those of his listeners.

Thus far, consideration has been given to the speaker's efforts to gain attention of his audience. Communication, however, is a joint process between the speaker and the observer. The listener himself has definite responsibilities, other than merely placing himself within hearing range of the speaker and assuming the proper listening pose.

One who listens pays attention to what is being said—i.e., he is "at-tension." This state of mind suggests that one is focusing his faculties on what he expects to receive from the experience. He *listens with a purpose.* The person who listens in a vague sort of way is likely to receive little benefit from the presentation. In an expository type of presentation, the hearer is interested in the soundness and relationships of the facts and ideas presented. This, in turn, will help him organize his listening for a purpose. After all, there will always be reports and lectures which are poorly organized. However, it may still be possible to profit from the experience, despite the speaker's limitations.

## What Presentation Techniques Are Recommended?

The effective presentation of a class lecture, demonstration, or report adheres to all the characteristics of effective speaking. First of all, the speaker must be heard. He needs to vary his voice in such a way as to drive home his points. The good speaker is enthusiastic about what he has to say; he looks directly at his listeners—talking "to" them rather than "at" them.

Techniques of delivery will be found in almost any basic speech textbook. The following elements of effective communication are basic:

1. He speaks in a conversational manner.
2. He thinks as he talks, and talks as he thinks.
3. He closely observes audience reactions.
4. He maintains poise at all times. (Some teachers violate this rule by sitting on the desk or leaning on a speaker's stand. In an attempt to appear casual or relaxed, they appear to some students as sloppy or lazy.)
5. He avoids annoying mannerisms. (One may develop "little habits" which detract seriously from what is being said. Often the teacher is unaware of these annoyances. Some teachers periodically provide students an opportunity to indicate the nature and extent of such annoying mannerisms. Anonymity is essential for valid suggestions.)

## What Function Is Served by the Question and Answer Session?

The question or discussion period following an informal lecture, demonstration, or report is of utmost importance. The lecture or report, being designed to inform the group, usually needs some clarification. This can come only from the group, as the speaker cannot know the type of mental images his discourse has produced. Five or ten minutes will usually suffice for a twenty-minute report.

The teacher then leads the class in a brief *review* of the main points made and brings them to bear upon the solution of a problem. The reader will recall that an informal lecture or report is meant to be a *basis* for problem-solving. It is concerned with the data-gathering (factual) step. There remains the evaluation of the data and their bearing upon an appropriate solution of the problem under consideration. In the process of review both students and teacher can bring related information to bear upon the problem.

A concomitant outcome of an oral report can be valuable training in evaluation of data. Students need training in assessing the validity and reliability of both the spoken and written word. Fallacies, improper deduction, and outright distortion of facts are among the most prevalent weaknesses of oral (and written) discourses. Adolescents, especially, are prone to confuse the issues by expressing their own value judgments along with the facts.

Most demonstrations are performed to help students visualize how conclusions are reached. Frequently the class group is expected to form certain conclusions on the basis of evidence produced by the demonstration. Teachers frequently violate sound scientific principles, however, by encouraging students to conclude too much on the basis of *one* experiment.

## How Are Oral Presentations Evaluated?

One of the most difficult and controversial aspects of oral presentations involves evaluation. Indeed, some teachers attempt to judge such presentations on the basis of purely general impressions. Some authorities, however, would seriously question or even deplore such a technique. Whether we like it or not, evaluations of oral discourses are highly subjective. Thus they are affected by certain predispositions of the evaluator. The personal factor involved can be substantially reduced by (1) having a number of people participate in the evaluation, and (2) establishing a number of bases for such an evaluation. Whenever practical, both techniques should be utilized.[1]

Since lecturing or reporting procedures are designed to facilitate the presentation of facts, students usually will be occupied in making notes of the main points, jotting down questions, and the like. Therefore, the teacher is the most logical person to make a formal evaluation. At least three bases which can be used are the following:

[1] For an illustration of how this dual approach can be applied, see Chapter 16, "Discussion Methods."

1. A presentation can be judged on the basis of the response of the group. Do students seem interested in the lecture or report during the actual presentation? Are there a number of appropriate questions following the report? Do students keep referring to the speaker's points in the follow-through session?
2. A presentation can be evaluated on the basis of the techniques of presentation. Was there evidence of planning? of proper body and voice control? Was eye contact maintained throughout?
3. A report can be judged on the basis of the adequacy of content coverage. Did the speaker present the facts fully? Was he able to maintain his role as impartial observer?

The fallacy of using audience reaction as a sole basis for evaluation is readily apparent. Many reportorial topics, for instance, may provoke enthusiasm because they are of immediate concern to the group. Or they may happen to support previous convictions of many of the listeners. Sometimes the reporter himself will be especially well liked by the group. Enthusiasm expressed under such circumstances can be high, even though the content be poorly stated or even invalid.

The immediate disadvantage of relying solely on techniques of delivery is inherent in the purpose of the talk. A lecture or report is designed to inform a group of people. Although recommended speech techniques correlate with effective communication, it is possible that the criterion of objective techniques will not be an effective measure for a particular individual.

Likewise, completeness and accuracy of content can be lost to the group if oral communication is ineffective. Many research specialists are weak in this respect. They often make up for the deficiency, however, by making copies of the report available to each member of the group. Under these conditions the desirability of having the report read in the first place might be questioned. In any event, the ordinary class report is dependent on adequate communication of ideas.

It can be seen, then, that all three bases of evaluation are needed. Few teachers can maintain a very high degree of accuracy by relying on general impressions only. Many teachers utilize rating scales which can be checked during and immediately following oral presentations.

The "Rating Scale for Oral Presentations" (Figure 21–1) illustrates the essentials of such a measure. It will be noted that all three of the bases for evaluation described above are included in the rating scale. In addition, there is a dimension for "general effectiveness." Different teachers, of course, favor different evaluation forms.

DIRECTIONS: Student will be marked with a check ($\sqrt{}$) on a continuum from one end of the line to the other. A check within the broken lines will be roughly equivalent to an average rating.

I. Delivery

   A. Lesson Beginning

| | | |
|---|---|---|
| Attention-getting, indicative of general content. | Beginning apparently planned, but effectiveness somewhat lacking. | Beginning poorly given; rambling statements; apologies. |

   B. Audience Contact

| | | |
|---|---|---|
| Looks directly at his listeners. | Depends heavily on notes, apparently does not "see" his listeners. | Reads from notes or looks above heads of listeners. |

   C. Enthusiasm

| | | |
|---|---|---|
| Intensely interested in topic. Stress is "natural" or "spontaneous." | Some interest evident. Occasionally lapses into a monotone. | Lack of interest; just another job to be done. |

   D. Use of Communication Skills (voice, posture and gestures, grammar, spelling, penmanship)

| | | |
|---|---|---|
| Communication skills above reproach. | One or two of the communication skills need further development. | Several communication skills need immediate attention. |

II. Content

   A. Major Points

| | | |
|---|---|---|
| Major points stressed and supported with pertinent examples. | Major points not very clearly defined and developed. | Content of the presentation confusing or extremely vague. |

   B. Objectivity

| | | |
|---|---|---|
| Distinguishes between "facts" and opinion. To me-ness evident. | Sometimes difficult to distinguish between facts and opinion. Tends to over-emphasize own opinions. | Facts and opinions generally indistinguishable. Apparently unaware of projections. |

III. Audience Reaction

| | | |
|---|---|---|
| Students attentive; take notes and ask pertinent questions. | Some audience interest evident. Note-taking and questions are brief. | Little evidence of interest. Only occasionally does a student take notes. Few questions. |

IV. General Effectiveness

| | | |
|---|---|---|
| High overall effectiveness. Appropriate "balance" maintained. | Presentation reasonably effective. | Presentation generally ineffective. Lacks needed "punch." |

**FIGURE 21–1.** Rating scale for oral presentations

# PLANNING FOR THE LECTURE

Techniques of informing others must be carefully planned. Students are painfully aware of teachers who "can't explain very well" or those who "are confusing or difficult to follow." Likewise, students and teachers recognize the difficulties that many students experience when asked to present oral reports. Most of these difficulties are related to inadequate planning. It is hoped that the illustrated plan which follows will clarify the problem somewhat. The plan is suggestive only.

LESSON PLAN ILLUSTRATION (social studies class)

*Concept:* Legal safeguards, based on the Bill of Rights, have been modified through various Supreme Court decisions.

*Problem:* What are the legal safeguards of the accused?

*Goals:* After this lesson on civil liberties the student should further understand the impact of recent Supreme Court decisions on one's protection under the law, as evidenced by:
1. His ability to relate (apply) recent court decisions to basic Constitutional guarantees.
2. The questions he asks in the subsequent discussion: "What protection should a youth offender have under the law?"
3. His application of the basic lecture concepts to a subsequent case analysis, involving procedural safeguards.

*Lesson Approach:*

"CATCH" TITLE:

"The thief is guilty: let's get on with the hanging!" These words ring out repeatedly from our favorite Western movies and TV shows. Almost without exception (in make-believe shows) the "thief" is not hung because his innocence is established—usually at the last moment.

INITIAL SUMMARY:

In our study of civil liberties thus far we have made reference to the Constitutional foundations of our legal safeguards, emphasizing the guarantees continued in the Bill of Rights. Through the study of cases we have seen how the basic Constitutional guar antees are implemented through our federal and state governments and how the Fourth Amendment serves both the ends and means of justice.

We will now direct our attention to the "innocent thief" who is almost hung in the Western movies. The rights of the accused are being continually reinterpreted through Supreme Court decisions. I am going to interpret some of these at this time. You will note that several of these decisions have been rendered since our textbook was written.

*Lesson Development:*
1. Preliminary hearing
   Differences between federal and state courts (Our own state practice)
   Arraignment—pleads guilty or not guilty

2. Grand Jury (if serious case)
   Purpose—To determine if the evidence warrants holding for trial (indictment)
   Not all states have one
   Federal—Consist of sixteen to twenty-four local citizens; serve as long as eighteen months
   Majority decision only
   Cassell v. Texas (1950)—Must not exclude important racial groups
3. Bail bond (in most cases)
   Purpose
   8th Amendment—No excessive bail
   Stack v. Boyle (1951)
4. Assurance against self-incrimination
   5th Amendment
   (Not sufficient grounds if just fear of being ridiculed by friends)
   Can be held in contempt of court
5. Coerced confessions
   (Another application of the self-incrimination privilege)
   Definition—a confession made after one's will has been broken down
   Can't be used—considered untrustworthy
   Techniques of obtaining confessions
   Chambers v. Florida (1940)—No brutality permitted
   Colombe v. Connecticut (1961)—No psychological coercion
   Miranda v. Arizona (1966)—All questions must be preceded by warning of rights
6. Can't be required to testify at one's trial
   Malloy v. Hogan (1964)—Extended the 5th Amendment to state courts (through the 14th Amendment)—thus no penalty for remaining silent
7. Counsel for indigent defendants
   (Approximately two-thirds of those charged with serious crimes cannot afford to hire a lawyer)
   State courts (until recently) required to provide counsel for capital offense cases only
   Gideon v. Wainwright (1963)—Required free counsel for all indigent defendants charged with serious crimes
8. Right to counsel prior to arraignment
   Escobedo v. Illinois (1964)—Right to a lawyer while being interrogated

*Deriving Generalizations:*

From the foregoing analysis of the rights of the accused a number of generalizations seem evident.

ILLUSTRATIONS:

1. Rights of the accused have varied from one period of time to another.
2. There is a decided trend toward a more liberal interpretation of the rights of the accused.
3. The Bill of Rights and the "Civil War Amendments" provide the basis for specific rights of the accused.

The foregoing lesson plan is more detailed than many teachers prefer; it is perhaps not detailed enough for others. The primary purpose of this plan is to provide information not readily accessible. The information is useful (along with other facts) in providing a factual *basis* for resolving fundamental issues in the area of civil liberties. Certain aspects of the lecture undoubtedly touched upon in text materials were *reorganized* and re-presented in the lecture. These aspects, of course, would be merely mentioned in the presentation.

## VALUES

Lecture is economical of time and materials.

The method serves to channel thinking of all students in a given direction.

Demonstrations, especially, enable the class leader to utilize activities which would be too dangerous for pupils themselves to perform within the ordinary classroom.

Lecturettes, and to some extent reports and demonstrations, are easy to prepare, as they are usually based on specialized knowledge of the leader.

Large-group instruction increases the accessibility of especially competent leaders.

## LIMITATIONS AND PROBLEMS

Information-giving methods can encourage the retention of facts as ends in themselves.

The method, in and of itself, is inadequate for teaching certain types of concepts. (Attitudes, feelings, and skills, for example, are not learned through pure telling or showing procedures.)

Some teachers have difficulty adapting their presentations to the comprehension levels of their students. (A passive audience is less able to indicate its lack of understanding.)

Social learnings are minimized during oral presentations.

This approach to teaching tends to encourage acceptance of the teacher as a final authority. In this way a teacher's bias and prejudices may be accepted at face value.

Exposition processes are extremely difficult to adapt to individual differences of students. Superior students, for example, frequently complain of boredom "after about the fifth explanation." Likewise, less able students often charge that lectures are "too fast."

## ILLUSTRATED LECTURE OUTLINES

I. Useful in art, home economics, and psychology classes

   *Unit:*    Color Relationships

*Concept:* The artist utilizes color in many ways.

*Problem:* How is color useful in creating mood, symbolizing ideas, and expressing emotions?

*Main Points:*
1. Plastic quality of color
2. Emotional quality of color
3. Aesthetic quality of color

II. Useful in English literature, world history, and social studies classes

*Unit:* The Aspiring Mind

*Concept:* The fusion of classical form of literature with the English context and exuberance (in the Elizabethan era) brought about a mature and artistic drama.

*Problem:* What are the basic elements of the drama in literary works?

*Main Points:*
1. Story line
2. Conflict
3. Plot structure
4. Character development
5. Interpretation

III. Useful in industrial arts classes

*Unit:* Precision Measuring Instruments

*Concept:* Precision measurement is essential to today's complex industrial system.

*Problem:* What methods do we use to measure units smaller than 1/64th of an inch?

*Main Points:*
1. Basic parts
2. Working principles
3. Different sizes
4. Different types

IV. Useful in history classes

*Unit:* Imperialism

*Concept:* China's relations with the West have been typified by one misunderstanding after another.

*Problem:* What were the circumstances and consequences of the First Opium War?

*Main Points:*
1. Causes
2. British bombardment of Chinese ports
3. Results

CHAPTER **22**

# Review Method

## OVERVIEW

### Key Concepts

1. Although recall is a basic aspect of review, it merely sets the stage for the extension of original learnings.
2. Emphasis in a review focuses upon application of concepts to related problems.
3. Related problems in a review are merely *identified;* they are not discussed extensively in a review lesson.
4. Review often occurs informally along with other instructional experiences. A carefully planned culminating review is an essential experience, however.
5. Practice is an effective method for polishing mental or motor skills; it is generally ineffective for cognitive and affective learnings. Such is a common misuse of review.
6. Review is most effective in increasing retention of that which is learned.

### New Terms

1. **Review**—A relook or new look at previous learnings. Thus the technique when employed appropriately may guide the learner in application of original learnings to new situations.
2. **Initial Learnings**—Previously learned concepts (ideas) which form the basis for review.
3. **Retention**—One's ability to remember (and use) that which is learned.

## Questions to Guide Your Study

1. "Review and practice may be used interchangeably." Defend or refute.
2. Why must students assume major responsibility for carrying a review discussion?
3. How does concept-learning contribute to effective review?
4. Why are review lessons (as typically conducted) so often dull and boring?

Mr. Krupp was looking forward to today's review lesson in world history. For some time now he had culminated each unit with at least one period of review, prior to his unit test. Even those students who had shown relatively little interest usually followed the review proceedings fairly well.

As usual, he began by asking the class to submit questions on points which needed clarification. Mary immediately opened the session by asking, "What do you think was the most important cause of World War I?" The instructor countered with, "How would *you* answer the question, Mary?" Thereupon, Mary proceeded to "review" two or three causes of the conflict which were either mentioned in the text or in previous class periods. Eventually Mr. Krupp indicated what he considered to be the major cause of the war. (Many of the class members made a note of this point, in preparation for the next day's test.) The succeeding questions were handled in a similar manner.

A casual observer might have noted that the session was "carried" by four or five individuals. Most of the instructor's questions were designed to determine if students could *repeat* important points studied, whereas the students' questions were primarily concerned with the opinions of the instructor on important points. Toward the end of the hour the group became quite restless. Some students apparently attempted to get Mr. Krupp "off the topic into more interesting avenues of thought."

Mr. Krupp's review is representative of many such experiences throughout the secondary schools of this country. While it does contain some aspects of an appropriate review experience, its effectiveness can be of little lasting value. The students obviously were interested in receiving help in passing a test. Instead of extending their associations in the area they were *repeating* or *practicing* factual material which had been "covered" at an earlier date. It would appear that Mr. Krupp's review lesson was predicated on two or three false premises.

In the first place, repetition or drill generally is inappropriate for such a lesson. The mere recall of content material does not ensure application. In fact, it has been demonstrated that such an experience often impedes the making of worthwhile associations. Both students and teacher have a tendency to think in terms of factual-type tests only. Like most other teaching methods, the review experience appropriately deals with the resolution of important problems. About the only problem being solved during the foregoing lesson was that of having the teacher "spot" the students for an examination. An important function of review is the *extension* or *transfer* of previous learnings to other areas.

Lacking a worthwhile purpose, class contributions were restricted to very few individuals. In most cases of this nature these are the relatively few persons who are able to excel on written examinations. Even when there is a worthwhile purpose involved, interest tends to lag unless variety is introduced. Instead of discouraging attempts to digress, Mr. Krupp might have encouraged them—so long as they dealt with inferences and relationships of a related nature. The term *review* is almost as ambiguous as class discussion. Teachers speak of reviewing *for* a test, reviewing the *results* of a test, reviewing important words or terms, reviewing the major points of a lesson, and so on. Too often a so-called review is little more than repetitive practice or drill. While there is a definite place for such practice, when drill is *substituted* for review the results *must* be disappointing. Review, literally, means a re-view or a re-look at something. Thus review might be better called a new view, i.e., a view of some problem from a new angle. It is a technique of guiding the student in the application of original learnings to related situations.

# FUNDAMENTAL PROPERTIES

In addition to enhancing transfer of learning to related life situations, review may substantially contribute to the permanence of that which is learned. Unlike class discussion which focuses attention to one particular problem, review emphasizes the recognition of many related problems. Its widespread misuse reflects a general misunderstanding of the essential properties involved.

### What Initial Learnings Are Necessary?

Before an individual can take a *re*-view of a situation, he must have viewed it at least once before. There is a tendency to assume adequate initial learning when the student has read his text or is able to verbalize answers to factual questions. Thus one loses sight of the basic nature of the learning process—that of coping with basic educational *problems*. The products of each educational experience consist essentially of centralized ideas, generalizations, or concepts. These, in turn, become the necessary data for review lessons. If previous experiences have emphasized the acquisition of knowledge only, it is logical (but fallacious) to conceive review as a mere repetition of these facts. Generalizations *must* be derived prior to effective review.

### What Role Does Recall Play in Review?

Recall is a fundamental aspect of review. Basic unit generalizations are brought together in one lesson for the first time. As a means of assisting students to recall major ideas or concepts, it is often desirable to recall the context from which they were developed. Consequently, the experience may begin with the question, "What have we done during this unit?" When an activity is mentioned (e.g., class discussion) attention will be directed to the major idea(s) which evolved from the experience. In like manner each major unit concept is identified. (They are usually listed, providing a basis for subsequent review activities.)

### Why Is It Important to Extend Learnings?

Once basic, previously derived generalizations have been brought before the group, their application to related problems is emphasized. Although specific lesson generalizations, like facts, may not apply readily to broad problems, it is relatively easy to combine them into broader concepts for this purpose. Review is usually most effective when generalizations are somewhat comparable in scope to unit concepts. (See Chapter 1, "Gaining the Concept.") They are most effectively utilized, however, when students themselves derive the concepts. Processes of reflective thought reach their peak as students identify related problems to which previous learnings apply.

## REVIEW PROCEDURE

Review is common; it can occur incidentally at any point within a lesson, or it can be the major portion of a lesson. Yet, most authorities suggest that teachers as a whole cannot, or at least do not, make adequate applications of the procedure. Burton,[1] for instance, states that he has seen several hundred reviews in progress, but practically none that amounted to anything more than drill. Why the difficulty? Is it because the technique is unusually difficult? (This does not seem likely.) Or is it due more to an incomplete understanding of the procedure involved?

Although it is recognized that a *re*-view or *re*-look is important at any point during a lesson, the emphasis in this chapter is on review lessons which occur at the culmination of a unit or block of work. The basic essentials, however, can be readily applied to other review situations.

### How Are Basic Unit Generalizations Used in Review?

Each lesson should be culminated with from two to five student-derived generalizations. These generalizations collectively embody a major lesson concept upon which the lesson rests. It should be noted that major unit concepts, developed by students during a review, will not be identical to individual lesson generalizations. Rather they will be similar to *unit* concepts developed by the teacher in preinstructional planning activities. (Each lesson is normally based upon one such concept.) The teacher does *not* provide the learner with his own list of unit concepts, however. Unit concepts, derived by students, are likely to more closely parallel actual learnings than those sought by the teacher.

---

[1] William H. Burton, *Guidance of Learning Activities,* 3rd ed. (New York: Appleton-Century-Crofts, Inc., 1962), p. 460.

This phase of a review involves clarifying, in some cases for the first time, the major ideas (concepts) of the unit. Since they are based upon a number of lesson generalizations, a process of abstraction, in addition to mere recall, is involved. Indeed there is a natural tendency to evolve broad concepts from lesson generalizations into broader concepts. This process should be encouraged. To illustrate from an art class concerned with "Color Relationships":

*Lesson Generalizations:*
1. Light, bright colors evoke a happy, gay mood.
2. Dark, somber colors generally evoke a depressing mood.
3. Different colors have different emotional impacts. (Red, for example, is happy, exciting.)
4. Colors symbolize ideas. (Blue, for instance, is associated with loyalty and honesty.)

In recalling these generalizations, students might be guided in evolving the following unit concept: *Color may be used to create mood and symbolize ideas.* The reader will note that the mere recall of specific facts is *not* an essential aspect of review.

## How Are Unit Concepts Extended to Related Problems?

Basic unit learnings are broadened and extended as the student perceives how they may be applied to related problems and situations. Such has been described as the heart of every review lesson. This expansion of original learning is achieved through a skillful process of questioning.

In this phase of review the higher order questions will be emphasized. (See Chapter 11.) The process is often introduced by asking questions of advocacy. Such questions often begin with the word *Should.* An advocacy question directs attention to one particular solution to a problem. Sometimes *How* or *Could* questions are useful in this respect. To illustrate from an art class that is studying "Color Relationships":

Should (*or* How could) we use color to improve our homes? Possible responses might include the following:

1. Light, cool colors make walls seem to recede.
2. A single dark wall may be used to correct the proportions of a large, square room.
3. Single light-colored walls give focus to a large, square room.
4. Dark, warm colors may be used to make large barnlike rooms cosier.

Each suggested application is discussed briefly for the purpose of clarifying the idea. No effort is made to resolve issues in a review lesson, as the function is merely that of *recognizing related problems for expansion of knowledge.* (In some instances, of course, such problems may reveal the need for further consideration of basic issues. In such cases, other appropriate techniques will be employed.)

In a review lesson, students should assist in recall of basic generalizations and derivation of concepts; they should bear the major responsibility for extending these learnings to related areas. It may be necessary for the instructor to offer a few suggestions as a means of preparing students for further analysis. There is a decided tendency to rush students through a review lesson, assuming that most of the important relationships are obvious. The evidence quite clearly suggests, however, that students transfer learnings only to the extent to which they are taught to transfer. Two or three class periods might be profitably devoted to such activities.

### How Is the Review Lesson Evaluated?

An appropriate review generates considerable enthusiasm and creativity. When individuals begin to understand how their school experiences can be applied to out-of-school problems, they tend to develop and maintain a high degree of interest. Such behaviors will be apparent in other class activities as well. The teacher himself will also become more conscious of the importance of transfer of learnings to related situations.

The effectiveness of a review lesson, perhaps more than with any other method, is reflected in a written unit test. Frequently, however, students complain when teachers emphasize the application of broad concepts in review, if their examinations are based largely on specific details. Such an inconsistency seriously undermines the effectiveness of instruction. The review lesson, designed to extend learnings to related problems, is closely akin to evaluational experiences. Test items, for example, serve a similar purpose. Test item situations, however, must include problems other than those introduced during reviews. The purpose is to determine if the individual can make such associations and relationships on his own.

## PLANNING FOR REVIEW

A major factor contributing to poor review lessons is inadequate planning. Teachers quite naturally are interested in clarifying facts and principles; they are less interested in extending these. Yet, it is through extension and association of ideas that adequate understanding is best revealed. The illustrated plan represents that review which is usually introduced at the culmination of a unit.

LESSON PLAN ILLUSTRATION (art or home economics class—basic design)

*Unit:* Color Relationships

*Concept:* (Will involve all the unit concepts as an essential aspect of the lesson.)

*Problem:* How can we relate what we have learned about color relationships to different situations outside the realm of fine arts?

*Goals:* After this lesson the student should have furthered his understanding of the basic principles underlying color relationships, as
evidenced by:
1. His ability to identify related problems in class review.
2. His ability to apply basic principles to related problems.
3. His ability to draw parallels with problems previously studied.

## Lesson Approach:

During the past few weeks we have emphasized the principles underlying color relationships. We have analyzed the properties of color and we
have seen how colors may be used to give spatial quality to the pictorial field,
to create mood and symbolize ideas, to attract and direct attention, to organize a composition, and to accomplish aesthetic appeal. We have seen
that color is one of the most expressive of art elements because its quality
affects our emotions directly and immediately.

Although we have spent the last few weeks exploring color relationships
in the context of the fine arts, color is not the sole property of the fine arts.
Actually, colors permeate every area of our lives. Today we will take a look
at some of the areas outside the realm of fine arts, areas where carefully
controlled color solves numerous problems.

## Lesson Development:

I. ANALYSIS OF THE PREVIOUS UNIT EXPERIENCES

What generalizations or big ideas evolved during our study of this
unit?

A. Color may be used to give spatial quality to the pictorial field.
1. The warm colors—red, orange, and yellow—will in general seem to advance.
2. The cool colors (containing blue), such as green, violet,
and blue-green, will in general seem to recede.

B. Color may be used to create mood and to symbolize ideas.
1. Light, bright colors evoke a happy, gay mood.
2. Dark, somber colors generally evoke a depressing mood.
3. Different colors have different emotional impacts, i.e.,
red evokes a happy, exciting mood; blue suggests a
dignified, sad, or serene mood.
4. Colors symbolize ideas. Examples: Blue is associated with
loyalty and honesty; red with bravery, passion, or danger;
yellow with cowardice; black with death; green with
life, hope, or envy; white with purity or innocence; purple
with royalty or wealth.

C. Color may be used to attract and direct attention and serve to
organize a composition.

D. Color may be used to accomplish aesthetic appeal by a system
of well-planned color relationships.

II. RECALLING HOW THE MAJOR CONCEPTS WERE DERIVED

A. Each student created a collage of simple planes overlapping
in space. These planes were cut from colored paper and pasted
on a neutral background. The colors were chosen to establish
spatial position of the forms.

B. Each student executed three small paintings expressing (1) a
happy mood, (2) a sad mood, and (3) either an angry or

dangerous mood using color (not subject matter) to establish the mood.

C. To illustrate color organization in a composition, each student executed three small paintings: (1) monochromatic, (2) analogous, and (3) complementary.

D. To illustrate aesthetic appeal, we discussed harmonious color combinations. We discussed selection of hues and arrangement of them in pictorial field. We also discussed variety and repetition and dominance. These activities were followed with a critique on the finished paintings and collages.

III. EXTENDING UNIT CONCEPTS TO RELATED PROBLEMS

With our ideas before us, let us briefly consider other areas to which they may apply.

*Examples:*

1. How could we use color to improve our homes?
   a. Light, cool colors make walls seem to recede, giving a small room a more spacious impression.
   b. A single, dark wall may be used to correct proportions of a long, narrow room.
   c. A single, light-colored wall gives focus to a large, square room.
   d. Dark, warm colors make walls appear to close in. They are often used to make large, barnlike rooms seem cozier.

2. Could we use color to improve our clothing?
   a. Color in everyday clothing can correct physical disproportion in appearances of individuals.
   b. Color in theatrical costumes can set a mood and help symbolize ideas.

3. Might we use color to improve industry?
   a. Illumination may be improved through the use of color.
   b. Accident frequencies may be lowered with use of color.

4. How could we use color to improve hospitals?
   a. The psychological effects of different colors are used.
   b. Visual variety is considered essential in the care of hospital patients.

5. How can color be used to improve architecture?
   a. Color is used to make buildings more aesthetic.
   b. Color is used to control heat reflection.

6. Should we use color to improve restaurants?
   a. Bright, cool colors make a restaurant appear clean.
   b. Warm, subdued colors place the customer at ease and presumably increase the size of his check.

7. How could we use color to improve sales?
   a. Colors attract attention to packaging.
   b. Colors can make advertising more emphatic.

DERIVING GENERALIZATIONS:

From our treatment of related problems, what big ideas seem to stand out?

*Examples:*

1. Color, when carefully controlled, is capable of improving every area of our environment.
2. Color deals with facts and principles which can be scientifically utilized.

It should be noted that the last phase of the illustrated plan (deriving generalizations) involves a further abstraction of unit concepts. Although this is not an essential aspect of a review lesson, it may be useful as a means of clarifying the basic theme of the unit.

# VALUES

Review is uniquely valuable for facilitating application or transfer of learnings to related situations. It has long been recognized by psychologists that individuals apply or transfer learnings to new experiences to the extent that they are taught to make this transfer. Review is designed for this purpose.

The formulation of new associations and relationships, through review, renders learning more permanent—forgetting is reduced.

Review enables the teacher to correct misconceptions and misunderstandings which inevitably arise in group learning situations.

Review procedures are extremely flexible. They may range from the informal five-minute review at the end of a class period to extended reviews of one or more class periods. This flexibility feature, however, has sometimes worked as a disadvantage, especially when review sessions have been ill-conceived and inadequately planned.

# LIMITATIONS AND PROBLEMS

Review has been widely misused. Often mistaken for review are recitation sessions in which the learner has been expected to recall specific facts for a test.

Prior to initial learning, review is a waste of time. To make a *re*-view of learning not thoroughly understood in the first place results in chaos.

Review is deceptively easy. Even when review is used for the purpose of expanding learning, it is extremely easy to get bogged down on some related issue. If this occurs, review purposes may be impossible to achieve.

Review, if inconsistent with anticipated tests, is extremely difficult to conduct. Too often reviews have served to "spot" students for a factual-type test. If, however, students anticipate tests of application, they will welcome timely reviews.

## ILLUSTRATED REVIEW PROBLEMS

I. Useful in history, government, and social studies classes

*Unit:*     Population Pressures

*Problem:* How can we relate what we have learned in this unit to other problems in the Far East?

*Unit Concepts:*

1. Many conflicts are indirectly related to inadequate food supplies.
2. Basic religious differences account for much strife within and among many nations of the Far East.
3. Problems of population control reflect religious, educational, and traditional problems.
4. Asian mistrust of the Western nations is related to past colonial problems.
5. Communism tends to have a special appeal to impoverished peoples.
6. Regional development is hampered by long-standing disputes and mistrust between neighboring countries.
7. "Have-not" peoples often assume that the wealthier nations have a moral obligation to provide economic assistance.

*Extending Concepts to Related Areas:*

1. Should we withdraw all our troops from Southeast Asia?
2. Should we attempt to establish a regional economic assistance program involving the Mekong Delta?
3. Should we encourage the establishment of birth-control clinics in nations like India and Pakistan?
4. Should we attempt to develop a regional economic assistance program with the cooperation of Communist China?

II. Useful in United States history, American literature, and social studies classes

*Unit:*     Responsible Individuals Make Up a Democracy

*Problem:* How can we relate what we have learned in this unit to other problems involving decision-making processes?

*Unit Concepts:*

1. Mature decision-making is part of becoming a responsible adult.
2. Both the individual and the group have responsibilities for the democratic judicial process.
3. In a democracy one must not be politically disinterested.
4. Duties and privileges in a democratic family unit parallel those of all citizens.
5. Participation in the arts is a privilege and responsibility of all citizens.

*Extending Concepts to Related Areas:*

1. Should the citizen try to influence television programming toward higher aesthetic levels?

2. Should an individual expound an unpopular philosophy in which he believes?
3. Should an adult let children share equally in family decisions?

III. Useful in physical education, group guidance, and sociology classes

*Unit:* Teamwork in Sports and Society

*Problem:* How can we relate what we have learned about teamwork to our lives as a whole?

*Unit Concepts:*
1. We are on teams all our lives.
2. Each player has a responsibility to the team.
3. It is as important to bring others into team participation as it is to make a large individual team contribution.
4. Principles of teamwork are readily transferred to teamwork in the larger society.
5. All people must be competent team workers to function effectively in society.

*Extending Concepts to Related Areas:*
1. How may teamwork be used in civic clubs?
2. How can we use teamwork principles in church groups?
3. How might we use teamwork principles in the family?
4. How can we use teamwork principles at work?

IV. Useful in mathematics classes

*Unit:* Equations and Formulae

*Problem:* How can we relate what we have learned about equations and formulae to related everyday situations?

*Unit Concepts:*
1. Parentheses must be cleared before any action is taken outside the parenthesis.
2. Equations are of three types: true, false, and conditional.
3. Every equation possesses roots which must be clearly understood for effective use.
4. Equations and formulae represent ways of expressing equivalence.

*Extending Concepts to Related Areas:*
1. Is it possible to find solutions without using parentheses?
2. How could equations be used to solve distance problems?
3. How could equations be applied to navigational problems?
4. How may equations be used to help us save money?

V. Useful in chemistry classes

*Unit:* The Gas Laws

*Problem:* How can we relate our learning about gas laws to practical aspects of living?

*Unit Concepts:*

1. Pressure is a force per unit of area.
2. Temperature is based on arbitrary scales.
3. Volume is a three-dimensional quantity.
4. Pressure is inversely proportional to volume.
5. Volume is directly proportional to pressure.

*Extending Concepts to Related Areas:*

1. How can we transport more electric power in existing power lines?
2. How can the power of electric magnets be increased manyfold?
3. How can living organisms be preserved for future use?

CHAPTER **23**

# Drill and Practice Procedures

## OVERVIEW

### Key Concepts

1. Drill or practice is an effective method for polishing mental or motor skills; it is often ineffective for cognitive and affective learnings.
2. Drill or practice basically is an individualized (rather than a group) method.
3. Modeled demonstrations are essential in the development of mental and motor skills.
4. To avoid monotony, the setting for drill and practice must be varied constantly.
5. Practice does *not* make perfect; it makes permanent. Unless it is corrective in nature, usually requiring supervision, it may be worse than useless.

### New Terms

1. **Drill**—Commonly used in connection with the teaching of mental skills. In this chapter the terms "drill" and "practice" are used interchangeably.
2. **Practice**—Commonly used in connection with the teaching of motor skills. In this chapter the terms "practice" and "drill" are used interchangeably.
3. **Initial Learnings**—Basic cognitive understanding or perception of the rudiments of the skill to be learned.
4. **Varied Contact**—Preliminary practice of the skill being developed.
5. **Repetitive Practice**—That practice which is designed to correct minor details (problems) associated with a skill. Often referred to as develop-

ing "polish" to the skill.

6. **Kinesthesis**—Usually used in connection with motor skill development, the term refers to muscular sensation or the "feel" for a desired movement. Verbal and visual kinesthetic cues are most useful in the early stages of learning, gradually giving way to internal cues as the skill develops.

7. **Overlearning**—Learning beyond the point of bare mastery. Up to 50 percent overlearning is recommended. Thus if basic mastery is achieved in thirty minutes, fifteen additional minutes could be profitably devoted to practice.

## Questions to Guide Your Study

1. Why is drill in the cognitive and affective domains generally discouraged?
2. What role do demonstrations play in skill development?
3. Why is variation encouraged in preliminary practice sessions?
4. Why is group drill generally discouraged?

Ask almost any college professor what training deficiencies, if any, are apparent in college freshmen and his response is likely to be direct and to the point. "They tend to be weak in the basic skills: reading, writing, and arithmetic." His solution: "More drill or practice in these areas!" Likewise, the lay public has repeatedly accused the schools of reducing or even eliminating drill from the schoolroom. Some teachers, however, dare not admit the use of drill as a teaching method, fearing they will be associated with a traditional approach to teaching. Although the technique has undoubtedly been misused in the past and accordingly associated with a memoriter type of instruction, the modern school does *not* advocate the elimination of drill or practice. In fact, current teaching techniques demand even *more and better* practice than did those in the earlier schools.[1]

Skill deficiencies, apparent among many high school graduates, usually can be more accurately attributed to *improper* drill procedures rather than to inadequate amounts. Listed below are some instances of *misuse and misapplication* of practice or drill:

A mathematics instructor asked his students to memorize formulae.
A biology teacher required students to repeat verbally the steps of the problem-solving process.
An industrial arts teacher asked his students to commit to memory safety regulations and certain work procedures.
An American history teacher requested his students to memorize the state capitals and a series of important dates.
A home economics teacher drilled students on certain basic cooking recipes.

[1] William H. Burton, *Guidance of Learning Activities*, 3rd ed. (New York: Appleton-Century-Crofts, Inc., 1962), p. 454.

An American literature instructor expected students to memorize selected
passages of prose and poetry, along with the names of important authors.
A physical education instructor required that his students memorize the rules
of tennis before participating in the activity.

The foregoing illustrations represent but a few of the inappropriate uses of
practice or drill. What is there about these experiences that renders them
inappropriate? Each of them violates at least one of the necessary conditions of
effective practice. In the first place, practice or drill must be contained within
the framework of a functional situation. Although students do need specifics,
they are useful only as a means of deriving generalizations. Furthermore, drill
prior to initial understanding is a waste of time. Finally, practice or drill must
be restricted to the acquisition of skills. Drill applied to the development of
understandings and attitudes is a useless endeavor.[2] Perhaps a thorough understanding of the meaning and function of practice or drill procedures will somewhat clarify the point.

# FUNDAMENTAL PROPERTIES

Drill or practice is an old, time-tested technique of teaching. It is essential to
every subject area. Unfortunately, however, the method has been grossly misused. Near the end of a long, illustrious career, William Burton[3] stated that
while he had seen several hundred reviews in progress practically none of them
amounted to anything more than drill. It seems likely that this state of affairs
reflects a basic misunderstanding of the place for drill in teaching. This section
emphasizes those fundamental processes which have a critical bearing upon this
issue.

### What Initial Learnings Are Necessary?

Prior to engaging in any form of practice, an individual must develop a
cognitive understanding of the basic function or purpose and the rudiments of
the skill to be mastered. This usually involves some preliminary reading, participation in a discussion, listening to a lecture presentation, and the like. In the
motor skills area the importance of basic cognitive understanding is readily
apparent; in the mental skills area, however, the problem is much less obvious.
Drill, in the absence of basic understanding, is often confusing and usually a
waste of time.

---

[2] A possible exception involves drill for mastering patterns, sequences, or order of
arrangement.

[3] Burton, *op. cit.,* p. 460.

## What Is the Role of Demonstrations in Drill or Practice?

The processes of skill development involve both the cognitive and the psychomotor domains. This means that a basic understanding must be translated into verbal responses or motor movements appropriate to the skill. Thus it is almost essential that the learner have an opportunity to observe a modeled demonstration of the skill involved. Such an experience must be as consistent with basic cognitions as possible. All minor discrepancies should be clarified. The learner is then able to mimic his observation in the preliminary stages of application.

## Why Is Drill or Practice Referred to As an Individualistic Process?

In translating any cognitive learning into somatic movements, each individual is unique. In skill development orthodox approaches are encouraged. Ultimately, however, those practice exercises necessary for learning "the correct strokes" become an individual matter.

Occasionally it may be necessary for an entire class to sound out certain words in unison in the early stages of drill. Otherwise, drill is something that each learner must perform on his own. The same principle holds for a motor skill. Even though several members of a team sport may be on the field at the same time, the "coaches" must observe the progress of each student as the skill is perfected. For this reason drill or practice outside of the class setting is usually encouraged.

## What Is the Role of Feedback in Skill Development?

Skill development basically consists of solving mechanical problems. Basic to this process is immediate knowledge of results. In the early stages of skill development the learner should receive such feedback from one exploratory trial to the next. In a motor skill, for example, he must realize what his muscles are doing *and* what his muscles should be doing to properly perform the skill.

Although verbal feedback is reinforcing, visual perception is better. Videotaped exploratory trials with immediate playback facilities are most desirable. Thus the learner is able to analyze his own performance and make necessary adjustments. Once an adequate perception of the movement is established, the learner is able to rely upon his own memory as a guide to performance. Verbal and visual cues, accordingly, are gradually eliminated.

## What Constitutes an Efficient Drill or Practice Session?

Frequent, short drill or practice sessions are preferred. Especially in the area of mental skills the learner soon becomes exhausted. Fifteen- to thirty-minute sessions are most efficient. When an individual becomes exhausted the frequency of mistakes increases. If repeated often enough they may become "stamped-in," rendering them especially difficult to dislodge. Although the same principle holds in the area of motor skills, it may be necessary to gradually lengthen practice sessions for the purpose of developing "polish." This is especially true in competitive sports, where individuals frequently must play under exhausting conditions.

Daily practice is recommended. Less than once a week is probably not often enough for maintaining efficiency. The polish phase of skill development represents overlearning (learning beyond the point of bare mastery). Drill in overlearning up to fifty percent is recommended. A foreign language skill, for example, that requires an hour to learn may be efficiently drilled for one and one half hours. Although the same principle holds for motor skills, the coach of a competitive sports team may go far beyond the point of maximum efficiency as a means of producing team excellence.

## What Is the Role of Kinesthetic Sense in Motor Learning?

In the early stages of skill development motor pathways are developed through "trial runs." Varied movement opportunities are provided as a means of calling attention to certain patterns. Accuracy is not important at this point. With practice, however, each movement is refined partially by "feel," e.g., the learner begins to internalize the movement(s). Less conscious effort is required for the task than was originally experienced. This process varies with the individual *and* the particular skill involved.

As skill development progresses the "feel" or "touch" for various movements becomes increasingly evident. In order to enhance this experience continued use of visual cues is desirable. Films, demonstrations, and the like help the learner "sharpen his mental image" of the skill to be mastered. Some teachers reinforce the kinesthetic sense of the learner by calling attention to sound, such as the "crack" of the bat, or the "swish" of the tennis racket. Such feedback seems to assist one in developing appropriate associations between sound and movement. In the advanced stages of motor learning kinesthetic sense comes mostly from within.

Motor skills sometimes are developed inappropriately prior to any organized instruction. Even so, this kinesthetic sense accompanies learning and provides necessary feedback for the learner. Relearning thus becomes extremely difficult, as a new set of guidelines (cues) must be established for developing the correct "feel" for the movement. The learner may revert to his old (outmoded) patterns without even becoming aware of the process. For this reason relearning is a slow, laborious process.

## In What Areas Is Drill or Practice Appropriate?

Practice is appropriate whenever a more or less fixed pattern of automatic responses is needed. It is designed to extend or polish *skill* learnings by adding

**361**

meaning and associations to original learnings. Motor skills, habits, and mental skills are made more useful and meaningful through appropriate practice procedures. Many courses in today's secondary schools are concerned, principally, with the acquisition of skills. Such skills as using the typewriter, developing laboratory techniques, driving an automobile, baking a cake, using shop tools, playing a musical instrument, and a host of others make heavy demands on practice or drill procedures.

Drill especially has been subjected to severe criticism due to its misuse. Except in a few specialized cases (e.g., developing sequences or patterns), its use must be restricted to the area of mental and motor skills. The traditional practice of asking students to memorize (drill) specific facts in history or literature, for example, represents a misuse of the method.

### How Does Drill or Practice Differ from Review?

Practice and review are alike in that they both add to or supplement initial classroom learnings. Moreover, there is a substantial amount of practice or recall in review procedures. It must be remembered, however, that in review a minimum of time is devoted to the recall of basic concepts and that these concepts serve as a *means* to the major issue to be resolved: "What related problems seem to bear upon the things we have learned?" Furthermore, both practice and review, when properly used, ensure more permanent learning. The deeper understandings and associations gained through review, like the polish developed through practice, tend to make learnings more functional, thus increasing retention.

As previously indicated, one of the major differences between practice and review has been too often overlooked. While practice techniques are most effective in the teaching of skills, they are not effective in the teaching of understandings, attitudes, and appreciations. In these areas, reviews are needed. Whereas review involves the processes of *group* deliberation or problem solving, practice techniques for the most part do not rely on group processes. Practice or drill can be considered an extension to the *group* problem-solving process—one of refining the *products* of deliberative processes. Another important distinction between the two techniques is that, whereas a review may involve the entire class group, the practice or drill procedure must be individualized. In a review lesson, for example, the relationships and associations developed by one member can be especially helpful to the other class members. Practice or drill, however, usually is much more effective when individualized. Most of us can remember instances when the class was asked to repeat something in unison. Perhaps it was the letters of the alphabet or a rule of grammar. Recent investigation, however, has discredited such practices when used for this purpose. One junior high school teacher even questions the time-honored practice of pledging allegiance to the flag, after having students write out what they were actually saying. Lack of understanding was readily apparent from such expressions as "one nation under guard," "I pledge a leagence," etc.

# DRILL AND PRACTICE TECHNIQUES

As with any other method of teaching, there are certain steps that, if followed closely, will greatly accelerate accuracy in the development of skills. Although the perfection of motor skills depends on inherited characteristics, these skills seldom will be fully realized in the absence of an effective training program. A basketball team, for example, may be limited by native endowment, but the difference between a well coached team and one with inadequate or improper coaching is obvious. The same principle holds for other skills. Teaching, likewise, is a complex of *skills* that can be developed. Although some individuals possess a more favorable native endowment than others in this area, appropriate training procedures can be of invaluable assistance to most students. The cliché that "teachers are born and not made" has been thoroughly disproved. Perhaps as a consequence of the earlier and false notion that skills cannot be taught, they were for a long time left to chance. Even today some teachers make relatively little systematic effort in the development of mental skills among students. These learnings all too frequently have been left to the resources of untrained young learners.

As a result of extensive investigation, educational psychologists have been able to offer many useful clues to the effective development of skills. It has been found that three steps may contribute greatly to the developmnt of skills: development of initial learning, varied contact, and repetitive practice. An illustrated lesson plan, featuring a mental skill, also has been provided. Generally the same processes apply to motor skill development.

### How Are Skills First Introduced?

A skill, like any other learning, is first introduced in such a manner as to permit the learner to perceive the problem. Once the purpose is thoroughly understood, verbal instruction on the essential rudiments of the skill are fully appropriate. Verbal instruction often is accompanied by a demonstration. The chief purpose is not to have the learner copy the model, but to promote full comprehension of the purpose of the activity and the general form and sequence of events to be followed.

Detailed explanations or demonstrations at this point should be avoided. If more than the gross aspects of the skill are presented, thinking processes may become confused. Detailed explanations are not only valueless, but learning actually may be retarded as a result. A speech teacher, for example, first introduces the art of speechmaking with a brief description of the following points:

1. Introduction—attention-getting
2. Body—two or three main points to be developed
3. Conclusion—restatement of the major theme of the presentation

This can be followed with a five-minute demonstration.

## What Function Does Varied Contact with the Skill Serve during the Early Phase of Its Development?

After being briefly introduced to a skill in a functional situation, the learner must have direct contact with the activity in a variety of meaningful situations. It is important that the learner have an opportunity to engage in exploratory trials, ask questions, observe skilled performers, inspect diagrams, and so on. In terms of the problem-solving process this might be called *evaluation of alternative proposals.* It is in this phase of development that the student will introduce his own innovations to be tried and tested. This is indeed the *creative* aspect of skill development. Through one's own diagnosis (often assisted by the teacher) a more complete understanding of the problem can be developed. For maximum benefit, conditions should resemble actual life situations as closely as possible.

The teacher can be especially useful in the exploratory phase of mastering a skill. The task of the student is to capitalize on strengths while minimizing weaknesses. By pointing out these factors the teacher can help the learner diagnose his or her own problems. Recognizing the importance of reinforcement or reward in learning, the teacher should make critiques as positive as possible. In the early stages of development, for example, it is desirable to minimize weaknesses. In any event, strengths should usually be emphasized prior to deficiencies. Some teachers, when enlisting the aid of a class group in diagnosing skill performance, call attention to weaknesses by asking the individual himself to point out perceived problem areas.

One of the greatest problems a teacher will encounter in skill development is that of helping the learner see mistakes as seen by others. The mere act of telling a person that he or she has a flat, nasal voice, for example, may have absolutely no effect on the learner for the simple reason that one hears his voice only through his own ears. A videotaped playback of a selected presentation, however, may produce almost immediate corrective efforts. Likewise, it may accomplish little to tell one that he or she gestures too much, or that posture tends to detract from performance. By merely placing a mirror in the back of the room, however, the problem is likely to become immediately apparent.

Oddly enough, some teachers assume that verbal instruction is all that is needed in the development of skills. The assumption is made that once a person understands how a skill is performed he can complete the process through individual initiative. An excellent example of such a fallacy can be found in the teaching of instructional methods courses at some colleges and universities. The complaint is often heard, "We tell (or less commonly, show) perspective teachers how to teach, but they tend to forget these learnings when they start teaching." A more accurate statement would be that the learners simply have not been prepared to utilize the skills involved. They need varied contacts with skills under controlled and closely supervised conditions that approach actual situations as nearly as possible. Simulated teaching experiences in a methods course cannot produce proficiency in the skills needed, but they can broaden understanding and perception of the intricate relationships involved. If a teacher is to use review, drill, sociodrama, class discussion, and the like effectively, verbal explanations, demonstrations, *and* varied direct contact with the skill, prior to practice teaching, are needed. It is in practice teaching and later that polish is achieved.

## How Does Repetitive Practice Contribute to Acquisition of Skills?

A basic skill must be repeated often for the purpose of refining or developing precision. The *situation* within which it is performed, however, is *varied* as often as possible. This variation not only avoids monotony and thereby facilitates sustained interest, but more importantly it enhances the likelihood of transfer of the skill to related situations. Let us take an example from the area of mental skills. A group of students in a beginning Spanish class could practice speaking the vocabulary by discussing a topic in class; they might visit the Spanish consul's office; they might take an imaginary trip to some South American country; or they could invite two or three Chicanos to class. The vocabulary drill is similar in all situations, but the situations have been varied.

Although repetitive practice is essential in the perfection of a skill, enforced practice may have no positive effect. The pupil must see its importance in terms of his or her own goals. Self-motivated practice leads to gradual improvement of a skill through *revision of details.* Following a period of accelerated learning that results from early practice sessions, many learners reach a *plateau* in which relatively little progress is obvious. This probably indicates a need for a more thorough understanding of the relationship of certain details to the total skill. At this point added encouragement and direction from the teacher are extremely useful. An individual chart that shows the individual's own progress tends to contribute to continued interest and improvement.

Practice or repetition can become monotonous very quickly, even under the most favorable circumstances. When the individual practices for a purpose that is very important to him, motivation can remain high for long periods of time. Too frequently, however, classroom problems are more remote to the learner than might be desirable. The very nature of the materials sometimes accounts for this difficulty. Drill, connected with important terminology, sequences of events, and the like may be important but not in itself very interesting. Short games offer excellent opportunities in certain areas in which practice would tend to become monotonous. The psychological damage that results from such games as the old-time spelling bees need not be present if due caution is observed. Conditions can be created in which winning is not essential.

## What Preplanning Is Necessary?

Development of motor skills has long been a familiar aspect of formal education. The technique is relatively easy to apply simply because the learner quickly becomes overtly active. The individual asks questions; difficulties can be observed and corrected as the skill is developed.

In the realm of mental skills, however, the task is much more complicated. Although the *processes* are comparable, there are fewer observable activities that are useful for effective guidance. While memorization is frequently stressed (sometimes inappropriately), seldom are memory techniques provided.

The illustrated lesson plan that follows can be applied to the development of mental skills in general, whether they be in the area of foreign language, drama, music, language selections, or mathematics.

# LESSON PLAN FOR DEVELOPMENT OF MENTAL SKILLS

**Subject:**  Foreign Language

**Problem:**  How can we best acquire vocabulary skills?

**Goals:**  After this lesson the student should have furthered his skill in aural-oral language techniques, as evidenced by:

1.  His ability to pronounce correctly selected exercises provided by the teacher.
2.  His ability independently to recreate a variety of language patterns.
3.  His ability to detect his own language problems by comparing his speech habits with those of imitated models.

**Lesson Approach:**

Learning a foreign language involves a series of steps, similar to those we follow when learning a motor skill, like playing tennis. It is extremely important that you follow the steps as outlined. You should concentrate on the task just as you would if you were learning to play tennis, for example.

**Lesson Development:**

I.  **Development of Initial Understanding:** (Listening-Comprehension)

This group of exercises is designed to help you understand the spoken language. It involves four basic steps: (List)

**Step 1.**  Material presented at a normal rate of speech.
**Step 2.**  Material repeated slightly faster.
**Step 3.**  Questions presented with pauses for the student to think of the answer. Correct answer then presented, following the pause.
**Step 4.**  Material repeated a third time.

From the following example, it will be noted that the questions emphasize concepts rather than minute details. (The conversational parts of the exercise would be presented in the foreign language involved.)

We are in Paris. Paul is talking to a policeman. Let's approach and hear what they are saying.

Excuse me, officer.
Yes, sir.
Where is the nearest post office?

Straight ahead to your left.
How far is it?
About three minutes' walk.

Now let's listen to them again. (Dialogue is repeated at a faster rate.)
Now you will hear three questions. After each question there will be a silent pause in which you will have time to think of the answer. Do not say the answer; just formulate it mentally. Then you will hear the correct answer to check your understanding.

What did Paul want to know? (pause—for student to think the answer)
He asked for the nearest post office.
Was the post office near or far? (pause) It was very near. Just three minutes' walk.
Was the post office to the left? (pause) No, it was straight ahead.
Now let's listen once again to Paul and the policeman in Paris. (Dialogue follows for the third time.)

**II. Initial Practice:** (Mimicry-Memorization)

This group of exercises is designed to aid you in developing correct pronunciation and intonation. It consists of short, oral dialogues, including the following steps: (List)

**Step 1.**  A four-to-six-line group is presented five to ten times in succession.
**Step 2.**  Each line is repeated at least three times, each time with a pause for repetition.
**Step 3.**  The four-to-six-line group is presented again in its entirety. Student repeats the group once.
**Step 4.**  When all the four-to-six-line groups composing the dialogue have been presented and practiced, as indicated in Steps 1, 2, and 3, the entire dialogue is reviewed, each sentence being heard once and repeated once by the student.

The example that follows is based on an analysis by Holton and others:

Listen, without repeating.
Can't you come along?
Sorry, I can't.
Well, then, some other time.
I hope so.
(Student hears the same dialogue several times more without repeating.)
Now listen and repeat.
Can't you come along? (pause) Can't you come along? (pause) Can't you come along? (pause)
Sorry, I can't. (pause) Sorry, I can't. (pause) Sorry, I can't. (pause)
Well, then, some other time. (pause) Well, then, some other time. (pause) Well, then, some other time. (pause)
I hope so. (pause) I hope so. (pause) I hope so. (pause)
Listen and repeat once more. Listen and repeat a third time.
Can't you come along? (pause)
Sorry, I can't. (pause)
Well, then, some other time. (pause)
I hope so. (pause)

Present entire group again in its entirety. Then you are to repeat the group once.
Now let us review the entire dialogue or selection (containing several four-to-six-line groups). You will hear and then repeat each sentence once.

### III.   Varied (Creative) Practice:

This group of exercises will help you bridge the gap between memorization of models and free conversation. They will help you recreate a variety of patterns (situations) *without* the help of a model immediately preceding. Every exercise will require you to change one element only. The following steps should be observed.

**Step 1.**   Saturation practice with at least five models. Student listens and repeats both the problem and solution.

**Step 2.**   Student hears a cue and attempts to provide the appropriate response.

**Step 3.**   Student hears the correct response and repeats it.

The following example involves pattern mutation:

I know George. (pause) I know him. (pause) (Four other similar models given as saturation practice)

| I know George. | I know her. | I know him. | I know him. |
|---|---|---|---|
| (Cue from master) | (Incorrect response) | (Correct response from master) | (Student repeats correct response) |

(It should be noted that there are four basic types of creative practice exercises: pattern recreation, pattern mutation, pattern rearrangement, and vocabulary building.)

### Deriving Generalizations

Now compare your speech habits with those of the perfect models imitated. (Use recorded mimicry-memorization exercises.)

What problems do you detect? Make a list of them for future reference.

The foregoing plan for mental skill development assumes use of recorded exercises. In the language laboratory, for example, each student has a separate booth and may have a separate set of exercises. If this is the case the teacher merely sets the stage and plugs in on the experience from time to time.

The sequence of experiences is based upon much careful investigation in the area of skills development. It is equally applicable to the development of motor skills.

# VALUES

Drill or practice is the basic instructional method for acquisition of mental and motor skills.

The individualistic nature of the method is conducive to direct pupil involvement. Especially in the motor skills area interest is easily maintained.

Drill or practice, when spaced appropriately, can reduce the rate of forgetting and contribute to continued development of the skill.

Practice develops habits. Thus desirable habits developed during the adolescent years tend to become a part of one's life style.

# LIMITATIONS AND PROBLEMS

Drill or practice in the cognitive domain often is inappropriate. It is in this realm that the method has been widely misused.

Since early drill or practice is largely exploratory, diagnosis is essential. Misguided drill or practice may impede appropriate skill development.

In the early stages of skill development accuracy rather than speed is emphasized. Skill development being largely individualistic in nature, it is sometimes difficult to achieve this balance.

Repetitive drill or practice may become monotonous unless a variable learning environment is provided.

Overlearning in the latter stages of skill development is desirable. Since the degree of overlearning will depend somewhat upon the learner's purpose, it may be difficult to work out appropriate practice sessions with each individual learner.

# ILLUSTRATED DRILL OR PRACTICE TECHNIQUES

I.  Useful in any motor skills area

    *Videotaped explorations*
    Set up your class into five-minute microteaching sessions. (This assumes basic understanding of the rudiments of the skill.) Provide opportunities for students to select either a progressive or a repetitive task sequence.

    Immediately following the experience, replay for study and analysis. Have the student critique himself in terms of delivery, continuity and sequences, specific techniques and styles used. Finally, ask the student to identify different ways of performing key phases of the experience. (This tends to expand thinking, thereby encouraging new insights in the area.)

II. Useful in foreign language (or almost any mental skills area)

    If, as has been emphasized in this chapter, mental skill development involves a form of mechanical problem solving, the traditional drill procedure may need to be lengthened.[4]

    A.  The teacher reads aloud the first line of the drill (often about four or five lines long) plus the cue word for the next line.
        *Model Sentence:* The chair is in the room.
                 *Cue:* table
            *Response:* The table is in the room.
                 *Cue:* book
                        etc.
        (Students repeat several times as they individually copy the model.)

---

[4] For a thorough analysis of how this process is related to transactional psychology the reader is referred to Earl W. Stevick, "The Meaning of Drills and Exercises," *Language Learning* 24 (June 1974): 1–22.

B. Students provide sentences from the drill in any order without cues.

C. Students take turns suggesting sentences that are grammatically similar to those in the drill but which contain other vocabulary.

D. Students use sentences derived from the foregoing steps that hopefully will draw reactions from the teacher or other students.[5]

Such an experience tends to make drill sessions less teacher-centered and has the advantage of encouraging pupil reflection, thereby broadening and expanding original learning.

III. Drill teams (both mental and motor skills areas)

The individual nature of drill provides an excellent opportunity for the use of student drill teams (in both mental and motor skills areas).

After the basic rudiments are understood, gross body movements follow. The participant must progress through a stage of "shaping" body movements or vocal patterns. Another student (who possesses basic understanding) can be extremely useful in providing much needed feedback and diagnosis.

Following short practice sessions and critiques (perhaps repeated once), the roles of the team members are switched. The technique permits the instructor to concentrate on common problems and unusual difficulties as he or she moves from one drill team to another.

IV. Use of games (both mental and motor skills areas)

Games in connection with the teaching of motor skills are so common that it is often difficult to think of them in any other context. Oddly enough, games as a vehicle for teaching mental skills have been strangely neglected even though the basic instructional method is the same for both mental and motor skills.

A. Useful in foreign language, business, or mathematics

Set up a party in a foreign country. Assign students specific roles, such as hosts and hostesses, visiting celebrities, young and old adults, children, etc. Have each participant plan an aspect of conversation that will offer a challenge to others.

Set up a mock business where shorthand must be taken (and dictated) under a variety of trying conditions. Include typists who must prepare manuscripts under a variety of pressure situations. Likewise include office workers and other personnel who might be found in any large business firm.

Develop a mock business firm that employs skilled mathematicians, accountants, tax specialists, and sales personnel. With imagination roles can be established for a variety of skill levels.

B. Useful in industrial arts, vocational agriculture, and home economics

Turn the school shop into an imaginary industrial shop. Accept a variety of orders from customers in the local area. Contract these jobs out to students, depending upon various skill levels. (Such a "game" will not only spark considerable interest but result in a wide range of projects.) If additional equipment is needed or additional skills must be developed, make the necessary arrangements as would be expected in any such firm.

[5] *Ibid.*, pp. 16–17.

If individuals are to be successful farmers they must have direct experience in many of the varied roles needed. Some schools have managed to establish demonstration farms both for future farmers and as a living demonstration for actual farmers in the area. With a little planning and imagination most of the needed land and supplies sometimes can be obtained for nominal cost from interested local farmers and public agencies. (Surplus property from federal projects represents an additional source.)

A home economics class can be divided into different types and sizes of families. Family living, meal preparation, sewing, budgeting, and many other aspects of family life can be included in the "game." Such an arrangement eliminates many sources of monotony and adds realism to class projects.

CHAPTER **24**

# Measurement and Evaluation Techniques and Devices

## OVERVIEW

### Key Concepts

1. A valid test must be reliable; a reliable test, however, may not be valid.
2. Specific behavioral outcomes, derived from instructional goals and basic concepts, provide the basis for measurement and evaluation.
3. Tests generally should emphasize the higher levels of cognition. (See Chapter 2.)
4. Multiple-choice items tend to be superior to other test items.
5. Test-taking behavior involves definite skills that may have a marked impact on test scores.

### New Terms

1. **Measurement**—A quantitative amount of some experience, such as a test score.
2. **Evaluation**—The quality of an experience, often based upon some measure.
3. **Validity**—The trustworthiness of a measure. For example: "Does it measure what it is supposed to measure?"
4. **Reliability**—The consistency of scores on a given measuring instrument.
5. **Situational Test Item**—An item that thrusts the student into a contrived situation. Designed to determine how well learnings may be applied.
6. **Performance Test Item**—An item that requires the learner to actually do (perform) a specified skill.

7. **Modified or Qualified Test Item**—Usually a supplementary item so designed as to probe depth of understanding or frame of reference.
8. **Subjective Test Item**—An item open to more than one type of response, based upon the frame of reference of the individual involved.
9. **Objective Test Item**—An item that can be scored objectively.
10. **Item Analysis**—A technique for determining which test items do and do not contribute to reliability.
11. **Criterion-referenced Measures**—Interpreting achievement in terms of a predetermined standard (criterion) of performance, without reference to level of performance of other members of the class. This may include both mastery and developmental measures.
12. **Norm-referenced Measures**—Interpreting achievement in terms of an individual's position relative to other members of the class.
13. **Minimum Essentials Measures**—Those criterion-referenced measures used to assess mastery or competence in specifically defined areas. Such measures are usually most appropriate in the skills areas; a minimum passing score of from 85 to 90 percent is usually established to allow for sampling and personal errors.
14. **Developmental Measures**—Those criterion-referenced measures used to assess a class of behaviors (often in the cognitive domain) that represent achievement beyond the minimum essentials level. Due to the complexity of such goals, degree of achievement is all that can be expected, often necessitating a norm-referenced assessment.

### Questions to Guide Your Study

1. What functions are served through classroom measurement?
2. Measurement and evaluation have been described as the weakest aspect of the instructional process. Why?
3. "Inasmuch as memory and recall are necessarily involved in the higher levels of cognition, recall test items are not necessary." Defend or refute.
4. Why are modified or qualified test items recommended?
5. "The nature of test item expected determines the nature of the learning experience." Defend or refute.
6. It has been said that objective test items are not objective. Explain.
7. "Mastery (minimum essentials) test items tend to be at the lower levels of cognition." Defend or refute.

The evening was hot and the hour was late. Mr. Becker heaved a sigh of relief as the last parent left his American history classroom. "These open houses for parents are always quite a strain," he thought as he filed the last of the student folders. Each parent had in effect asked the same question: "How is my Johnny doing in American history class?" As Mr. Becker reflected on his responses he heard himself saying:

"He's doing fine. In fact, he made one of the highest grades on our midterm examination."

"The boy is experiencing a little difficulty in concentration. You will notice from his responses on this test that his answers are often vague and sometimes a bit farfetched."

"Johnny appears to be confusing some of the important facts. You will notice here that he was not sure of the basic causes of World War I."

"Mary is a quiet girl, but she does well on tests. I would say she is doing outstanding work."

Mr. Becker's experience is repeated in much the same manner in thousands of schools throughout this country. Parents want to know "how well Johnny is doing." The instructor reports he is "doing fine" or "not doing so well" on the basis of a test or tests. Both parties may feel a bit dissatisfied with the experience, but lack the ability to analyze the situation. Most of the assumptions implied in Mr. Becker's responses indicate sources of error that can render measurement and evaluation much less effective than expected:

1. Mr. Becker seemed to be confusing measurement with evaluation. Although the two processes are related, evaluation includes much more than assessment of test performance.
2. By alluding to facts, such as the causes of World War I, Mr. Becker appeared to equate factual retention with learning. Although facts are indeed essential in the learning process, they more appropriately serve as means to ends rather than as ends in themselves.
3. Neither the parents nor Mr. Becker displayed evidence of understanding the meaning of specific, observable outcomes of learning. While test performance is considered *one* important observable product of learning, other behavioral evidences of goal fulfillment are also important.
4. Mr. Becker seemed to be measuring a student's progress wholly on the basis of the progress of other students in class. Most teachers are aware of the extremely wide variation in abilities among students. Yet, these same teachers often will measure and evaluate student progress on the assumption that all have an equal chance. A score of 80 by one student might represent "high" performance while the same score by another might represent "low" performance.
5. Mr. Becker, in his concept of evaluation, seemed to be neglecting certain important intangible factors, such as attitudes and opinions, critical thinking ability, mental health, work and study habits, and social skills. Such intangibles can be measured by translating goals into expected behavioral outcomes.

Tests are designed to provide the teacher with a quantitative measure of some experience. The quality of a test, on the other hand, is an assessment of the value of the quantity being measured. Since evaluation, to a substantial degree, is based upon the tests that teachers themselves produce, this chapter is designed specifically for those who desire to improve the quality of test items. It is recognized that other measurement and evaluation tools, such as rating scales, checklists, and anecdotal records, must be used in conjunction with tests.

# FUNDAMENTAL PROPERTIES

The quality of any test rests upon a number of basic properties, some of which relate to the purposes being served. Some understanding of the properties, treated in this section, is essential if the teacher is to profit fully from the techniques offered in the latter portion of this chapter.

## What Is the Place for Concept Application?

Learning for what? This is a basic question that every teacher must ask himself repeatedly. Teachers and students quite naturally become engrossed in the content details of subject matter. A mere acquisition of specific facts, however, may provide a rather poor means of assessing the usefulness of the learning experience. It has been established that students quickly forget specific details. They may remember basic concepts (big ideas), however, for an indefinite period of time. (Refer to Chapter 1, "Gaining the Concept.") Basic concepts, then, become the fundamental ingredients for subsequent experiences. Many test items are designed to determine if such concepts can be applied appropriately in related situations.

## What Role Do Behavioral Objectives Play?

As indicated in Chapter 2, behavioral outcomes set the stage for instructional and evaluational activities. Once a basic concept has been reworded as an instructional goal, the teacher is able to predict (in terms of actual behavior) terminal behaviors and products of the learner. Tests are valuable tools for making an assessment of that which is learned. If, for example, an electronics student should be able to construct a radio transmitter out of common household items after he has been exposed to certain class experiences, a performance test (with certain items supplied) would become a suitable means of determining achievement. Another evidence of achievement might be one's ability to recognize complete circuits. In this case, a situational multiple-choice item could be employed.

## How Are Reflective Processes Involved?

It seems reasonable to assume that a substantial portion of school learning is based upon a more-or-less orderly process of critical or reflective thinking. In short, an individual when confronted with a difficulty will assess the situation in terms of the available facts, will consider possible solutions or courses of action to take, and will finally select or act upon the solution that seems most compatible with the data available. Instructional methods are viewed as different approaches to the reflective process. In assessing one's ability to apply that which is learned, then, selected reflective or problem-solving situations must be developed. They may be new to the individual but involve application of definite concepts gained from the educational experience.

## What Is Validity?

A valid test is one that measures what it is supposed to measure. If, for example, ten major concepts have been identified and emphasized during a unit, the test must be based upon these concepts. While it is appropriate to include some items dealing with specific facts pertaining to concepts, major emphasis must be focused on the learner's ability to *use* the concepts in related situations. Generally the number of test items pertaining to any given concept should approximate its relative emphasis during the instructional program. If, for example, three class periods were given to one concept while a single class period was devoted to a second concept, three times as much test emphasis might be placed on the first concept.

## What Is Meant by Reliability?

Every teacher is concerned with the trustworthiness or consistency of his test results. Does Johnny's poor mark, for example, indicate a general lack of understanding in the area, or might it merely reflect errors due to chance and poor test items? How much would his score change if the test were administered several times without the influence of his previous test experiences?

Although it is impossible to eliminate all chance error, a simple item analysis will reveal those sources of inconsistency due to poor and/or ambiguous items. An accurate index of item difficulty and discrimination can be obtained by determining how well a given item is related to success on the test as a whole. The most accurate procedure entails contrasting the responses of the highest 27 percent of the examinees with the lowest 27 percent. The procedure is long and laborious, however. It is possible, nevertheless, to conduct an item analysis in ten to twenty minutes by using students. This slightly different procedure, as described by Paul B. Diederich,[1] involves separating test papers into top and bottom *halves*. Use of test *halves* renders small and fuzzier differences, since some papers will fall into one or the other half by chance. On the other hand, the procedure has the practical value of involving *all* students while the analysis is being made. (The top and bottom *quarters* analysis leaves one-half of the class idle during the procedure.)

The difference between the high and low *halves* should be 10 percent, i.e., 10 percent more of the top half should respond correctly to an item than those in the bottom half. In a class of forty students, for example, at least four more students in the top half than in the bottom half should select the correct response. The minimum acceptable high-low difference of 10 percent (for halves only) is accurate for the *middle range* of item difficulty, i.e., if a total of from 25 to 75 percent of the students make correct responses to the item. This approximation is reasonably accurate until one reaches items that fewer than 20 percent or more than 80 percent of the class answered correctly. In a class of forty students the 20 to 80 percent range (for which the 10 percent discrimination difference is reasonably accurate) would fall between eight and thirty-two students. Any difference of four or more within this range would be reasonably acceptable. As

[1] Educational Testing Service, *Short-Cut Statistics for Teacher-Made Tests,* Bulletin no. 5 (Princeton, New Jersey, 1960), p. 7.

noted earlier, most items that fall outside this range would be too hard or too easy.

By separating test papers on the basis of scores, equally between the upper half and the lower half, and passing them to the right half and the left half of the students in the room, the teacher is ready to conduct his item analysis. He will want to obtain four figures for each item, labeled and defined as follows:

H = the number of "highs" who got the item correct
L = the number of "lows" who got the item correct
H + L = "SUCCESS" − total number who got the item correct
H − L = "DISCRIMINATION" − the high-low difference

As the teacher calls out the item number, he may have selected students count the show of hands for him and do the necessary adding and subtracting.

A teacher will soon discover that the high-low difference for some of the items will be zero or negative. This indicates that the better students are doing no better, or perhaps worse, on an item than the poorer students. An inspection of the item will often reveal the cause. Accordingly, the item can be improved prior to its use on a subsequent test. Eventually one may be able to build up quite a reservoir of *discriminating* test items.

There may be two or three items on a test that did not discriminate satisfactorily for no apparent reason. When there is time, a teacher may want to subject these to a second stage of item analysis (assuming a multiple-choice item). This may be accomplished by determining how many of the "highs" chose each response and then how many of the "lows" chose each response. Thus a response that tended to confuse the "highs" may be easily identified. Perhaps this group suspected a trap or thought it too obvious.

### What Is Meant by Objectivity?

A test item is said to be objective if it is clearly stated. Most words have several meanings. Therefore, it is important for a teacher to clarify intended meanings so that students will understand the question in the same way. Both essay- and objective-type items run the risk of being misunderstood. The qualified essay item described later in this chapter may greatly increase objectivity. Likewise, modified multiple-choice and true-false items enable the student to indicate his particular frame of reference when responding to the item.

Another aspect of objectivity is associated with scoring procedure. Use of a scoring key reduces the effect of personal bias. A scoring key usually consists of a copy of the test with an indication of the acceptable responses and the various weights to be assigned to each item.

### What Should Be the Difficulty Range of Items?

The difficulty range of criterion-referenced items used to determine mastery level must be interpreted quite differently from that of norm-referenced and criterion-referenced items or tests at the developmental level. In the former, student achievement is assessed in terms of type of behavior or performance a student is capable of demonstrating. Level of performance, usually predetermined, is stated as a part of each instructional goal and behavioral outcome. In this manner an absolute standard (*criterion*) is established for assessing an individual's achievement. *One's position relative to other students in class is not a factor.* In testing for minimum essentials, mastery within reasonable limits is expected. Thus a spread of scores is not expected. The difficulty of a test item (or task) should correspond to the difficulty of the performance task described in the specific learning outcome.

Difficulty range becomes an important concept in all norm-referenced and criterion-referenced measures at the developmental level. Here one is interested in the student's relative standing in class. Achievement is assessed in terms of how the learner compares with the achievement of other students in class. Thus a spread of scores becomes important. Since complete mastery is not expected, a range of item difficulty is needed if one is to assess relative degree of progress toward a given objective.

It has been established that norm-referenced items chosen for maximum discrimination will tend to have a difficulty value of approximately 50 percent, i.e., one out of two students will respond incorrectly to the item. Allowing for chance clues and the like, the point of maximum discrimination usually is placed slightly higher. Although an item ideally will be answered correctly by 50 to 60 percent of the students, it may be desirable to include a few easy items (for encouragement) and a few hard items for the purpose of discriminating among top students. Since a few "easy" items, along with a few "hard" ones, are included, the minimum level of about 70 percent is usually considered a "passing" level.

## What Time Limitations Should Be Observed?

Tests are of two types with respect to time: power and speed. A *power* test provides the student with ample time to respond to all items, whereas a *speed* test limits the amount of time allowed for separate sections and/or the total test time. Most teacher-made tests are designed as power tests. In attempting to include as many items as possible within the limits of a class period, tests are sometimes too long for weaker students. Thus a power test, in effect, becomes a speed test for *some* students. Such a condition may produce unreliable test results.

In those areas in which criterion-referenced items can be used, the problem becomes especially critical. A representative sample of a student's performance within a given area is necessary. If a complex of skills is involved (as in mathematics) each separate skill must be adequately tested. Gronlund[2] suggests as a rule of thumb that at least ten items for each instructional objective be in-

[2] Norman E. Gronlund, *Preparing Criterion-Referenced Tests for Classroom Instruction* (New York: The Macmillan Co., 1973), p. 14.

cluded. Thus in order to keep such tests of reasonable length subunit tests, involving a week or two of class time, may become necessary.

### What Functions Do Tests Serve?

Tests can serve a variety of purposes that contribute to the learning process. Perhaps the least used but potentially the most valuable is the *pretest.* A pretest can be extremely useful in assessing the learner's readiness for the material to be learned. If, for example, one does not possess the needed entry level skills he has little chance of success until such skills have been mastered. Likewise, a pretest reveals those portions of an instructional unit that students have already mastered. A pretest also can serve as a baseline from which to assess an individual's progress. For most pretests an individual's relative standing with his peers is not important.

Tests perhaps serve their greatest function as an instructional activity for *improving learning.* Often known as *formative testing,* such tests may be administered at intervals throughout a given unit. Such tests may be self-administered; sometimes they take the form of open book tests. Occasionally a teacher may administer a test that parallels a regular unit test but then permits students to grade their own papers. If basic essentials are involved the test may be repeated until mastery is achieved.

*Diagnostic tests* are somewhat similar to formative tests. They are representative of the various tasks involved but feature especially the common errors that students make. It is essential that these errors be analyzed in terms of degree of complexity. Thus such tests tend to be somewhat longer than the typical formative test.

Tests given at the end of a unit or course for the purpose of assigning grades are often called *summative tests.* Such tests may consist of both mastery and developmental level items, separated into two parts and arranged by instructional objective. Where it is necessary to report test performance in terms of letter grades, Gronlund suggests the following:

A—Achieved all mastery objectives and *high* on developmental objectives
B—Achieved all mastery objectives and *low* on developmental objectives
C—Achieved all mastery objectives only

Students who fail the mastery portion of the test are recycled through the instructional process until mastery has been achieved. If recycling is not possible, letter grades of D and E can be assigned to such students.

### What Test-taking Behaviors Are Important?

As indicated, teachers who would establish test validity must follow a carefully outlined procedure. This entails testing in terms of instructional goals and anticipated behavioral outcomes. Test items will be so constructed as to emphasize the higher levels of thinking. If the student is unable to *demonstrate* the extent of his learning, however, the best test is of no avail. In order to minimize this hazard appropriate test-taking behaviors must be emphasized. As in any other aspect of learning, there are certain essential skills involved.

In the first place there is no substitute for thoroughness. This, above all else, tends to eliminate "examination panic." By following the SQ4R method of study described on pp. 235-36 and then distributing review sessions evenly throughout the week preceding the examination, one is likely to not only know his material but *feel that he knows it as well.*

Some students, mistakenly, associate thoroughness with "cramming," e.g., spending long hours the night before the examination going over and over the materials. On the contrary, the evidence clearly indicates that cramming is not a desirable procedure; instead, one should probably stop studying the day prior to the test. Daily working, eating, and sleeping habits should be continued as usual.

In addition to thoroughness, security is enhanced by carrying one's notebook to the examination *without opening it.* As Smith[3] points out, this has the effect of assuring oneself that he could check a question if he needed to (prior to the examination, of course). Smith also recommends that one should avoid the temptation of discussing points with other students just prior to the experience. *Panic is contagious!*

One most appropriately responds to *objective test items* by working directly through them, answering first those that he obviously knows. Those items that pose some uncertainty should be checked and answered tentatively (in a separate place). Those that are confusing or apparently not known should be checked for later reference (in a different manner than uncertain items). Above all, one should avoid pondering over such items during the first time he works through the test.

After responding to the items he knows, the test-taker rereads those items he thinks he knows and compares his answers with his first impressions. (The first impression is often best.) Finally, he grapples with those items that baffle him. It often helps to reword the question in one's own words and then compare it with the original version. Many times confusion is a result of misreading the item.

Since words often carry many meanings, one must avoid thinking too hard about an item or its alternatives. Bright students especially tend to read meaning into items that was never intended. For those items that remain in the "unknown" category, one can usually increase his chances by looking for test clues. A foil (alternative) that is longer or shorter than the other choices is often the correct one. In addition, such qualifying words as *usually* or *sometimes* tend to denote correct choices; whereas such words as *always* or *never* suggest incorrect ones.

In responding to essay items one should set up a time schedule, allowing a few minutes at the end. He should write until his allotted time is up and then

---

[3] Donald E. P. Smith, gen. ed., *Learning to Learn* (New York: Harcourt, Brace and World, Inc., 1961), p. 42.

move to the next item. (Six incomplete answers usually will receive more credit than three complete ones.) He appropriately reads through all test items prior to writing out any answers. As he does this, answers that come to mind should be denoted with key words, designed to provide cues for later reference.

As with confusing objective items, one should put confusing essay items in his own words and then compare them with the original. This materially increases his chances of deriving intended meaning. It also helps to briefly outline a proposed answer and then expand this outline as one answers the item. This not only contributes to thoroughness and accuracy, but it also tends to create a favorable mind set with the evaluator. The practice of beginning an answer with the hope that the right cues will somehow appear is wasteful and usually unproductive. Finally, one should check for misspelled words, grammatical errors, and misleading and/or dogmatic or very definite statements. In emphasizing the importance of qualified answers, Smith points out, "It is better to say 'Toward the end of the 19th Century' than to say 'In 1894' when you can't remember whether it's 1884 or 1894."[4] If the test contains both essay and objective items, the essay items should be answered first.

Adequate test-taking skills often make the difference between letter grades; they sometimes make the difference between passing and failing. For the teacher who is interested in increasing validity of test results, test-taking skills are of utmost importance.

# TECHNIQUES OF MEASUREMENT

The construction of effective class tests demands careful attention to content, purpose, and level of goal achievement expected. Thus testing procedures vary considerably. Those which follow, however, should provide the teacher with a useful guide that is consistent with the other instructional strategies presented in this book.

### How Are Concepts and Goals Identified?

If the instructional process rests upon basic unit concepts (as advocated in this book), testing procedures, likewise, must be based upon such a foundation. The reader will recall that the first step in the instructional process is concept identification. Each unit concept (usually six to ten per unit) provides a basis for development of unit goals, with their accompanying behavioral outcomes. As illustrated in Chapter 2, "Establishing Instructional Objectives," the outcomes are usually more useful as guides to instruction than as guides to evaluation. When behavioral outcomes are first identified, the instructor is quite naturally most interested in those *intermediate* behaviors which indicate *progress toward*

---

[4] Smith, *op. cit.*, p. 43.

goal achievement and concept attainment. To illustrate the point, the goal illustration used in Chapter 2 has been reproduced.

> After this unit in American literature the student should further appreciate the social inequalities resulting from a social class structure, as evidenced by (1) his realistic *responses* in a class discussion on the problem "What should be the United States's policy with respect to migrant workers?" (2) his willingness to examine feeling reactions resulting from a sociodrama designed to portray feelings in a specified social situation, and (3) his greater cooperation with underprivileged students in class and society.

It will be noted that outcomes (1) and (2) are to be elicited *during* the instructional process. Although the third outcome is a *terminal* behavior, it can hardly be used for evaluational purposes in its present form.

Behavioral outcomes, to be most useful for evaluational purposes, must be redefined as *terminal* behaviors. Such behaviors must be much more explicit than the intermediate behaviors described in Chapter 2. The first outcome from the foregoing illustration, for example, reads: "his realistic responses in a class discussion on the problem: What should be the United States's policy with respect to migrant workers?" As a result of the class discussion, what specific outcomes might be expected? From such an experience one might expect (among other things) the learner to evaluate evidence in the area and to draw warranted conclusions from the evidence available. The unit concept, "A social class structure produces social inequalities," is used as a guide for constructing test items designed to determine how well the learner can evaluate evidence and draw warranted conclusions in the area. Likewise, the second outcome, concerned with the learner's willingness to examine feelings portrayed through a sociodramatic experience, must be more specifically stated for evaluational purposes. The instructor asks himself what such an examination of feelings might produce as terminal behaviors in the student. Perhaps it will be increased empathy or increased skill in interpersonal relationships in the area. Test items, and other evaluational tools, are then constructed for assessing progress in this direction. The third outcome, although already stated as a terminal behavior, must be more specifically qualified if it is to serve for evaluational purposes. (As a terminal behavior it does not directly serve instructional purposes.) Further refinement of the outcome can be achieved by specifying the important *conditions* under which "greater cooperation with underprivileged students" might be expected. One condition, for example, might include the learner's willingness to accept such students in specific group activities. Such an outcome is probably most appropriately evaluated through direct observation.

### How Are Instructional Objectives, Behavioral Outcomes, and the Content Outline Integrated?

Prior to actual construction of test items, one must assemble instructional unit goals (which are culminated with anticipated pupil behavioral outcome samples). Instructional goals, of course, are evolved from basic unit concepts.

All these are developed in preinstructional activities. They must be modified, however, on the basis of the actual instructional experience. Utilizing the Bloom taxonomy as a frame of reference, unit goals are listed from simple to complex.[5] The essential elements only are listed. The list that follows is illustrative only. The reader may want to identify his own major field by filling in the blank spaces provided.

Objectives for a Unit in _____

1. Knows important facts or terms
    a. Reproduces word meanings
    b. Matches terms that fit given definitions
    c. Uses terms correctly in describing _____ problems
2. Understands _____ principles
    a. Derives _____ concepts from provided class experiences
    b. Describes _____ principles in his own words
    c. Transposes _____ selections into his own language
    d. Points out the relationship among _____ principles
3. Applies _____ principles to related situations
    a. Identifies the _____ factors needed to solve a practical problem
    b. Relates practical life problems to the _____ principles involved
    c. Uses _____ correctly in selected problem situations
    d. Predicts the probable outcomes of an activity involving _____ principles
4. Interprets _____ data
    a. Distinguishes between facts and assumptions
    b. Formulates appropriate problems from provided data
    c. Identifies bias in provided data
    d. Differentiates between essential concepts and related details
5. Synthesizes _____ concepts
    a. Derives hypotheses from provided data
    b. Compiles the essential properties from selected class experiences
    c. Reconstructs basic _____ concepts from provided materials
    d. Creates a new story, formula, music selection, etc., from provided data
6. Evaluates the adequacy of _____ principles
    a. Justifies his point of view, based upon sound _____ principles
    b. Compares contrasting views within a given context
    c. Appraises the adequacy of data
    d. Derives logical conclusions from provided data

Although a completed outline of instructional objectives applies generally to the subject matter of a course, it does not describe specific content material. Under the objective of *knowing*, for example, the specific terms to be reproduced are not identified. As Gronlund points out, this makes it possible to apply

[5] Benjamin S. Bloom, ed., *Taxonomy of Educational Objectives, Handbook 1: The Cognitive Domain* (New York: David McKay Co., Inc., 1956).

such an outline to various subject areas and thus to various units within a given course.[6]

The reader will recall (pp. 29-30) that some authorities insist that behavioral outcomes must specify the conditions under which the behavior is to be exhibited and the minimum level of performance expected. It was pointed out that such a procedure is desirable for *minimum essentials* but that it is not appropriate for *developmental outcomes*. The foregoing outline is representative of the latter. Although items designed to test for *minimum essentials* may be included in the same instrument, they must be evaluated separately as indicated in the chapter that follows.

The next step in preparation for a test is to develop a table in which the instructional objectives are related to the basic concepts of the unit. These concepts will correspond to those which were developed for instructional purposes. They must be modified in light of actual experience, however. Table 24-1 is based upon the concepts developed in the illustrated teaching unit offered in Appendix A.

The identified concepts represent the major content emphasis, while the instructional objectives correspond to the six categories of Bloom's taxonomy.[7] The numbers in each cell suggest the number of items to be prepared at that level for each concept. The reader will note that emphasis is placed upon the higher levels of cognition. If instructional methodology is based upon processes of reflective thinking (as assumed in this book), this is a valid point of emphasis. Moreover, it must be remembered that the higher objectives necessarily involve attainment of the lower ones. The total number of items in each column indicates the relative emphasis to be given to each of the concepts. It is seen that concepts B and F are to receive the greatest emphasis in the test. This will roughly correspond to the emphasis placed upon each area during the instructional process.

## How Are Test Levels and Types Selected?

After the terminal behaviors for each unit concept have been explicitly identified, the instructor must decide which of these can best be examined through the use of test items. He then ascertains the level of goal achievement expected. By referring to Chapter 2 the reader will note that the cognitive domain contains six levels, the affective domain five, and the psychomotor domain four. The three domains range from the simple to the complex, and the lower-level objectives are each necessary to the attainment of each succeeding higher-level objective. In terms of the actual instructional experience(s), the teacher decides what level of goal attainment might be expected. If, for example, oral reports

[6] Norman E. Gronlund, *Stating Behavioral Objectives for Classroom Instruction* (New York: Macmillan Co., 1970), p. 40.

[7] Progress toward affective goals is usually best measured by actual behavior records. This will involve various techniques of observation, e.g., rating scales, checklists, and anecdotal records.

**TABLE 24–1.** Table of specifications for a sixty-item test on a unit in general business (Sales Promotion and Advertising)

| Content Areas | Instructional Objectives | | | | | | Total |
|---|---|---|---|---|---|---|---|
| | 1<br>Knows Basic Terms | 2<br>Understands Concepts and Principles | 3<br>Applies Principles | 4<br>Interprets Data | 5<br>Synthesizes Principles | 6<br>Evaluates Principles | |
| A. Customer satisfaction is the most important product. | 1 | 4 | 3 | | | | 8 |
| B. Customer needs are the prompters for purchasing decisions. | | | 5 | 5 | 4 | 2 | 16 |
| C. Advertising can be an effective means of preselling products. | 2 | | 2 | 4 | | | 8 |
| D. Advertisements use customer motives that can be restated in the personal selling approach. | | 1 | 3 | | 3 | | 7 |
| E. The customer market is in a state of constant change and therefore requires continuous study to stay abreast of current developments. | 1 | 1 | | 2 | 3 | 2 | 9 |
| F. Sales appeals must be consistent with ethical standards of advertising. | 2 | | 4 | 3 | 3 | | 12 |
| Total number of test items | | | | | | | 60 |

were employed as the basic means of attaining a given concept, the teacher must judge how effective they were. If they were not as effective as anticipated, test items dealing with the specific concept(s) involved might be restricted to the knowledge or comprehension levels of the cognitive domain.

Identification of goal achievement level provides a sound basis for ascertaining the type of test item to be employed in each case. As indicated in the sections that follow, different test types correspond broadly to goal levels as identified in each of the three instructional domains.

## How Are Performance Test Items Constructed?

For many years one of the leading controversies in the area of test construction has focused on the level of item difficulty needed to determine progress toward goals. Some teachers have assumed that a knowledge of the essential facts in given areas should be sufficient evidence of goal achievement. Others, pointing out the wide gap between knowledge and application, have suggested that more than retention is needed. Although some indication of learning can be ascertained from how well one knows the facts, most teachers would readily agree that the best indication of learning is application in natural life situations.

In many areas, especially in the area of motor and mental skills, it is relatively easy to provide test situations that demand actual life applications of the concepts involved. The illustrations that follow suggest the wide applicability of performance test items to different areas of specialization.

- —adds fractions correctly
- —prepares and delivers persuasive speeches effectively
- —recognizes plant species in the local area
- —summarizes effectively
- —speaks in a foreign language
- —selects art objects that portray a given mood
- —plays music according to directions
- —analyzes current events in terms of selected concepts gleaned from history
- —types _____ words per minute with a maximum of two errors

It is evident from the foregoing illustrations that performance test items can be employed in most subject fields. In skills subjects, some tests may be entirely of the performance nature. Such items are relatively easy to construct once the desired application has been identified. The major task is to establish the conditions and criteria of acceptable performance. For example, how many plant species in the local area should a student be able to identify and under what conditions? How well must he speak a foreign language under what circumstances? How many words per minute should he type?

## How Are Situational Test Items Constructed?

Unfortunately, it is not always possible to measure behavioral changes directly. In the first place, the instructor may not have an opportunity to see each pupil in a realistic situation that demands a direct application of the learning involved. Frequently the outcome will not be applied to any real-life situation for several weeks or even months, simply because the learner will not find himself in a situation demanding such application. The teacher, in an effort to determine degree of understanding, will be obliged to resort to less direct measures. In such instances he can do no better than *simulate* an experience involving an appropriate application. In other words, he builds a realistic situation that demands an application of that which has been learned. For example, in a unit on first aid, one evidence of understanding the principles involved would probably be: "He recognizes and administers first aid properly in case of shock." It is impractical to induce a case of actual shock for test purposes; it is possible, however, to simulate or act out the experience. Since it is impossible objectively to evaluate such an experience for all thirty-five to forty students in a class, a written description of a realistic situation may be as close to reality as is possible. Thus one is measured on the basis of what he would *plan* to do in the situation rather than on his *actions* in the situation. Such a procedure obviously is a compromise with what is desired, because people do not always behave the way they plan to behave. For instance, in the foregoing illustration one might describe a fully adequate plan of action, whereas in the actual situation he might become hysterical and do nothing. Despite the exceptions, however, an indication of what one *thinks* he would do in a lifelike situation is a reasonably sound prediction of what he actually would do. For this very reason people plan ahead.

*Multiple-choice Test Item.* Learning has been described as, basically, that of resolving issues—both great and small. Testing, then, ideally would become an additional experience in the resolution of issues. The multiple-choice item can be readily adapted to the problem-solving situation. Many of man's most difficult problems involve the making of choices between known alternatives. The choices made in relatively simple problem situations often materially affect his degree of success and/or happiness in life. This is not greatly different from the problem of a student choosing between alternatives on a multiple-choice test item. The long test of time has convinced test constructors of the generally superior versatility and convenience of multiple-choice items. While other forms can be used effectively in special situations, the multiple-choice is more widely applicable and generally effective.

The multiple-choice question consists of an item stem and four or five responses, only one of which is the best answer. The other answers are usually referred to as foils or distractors. The item stem can be in the form of a direct question or an incomplete sentence. In essence, the item stem poses the problem situation and the possible answers represent the alternative solutions. The student "solves" the problem by making a choice. All of the foils or distractors should be plausible to those who lack the necessary understanding of the concept application involved. Some teachers include distractors that on the surface are all quite acceptable, i.e., they represent accurate statements. Only one of the possible answers is best, however, *in terms of the situation posed.* As a general frame of reference the possible answers should include one *preferred* answer; one distractor will represent a near miss; another will indicate a crude error; while the remaining distractors will tend to fall some place between those two extremes. Teachers sometimes make use of the distractors "'all of these" or "none of these." These responses can be used effectively only when the question calls for a highly specific answer that is either completely correct or incorrect.

There are likely to be a number of reasons why a student makes an inappropriate application to a multiple-choice test item. He could misunderstand the item stem or any one of the distractors; he could interpret the question in a unique way; or he simply may not possess an adequate understanding of the concepts necessary for the application. If the first two reasons are involved, the item is not valid for *that particular individual.* Sometimes a teacher desires to achieve greater validity by giving the student an opportunity to qualify or otherwise justify his answer. This enables the instructor to give credit for a choice that might have been justifiably selected *from the student's point of view,* even though it ordinarily would have been considered incorrect. Ultimately, however, the teacher must decide whether or not the reason given is sufficient to warrant either full or partial credit for the response.

A modified, situational form of the multiple-choice item is illustrated below.

*Subject:* Art

*Concept:* Color is derived from light.

*Item:*   A.  Suppose you were asked to paint a desert landscape that will convey the impression of intense heat, extreme aridity, and yet contain a "typical" beauty. How would you choose the colors you would use?
1. Hold your palette up close to the sand and then hold it close to a cactus in order to mix the exact colors of the objects you are painting.
2. Mix your colors according to directions in a book that gives precise formulae for mixing sky color, a desert color, and a cactus color.
3. Take a photograph of the desert and match the colors in the photograph.
4. Study the color of light reflected on the desert at various times of the day before deciding what colors you will use.
5. Study the color of the sand, the rocks, and several different varieties of cactus before deciding what colors you will use.

      B.  Defend your answer.

*Subject:* American literature

*Concept:* Realities of life are not always consistent with ideals.

*Item:*   Crèvecoeur's view of "The American Dream" indicated a concern for the people's ideals. Assuming that ideals can act as a force to help overcome harsh realities, which of the following would be most consistent with Crèvecoeur's views?
1. Setting our goals as high as possible to utilize the greatest force.
2. Accepting reality as it is, eliminating the stress of striving.
3. Setting concrete and absolute goals for which to strive.

4. Setting our goals at the upper limits of what is reasonable and attainable.

Indicate a reason for your choice consistent with the idea that ideals can be a force.

It should be noted that the second item is to be answered in terms of Crèvecoeur's views. Teachers sometimes err when they merely ask students to respond with no specific frame of reference indicated. This in effect forces the student to "outguess" the teacher. The correct answer, under such conditions, is based upon the opinion of the teacher only.

If it can be assumed that, during the instructional process, the teacher did not use the specific situation employed in the items, the test questions demand knowledge of the facts, *in addition to* application of basic ideas (concepts). Thus the student must "go the second mile" to respond properly to the questions. The "defend your answer" part of the items serves to probe, still further, one's depth of understanding.

*Essay Test Item.* Like the multiple-choice item, the essay item is readily adaptable to a specific situation. Unlike other test item types, it may elicit a detailed written response. The item can involve the making of complex relationships, the selection and organization of ideas, formulation of hypotheses, the logical development of arguments, and creative expression.

The essay item is particularly vulnerable to unreliability, discussed earlier. Unlike objective items, however, it is also subject to scorer unreliability. To some extent, a student's mark on such an item is dependent on the reader rather than on the actual quality of a response. Such weaknesses, however, can be minimized with due precautions.

The essay item can be substantially improved if it is so constructed as to elicit an application of learnings to new or different situations. Test reliability can be improved by giving hints concerning the structure of the answer expected. Sometimes this is called the *qualified* essay question. Illustrations of the *situational* essay, in which the answer is somewhat *qualified,* follow:

*Subject:* Art

*Concept:* Color is derived from light.

*Item:* Every color can be described in terms of physical properties: hue, value, and intensity. Discuss the color blue in terms of these properties.

*Subject:* United States history

*Concept:* Bitter feelings between individuals and nations (e.g., the Allies toward the Central Powers following World War I) make peaceful relationships difficult to establish and maintain.

*Item:* Wilson urged "peace without victory" at the Versailles Peace Conference. How does this statement reflect upon our relationships in the Middle East today? Be sure to tie in Wilson's statement to the attitudes and feelings of other members of the peace conference and relate your feelings to the situation in the Middle East today.

It should be noted that the second item not only asks the student to draw relationships, but he must also relate to current situations. This is especially difficult (but essential) in a subject such as history.

Scoring reliability is substantially improved by formulating an answer key in advance of marking the questions. Sometimes it is desirable to underline or otherwise call attention to key points. Students, likewise, may be asked to underline key phrases to call attention to important points. Scoring reliability can be increased if the student is not identified until *after* all items have been marked. This may be accomplished by asking him to enter his name on the back of his test paper. The practice of marking all students on each essay item before proceeding to the next one and completing the process without interruption also may greatly enhance one's scoring consistency.

### How Are Recall Items Constructed?

Sometimes teachers assume that if a person can recall the important facts in an area he will make actual applications when needed. Using an illustration cited earlier, one could assume that a student who could describe the symptoms and appropriate treatment for shock could be reasonably expected to apply that knowledge. It is assumed that the student will use such information to *plan* his actions and that he will *behave* according to his plans. There is considerable evidence, however, indicating a broad gap between *verbal* understanding and actual behavior experienced in the original learning situation.

*True-False Item.* The true-false item has lost much of its original popularity within recent years. There are many serious limitations associated with its use. Among the most serious is a tendency for the user to emphasize isolated facts that often hold slight validity in relation to the course objectives. Contrary to popular belief, the true-false item is so difficult to construct that it has little usefulness. This type of question tends to penalize the brighter student, as he is more likely to think of the exception that can alter the intended meaning. Furthermore, test makers tend to make more items true than false, to use specific determiners (all, never, entirely, and so on), and to use textbook language.

It is possible, however, to improve the true-false item substantially so that it can serve a useful function. Even if one desires to emphasize broad concepts and selection among alternatives on a test, it is quite likely that he also will desire to test for certain specific data. In such a case the true-false test item becomes quite useful. The item can be substantially improved by encouraging students to apply a minor concept or generalization in some way. To illustrate in the field of art:

*Concept:* Color is derived from light.

*Item:* A red coat will appear red to the eye *because it absorbs red color waves and reflects blue color waves.*

One of the most important means of improving items is to use the *modified* form. Such items are designed to permit a student to justify or to improve

**391**

an answer so that it will become a correct answer. The student is asked to to correct all incorrect items. In order to guard against the addition or deletion of something like the word "not" as a means of correcting an item, it usually is necessary to underline certain key clauses or phrases. The student is asked to change the underlined portion in such a manner as to make the statement correct. If change is necessary, the student should alter the underlined portion only. Students may be allowed some credit for the mere recognition of a true or false statement and additional credit for their ability to make appropriate corrections.

*Completion Test Item.* The completion test item has also been overemphasized. Like the true-false item, its answer is easy to defend merely by referring the student to a particular page in his textbook. As a consequence, specific details and, all too often, meaningless verbalisms are emphasized. The objectives of the course often are forgotten when tests are being constructed. The inevitable result is a tendency to gear the entire instructional process to memorizations. Students, likewise, realizing they will be tested in such a manner, tend to emphasize the recall of specific details and terminology. Thus cramming for tests becomes popular.

Despite the inherent weaknesses involved, there are occasions when the meaning of a term and the like is important enough for the inclusion of some such items. In fact, most tests will contain a limited number of these. As its name implies, the item is answered by the completion of a statement. There is an ever-present danger, however, of a statement so mutilated that the respondent is unable to understand the meaning intended. For this reason, some teachers have changed the uncompleted statement to a question form. The following example illustrates the item.

*Subject:* Art

*Concept:* Color is derived from light.

*Item:* The color purple is a combination of _____.
What colors are combined to produce a purple color? _____.

Although both forms elicit the same information, the second one is probably easier to answer because it is worded as a complete thought. Furthermore, the answers can be placed in a column to facilitate marking.

*Matching Test Item.* Like the completion item, the matching question is of relatively minor importance. It is used when teachers desire students to relate such things as dates and events, terms and definitions, persons and places, or causes and events. Its chief disadvantage is that it is not very well adapted to the measurement of real understandings as opposed to rote memory. Because the separate items in the exercises should be homogeneous in nature, there is the likelihood of test clues that reduce validity. Multiple-choice items should be used whenever possible to replace the matching test item.

Appropriate use of the item is facilitated by (1) having at least five and not more than twelve responses, (2) including at least three extra choices from which responses must be chosen, and (3) using only homogeneous items or related materials in any one exercise.

## How Are Rating Scales Employed?

Although rating scales have been developed and used as effective *measuring* instruments, they are usually most effective as *gross guides to evaluation.* Rating scales are used for evaluating situations or characteristics that are present in varying degrees. The word *scale* indicates a graduated scaling instrument. It seems to work best for judging behavior or products that are easily observable. Due to their subjective nature, rating scales are usually used as supplementary evaluations or in areas in which more objective instruments are not available.

As in the case of other instruments used for evaluative purposes, the teacher first must decide what is to be judged. If he has already stated goals in terms of behavioral outcomes, the task is relatively easy. The instructional objectives often form the main points on the scale. Each trait or dimension to be evaluated is then broken down into three or more descriptions, representing qualities of performance. These are usually arranged systematically below a horizontal line. When completed the evaluator checks any point along the line from an indication of a very strong to a very weak performance. By writing out somewhat detailed descriptions greater validity may be assured. The illustration that follows was one teacher's attempt to devise a scale for evaluating the *approach* or *beginning* of an oral presentation: (A complete rating scale is provided on Figure 21–1, p. 340.)

| | | |
|---|---|---|
| Attention-getting, indicative of general content. | Beginning apparently planned, but effectiveness somewhat lacking. | Beginning poorly given; rambling statements, apologies. |

The number of categories for each trait or dimension being scaled has been a subject of some discussion. Generally, the greater the number of categories available the greater the accuracy of observation will be. Due to the difficulty of constructing and using instruments of several categories, many teachers prefer scales with three to five categories.

Reliability of a rating scale can be improved if the rater is permitted to disregard any dimension(s) that does not seem to be present in sufficient quantity for an evaluation. Somewhat related to this is the problem of agreement between observations or observers. For many purposes at least three observations should be obtained. By pooling the judgment of a number of persons, greater reliability can be achieved.

As indicated in the foregoing discussion, validity is increased by establishing somewhat detailed descriptions of the factor being evaluated. Another technique for increasing validity is use of an *anchor item,* enabling the observer to make a general appraisal of the effectiveness displayed. An anchor item may be necessary for several reasons. In the first place, construction of a rating scale makes it necessary for the user to predict all dimensions of importance in the performance. Seldom is this possible, especially when one considers the wide variability of student personalities represented in a heterogeneous group of people. Furthermore, there is some evidence that a general impression dimension, although woefully inadequate as the *only* criterion, may effectively serve as *one* criterion.

The fallacy of using a rating scale as a *measuring* instrument becomes evident when one realizes that, based upon normal variability, the units or categories are arbitrary, and the comparative interval sizes are not equal at all points along the continuum. For example, small differences at the extreme "desirable" or "undesirable" end of the scale indicate a greater variation than an equal difference at the middle of the scale. Thus one person may earn an "average" score on the basis of "average" ratings on all dimensions. On a similar scale, another student may receive a better-than-average score even though one or two dimensions are extremely weak. The scores may not be indicative of the relative worth of the performances, as indicated in the following illustrations:

> Mary was awarded a numerical score near the average category on the basis of the following dimensions deemed important in an oral report: Lesson Beginning; Audience Contact; Enthusiasm; Content; Audience Reaction; Objectivity; Use of Communication Skills (voice, posture, articulation, etc.). She was related near average on *all* dimensions.
>
> Susie was awarded an above-average score on the basis of the same dimensions. Although she was especially strong in most traits, she received very low ratings on Content and Communication Skills. These low ratings, however, still enabled Susie to earn more points than Mary.

It should be obvious, therefore, that extremely low (or high) ratings on one or more dimensions can, in effect, render all other dimensions almost valueless. A *numerical score* sometimes fails to reveal special weaknesses or strengths.

Many teachers, instead of attempting to use the rating scale to *measure* dimensions of a performance, use the ratings as mere *guidelines* in *evaluating* the performance. The need for some systematic scheme or measure is, however, a real one. Students frequently experience difficulty in understanding the limitations, and teachers themselves often want an instrument that can be somewhat more standardized. This has led to interesting modifications. Among them is a common practice of grouping the traits or dimensions being evaluated into three or four broad categories. When using such a scheme, it must be understood that a very low rating on any one dimension within a given group or category will render the entire category ineffective. Three such categories as bases for evaluating oral presentations might be: Delivery; Content; and Audience Reaction. In some cases the teacher-made rating scale is used as a *measuring* instrument if the likelihood of extremely low ratings appears remote.

Figure 21-1 represents a rating scale for evaluating oral presentations. The instrument is illustrative of four broad categories or dimensions, suggested to minimize the effect of extremely low (or high) ratings on certain dimensions.

In addition to the foregoing problems associated with the use of rating scales, the user should be aware of certain other factors that can limit their usefulness:

1. *"Halo" effect.* This factor seems to be associated with a response set of the person or object being rated. While there is some basis for the belief that

it helps to reverse some of the dimensions being evaluated, some teachers find the practice a bit confusing.

2. *Tendency to avoid extremes.*

3. *Personal bias.* This factor can cause a rater to exaggerate certain dimensions, while minimizing others in terms of his own preconceived notions.

Despite the many sources of error commonly associated with rating scales, they can serve a very useful purpose and should find a place in every instructional program. There are numerous traits that can be assessed only through observational procedures. A number of personality traits are amenable to rating. These are: efficiency, originality, perserverance, quickness, judgment, energy, scholarship, and leadership. As more precise trait definitions are developed other personality traits may soon become amenable to reliable rating.

## When Are Checklists Used?

A checklist differs from a rating scale in that no effort is made to evaluate the dimensions. It consists of items or dimensions, such as activities or characteristics, which are checked if present. Its chief function is to call attention to the items themselves rather than to their relative importance. The instrument has many uses. It often is used when some standardized sequence of operation is involved, such as laboratory techniques. Sometimes it is used as an aid in checking off certain characteristics, such as the qualities of some finished product. Examples are the completion of some class project in art, industrial arts, or home economics. The dramatics teacher frequently employs a checklist when preparing for stage productions. Likewise, the physical education instructor finds various uses for such an instrument.

## What Role Do Anecdotal Records Play?

An anecdotal record is a factual, observational record of specific incidents in the life of a student. Each anecdote should be *significant* of the trait or dimension under consideration. Such observations are recorded often enough to indicate *direction* of growth. Although the anecdotal record has many obvious limitations, it is useful when one must evaluate progress toward goals that cannot be judged in any other way. Social adjustment and growth, personal and emotional adjustment, and related factors can be effectively evaluated on the basis of cumulative anecdotal records.

The instrument consists of (1) identifying data, such as date, time, and place of the incident; (2) a description of the situation in which the incident occurred; and (3) a *factual* description of the incident.

The user must continually guard against mixing his personal evaluations with his report of the incident. It has been found that evaluations should be withheld until a number of incidents are recorded. Teachers tend to make their recordings too general for effective use. By quoting what was said, one is much

**395**

more likely to make an accurate record of the actual event than by merely interpreting what happened. Elementary teachers have made use of the instrument for several years, but secondary teachers in many areas are just beginning to discover its usefulness, as the following illustration exemplifies:

> Mr. Blackburne was preparing report cards for midterm distribution. After working long hours in arriving at achievement marks, his attention was directed to the mark requested for *Personal Adjustment and Growth.* Mr. Blackburne was tired and annoyed. Possessing no actual data, he was obliged to mark on the basis of general impressions.
>
> Within a few days a number of parents called on Mr. Blackburne for a further explanation of their children's marks on *Personal Adjustment and Growth.* Mr. Blackburne was able to make a few general statements and, in some cases, recall one or two incidents indicative of the problem. He was, however, unable to justify his indications of inadequate *growth* in the area.

In using anecdotal records it is not essential that a record be kept on *every* student. Perhaps such a situation would be ideal, but with five daily classes of thirty-five students each the task would be impractical for most teachers. As a beginning, a teacher usually finds it desirable to keep records on those students who seem deficient in the dimensions under consideration. After a few days most such individuals stand out from their peers. The number is usually small, seldom exceeding four or five individuals in a class of thirty-five to forty. The number of records needed for a reasonably accurate evaluation has long been a subject of discussion. Obviously, the more usable anecdotes one has on file the more likely he is to obtain an accurate picture of the dimension under investigation. By averaging just one anecdote per week, a teacher usually can present a defensible case if necessary. It is extremely important that the user avoid the collection of data only for the purpose of confirming a preconceived point of view. As in all other aspects of teaching, the instructor must be as objective as possible— recording both positive and negative data that seem significant. In an attempt to attain maximum objectivity, some teachers have established a *time-sampling* system. For example, one may decide that an anecdote will be made of Johnny's behavior on Thursday of each week. The actual anecdote will consist of the first significant incident that occurs on the prescribed day. A few anecdotes on students with problems, when combined with those of other teachers, are extremely valuable in helping the guidance counselor develop a program of remedial treatment.

## How Are Test Results Used?

As indicated earlier, tests are utilized for different purposes. The instructor must, of course, determine how well basic concepts can be applied in life or lifelike situations. Test results also may provide him with clues to deficiencies in the learning experiences and the need for reteaching certain concepts. Using tests as a basis for ascertaining weaknesses in the instructional process is a sound, but frequently neglected, technique.

Any test that is worth giving is worthy of a thorough review. This, of course, entails much more than merely correcting those items which were missed. The concept (upon which each item is based) must be clearly identified and other illustrations provided, enabling the learner to perceive the necessary applications. Some teachers systematically go over all major tests with students, item by item. Generally such a practice is to be discouraged, since the lesson can easily deteriorate into a bickering session with students who see an opportunity of talking the teacher into "additional credit." A better procedure involves analysis of general areas of difficulty as a basis for going over items selectively.

A student who incorrectly responds to a given test item is, in effect, communicating evidence of a learning deficiency. By examining all items devoted to each concept, the teacher may obtain a reasonably sound basis for remedial instruction. If all or most of the group display similar problems, special group activities may be provided. Many, if not most, deficiencies, however, will be of an individualized nature. This necessitates individualized remedial instructional processes. Generally, each individual, utilizing his test paper as a basis, should be provided additional opportunities to make conceptual applications in areas of deficiency. This may eventually take the form of a subsequent test, or it may merely entail informal written statements pertaining to areas of deficiency. When the instructor is satisfied that deficiencies have been corrected, at least partial credit may be allowed for purpose of evaluation.

## VALUES

When used appropriately, test items offer a sound measure of the learner's ability to apply that which has been learned.

When used for diagnostic purposes, tests are especially useful to the learner and to the teacher for identifying areas in which relearning and reteaching are needed.

The quantitative nature of test results accommodates group evaluation. Thus test results are often more valid than results obtained through other measures.

Test items are extremely flexible. By using various types, the teacher can test for almost any level of goal attainment. This applies especially to the cognitive domain.

Tests, when used appropriately, can motivate the learner to greater effort. Students must be assured a reasonable chance of success, however. Competition with bright, or even with average, students for class marks is self-defeating for the less able student.

## LIMITATIONS AND PROBLEMS

Achievement on teacher-made tests is often *inappropriately* assessed in terms of all other students in class. Such a practice actually attempts to combine ability with achievement. (Standardized IQ tests are especially designed for, and accordingly are much more effective than, teacher-made tests for measuring *ability* to do schoolwork.)

Overemphasis upon competitive class marks may develop an unhealthy form of competition. Competition with one's own past achievement record or competition with other equivalent subgroups is preferred.

Tests that demand mere recall of information tend to relegate learning to this level. While some items appropriately should test learnings at this level, many important class goals and instructional techniques should stress problem-solving techniques. Accordingly, testing devices should seek to determine progress in these areas.

Passing tests has often become the end of education, at least in the minds of many students. While appropriate tests themselves should measure progress toward more basic goals, the *intent to remember and to apply* is an extremely important psychological principle.

Tests, as often used in today's schools, tend to encourage cheating and other forms of dishonesty. Also involved may be the development of some form of status order that is often closely related to community social class lines.

Evaluation, when overemphasized, tends to be made at the expense of other, more effective instructional procedures. Furthermore, the difficulty of evaluating certain basic educational goals (affective goals, for example) tends to limit the extent to which they will be taught.

## ILLUSTRATED TEST ITEMS

Whenever possible, situational items are emphasized in the selected illustrations.

MULTIPLE-CHOICE ITEMS

    I.   Useful in biology classes

          *Unit:*     Similarities and Variations

          *Concept:*  Mendelian ratios provide the basis for inheritance.

          *Item:*

          A.  You purchased certified hollyhock seeds two years ago and their quality was exceptionally high, producing double white flowers. Those seeds that germinated the following year, however, produced many unsightly, single-petaled flowers. Which of the following probably accounts for your inferior flowers?

              1.  Double whites were pollinated by red, recessive singles.

              2.  Dominant, red singles pollinated the double whites.

              3.  A mutation accounted for the changes.

              4.  The multiple whites were incompletely dominant for color and petal.

              5.  All hybrid flowers in the second generation revert back to the original characteristics.

          B.  Defend your answer.

II. Useful in chemistry classes

    *Unit:*    The Gas Laws

    *Concept:* The volume of a gas is directly proportional to the temperature.

    *Item:*

    A. The main function of baking powder is to furnish $CO_2$ gas in order that the cake will be light. Which of the following would be most appropriate at 20,000 feet altitude?
      1. Increase the measure of baking powder.
      2. Decrease the measure of baking powder.
      3. Leave it out altogether.
      4. Use the amount you would use at sea level.
    B. Explain your answer.

III. Useful in mathematics classes

    *Unit:*    Financial Matters

    *Concept:* Taxes are an essential part of the American scene.

    *Item:*

    A. If the tax on your property is 3 percent of the assessed valuation, which one of the following would be representative of this assessment?
      1. 30¢ per $1.00 assessed valuation
      2. $10.00 per $1,000 assessed valuation
      3. 30 mills per $1.00 assessed valuation
      4. $30.00 per $100 assessed valuation
    B. Support your answer by computing a 3 percent property tax for assessed values of $1.00, $100, and $1,000.

IV. Useful in home economics classes

    *Unit:*    Marriage

    *Concept:* Each marriage partner must be flexible for a satisfying marriage relationship.

    *Item:*

    A. Because of financial difficulties, Pam has decided to take a job, even though both partners would prefer that she not work. Which of the following adjustments is probably most basic?
      1. Changed role patterns for each partner
      2. Changed decision-making pattern relative to financial matters
      3. Changed attitude toward each other's work
      4. A flexible scheduling of meals
      5. All of these of equal importance
    B. Defend your answer

ESSAY ITEMS

    I. Useful in biology classes

      *Unit:*    Similarities and Variations

*Concept:* Mendelian ratios provide the basis for inheritance.

*Item:*

> The offspring of a cross between a white snapdragon and a red snapdragon yields a plant with pink flowers. A cross of two of the pinks yields white and red offspring. Explain the Mendelian law implied here, illustrating the expected ratios of the second filial generation.

II.  Useful in English literature classes

*Unit:*  The Aspiring Mind (of the Elizabethan Period)

*Concept:* Fusion of classic with English content and exuberance brought about a mature, artistic drama.

*Item:*

> A drama, to be popular, has to contain an appeal. Discuss features of *Macbeth* that have such an appeal. Treat the following aspects: atmosphere, movement, poetry, and character development.

III.  Useful in American literature classes

*Unit:*  The Beginnings of the American Tradition

*Concept:* Political writers influenced the development of democratic ideals.

*Item:*

> Select three of Thomas Jefferson's political ideals, formed in the Declaration of Independence, and tell what they mean today.

IV.  Useful in industrial arts classes

*Unit:*  Precision Measurement and Systems Used

*Concept:* Proper care and use of precision measuring instruments are essential to their accuracy.

*Item:*

> In cutting a block of steel to 1.500″ square on a milling machine, give the sequence to follow, including precautionary steps to take before and during the squaring operation.

V.  Useful in physical education classes

*Unit:*  Teamwork in Sports and Society

*Concept:* Teamwork is an excellent method of goal attainment.

*Item:*

> John and five of his classmates have been assigned the problem of reporting the life of Babe Ruth. John feels the other members are not putting forth a very effective team effort. Discuss the steps that John should take to provide effective teamwork for this group.

TRUE-FALSE ITEMS

   I. Useful in home economics classes

      *Unit:*    Marriage

      *Concept:* Many factors influence marriage success.

      *Item:*

          In the film *Are You Ready for Marriage?* Bill and Mary's marriage was threatened because *Mary was career minded.*

      *Concept:* Marriage customs vary from one culture to another.

      *Item:*

          In the child-rearing customs of Japan, the male was highly favored because *he would someday carry the authority of the household.*

  II. Useful in English literature classes

      *Unit:*    The Aspiring Mind (of the Elizabethan period)

      *Concept:* Ambition can work to the benefit or detriment of the individual.

      *Item:*

          If a person is told he will accomplish something, he should *do anything he is told to do in order to accomplish that goal.*

      *Concept:* Emancipation of restricted classes provides new opportunities for the individual in all aspects of life.

      *Item:*

          The lower social classes accomplished more during the Elizabethan period than in the Middle Ages because *the European governments paid them extra for overtime.*

# CHAPTER 25

# Evaluation and
# Reporting Procedures

## OVERVIEW

### Key Concepts

1.  Minimum essentials objectives, to be achieved by *all* students, are judged by absolute measures rather than by the scores of other individuals in class.
2.  Developmental objectives, to be achieved in varying degrees by different students, may be assessed in terms of the class norm.
3.  Evaluational experiences, when interpreted in terms of group performance, are recorded as *standard* (as opposed to *raw*) scores.
4.  Standard scores (letter or stanine marks) are based upon the normal probability curve and thus can be weighted directly and combined for marking purposes. (Raw scores cannot be so combined.)
5.  A good test item (when used to measure developmental objectives) has a difficulty value of between 50 and 60 percent.
6.  Validity of class marks is increased when many different dimensions of performance are assessed.
7.  Marks based upon the normal probability curve are based upon the assumption that every individual has a reasonably equal chance of success.
8.  Report cards provide a poor but sometimes the only direct avenue of communication between parent and teacher.
9.  Evaluation most appropriately is based upon actual achievement, rather than ability to achieve.

### New Terms

1. **Normal Probability Curve**—The expected frequency distribution (bell-shaped) in any unselected group.. Scores characteristically cluster near the middle and taper off uniformly toward each extreme.
2. **Standard Score**—Derived from a raw score, a standard score is based on a uniform standard scale (*normal probability curve*). Its use simplifies comparisons and interpretations of scores on different tests.
3. **Item Analysis**—A technique for assessing the difficulty and discriminating power of a test item, based on actual student responses. *Item difficulty* usually is expressed as a percent of those who failed to answer an item correctly; *item discrimination* usually is expressed as a ratio between good and poor students who answered an item correctly.
4. **Minimum Passing Score**—The lowest score that satisfies a particular requirement. It essentially separates students into "pass" or "fail" groups. Determination usually involves a number of somewhat arbitrary decisions.

### Questions to Guide Your Study

1. What problems are associated with identical standards for all students?
2. What would be the theoretically lowest acceptable score on a minimum essentials test? Why would acceptable standards vary in practical class situations?
3. What basic assumptions are associated with the "normal probability curve"? How valid are such assumptions in today's secondary school?
4. Why is marking on the basis of the normal probability curve more appropriate in "homogeneously grouped" classes than in nonselected groups?
5. What is the relationship between traditional percentage marks and the normal probability curve? Which of the two is more realistic today?
6. What advantages do standard scores have over the mere accumulation of raw score points?
7. "Class marks should be reduced to pass or fail." Defend or refute.

Although certain measuring instruments can be scored objectively, evaluation and reporting techniques are highly subjective. In the final analysis, the instructor *and* students must pass judgment on the worth of basic learning experiences. The process, however, need not be haphazard or "nonscientific." Some traditional practices are based on faulty assumptions; others are used for purposes of expediency. Therefore, the problems treated in this chapter are selected with a view of disclosing certain misconceptions (as in the case of combining test scores) and offering sound techniques that are economical of time and effort, as illustrated in stanine distribution techniques.

## FUNDAMENTAL PROPERTIES

Evaluation, perhaps more than any aspect of teaching, reflects a teacher's value system. This rationale must be thoroughly examined and then reexamined as time and local conditions change. It is hoped that this section will enable the practitioner to develop an evaluational procedure consistent with current instructional technology.

## What Are the Relative Merits of Maximum, Minimum, and Multiple Standards?

*Maximum standards* usually are set above the ability level of all but the most capable students in class. In actuality, they have been passed down from a school practice that no longer exists. Even as late as the early decades of the twentieth century most high school classes were made up of the more scholastically able students only. Although some students were brighter than others, the difference could be more or less equalized through additional effort. By accepting as satisfactory 60 or 70 percent of the maximum, most students had an opportunity to succeed. Such a system works fairly well in relatively select groups. Most secondary school classrooms of today, however, are characterized by heterogeneity. Often as much as half the group may be *unable* to achieve acceptable standards. Realizing the state of affairs, many individuals cease to try. Thus both teacher and student often become extremely frustrated.

Some teachers have attempted to modify the procedure by lowering the level of maximum standards to enable most students to succeed. Although rewarding to the average or slightly-below-average student, it tends to create problems with the more able student. Now they find it possible to succeed with a minimum of effort. High standards of achievement cease to hold meaning for them.

Other teachers have attempted to resolve the difficulty by applying the normal distribution curve to the various degrees of achievement. (The normal distribution curve is discussed more fully later in this chapter.) A rigid interpretation of the normal curve guarantees a fixed number of top marks and an equal number of low marks. Too frequently this results in *ability* marks rather than *achievement* marks. In effect, the solution may eventuate into a complete lack of standards as students and teachers come to realize the futility of competition with those of different abilities.

In achieving the goals of a particular course or unit, a teacher expects every student to demonstrate certain *minimum standards*. Such standards are within the capacity range of all students. At the same time, those with greater ability and interest will be able to advance well beyond such standards. They are encouraged to do additional assignments on the basis of their own or the teacher's suggestions. Students are expected to meet *all* minimum requirements. Scores on a *minimum essentials test* should be almost perfect—allowing for errors of reliability and validity. Deficiencies would be corrected through repeated teaching and testing.

Work beyond the minimum is evaluated *on the basis of the individual involved*. As all students are expected to progress beyond the minimum, even the most menial tasks will warrant due credit for some. Evaluation of work beyond the minimum is based on a number of factors, such as effort, achievement, thoroughness, neatness, time involved, and so on. Due recognition can be given through displays, special reports, and the like. Whenever possible, the student is given an opportunity to pursue special interests *after* minimum standards have been satisfied. Some teachers have constructed tests of two parts: one part containing questions designed to measure achievement of minimum essentials; the other to determine degree of progress toward developmental instructional goals. Near perfect scores are expected on minimum essentials tests (items). Tests designed to determine progress toward developmental goals may be evaluated in terms of the scores of other comparable students in class.

By establishing *multiple standards* to operate in parallel, a teacher may allow students to pursue special interests while meeting basic course requirements. Vocational courses have been set up in this manner. Sometimes such standards are applied to project work of all kinds. There would be no necessity for lowering standards to reduce failures. Pupils could find success in any one of a variety of ways. Each pupil would be judged separately on his own merits.

Although multiple standards have been used effectively in small classes, the method soon becomes unwieldy in large classes. With thirty-five to forty students in five different classes, there may be little chance of making the procedure operational.

In the foregoing discussion little attempt has been made to recommend one type of standard over another. As indicated, much of the decision must be based on the particular set of circumstances in which the teacher finds himself. Teachers have effectively solved the problem by the application of a combination of minimum and multiple standards. Others have developed a scheme of flexible subgrouping within the classroom to facilitate the establishment of maximum standards. Each teacher will, no doubt, want to evolve his own set of standards— subject to modification as circumstances permit. What *does* seem important, however, is that every student must be given an opportunity to succeed relative to his own capacities, according to some defensible standard of performance.

## What Are the Relative Merits of Growth vs. Status Marking?

Recognizing extreme differences in ability, some teachers prefer to assess achievement in terms of individual growth rather than in terms of one's status among his peers. Such a practice is defensible when *assessing mastery of minimum essentials*. As indicated in the previous chapter, however, minimum essentials marking is most effective in the skills area and at the lower levels of cognition. Logically, it might seem reasonable to merely carry the procedure one step further by establishing initial base performance on the basis of a pretest and other preliminary observations. Differences between these and subsequent test scores and other measures would thus provide a reasonable estimate of growth.

Unfortunately such a procedure is fraught with a number of serious hazards. Among the most serious is the absence of an assessment of relative competence. A weak student, for example, may make remarkable progress in an area such as mathematics but still be well below the competence level of his class. A "high" mark on a test in terms of growth does little to encourage an individual when he realizes that his progress was poor relative to the rest of the class. The student realizes, quite appropriately, that competence is what counts; that rate of growth is important only to the extent that it contributes to status.

Each test contains errors of measurement.[1] For most teacher-made tests the estimated error of measurement is approximately three score points. Thus differences between individual pre- and posttest scores frequently will consist mostly of errors of measurement.

Still another difficulty is the ceiling level for the better students. An individual who already knows the answers to a considerable number of pretest items, for example, may find it extremely difficult to demonstrate actual rate of growth. He has little room for progress on the measures provided. In actual practice, of course, students soon get testwise, making sure that their pretest scores will be low enough to allow for reasonable "improvement."

It can be seen from the foregoing that the teacher is caught in the horns of a dilemma. On the one hand, the weak student is encouraged when he is rewarded for mediocre work that may indeed represent superior progress for the individual involved. On the other hand, the student soon realizes that his achievement does not really measure up to the rest of the class. If status marking is employed, however, such an individual meets continuous frustration and discouragement if he happens to be in a class with students of much higher ability.

In resolving the dilemma the teacher, first, expects all students to master the minimum essentials. Individuals who do not are recycled through the program until they do achieve this minimum level. (If the existing school program does not permit this type of recycling, such persons should be failed. It is unrealistic to "pass" an individual who cannot cope with the minimum essentials of a course.) Such criterion-referenced measures are assessed independently of the achievement of other students in class. Progress beyond the minimum essentials (achievement of developmental objectives) should be made on the basis of status relative to the rest of the class. As Ebel[2] suggests, the alert teacher provides opportunities for various kinds of achievement. Thus status or norm-referenced marking need not mean that some students will always "win" while others will always "lose." Success is important to each person but none of us should expect to succeed all the time. By the same token, none of us should be placed in a position of failing all the time.

## How Is the Minimum Passing Score Determined?

As indicated earlier, the minimum passing score on a minimum essentials criterion-referenced test theoretically is a perfect score. Since test perfection and

---

[1] An *error of measurement* is the difference between an obtained score and the corresponding true score. If it were possible to administer a test several times then each individual's average score could be said to represent his true score. Usually, however, a test is administered only once. Thus allowances must be made for expected differences between the actual score and one's theoretically true score.

[2] Robert L. Ebel, *Essentials of Educational Measurement* (Englewood Cliffs, N.J.: Prentice-Hall, Inc., 1972), p. 331.

flawless performance are ideals seldom reached in practice, a minimum passing score of 80 or 90 percent is usually recommended. It should be pointed out that at the present time this figure is more-or-less arbitrarily established.

In norm-referenced tests a minimum passing score is perhaps more arbitrary than in minimum essentials tests. Yet this is a decision that must be made constantly. The actual scores are influenced by many factors such as type of item, whether the test is "hard" or "easy," the ability level of the student, how well the concepts have been taught, and so on. With true-false items, for example, there is an expected chance score of 50 percent. Likewise, the multiple-choice item (with four alternatives) produces an expected chance score of 25 percent. Ebel described several ways of ascertaining an appropriate minimum passing score. Unfortunately, some of the techniques are somewhat laborious or difficult in design. As a general rule of thumb the passing score may be defined as the midpoint between the mean or average score and the lowest score. Since this is a rather arbitrary determination, considerable flexibility and good judgment must be exercised.

## What Are Some Problems in Combining Test Scores?

Mr. Martin had developed a point system to assist in evaluational procedures. Although he gave students some indication of mark equivalents on each test or exercise, he made a practice of entering raw scores in his record book. He reasoned that the raw scores on each test could be added, with perhaps some additional weight being given to the final test. He considered the individual tests as actually constituting parts of one big test over the entire course.

While Mr. Martin's system of evaluation could be defended on logical grounds, it contained at least two serious disadvantages:

1. *Mark equivalents on each test are not likely to correspond to the final letter-grade standing at the end of the course.* Although it is not always necessary to indicate mark equivalents on separate tests, most students like to know where they stand. Furthermore, knowledge of progress is a sound psychological principle that seems to enhance learning.

2. *When several tests are combined, those with greater variability have greater weights.* The point can be very simply illustrated by the following example:

Johnny made the top score (80 points) on a three-week unit test. At the end of the next unit (also three weeks long) he made a top "C," with a score of 50 points. When the two numerical scores were combined he had a total of 130 points.

Nadine, on the other hand, made a top "C" mark on the first test, but due to less variability in the scores she made 60 raw score points. On the next test, however, she made the top score, which was 80 points. When the two test scores were combined she had a total of 140 points.

If the tests were supposed to be of equal importance they were not serving such a function in Mr. Martin's class. The discrepancy tends to become even more pronounced when a unit test is compared to a final examination. Let us suppose that the range for one unit test in Mr. Martin's class is 30 points, whereas the range in the longer, final test is 90 points. If the raw scores are added, the final test actually counts three times as much as the unit test because it has three times the variability of the former. A teacher (unaware of the influence of variability) may decide to double the weight of the final test by multiplying the scores by two. Actually, however, the final test receives a weight of six, instead of two as supposed.

While it is true that a test of greater variability *may* indicate greater reliability, the difference in variability is more likely attributable to the arbitrary nature of different units of measurement in the two cases. In a practical classroom situation it is extremely unlikely that variability of tests of equal importance can be kept equal. The range difference between two tests will differ as much as 30 points for no apparent reason. It is possible to correct for this by adding a constant to the test with least variability, but most students are unlikely to understand the real reason for such a practice.[3]

The most reliable procedure seems to be to convert scores on each test to some type of standard score.

Teachers traditionally have used a five-point system of letter marks for this purpose. It should be pointed out, however, that through such a procedure information is lost unless a plus-and-minus system is added. This, of course, takes considerable time and effort. A preferable system involves the use of stanine scores, described later in this chapter. This has the advantage of units that can be readily added at the end of the course. Furthermore, it divides the distribution into more divisions (nine instead of five), thereby making the standard score more accurate. In other words, there are likely to be fewer objections from those who miss a mark by one or two score points. A "C" is automatically divided into three categories, with stanines of 4, 5, and 6. By converting each set of scores into standard scores, it is relatively easy to assign different weights to these when they are combined at the end of the course.

There is one hazard, however, that should be taken into account when standard scores are averaged. There is a tendency for marks to *regress toward the mean or average*. Thus actual progress of the weaker students will tend to be less than indicated. Likewise, actual progress of the better student will tend to be more than is readily apparent. To illustrate:

Jack made a top mark on one test, but could do no better than a "B" on the next one. Even if he made "A's" on every subsequent test it would be difficult to bring his mark up to an "A," simply because this represents the topmost mark possible.

Tommy, however, made a "D" on one test. By a reasonable amount of effort he can earn a "B" on the next one. Thus it will not be too difficult for him to maintain a "C" average.

The problem may be corrected at the end of the course by subjecting the final average stanine (or letter mark) to a frequency distribution. Thus a stanine of

---

[3] For a thorough description of the technique the reader is referred to Ebel, *op. cit.,* pp. 348–51.

7.3 *may* be sufficient for a mark of "A." Such an evaluation would depend on the percent of "A's" deemed appropriate by the instructor.

There has been a great deal of controversy concerning the relative percentages of marks to be administered. Much depends on the *quality* of student performance—which reflects on the teacher himself. As indicated earlier, marking on the basis of the normal curve is dependent on each student having a *fairly equal chance* and *a representative sampling* of students. When these two conditions are met, the percentages developed for the use of stanines seem to be reasonable. A teacher must bear in mind, however, that "normal" achievement might be expected under normal conditions only. Through his own efforts he may have helped his group make greater achievement than under normal conditions. If so, he would be fully justified in assigning a higher percentage of high marks than low marks. In the final analysis it is the teacher's judgment as to the number (if any) who should fail, the number who should make "A," and the like. The normal curve concept can serve as a useful guide only.

## What Are the Basic Problems Associated with Reporting Procedures?

The basic premise underlying the use of report cards is sound. Parents do need periodic reports on the progress of their children; they need guidance in techniques of cooperating with the school. Indeed, report cards have become traditional. Efforts to replace them with other techniques of reporting have usually met with strong parental resistance.

The most common report card is the A-B-C-D-F form, representing a range from exceptional to unacceptable work. The marks are usually based on where a student stands in relation to the rest of his class. The distribution of marks is usually based on some modification of the normal curve of probability, described in a previous section.

While the five-letter system of reporting appears simple enough, it has proven most unsatisfactory in practice. Marks of this kind are extremely abstract. What does a "C" mean, for example? Does it mean that Johnny has been content with mediocre work? What elements of the educational process were included in the mark? What can his parents do to help him improve his class achievement? The traditional report card reveals none of this. Furthermore, a "C" in one class usually is not equivalent to a "C" in another class.

Many parents and teachers alike object to report card grades based on total class achievement only. It is recognized that, under such a system, some students can make "A's" with a minimum of effort, while others are destined to fail because of their limited abilities. In an effort to minimize the competitive effect of letter grades, some schools have resorted to reports of "satisfactory" and "unsatisfactory," with an honor grade for outstanding achievement. Thus a "U" indicates a student's achievement falls below his ability; an "S" indicates the student's work has been consistent with his ability. Students who do much more than expected are marked with an "H." The faults of this system soon became apparent, however. Lumping together excellent, good, and fair achievement in some cases tends to decrease pupil effort. Furthermore, marking students according to their capacities to achieve is no simple matter. Parents still want to know how their children stand in relation to the rest of the class.

In the elementary school, report cards have been supplemented and sometimes replaced by letters and/or parent-teacher conferences. While such contacts are preferred, they have not been found very practical at the secondary school level. Unlike the elementary teacher who often has the same group of thirty to thirty-five students most of the school day, the secondary teacher may teach 200 students during a single day. This many parent-teacher conferences or individual letters every six weeks would be prohibitive.

Other reporting innovations have included separate marks for a variety of characteristics associated with learning. Some of these factors included initiative, cooperation, attitude, social habits, work habits, and so on. In addition, spaces have sometimes been provided on the report card for teacher and parent comments. These too have often been disappointing in practice. How does one measure such factors as initiative and attitude? Does lack of initiative always reflect on the learner? Is it not likely that, in some cases, the difficulty might be more closely associated with the teacher than with the student? How accurate are teacher comments when 200 different report cards are being prepared for distribution? Although satisfactory answers to such questions have not emerged, a number of trends are treated in the next section of this chapter. It seems that achievement, status, and various affective qualities of a student might be included (separately) in effective reports to parents.

# TECHNIQUES OF EVALUATION

The measuring instruments treated in the foregoing chapter are merely tools to facilitate evaluation. A superior test is of minimal value in the hands of an incompetent evaluator. Unfortunately, many malpractices do exist. At least some of the difficulties can be attributed to the rapidly changing nature of the school.

Today's secondary school teacher, in attempting to accommodate the needs of all students, finds many conventional evaluational techniques partially or wholly invalid. The "time-honored" practice of evaluating each individual in terms of his relative class standing, for example, is highly questionable in classes where the ability range is great. It is equally inappropriate when the economic and cultural backgrounds of various class members are marked.

## What Statistical Concepts Are Essential?

Time after time the classroom instructor finds himself with a group of raw scores that somehow must be made meaningful. The scores, in and of themselves, have very little meaning until they are compared to some sort of previously developed criterion or standard. *Ideally* this standard would be a comparison of one's performance with his own capacities. In courses that rely heavily on performance, it is relatively easy to evaluate a student on this basis.

Mary was delivering a prepared speech. This represented her fourth such performance in speech class. Mr. Brody noted definite and consistent progress in several areas. He had before him a rating scale of each of Mary's previous performances. Although Mary's speech performance was below that of many of the other students in class, *for her* the record disclosed satisfactory and consistent improvement.

Tom's performance was at least as good as Mary's, but *for Tom* it was indicative of unsatisfactory progress. A glance at the records of his previous performances indicated a steady decline. Tom had started the year off with a superior performance. Mr. Brody noted, however, that many of the suggestions for improvement were repeated on each succeeding speech critique. He guessed that Tom had selected his speech after he entered the classroom that day.

The foregoing illustrations indicate a technique of evaluation that can be applied to such courses as speech, many phases of home economics, industrial arts, vocational agriculture, music, art, typing, and certain phases of many other courses. For the more "academic" courses, however, a teacher will find it extremely difficult to assess progress on the basis of one's capacity for progress. Although pretests often reveal useful data. They are usually insufficient bases for later comparisons of individual progress. While some teachers have been able to develop techniques for accomplishing such a feat with very small classes, too often classes are large, and the trend is toward even larger classes. Consequently, this discussion is aimed primarily at helping those who have large, "academic" classes.

*Normal Probability Curve.* Lacking adequate means of evaluating progress on the basis of one's capacity for progress, one must turn to techniques of assessing an individual's progress in terms of that of the *group* (norm-referenced evaluation). An extremely useful device widely used in secondary school and college classes is the *normal probability curve.* It has been found that almost any characteristic, trait, or dimension is present in varying degrees in any *representative* population. The *pattern* of variation expected will *always* approach a bell-shaped curve. For example, the weights of a large number of randomly selected 16-year-old girls would vary from extremely light to extremely heavy as compared to most of the girls, whose weights would fall some place between the two extremes. Most of the girls would tip the scales fairly close to the *average.* A graphic picture of this dimension is reproduced in Figure 25–1.

A repetition of our investigation, as long as it were *representative* of all girls in the population, would tend to show the same pattern. Likewise, with any such group and with *any* dimension, measurements tend to distribute in the form of a bell-shaped curve. In common practice this concept is often identified as the *normal distribution or probability curve.* One important assumption involved must be emphasized, however: the group must be *representative* of the entire population. Small groups (fewer than thirty), by chance, usually distribute

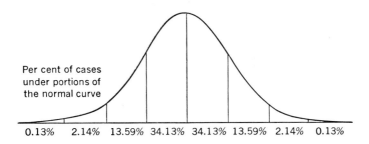

Per cent of cases under portions of the normal curve

0.13%   2.14%   13.59%   34.13%   34.13%   13.59%   2.14%   0.13%

**FIGURE 25–1.** Normal probability curve

unevenly along the curve. In some cases chance factors will skew the distribution toward the right or left. Although a perfect bell-shaped curve exists in theory, only normal class size groups may be applied to the curve concept, as long as the user employs it as a rough guide only, and as long as he has reason to believe that his group is somewhat representative of the entire population on the trait being measured.

One of the more important developments of the present century was the scholastic aptitude test—commonly referred to as the *IQ test*. Through the use of IQ tests a teacher sometimes can predict a child's *capacity* to do school work. It has been established that one's capacity for school work remains relatively constant throughout life. Thus it becomes quite possible for a teacher to predict, within reasonable limits, a student's potential for academic achievement. Assuming a representative group, in terms of academic aptitude, we could expect about two-thirds (68.13 percent) of our group to fall within the *average category* of aptitude, but the remaining third would be evenly distributed between below-average and above-average range of aptitude. Now if we have a *representative amount of progress*, an application of the normal curve would give those students with lowest ability failing marks, and those with highest ability the highest marks. In effect, *we are awarding a class mark on the basis of one's ability rather than on the basis of actual achievement. In other words, when a teacher uses the normal probability curve as a basis for the distribution of test marks, he is assuming that all students have a fairly equal chance.* Yet, through a similar process, it has already been discovered that all students do *not* have an equal chance.

Until just a few decades ago the assumption that students had a "fairly equal chance" was reasonably valid. Most of the weaker students dropped by the wayside prior to high school. The average student, by working hard, could compete fairly well. (A similar situation exists today in most colleges and universities.) In certain classes, open only to those with average or above-average ability, the use of a curve may still be quite appropriate. But in classes open to *all* students, the practice is indefensible as long as scholastic aptitude is not taken into account.

At this point the reader may be surprised to learn that most judgments based on student progress are either directly or indirectly based on the normal distribution curve.

Mr. Burton boasted that he had no use for the normal curve. He proudly announced that he was sticking with the "tried and tested" *percentage* system of marking, i.e., students making 93–100 points received "A"; 86–92–"B"; 78–85–"C"; 66–77–"D"; all marks below 65 were rated as failing. In this manner all students could theoretically earn "A," or they could all fail.

Marks, to Miss Knox, should be based on acceptable standards of performance identified by each student. If, after marking a test, it appeared a little difficult, she made the passing score lower than usual, likewise with the other points of her scale. Her decision was dependent on the marks of certain "key" students in her class.

Both of the foregoing illustrations are based on the concept of the normal curve. The percentage distribution employed by Mr. Burton is derived from a normal distribution. His assertion that all could theoretically make "A" or "F" was truly *just* theory. Unless the test was extremely hard or easy, or unless all his students were by chance below or above average in ability, this could not possibly happen. By utilizing such a technique Mr. Burton was assuming that all of his test items were reliable and valid. Such is highly unlikely. Likewise, Miss Knox's reasoning was fallacious. Subconsciously perhaps, she was using the concept of a normal distribution, but instead of basing the distribution on what might be reasonably expected she was bringing in personal judgment. Although personal judgments are frequently necessary, when one relies on them alone personal favoritism is almost certain to become an important factor.

What basis should a teacher use in evaluating test marks? There seems to be more than one solution. It is likely that some combination of methods may be useful.

1. *Minimum, combined with multiple, standards.* As indicated in the foregoing topic, minimum standards can be used effectively *as long as every student can reach them.* Then, all students, in cooperation with the teacher, should select *additional* tasks according to their interests and abilities. Hence one is evaluated on the basis of achievement in relation to ability.

2. *Subgrouping within the classroom.* If the below-average, the average, and above-average students are arranged in subgroups *for the purposes of evaluation,* the normal curve can be appropriately applied to each group; each student thus will have an approximately equal opportunity for success. (See Chapter 6).

3. *Use of the normal distribution curve.* In classes limited to average and above-average students the inaccuracies will be minor, i.e., each student will have a fairly equal opportunity for success. Likewise, a class of below-average students can be evaluated on the basis of a normal curve. Quite understandably a comparison of marks between these classes will not be comparable. It must be remembered, however, that marks supposedly represent *achievement* rather than ability. Ability can best be predicted from other types of measures.

4. *Performance ratings.* In some skills areas a direct observation of performance is possible. Marks can then be based on observable progress in terms of one's ability.

Because the normal curve is so frequently used, the section that follows will introduce a system that has many advantages. It probably represents the simplest, yet most accurate, application of the normal curve that a busy teacher can make. The *stanine distribution* can be constructed by most teachers in five to ten minutes after raw scores are derived.

*Stanine Distribution.* The stanine distribution is a simple nine-point scale of standard scores. The word *stanine* is derived from the words ST*Andard NINE.* Raw scores are converted to standard scores, ranging from 1 (low) to 9 (high). Thus raw scores can be grouped into intervals or classes. Just as the traditional A, B, C, D, and F scale represented five divisions of a normal distribution curve, so does the stanine represent nine divisions of a normal distribution. The stanine has at least two practical advantages over the five-letter scale distribution system:

1. It enables a teacher to divide class scores directly into nine intervals or classes of whole numbers. In actual practice the use of the traditional five-letter procedure often is somewhat time-consuming. Traditional letter marks, when combined, must be transposed into numbers and then back again into letter marks for student interpretation. Furthermore, if greater accuracy is sought through the use of plus and minus signs, the use of decimals becomes necessary.

2. Stanine scores for one test or project are easily weighted, for the purpose of combining with other stanine scores. For example, if a teacher decides that a given test should count twice as much as another test, he merely multiplies the stanine scores of the more important test by 2 and adds the product to stanine scores of other tests.

Stanine scores will conform to the proportions of the *normal curve.* Percentages of the class group(s) that fall within each of the nine stanine classifications for a normal population are shown in Figure 25–2. A useful characteristic of stanines is the equally-distanced steps involved.

Stanines can be just as readily applied to written papers, drawings, products, or other exercises as they can to test scores. The only requirement is that the papers or products be serialized or ranked from high to low. For example, individual class projects in industrial arts can be assigned ranks of *Excellent, Very Good, Good, Fair,* and *Poor.* Then each project *within each rank* can be

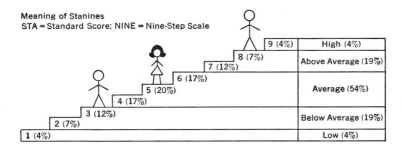

**FIGURE 25–2.** Percentage of cases at each stanine level

Reproduced from *Test Service Notebook,* No. 23 (New York: Harcourt, Brace & World, Inc., 1961). Used by permission of the publisher.

serialized from high to low. After serializing or ranking all of the projects in this manner, it is easy to determine the number of cases at each stanine level.

For convenience, a table of percentages for stanine scores has been prepared (Table 25–1). The reader will note that percentages have been computed for 100 cases. If the group is larger than 100 the appropriate number of actual cases for each stanine score can be readily determined by multiplying the number by the percentage of cases at each stanine level.

In referring to Table 25–1 the teacher merely reads across to determine the theoretical number of students who should receive a given stanine score. In a class of forty students, for example, the stanine distribution would be as follows: 1–1; 2–3; 3–5; 4–7; 5–8; 6–7; 7–5; 8–3; 9–1. This is only a theoretical grouping, however, based on a normal distribution. In relatively small groups the distribution usually is skewed to the right or left. As in any evaluation scheme, the teacher must use his best judgment as to desirable adjustments. In any event, however, *all students with identical raw scores or identical ranks receive the same stanine score.*

Use of the stanine distribution has been effectively illustrated by Durost in Table 25–2.[4]

*Directions for Table 25–2:*
1.  Arrange test papers on answer sheets in rank order from high to low. On a separate piece of paper, list every score in a column from the highest obtained score to the lowest (column A). Opposite each score write the number of individuals who obtained that score. This may be done by counting the papers or answer sheets having the same score, or it may be done by tallying the scores in the manner shown in column B.
2.  Add the frequencies (C) and write the total at the bottom of the column (D). This is shown to be 90.
3.  Beginning at the bottom, count up (cumulate) to one-half the total number of scores, in this case 45 (one-half of 90). This falls opposite the score of 34 (E), which is the median to the nearest whole number.
4.  In the column at the extreme left of the Stanine Table (Table 25–1), look up the total number of cases (90). In this row are the theoretical frequencies of cases at each stanine level for 90 cases (18) to which a stanine of 5 should be assigned. Starting with the median, lay off as nearly this number (18) of scores as you can. Here it is 20.
5.  Working upward and downward from scores falling in stanine 5, assign scores to stanine levels so as to give the closest approximation possible to the theoretical values. It is helpful to bracket these scores in the manner shown in column A.

After having made a tentative assignment, make any adjustments necessary to bring the actual frequencies at each level into the closest possible agreement with the theoretical values. Remember, however, that all equal scores *must* be assigned the same stanines.[5]

---

[4] Walter N. Durost, "The Characteristics, Use, and Computation of Stanines," *Test Service Notebook*, No. 23 (New York: Harcourt, Brace & World, Inc., 1961), p. 6.

[5] *Ibid.,* p. 6.

**TABLE 25-1.** Stanine table, showing number of cases falling at each level of a 9-point normalized standard score scale when the mean equals 5 and the standard deviation equals 2

DIRECTIONS. Under N, find the number corresponding to number of cases in the group. Entries in columns 1 to 9 give the number of cases that should receive the stanine score indicated at the top of the column. These figures are computed by multiplying the total number of cases in the group by the percentage of cases at each level. The figures are rounded-off values to give a symmetrical distribution of cases for any value of N given in the table.

| | *Percentage of cases at each level* | | | | | | | | |
|---|---|---|---|---|---|---|---|---|---|
| Number of cases | 4% | 7% | 12% | 17% | 20% | 17% | 12% | 7% | 4% |
| | | | | | *Stanines* | | | | |
| N | 1 | 2 | 3 | 4 | 5 | 6 | 7 | 8 | 9 |
| 20 | 1 | 1 | 2 | 4 | 4 | 4 | 2 | 1 | 1 |
| 21 | 1 | 1 | 2 | 4 | 5 | 4 | 2 | 1 | 1 |
| 22 | 1 | 2 | 2 | 4 | 4 | 4 | 2 | 2 | 1 |
| 23 | 1 | 2 | 2 | 4 | 5 | 4 | 2 | 2 | 1 |
| 24 | 1 | 2 | 3 | 4 | 4 | 4 | 3 | 2 | 1 |
| 25 | 1 | 2 | 3 | 4 | 5 | 4 | 3 | 2 | 1 |
| 26 | 1 | 2 | 3 | 4 | 6 | 4 | 3 | 2 | 1 |
| 27 | 1 | 2 | 3 | 5 | 5 | 5 | 3 | 2 | 1 |
| 28 | 1 | 2 | 3 | 5 | 6 | 5 | 3 | 2 | 1 |
| 29 | 1 | 2 | 4 | 5 | 5 | 5 | 4 | 2 | 1 |
| 30 | 1 | 2 | 4 | 5 | 6 | 5 | 4 | 2 | 1 |
| 31 | 1 | 2 | 4 | 5 | 7 | 5 | 4 | 2 | 1 |
| 32 | 1 | 2 | 4 | 6 | 6 | 6 | 4 | 2 | 1 |
| 33 | 1 | 2 | 4 | 6 | 7 | 6 | 4 | 2 | 1 |
| 34 | 1 | 3 | 4 | 6 | 6 | 6 | 4 | 3 | 1 |
| 35 | 1 | 3 | 4 | 6 | 7 | 6 | 4 | 3 | 1 |
| 36 | 1 | 3 | 4 | 6 | 8 | 6 | 4 | 3 | 1 |
| 37 | 2 | 3 | 4 | 6 | 7 | 6 | 4 | 3 | 2 |
| 38 | 1 | 3 | 5 | 6 | 8 | 6 | 5 | 3 | 1 |
| 39 | 1 | 3 | 5 | 7 | 7 | 7 | 5 | 3 | 1 |
| 40 | 1 | 3 | 5 | 7 | 8 | 7 | 5 | 3 | 1 |
| 41 | 1 | 3 | 5 | 7 | 9 | 7 | 5 | 3 | 1 |
| 42 | 2 | 3 | 5 | 7 | 8 | 7 | 5 | 3 | 2 |
| 43 | 2 | 3 | 5 | 7 | 9 | 7 | 5 | 3 | 2 |
| 44 | 2 | 3 | 5 | 8 | 8 | 8 | 5 | 3 | 2 |
| 45 | 2 | 3 | 5 | 8 | 9 | 8 | 5 | 3 | 2 |
| 46 | 2 | 3 | 5 | 8 | 10 | 8 | 5 | 3 | 2 |
| 47 | 2 | 3 | 6 | 8 | 9 | 8 | 6 | 3 | 2 |
| 48 | 2 | 3 | 6 | 8 | 10 | 8 | 6 | 3 | 2 |
| 49 | 2 | 4 | 6 | 8 | 9 | 8 | 6 | 4 | 2 |
| 50 | 2 | 3 | 6 | 9 | 10 | 9 | 6 | 3 | 2 |
| 51 | 2 | 3 | 6 | 9 | 11 | 9 | 6 | 3 | 2 |
| 52 | 2 | 4 | 6 | 9 | 10 | 9 | 6 | 4 | 2 |
| 53 | 2 | 4 | 6 | 9 | 11 | 9 | 6 | 4 | 2 |
| 54 | 2 | 4 | 7 | 9 | 10 | 9 | 7 | 4 | 2 |
| 55 | 2 | 4 | 7 | 9 | 11 | 9 | 7 | 4 | 2 |
| 56 | 2 | 4 | 7 | 9 | 12 | 9 | 7 | 4 | 2 |
| 57 | 2 | 4 | 7 | 10 | 11 | 10 | 7 | 4 | 2 |
| 58 | 2 | 4 | 7 | 10 | 12 | 10 | 7 | 4 | 2 |
| 59 | 3 | 4 | 7 | 10 | 11 | 10 | 7 | 4 | 3 |
| 60 | 3 | 4 | 7 | 10 | 12 | 10 | 7 | 4 | 3 |
| 61 | 3 | 4 | 7 | 10 | 13 | 10 | 7 | 4 | 3 |
| 62 | 3 | 4 | 7 | 11 | 12 | 11 | 7 | 4 | 3 |
| 63 | 3 | 4 | 7 | 11 | 13 | 11 | 7 | 4 | 3 |
| 64 | 3 | 4 | 8 | 11 | 12 | 11 | 8 | 4 | 3 |

TABLE 25–1. (continued).

| Number of cases | 4% | 7% | 12% | 17% | 20% | 17% | 12% | 7% | 4% |
|---|---|---|---|---|---|---|---|---|---|
| | | | | | *Stanines* | | | | |
| N | 1 | 2 | 3 | 4 | 5 | 6 | 7 | 8 | 9 |
| 65 | 3 | 4 | 8 | 11 | 13 | 11 | 8 | 4 | 3 |
| 66 | 3 | 4 | 8 | 11 | 14 | 11 | 8 | 4 | 3 |
| 67 | 3 | 5 | 8 | 11 | 13 | 11 | 8 | 5 | 3 |
| 68 | 3 | 5 | 8 | 11 | 14 | 11 | 8 | 5 | 3 |
| 69 | 3 | 5 | 8 | 12 | 13 | 12 | 8 | 5 | 3 |
| 70 | 3 | 5 | 8 | 12 | 14 | 12 | 8 | 5 | 3 |
| 71 | 3 | 5 | 8 | 12 | 15 | 12 | 8 | 5 | 3 |
| 72 | 3 | 5 | 9 | 12 | 14 | 12 | 9 | 5 | 3 |
| 73 | 3 | 5 | 9 | 12 | 15 | 12 | 9 | 5 | 3 |
| 74 | 3 | 5 | 9 | 13 | 14 | 13 | 9 | 5 | 3 |
| 75 | 3 | 5 | 9 | 13 | 15 | 13 | 9 | 5 | 3 |
| 76 | 3 | 5 | 9 | 13 | 16 | 13 | 9 | 5 | 3 |
| 77 | 3 | 6 | 9 | 13 | 15 | 13 | 9 | 6 | 3 |
| 78 | 3 | 6 | 9 | 13 | 16 | 13 | 9 | 6 | 3 |
| 79 | 3 | 6 | 10 | 13 | 15 | 13 | 10 | 6 | 3 |
| 80 | 3 | 6 | 9 | 14 | 16 | 14 | 9 | 6 | 3 |
| 81 | 3 | 6 | 9 | 14 | 17 | 14 | 9 | 6 | 3 |
| 82 | 3 | 6 | 10 | 14 | 16 | 14 | 10 | 6 | 3 |
| 83 | 3 | 6 | 10 | 14 | 17 | 14 | 10 | 6 | 3 |
| 84 | 4 | 6 | 10 | 14 | 16 | 14 | 10 | 6 | 4 |
| 85 | 3 | 6 | 10 | 15 | 17 | 15 | 10 | 6 | 3 |
| 86 | 3 | 6 | 10 | 15 | 18 | 15 | 10 | 6 | 3 |
| 87 | 4 | 6 | 10 | 15 | 17 | 15 | 10 | 6 | 4 |
| 88 | 3 | 6 | 11 | 15 | 18 | 15 | 11 | 6 | 3 |
| 89 | 4 | 6 | 11 | 15 | 17 | 15 | 11 | 6 | 4 |
| 90 | 4 | 6 | 11 | 15 | 18 | 15 | 11 | 6 | 4 |
| 91 | 4 | 6 | 11 | 15 | 19 | 15 | 11 | 6 | 4 |
| 92 | 4 | 6 | 11 | 16 | 18 | 16 | 11 | 6 | 4 |
| 93 | 4 | 6 | 11 | 16 | 19 | 16 | 11 | 6 | 4 |
| 94 | 4 | 7 | 11 | 16 | 18 | 16 | 11 | 7 | 4 |
| 95 | 4 | 7 | 11 | 16 | 19 | 16 | 11 | 7 | 4 |
| 96 | 4 | 7 | 11 | 16 | 20 | 16 | 11 | 7 | 4 |
| 97 | 4 | 7 | 12 | 16 | 19 | 16 | 12 | 7 | 4 |
| 98 | 4 | 7 | 12 | 16 | 20 | 16 | 12 | 7 | 4 |
| 99 | 4 | 7 | 12 | 17 | 19 | 17 | 12 | 7 | 4 |
| 100 | 4 | 7 | 12 | 17 | 20 | 17 | 12 | 7 | 4 |

Reproduced from *Test Service Notebook*, No. 23 (New York: Harcourt, Brace & World, Inc., 1961). Used by permission of the publisher.

## How Should Class Marks Be Derived?

By this time the reader has probably reached the conclusion that class marks should be abolished. However, marks, like money and motherhood, presently must be accepted as essential. For the time being at least, the major task is to reduce their unwholesome influence on the educational endeavor.

The following guidelines are not ideal, nor would all educational authorities agree with them. They do appear to be consistent with the analysis presented in this book. Furthermore, they go at least one step beyond most current practices.

**TABLE 25–2.** Distribution of raw test scores in a stanine distribution

| Stanine | Score Interval | Tallies | Frequencies | Grouping Actual | Grouping Theoretical |
|---|---|---|---|---|---|
| 9 | 58 | / | 1 | 4 | 4 |
|  | 57 |  | – |  |  |
|  | 56 | / | 1 |  |  |
|  | 55 | // | 2 |  |  |
| 8 | 54 |  | – | 7 | 6 |
|  | 53 |  | – |  |  |
|  | 52 |  | – |  |  |
|  | 51 | / | 1 |  |  |
|  | 50 | / | 1 |  |  |
|  | 49 | // | 2 |  |  |
|  | 48 |  | – |  |  |
|  | 47 | /// | 3 |  |  |
| 7 | 46 | / | 1 | 12 | 11 |
|  | 45 | /// | 3 |  |  |
|  | 44 | // | 2 |  |  |
|  | 43 |  | – |  |  |
|  | 42 | ⊬⊬⊓ / | 6 |  |  |
| 6 | 41 | // | 2 | 12 | 15 |
|  | 40 | // | 2 |  |  |
|  | 39 | // | 2 |  |  |
|  | 38 | / | 1 |  |  |
|  | 37 | ⊬⊬⊓ | 5 |  |  |
| 5 | 36 | ⊬⊬⊓ | 5 | 20 | 18 |
|  | 35 | // | 2 |  |  |
|  | 34 | ⊬⊬⊓ // | 7 |  |  |
|  | 33 | /// | 3 |  |  |
|  | 32 | /// | 3 |  |  |
| 4 | 31 | ⊬⊬⊓ | 5 | 14 | 15 |
|  | 30 | / | 1 |  |  |
|  | 29 | /// | 3 |  |  |
|  | 28 | /// | 3 |  |  |
|  | 27 | // | 2 |  |  |
| 3 | 26 | //// | 4 | 13 | 11 |
|  | 25 | ⊬⊬⊓ / | 6 |  |  |
|  | 24 | /// | 3 |  |  |
| 2 | 23 | / | 1 | 4 | 6 |
|  | 22 | / | 1 |  |  |
|  | 21 | // | 2 |  |  |
| 1 | 20 | / | 1 | 4 | 4 |
|  | 19 |  | – |  |  |
|  | 18 | / | 1 |  |  |
|  | 17 | // | 2 |  |  |

90

Reproduced from *Test Service Notebook*, No. 23 (New York: Harcourt, Brace & World, Inc., 1961). Used by permission of the publisher.

**419**

*First,* at least some marks might be based upon a criterion-referenced score. *As previously indicated, this is a point along a continuum of subject matter or skill that indicates the degree of proficiency achieved by an individual without reference to anyone else.* It is most easily applied in areas where there is some absolute unit of measurement, as in a motor skill such as tennis. Also in the areas of typing or shorthand, the most accurate marks are determined by letters or words per minute. The same principle applies to such areas as physical education, foreign language, and speech. As Trow[6] points out, the establishment of a criterion-referenced score in an area like social studies is more difficult but not impossible. But, as he adds, almost any planned continuum would result in a more meaningful score than we now have.

The task would essentially involve establishing one or more continuums from zero to 100 for each class subject. Degree of proficiency along this continuum would provide a basis for class marks. Instruction would be adapted to the person's beginning position on the continuum. (Some students would be farther along than others, so subgroups would be essential.) An advanced typing student, for example, who could type 60 words per minute would be marked on the basis of *his own progress* on a scale of proficiency set for such a course. A proficiency level of 80 words per minute, for example, might be worth a mark of "A." Indeed such a procedure is *already being used* in the skills areas such as typing and shorthand. *It could be applied to all areas!*

In those areas where more than one continuum is deemed necessary a composite score might be employed. For example, social studies outcomes have been evaluated on the basis of critical thinking skills. These have been identified as (1) identification of critical issues, (2) recognition of underlying assumptions, (3) evaluation of evidence or authority, and (4) making warranted conclusions. Each is necessary for the entire process of critical thinking. Thus proficiency levels along the four continuums could be averaged for marking purposes.

A *second* guideline for the derivation of class marks could be based on some normative procedure involving use of the normal curve of probability. For example, for those students who start at a given level, there may be times when none would reach the predetermined level of proficiency set for an "A" mark. If the predetermined proficiency level were realistically determined (based on the attained proficiency levels of other students), generally low achievement levels would suggest the presence of a class problem, possibly beyond the control of the student. Thus adjustments could be made on the basis of group progress.

As Trow suggests, introduction of the criterion-referenced system can begin in a small way with those skills that are most easily identifiable. During the transition period at least, both criterion-referenced and normative scores would be essential in the derivation of marks.

## How Are Several Class Marks Combined for Grading Purposes?

In most classes today students are marked in many ways. In one class there may be marks on short quizzes, reports, discussions, debates, tests, and many

---

[6] William C. Trow, "On Marks, Norms, and Proficiency Scores," *Phi Delta Kappan* 48 (December 1966): 171–3.

other activities. How may such disparate elements be combined into one class mark?

The *first* task is to record the results of *each* measure as a standard score. (The stanine has been offered as a useful device for this purpose.) It is worth repeating that raw scores are not comparable. *Thus they are not usually recorded at all* unless the teacher is able to develop an elaborate weighting system.

*Second,* the teacher decides the major dimensions that appropriately enter into derivation of a class grade. For example, ten quizzes, four class papers, two oral presentations, and the midterm test might be judged as of equal importance. The final test might be considered equal to *two* of the foregoing dimensions.

*Third,* the *standard* scores for each dimension are averaged. For example, the ten quizzes would be averaged, then the four class papers, followed by the two oral presentations.

*Fourth,* each of the *averaged* marks, in turn, will be averaged. This will provide the teacher with an average standard score. Since averaging of averages tends to produce a regression effect toward the mean (previously explained), the final average standard scores can be evaluated on the basis of a normal curve. From this, class grades may be assessed.

It should be noted that such a procedure is considered inappropriate if it is possible to evaluate an individual on his own performance, as in skills areas. Until such time as teachers have developed adequate criterion-referenced scales (as described in the foregoing problem) in the academic areas, some such approach may be used. In the final analysis, however, marks must be adjusted in terms of the particular class group (as well as the individual). In short, the normal curve is merely a tool to be used as a starting point in determining grades.

If criterion-referenced assessment is used, all students who meet the minimum standards (usually about 90 percent) for each assignment should be passed. It should be noted that optional experiences merely provide additional experiences for those who find the minimum number of learning experiences inadequate for meeting acceptable levels of competency.[7] They in no way suggest exceptional performance quality. Those who do not meet minimum requirements are recycled through parts of the programs until they do pass or else they are failed. If, as in many cases, criterion-referenced measures are combined with norm-referenced measures, a standard "C" or average mark may be used for those who meet the minimum essentials only. "A's" and "B's" might be used for those who also achieve highly on norm-referenced measures. Relatively few classes today are set up wholly on the basis of criterion-referenced measures only.

## What Are Some Trends in School Reports?

In an effort to correct at least *some* of the inherent weaknesses of report cards, a number of changes are becoming fairly common. Today many school

---

[7] Some teachers have developed "learning contracts" that in some ways parallel LAPs, except that in such cases optional experiences are frequently viewed as extra work that may warrant a higher grade for the student.

systems have adopted a dual marking system. Such reports contain one mark for achievement in relation to the entire class and another mark for the student's estimated individual ability to achieve. One student, for example, may receive an "A" grade based on the progress of the rest of his class, but may receive only a "C" for effort. This simply means that he has not been working very hard for his "A." On the other hand, another student may receive a "C" grade, but an "A" for effort. This indicates to the parents that the individual has been working very hard for his "C." Thus no further encouragement from his parents is in order. Today's report card frequently contains a few spaces for comments. A teacher may or may not elect further to clarify a report by making written comments. In addition, parent-teacher conferences are being urged in some school systems whenever they seem necessary.

Various surveys have been conducted to ascertain what parents want in school reports. Generally they are in favor of traditional report cards, consistent with the above, but they want more. Since the report card is about the only direct line of communication between teacher and parent, he wants to be informed if and when his son or daughter experiences difficulty. Moreover, the parent needs specific direction relative to the role he might play in helping his child overcome the difficulty. A common complaint is that the report card arrives when it is too late to take appropriate corrective action.

It is seen from the foregoing that parents want to know immediately when a child encounters difficulty. Parents apparently conceive of themselves as being active participants in the educative process. They want to know of the difficulty *in time,* so that appropriate remedial action can be taken. A teacher who fails to meet this responsibility is justifiably criticized.

While it seems highly unlikely that *all* parents would be able and willing to cooperate as much as desired, such surveys do indicate a healthy trend: *parents are coming to recognize their role in the educative process.* The report card is a form of communication. While it still leaves much to be desired, at the secondary school level it is often the *only* direct form of communication, and, as such, is an extremely important aspect of teaching. Reporting methods and understandings need to be developed with a view of getting away from teachers' reporting *to* parents except as a temporary station on the way toward reporting as communication between teachers, parents, and pupils.

The psychological impact of report card grades is tremendous. In teacher education so much time has been devoted to studying content, along with instructional methods and techniques, that the central position of grades and reporting often comes as a shock to the new teacher. Yet the report card is sometimes the only remaining link that connects parents and teacher—both of whom have a vital interest in the education of the adolescent. Both parties can and *ought* to be cooperating participants in the educative process. It is the responsibility of the school to initiate and encourage such a relationship.

## What Is the Place of Parent-teacher Conferences?

There is no substitute for sitting down with a student's parents and discussing his progress and problems in a face-to-face manner. Rather than merely providing a "grade," the teacher must be prepared to justify his assessment and perhaps offer timely suggestions for parental cooperation. Moreover, the home environment has a tremendous impact on an individual's behavior at school. The parent can provide needed insights into the home situation.

The parent-teacher conference has become the most widely used method of reporting at the elementary level. The self-contained class (a teacher working with one group of students for a considerable portion of the school day) is ideally suited for the parent-teacher conference. In many elementary schools, classes are dismissed early at regular intervals to accommodate such conferences. In most conventional high schools, however, teachers have a different group of students each class period. Thus conferences might entail meeting 200 or more parents (instead of 30 or 40, as with the elementary teacher). When handled in this manner the technique tends to become unwieldy.

Recently some schools have experimented with various group conference techniques. Parents of students with similar problems can be asked to attend an open meeting involving a "give and take" discussion with those teachers involved. As a follow-up, parents may be asked to supply certain written information that might aid teachers in working with their sons and daughters. Obviously such techniques of reporting have their limitations. Nevertheless, most of them are superior to the traditional report card.

## VALUES

Evaluation is a valuable communication link between teacher and student as well as between teacher and parent. It may be the *only* major communication link between teacher and parent.

Evaluation enables the learner to ascertain how well he compares to the rest of the class. While evaluation is fraught with numerous psychological hazards, most individuals need such information in coping with the realities of the school environment.

The best form of evaluation enables the learner to assess progress and to compete with his own past record.

Evaluation can be systematized to include both norm-referenced and criterion-referenced measures.

Evaluation of students may necessitate a teacher's reflectively examining his own teaching efforts and may produce attempts to create a better learning situation.

## LIMITATIONS AND PROBLEMS

Evaluation at its best is somewhat subjective. Unfortunately evaluative judgments, reflected in marks and letter grades, have an important bearing upon the learner's future.

Norm-referenced evaluation may be self-defeating to weak students if assessment is made solely on the basis of class performance.

Criterion-referenced evaluation in many respects is still rather arbitrary. How well a criterion has been achieved ultimately rests with the evaluator.

A poor student may interpret inadequate achievement as indicative of personal inadequacy.

In classes where norm-referenced evaluation predominates, able students may not be sufficiently challenged to do their best work.

Evaluation, to a marked degree, depends upon the values of the teacher involved. Thus grades in different classes are not fully comparable. This may create considerable misunderstanding between student and teacher as well as between teacher and parent.

## ILLUSTRATED EVALUATIONAL APPLICATIONS

I.  Deriving stanine marks and letter grades from a written test

| | *Raw scores* | (N = 40) |
|---|---|---|
| 1)2 | 122 | |
| | 120 | 9 |
| | 115 | |
| 3)3 | 114 | 8 |
| | 112 | |
| | 108 − 2 | |
| 5)5 | 106 | |
| | 104 | 7 |
| | 103 | |
| | 101 | |
| 7)6 | 99 − 3 | 6 |
| | 96 | |
| | 93 | |
| | 90 − 2 | |
| 8)8 | 89 | 5 |
| | 88 − 3 | |
| | 85 | |
| | 79 | |
| | 76 | |
| 7)8 | 75 − 2 | |
| | 74 | 4 |
| | 73 − 2 | |
| | 69 | |
| | 68 | |
| 5)4 | 66 | 3 |
| | 63 | |
| | 60 − 2 | |
| | 52 | |
| 3)3 | 50 | 2 |
| | 46 | |
| 1)1 | 38 | 1 |

It should be noted that slight variations from the theoretical stanine are sometimes advisable (as in stanine 9 of the illustration). Certainly, all students receiving the same test score will be awarded the same stanine grade. Normally stanines only are recorded.

If the user prefers to record letter grades (instead of stanines) the following guide is recommended:

$$
\begin{array}{ll}
9\text{-}8 = A & 3 = D \\
7 = B & 2\text{-}1 = E \\
6\text{-}5\text{-}4 = C &
\end{array}
$$

It should be noted that the foregoing stanine and letter grade assessment is based upon the assumption of a normal curve of probability. Although adjustments (to fit a unique class group) can be made for each set of data, many teachers prefer to make adjustments at the end of the course after all data have been averaged.

II.   Deriving an average term stanine for each student from a variety of data

As the illustration suggests, the teacher's first task is to develop a series of stanine units that can be averaged. For example, in the illustration the teacher decides that seven class quizzes will equal one stanine dimension (unit). This is derived by adding all seven quiz stanine marks and finding an average stanine. Since it is deemed advisable (in the illustration) to let the final test count more than one-sixth, an additional stanine is added. (This makes the test count 2/7 of the total assessment (except for those who completed optional assignments).

$$N = 30$$

| Name | Seven Quizzes | 15 Periods of Class Partici-pation | Four Reading Analysis Reports | Midterm Exam. | Term Project | Opt. Work | Final Exam. | Term Average |
|---|---|---|---|---|---|---|---|---|
| George | 2.4 | 5 | 6.3 | 7 | 8 | 7.6 | 2 2 | 5.0 |
| Grace | 3.7 | 3 | 7.3 | 5 | 7 | | 5 5 | 5.1 |
| Mary | 3.9 | 9 | 7.7 | 4 | 9 | 9.0 | 7 7 | 6.8 |
| Jo | 3.7 | 6 | 5.7 | 4 | 7 | | 7 7 | 5.5 |
| Bill | 5.4 | 9 | 8.0 | 3 | 6 | | 4 4 | 5.6 |
| Tom | 6.3 | 7 | 8.0 | 9 | 4 | | 8 8 | 7.2 |
| Wilson | 2.3 | 6 | 8.3 | 7 | 4 | | 4 4 | 5.1 |
| Debra | 5.1 | 6 | 7.7 | 2 | 8 | | 6 6 | 5.8 |
| Sue | 5.0 | 5 | 1.0 | 5 | 8 | | 6 6 | 5.1 |
| Glenda | 2.7 | 5 | 5.7 | 3 | 6 | | 5 5 | 4.6 |
| Mike | 2.1 | 6 | 5.7 | 3 | 1 | | 5 5 | 4.0 |
| Rhonda | 2.7 | 6 | 5.0 | 2 | 6 | 5.0 | 5 5 | 4.5 |
| Debbie | 1.7 | 2 | 7.7 | 8 | 9 | | 5 5 | 5.5 |
| Wanda | 1.9 | 6 | 8.0 | 6 | 6 | 8.0 | 2 2 | 5.0 |
| Allan | 5.3 | 7 | 8.0 | 2 | 8 | | 9 9 | 6.9 |
| June | 4.2 | 7 | 3.0 | 7 | 8 | | 5 5 | 5.6 |
| Virgie | 6.1 | 6 | 4.7 | 4 | 6 | | 4 4 | 5.0 |
| Gary | 4.9 | 6 | 7.7 | 9 | 7 | 8.9 | 3 3 | 6.2 |
| Fred | 4.0 | 6 | 2.0 | 5 | 7 | | 7 7 | 5.4 |
| Cathy | 5.7 | 5 | 3.7 | 5 | 7 | | 4 4 | 4.9 |
| Billy | 2.3 | 2 | 7.3 | 6 | 5 | | 4 4 | 4.4 |
| Greg. | 3.0 | 4 | 5.0 | 4 | 7 | | 4 4 | 4.4 |
| Meg. | 7.0 | 7 | 5.0 | 4 | 6 | | 1 1 | 4.4 |

| | | | | | | | | | |
|---|---|---|---|---|---|---|---|---|---|
| Ruth | 3.4 | 7 | 7.0 | 7 | 5 | 8.6 | 3 3 | 5.5 |
| Linda | 1.4 | 7 | 8.7 | 8 | 7 | 8.0 | 6 6 | 6.6 |
| Hank | 7.2 | 5 | 7.0 | 4 | 6 | | 8 8 | 6.5 |
| Bob | 7.4 | 5 | 6.7 | 9 | 5 | | 7 7 | 6.7 |
| Larry | 6.6 | 5 | 7.0 | 5 | 7 | 7.3 | 7 7 | 7.4 |
| Yvonne | 4.9 | 4 | 6.7 | 5 | 7 | | 8 8 | 6.2 |
| Judy | 4.1 | 8 | 8.0 | 5 | 9 | | 6 6 | 6.6 |

III. Deriving a course average from an average stanine
(Based upon data in Problem II)

$$N = 30$$

| | | |
|---|---|---|
| 1)1 | 7.4 | 9 |
| | 7.2 | |
| 2)2 | 6.9 | 8 |
| | 6.8 | |
| 4)4 | 6.7 | 7 |
| | 6.6 – 2 | |
| | 6.5 | |
| 5)4 | 6.2 – 2 | 6 |
| | 5.8 | |
| | 5.6 – 2 | |
| 6)6 | 5.5 – 3 | 5 |
| | 5.4 | |
| | 5.1 – 3 | |
| 5)6 | 5.0 – 3 | 4 |
| | 4.9 | |
| 4)3 | 4.6 | 3 |
| | 4.5 | |
| 2)3 | 4.4 – 3 | 2 |
| 1)1 | 4.0 | 1 |

The reader will recall that when averages are averaged there is a regression toward the mean. In effect, this eliminates extremes. In assessing letter grades the teacher decides (somewhat subjectively) whether or not any "E's" or "A's" will be awarded. Students who receive the same stanine, however, must be awarded the same letter grade.

IV. Assessing criterion-referenced data

11 Students completed all required activities and all optional requirements with a 90 percent accuracy level.

6 Students completed all required activities with a 90 percent accuracy level.

9 Students originally completed all required activities with a 75 percent accuracy level. After reworking the assignments all achieved a 90 percent accuracy level.

4 Students completed all required activities with a 50 percent accuracy level and did not bother to rework their assignments.

11 –A Since optional work is a choice of the student, its completion
6        should not play a part in this type of assessment.

9 –B The teacher *may* want to award "A's" to this group also. However, reworked assignments may be viewed as warranting a lower grade than those which were satisfactorily completed the first time.

4 –E Students who fail to meet the minimum standards (90 percent in the illustration) should not pass.

V.    Combining norm-referenced and criterion-referenced assessments

| Student | Norm-referenced Average | Criterion-referenced Mark | Letter Grade |
|---------|:-----------------------:|:-------------------------:|:------------:|
| George | 5.0 | A | B |
| Grace | 5.1 | A | B |
| Mary | 6.8 | A | A |
| Jo | 5.5 | B | C |
| Bill | 5.6 | B | C |
| Tom | 7.2 | A | A |
| Wilson | 5.1 | B | C |
| Debra | 5.8 | A | B |
| Sue | 5.1 | A | B |
| Glenda | 4.6 | E | E |
| Mike | 4.0 | B | D |
| Rhonda | 4.5 | A | C |
| Debbie | 5.5 | A | B |
| Wanda | 5.0 | B | C |
| Allan | 6.9 | A | A |
| June | 5.6 | A | B |
| Virgie | 5.0 | A | B |
| Gary | 6.2 | E | E |
| Fred | 5.4 | B | C |
| Cathy | 4.9 | E | E |
| Billy | 4.4 | B | D |
| Greg | 4.4 | A | C |
| Meg | 4.4 | A | C |
| Ruth | 5.5 | A | B |
| Linda | 6.6 | A | A |
| Hank | 6.5 | E | E |
| Bob | 6.7 | A | A |
| Larry | 7.4 | A | A |
| Yvonne | 6.2 | B | B |
| Judy | 6.6 | B | B |

The assumption in this illustrated grade assessment is that norm-referenced and criterion-referenced measures should be counted equally. The relative weight assessment will vary from one class situation to another. In academic courses, for example, most marks are likely to be norm-referenced and thus will receive most weight in evaluation. In some skills subjects most marks are likely to be of the criterion-referenced variety and to carry the most weight in assessment procedures.

# SELECTED BIBLIOGRAPHY

Ackerman, J. Mark. *Operant Conditioning for the Classroom Teacher* (Grandview, Ill.: Scott, Foresman and Co., 1972).

Beggs, Donald L., and Lewis, Ernest L. *Measurement and Evaluation in the Schools* (Boston: Houghton Mifflin Co., 1975).

Chase, Clinton I. *Measurement for Educational Evaluation* (Reading, Mass.: Addison-Wesley Publishing Co., 1974).

Clark, B. M., and Ramsey, M. E. "Why Small Group Instruction?" *Bulletin of the National Association of Secondary School Principals* 57 (January 1973): 64–73.

Ellis, G. B. "Teaching Psycho-Motor Skills with Sequenced Photographs." *School Shop* 32 (February 1973): 38–39.

Epstein, Charlotte. *Affective Subjects in the Classroom* (San Francisco: Intext Educational Publishers, 1972).

Hamm, Russell L. *Intraclass Grouping in the Secondary School* (Danville, Ill.: The Interstage Printers and Publishers, Inc., 1971).

Keller, C. W. "Establishing an Environment for Inquiry." *The Social Studies* 64 (March 1973): 106–14.

Kryspin, William J., and Feldhusen, John F. *Developing Classroom Tests: A Guide for Writing and Evaluating Test Items* (Minneapolis: Burgess Publishing Co., 1974).

Mager, Robert. *Measuring Instructional Interest* (Belmont, Calif.: Fearon Publishing Co., 1973).

National Education Association. *Discussion in the Classroom.* Rev. ed. (Washington, D.C.: National Education Association, 1972).

———. *Evaluating and Reporting Student Achievement: What Research Says to the Teacher* (Washington, D.C.: National Education Association, 1974).

———. *Teaching Toward Inquiry* (Washington, D.C.: National Education Association, 1971).

Rasor, J. E. "Skill Acquisition: A Practical Illustration." *Physical Education* 28 (October 1971): 155–57.

Ryan, Frank L., and Ellis, Arthur K. *Instructional Implications of Inquiry* (Englewood Cliffs, N.J.: Prentice-Hall, Inc., 1974).

Shaw, Marvin E. *Group Dynamics: The Psychology of Small Group Behavior* (New York: McGraw-Hill Book Co., 1971).

TenBrink, Terry D. *Evaluation: A Practical Guide for Teachers* (New York: McGraw-Hill Book Co., Inc., 1974).

Thyne, James M. *Principles of Examining* (New York: John Wiley and Sons, 1974).

Wick, John W. *Educational Measurement* (Columbus: Charles E. Merrill Publishing Co., 1973).

# ANNOTATED FILM LIST

*Evaluation of Student Performance*
    16 mm film; 30 minutes
    Treats the essential techniques of student performance.
    From the *Teaching Role* Series
    Minnesota Video Nursing Education
    801 E. 26th
    Minneapolis, Minn. 55404

*Group Dynamics—Groupthink*
    16 mm film; 20 minutes
    Deals with critical elements in decision-making groups.
    From the *Educational Psychology* Series
    1011 Camino Del Mar
    Del Mar, Calif. 92104

*The Lecture and Role-Playing Strategy*
    16 mm film; 30 minutes
    Depicts principles associated with meaningful lectures and demonstrations.
    From the *Nursing Where Are You Going and How You Will Get There*
    Series.
    University of Nebraska Television Council for Nursing Education, Inc.
    University of Nebraska
    1800 N. 33rd
    Lincoln, Nebr. 68503

*Planning Classroom Tests*
    16 mm film; 28 minutes
    Identifies strengths and weaknesses of objective tests and provides practice
    in constructing different types.
    From the *Nursing Effective Evaluation* Series.
    University of Nebraska Television Council
    University of Nebraska
    1800 N. 33rd
    Lincoln, Nebr. 68503

*Review Lesson, Biology*
    16 mm film; 41 minutes
    Depicts an unrehearsed class engaged in a review of a unit of work.
    Pennsylvania State University
    Psychology Cinema Register
    AV Series
    6 Willard Building
    University Park, Pa. 16802

*Small Group Instruction*
    16 mm film; 28 minutes
    Dwight Allen (Stanford University) treats the elements essential for pro-
    ductive small group interaction and control.
    From the *Innovations in Education* Series.
    Stanford University
    Stanford, Calif. 94305

# SELECTED FILMSTRIPS

*Alternative Measurement Tactics for Education Evaluation*
Sound filmstrip
Offers a conceptual system for developing different types of measurement schemes.
Vimcit Associates
P.O. Box 24714
Los Angeles, Calif. 90024

*Current Conception of Educational Evaluation*
Sound filmstrip
Distinguishes between measurement, evaluation, formative and summative evaluation, process and product criteria, etc.
Same source as above.

*Establishing Performance Standards*
Sound filmstrip
Illustrates both qualitative and quantitative techniques for assessing learning. Includes the three domains: Cognitive, affective, psychomotor.
Same source as above.

*Evaluation*
Sound filmstrip
Treats test construction, item sampling, and preassessment techniques.
Same source as above.

*Field Trips*
Filmstrip with captions
Indicates how to plan a successful field trip.
Simmel Meservey, Inc.
9113 W. Pico Blvd.
Los Angeles, Calif. 90035

*Improving the Use of the Chalkboard*
Filmstrip
Illustrated ways for improvement are provided.
Ohio State University
Teaching Aids Laboratory
1988 N. College Rd.
Columbus, Ohio 43210

*Interaction Analysis Observation System*
Sound filmstrip
Offers a technique for determining classroom interaction.
Multi-Media Associates
4901 E 5th St.
Tucson, Ariz. 85732

*Techniques for Measuring Behavior*—A Series: Cognitive, Affective, Psychomotor
Sound filmstrip
Offers guidelines for developing valid techniques in all three of these domains.
Multi-Media Associates
4901 E. 5th St.
Tucson, Ariz. 85732

# SELECTED OVERHEAD TRANSPARENCIES

*Educational and Psychological Measurement*—A Series
    8 x 10 transparencies
    Covers basic factors essential for sound measurement and evaluation.
    Research Media, Inc.
    4 Midland Ave.
    Hicksville, N.Y. 11801

*The Effect of Maturation and Instruction on the Learning of Motor Skills*
    10 x 10 prepared transparency
    Langford Publishing Co.
    P.O. Box 8711
    1088 Lincoln Ave.
    San Jose, Calif. 95155

*Guiding Student Learning*—A Series
    8 x 10 prepared transparencies
    Same source as above.

*Stages in Collaborative Problem Solving: Strategy for Change*
    8 x 10 prepared transparencies
    Langford Publishing Co.
    P.O. Box 8711
    1088 Lincoln Ave.
    San Jose, Calif. 95155

*Teaching Reading*—A Series
    8 x 10 transparencies
    Same source as above.

# FREE AND INEXPENSIVE LEARNING MATERIALS

*The Art of Teaching*
    25 cents
    Aids for teachers in writing tests.
    Charles Baseler Co.
    8 Fernwood Rd.
    Florham Park, N.J. 07932

*Educational Media.* No. 387-11826.
    50 cents
    *What Research Says to the Teacher* Series.
    National Education Association
    1201 16th St., N.W.
    Washington, D.C. 20016

*Evaluating and Reporting Pupil Progress.* No. 387-11812.
    50 cents
    *What Research Says to the Teacher* Series.
    Same source as above.

*Improving Teaching Effectiveness*
>50 cents
>Uses research findings as a basis for looking at class size, lecture versus discussion, programmed learning, and the like.
>Superintendent of Documents
>Printing Office
>Washington, D.C. 20402

*Integrated Media in the Modern School*
>$1.75
>Looks at both traditional and new media potentials.
>Professional Educators Publications, Inc.
>Box 80728
>Lincoln, Nebr. 68501

*Test Services Bulletins*
>Free
>Various titles in the area of measurement and evaluation.
>The Psychological Corporation
>304 E. 45th St.
>New York, N.Y. 10017

*Understanding Intergroup Relations.* No. 387-11840.
>50 cents
>*What Research Says to the Teacher* Series.
>National Education Association
>1201 16th St., N.W.
>Washington, D.C. 20016

# An Illustrated
# Teaching Unit

## THE YEARLY PLAN

*Subject:* General Business

*Course Introduction:*

Perhaps most of us are wondering how a study of general business methods will benefit us. What is meant by distribution of goods? As consumers what effect does distribution of goods have on our lives? How is distribution related to production? To business policies? What effect does distribution have on the progress of our economy?

To answer these questions and many more that might arise let's make a quick overview of the development of distribution or marketing—the words can be used interchangeably.

Early man eked out a bare existence. He picked berries, caught fish, and in general lived off the countryside. He was barely able to provide for his own needs. This is described as a subsistence living.

As the population expanded and people began to live in communities they began to divide up the work—men doing the hunting and fishing and the women taking care of the children and preparing the food and clothing. This type of arrangement was better than one in which one person did it all, but it was still on a subsistence level. What countries in the world today still live under this type of existence? (India, 85 percent of the people still live in such circumstances; and so do the people of Africa.)

As these communities began to rise above the subsistence level, they began to specialize and develop special talents. Maybe one community of people living along the river would specialize in pottery and fishing, whereas another nearby community would specialize in hunting. As each of these communities developed surpluses they naturally began to exchange commodities. Thus marketing began.

As specialization and surpluses increased, marketplaces sprang up. They were usually about two to fifteen miles apart, depending on the density of the population in the area. Slowly towns grew around these market areas and often would build a market hall to protect customers and wares. What countries of the world today have common marketplaces? (Mexico, for one. Show slides of Mexico's marketplace.) This is the state of development in many of the countries of the world today.

Starting about 1700 many nations began to be involved in what we call the industrial revolution. The development of new and better machinery increased productivity and allowed the production of new and old commodities at lower prices. With more products available for sale, trade increased and markets expanded.

Here in the United States trade developed along the seacoast and then spread inland. Local markets were established and grew into permanent establishments. Many of the early colonies were settlements established by traders who wanted an outlet for their products in the new world—not only as an outlet for new products but also as a source of raw materials for the factories in the mother country.

However, as this nation's people moved west, away from the seacoast, they began to develop manufacturing centers of their own. Coastal towns became wholesale and manufacturing centers for the inland towns. This gave rise to one of the innovations in marketing—the Yankee peddler. This individual would visit the eastern port cities and fill up a wagon with his wares and then make regular circuits to the inland farm areas. He had pots and pans, cloth, herbs, and almost anything that the farmers could not produce for themselves. Peddlers became known in a certain locality and they would sometimes settle down and establish general stores. These stores would carry about the same variety as the peddlers but in a little more depth. They were in one place and the local people came to the store rather than wait for the store to go to them.

As populations shifted, many of these early general stores became wholesale houses, supplying goods to other retailers, and others became specialized merchants. Many internal developments in the history of the United States led to this expansion. Wars, railroads, and capital all did their parts.

By the late 1800s many manufacturers became dissatisfied with the distribution system and thus began to send out their own salesmen to advertise their products. As the economy moved from one of subsistence to production of luxury items, increased interest in the needs of the consumer became apparent.

This eventually led to the establishment of chain stores, supermarkets, and discount houses common to today's market.

From our brief discussion on the development of retailing let us make a list of the processes involved in distribution or marketing. This list should include: (1) buying; (2) selling; (3) transporting; (4) storing; (5) grading; (6) financing; (7) risk-taking; and (8) market information.

In this course we will study consumer wants and demands as related to our personal situations. We will also look into the effects of advertising and sales promotion as they help a producer introduce his goods to the consuming public.

### Course Concepts

1. Production standards in the United States make this nation the distribution center of the world.
2. Retail markets in the United States are consumer-oriented.
3. Selling is a joint process of communication between the buyer and the seller.
4. The customer market is in a state of constant change and therefore requires continuous study to stay abreast of current developments.

5. Differences in the structure and style of a product can be stated as sales appeals.
6. A sound business enterprise is based upon adequate financing.
7. Business decisions are based upon market trends.

*Major Unit Titles*

|  | *Length* |
|---|---|
| The United States: Distribution Center of the World | 4 weeks |
| The Consumer Determines the Market | 6 weeks |
| Sales Promotion and Advertising | 4 weeks |
| The Consumer: A Constantly Changing Variable | 4 weeks |
| Sales Appeal | 5 weeks |
| Financing a Business Enterprise | 6 weeks |
| Market Trends | 3 weeks |

# THE UNIT PLAN

*Unit:* Sales Promotion and Advertising

*Unit Introduction*

The marketer, to succeed, must understand the needs, attitudes, and expectations of the consumer. He needs to be sensitive to the human factors that combine to motivate behavior. Consumers are motivated by primary and secondary needs.

Basic or primary needs include physiological and security or safety needs. What type of items might be included under physiological needs? This list might include: Food, clothing, shelter—the basics of existence. Safety and security needs include such things as insurance, fringe benefits, safety guarantees.

The secondary needs are psychological. They include recognition, social and self-actualizing needs. Examples of recognition might include being the first in a neighborhood to own a new product, some distinctive piece of furniture or style of golf clubs. Social needs might include such considerations as being part of a group, the individuals of which all own similar merchandise. In other words, it involves the bandwagon philosophy. Self actualization is involved when an individual can make creative use of his natural ability such as do-it-yourself projects, acquiring information and education. Basic needs must be satisfied before an individual has a desire to satisfy higher needs. For example, people in a subsistence condition are not interested in an education, do-it-yourself projects, or being the first to own a new product. They are interested in where the next meal is coming from.

Needs seem to follow a circular pattern. A need will lead to a drive which will result in a behavior pattern, which, in turn, will lead to need satisfaction or frustration. This in turn will lead to new needs and the pattern starts all over again.

The different socioeconomic groups in the U.S. tend to be motivated by different need levels. Lower-class members tend to be motivated by the first three need groups: physiological, security-safety, recognition. The middle and upper classes are motivated more by social and self-actualization needs.

Behavioral psychologists have established that rewards are better motivators than threats. We remember pleasant experiences and tend to forget unpleasant ones. Since people forget rapidly, repetition in a sales promotion campaign is necessary for driving the point home.

How can these factors affect our response to customers as they enter the store? What stores do you like to shop in? Why do you like to shop in them? (Develop through informal class discussion.)

We mentioned that an advertising campaign should have in it an element of repetition. This is necessary in order to presell an individual on a product and to start his responding positively to the five basic buying decisions: (1) the need, (2) the source, (3) the product, (4) the price, and (5) the time. By preselling the product through advertising, the amount of personal salesmanship is minimized. To help the potential customer through the process of making a decision to buy, the marketer follows the AIDA formula: A—Attention, I—Interest, D—Desire, A—Action to close the sale.

As we know, not all people want the same products, and thus each manufacturer must decide who the people are his product will appeal to. This is known as the target market. The target market is determined through an analysis of the current market situation and the expected trends of the future. The market is changing, and therefore there is a constant need for the evaluation of the consumer market. There is a need to know about people's buying habits, what products they want, their knowledge of existing similar products, and what they can afford. There are many sources of market information available, both public and private.

Once the consumers for a new product are determined, the advertisements that will appeal to this particular consumer's wants and desires can be written. The advertiser's job is to organize the pictures and written materials in such a way that preselling of the product can take place.

### Content Outline

While discussing this unit we will place major emphasis on the customer as his need satisfaction influences the development of new products and the appeals made by producers to attract consumer interest to buy their products.

1. Markets Are People
   a. The roots of human behavior
   b. Psychological guidelines
   c. The appeal
2. Marketing Strategy
   a. Steps in the marketing process
   b. Marketing as a continuous process
3. Determining Consumer Demand
   a. Market trends
   b. Market information
4. Influencing Consumer Buying Decisions
   a. Kinds of advertising copy
   b. The sales message

### Unit Concepts

*Important Concepts*

1. Customer satisfaction is the most important product.
2. Customer needs are the prompters for purchasing decisions.
3. Advertising can be an effective means of preselling products.
4. Advertisements use customer motives that can be restated in the personal selling approach.
5. The customer market is in a state of constant change and

therefore requires continuous study to stay abreast of current developments.

6. Sales appeals must be consistent with ethical standards of advertising.

## Instructional Goal and Outcomes

*Concept I:* Customer satisfaction is the most important product. After this unit the student should have furthered his understanding of the importance of customer satisfaction in sales promotion and advertising, as evidenced by:

1. His ability to synthesize various aspects of customer satisfaction from a case study.
2. His ability to analyze the merits of a debate on customer satisfaction.

## Learning Activities

1. *Case analysis*
   *Problem:* What psychological factors should be considered in selling?
   *Case:* "The factors that count!"
2. *Debate*
   *Proposition:* Resolved, that a dissatisfied customer should have the privilege of returning his goods.

## Instructional Goal and Outcomes

*Concept II:* Customer needs are the prompters of purchasing decisions. After this unit the student should have furthered his understanding of the role of basic human motives and wants in selling, as evidenced by:

1. His ability to apply appropriate psychological principles in a simulation game.
2. His interpretation of sales resistance in a sociodrama.

## Learning Activities

1. *Simulation Game:* "People, U.S.A."
2. *Sociodrama*
   *Problem:* How might a customer feel when he is pressured into buying a product?
   *Broad Situation:* Mary wants to buy a gift for her husband's birthday. Jim is a salesman in a department store.

## Instructional Goal and Outcomes

*Concept III:* Advertising can be an effective means of preselling products. After this unit the student should have furthered his understanding of the relationship between impulse buying and advertising, as evidenced by:

1. His ability to test hypotheses of impulse buying in a class discussion.
2. His ability to apply appropriate advertising principles in role-played situations.

## Learning Activities

1. *Class Discussion*
   *Problem:* What can we as marketers do to stimulate buying?
2. *Role Playing in Buzz Groups*
   *Buzz Groups:* What are the essentials of a good advertisement?

*Instructional Goal and Outcomes*

**Concept IV:** Advertisements use customer motive that can be restated in personal selling approach. After this unit the student should further appreciate the role that basic motives play in advertising, as evidenced by:
1. His ability to evaluate selected advertisements on the basis of the basic motive appeal.
2. His ability to develop an acceptable advertisement, using basic motive as a basis.

*Learning Activities*
1. *Project:* Selected Advertisements
   *Problem:* Evaluate the basic motives employed in the selected advertisements.
2. *Written Assignment:* Develop an advertisement utilizing the basic motives provided.

*Instructional Goal and Outcomes*

**Concept V:** Since the customer market is constantly changing, continuous study is essential if one wants to stay abreast of current developments. After this unit the student should have furthered his understanding of factors determining products market, as evidenced by:
1. His ability to predict the market value of selected new products.
2. His analysis of consumer demands as reflected in selected advertisements.

*Learning Activities*
1. *Written Analysis*
   *Problem:* What is the market value of the products before you?
2. *Project*
   *Problem:* From the selected advertisements, predict the elements of consumer demand, as reflected in the sales appeal.

*Instructional Goal and Outcomes*

**Concept VI:** Sales appeal must be consistent with advertising ethics. After this unit the student should have furthered his appreciation of the ethics of motivational appeals in advertisements, as evidenced by:
1. His evaluation of selected sales campaigns in terms of basic civil liberties.
2. His development of an advertising slogan which is consistent with advertising ethics.

*Learning Activities*
1. *Case Analysis of Sales Campaign*
   *Problem:* What are the appropriate ethical limits of selling?
   *Case:* The "Quick Buck" Auto Sales Co. sells a car.
2. *Written Assignment*
   *Problem:* What are the prudent limits of advertising?
   *Assignment:* Develop an advertising slogan for a new home.

Note: The foregoing represents the extent of preplanning experiences for teaching. As one teaches he will develop lesson plans for many of the learning activities. Finally, he will develop test items and evaluational devices for assessing concept attainment.

# Index